THE VENDOR CO
HANDBO

2nd Edition

INCLUDING FORMS AND DATA TEMPLATES CD

by David Secul

A Manual of Compliance Guidelines, Procedures and Standards for Product Development and Apparel Production.

The Fashiondex, Inc. New York, NY www.fashiondex.com
info@fashiondex.com 212 647 0051

Copyright © 2010 by The Fashiondex, Inc. All rights reserved.
No part of this publication may be reproduced or transmitted in any form or by any means, including but not limited to mechanical, electronic, photocopying, or any information storage or retrieval system, without the prior written permission of The Fashiondex, Inc.
The Fashiondex cannot accept responsibility for the accuracy or completeness of such information or for loss or damage caused by any use thereof.
The Fashiondex, Inc.
New York NY 10001
212 647 0051
E-Mail: info@fashiondex.com
Web Site: www.fashiondex.com
Printed in the United States of America
ISBN:0974101187

Also published by Fashiondex:

The Apparel Industry Sourcebook
The Apparel Production Sourcebook/America
The Apparel Production Sourcebook/Asia
The Apparel Design and Production Handbook (A Technical Reference)
The Small Design Company's Guide to Wholesale Fabrics and Trims
The Directory of Brand-Name Apparel Manufacturers
The Design Detail Book/Editions 1 and 2
The Color Book/Editions 1, 2 and 3
The Designer's Book of Bridal Gowns
Birnbaum's Global Guide to Winning the Great Garment War
Birnbaum's Global Guide to Material Sourcing
Crisis in the 21st Century Garment Industry
The Birnbaum Report/Strategic Sourcing for Garment Importers
Sourcing A,B,C'S
Poses

ACKNOWLEDGEMENTS

I would like to express my sincere gratitude to the following people for their help:

Bill Brandt, for his hard work editing all the text.
The Medium Group, for the book design.
Carlos Aponte, for his illustrations.
And most importantly, Angela Gengaro-Secul for her continued love and support and my son, Nicolo Secul, just for being around to make us smile.

-David Secul

PREFACE

This book outlines everything a designer or a garment manufacturer needs to know about producing a garment from start to finish. The book includes all the steps needed to perform or to avoid disconcerting incidents, such as chargebacks and late deliveries.

In 1996, I led a group of people that worked in a large production facility. It was then that I began to put together the pieces of this manual. Everyday, I saw things slip through the cracks and problems occur. I thought, if I can develop a book that would help avoid the everyday problems, it would be beneficial to me and my team.

I put the manual together, and as the years progressed and my position in the industry changed, I used the manual and passed it on to the people that I worked with each year. Being able to offer co-workers guidelines when creating a garment and offering factories solutions to problems prior to them occurring, really made this grueling process less complex than it had been in years. Let's face it, the fashion industry is always working behind schedule. It is always yesterday that the retailer wanted the garments or the sales office wanted the samples. If I can alleviate things that generally delay production, then I can make more people's jobs less painful, and ultimately make more people happy.

This book illustrates what it is that makes a designer succeed, as well as ways to make a production office run more smoothly. It outlines the way to manufacture a garment from the development of a sales sample to shipping the finished garment on time, and all of the "how to's" in between. The book demonstrates how to apply these ideas to an existing organization or to a start-up company. The book is ideal for the young designer, who is looking to begin a business, or for an existing company, that is having trouble with anything from poor or inconsistent fit to late shipping and charge backs. Included in the book are examples of forms and templates that you can compare to your existing ones. In addition to forms and templates, it gives you a sample plan and action calendar that will help with your organization of all the development stages. All these forms will be useful to keep you organized through this long and tedious process.

This book answers the questions of any new designer: "How do I produce a garment?", "Where do I start?", and "What standards should I use?" The book should help all those that are beginning in the fashion industry, and also facilitate those with existing loopholes that have been making their daily jobs grueling and hurting their businesses over time.

THE VENDOR COMPLIANCE HANDBOOK

A Manual of Compliance Guidelines, Procedures and Standards for Product Development and Apparel Production

INTRODUCTION

With the increasing amount of off-shore and outsourced production in the apparel industry, it is vitally important for start-up and small- to mid-sized companies to have all the necessary tools and formulas at hand, in order to assure a clear and precise exchange of information. Additionally, companies need an understanding of the scope and entitlements they have as a customer of goods and services.

In the past, merchandising and product development existed hand-in-hand with manufacturing, often within the same company. But with the advent of outsourced production and contracting, the apparel company no longer has the easy and direct links to production that formerly existed. Sourcing, production issues, and follow-up must be conducted over great distances. The modern apparel company must maintain constant contact and supervision with its suppliers and contractors through technological avenues such as email, Web PDM and other electronic forms of communication and notification.

This handbook presents an overview of the apparel development and production process. Its goal is to provide the designer, start-up company, manufacturer, and/or apparel producer with a comprehensive understanding of what occurs behind the manufacturing of a product, detail how to get garments shipped the precise way, and leave the reader with a clear understanding of the correct methods to be used with a vendor. The book should be used as a reference source for answers to questions encountered from development through finished production. This handbook specifies procedures and minimum standards that must be met or exceeded.

Included is instruction on development standards, the importance of tech packages and work-in-progress reports, the fabric and garment inspection process, sales sampling procedures, labeling procedures, the packaging and shipping of garments, and explanations of what constitutes compliancy in details of garments, including seams, snaps, finishing and more. Furthermore, the book explains reasons for chargebacks and ways to avoid receiving them, discusses expediting letters of credits, which are used to secure payments of goods delivered, and includes examples and explanations of sample forms that can be altered to fit most businesses.

This manual was developed as a clear, concise, user-friendly guide to procedures, standards and requirements for apparel production, and the aim is to provide all the items and steps that designers sometimes forget, and could ultimately lead to the success, or failure, of their line or company.

The book may be used as a supplement to a manufacturing agreement or contract between you and your vendor. If additional questions arise, which are not answered within the handbook, or if clarification is required for a standard or procedure, then your vendor should contact the appropriate person at your firm.

If there is anything that you believe is unclear or incomplete with this manual, please let us know. We encourage and appreciate feedback on any improvements for future editions.

NOTE TO READERS

The Vendor Compliance Handbook is to be used as a guideline. The compliances listed here are not the only set of rules that are utilized within the fashion industry. Before beginning any production, you should check with your retailer or factory to see if they use their own individual set of compliances that may vary with the ones listed in this book.

Please also note that this book is not specific to any particular apparel category. You will find a chart or template listed for most apparel categories, but it is impossible to be category-specific for every grouping in the industry, as there is an immense amount of categories in the fashion industry (everything from children's wear to plus sizes). Most likely, the categories can be adjusted to fit your particular needs. If there is a category that you would like a chart or template on, please e-mail us at info@andconsultants.com. Again, remember to check with your retailer or factory to see what compliances they have used in the past, so that you can compare them with those listed in this book. You can eventually create your own set of guidelines.

TABLE OF CONTENTS

CHAPTER 1

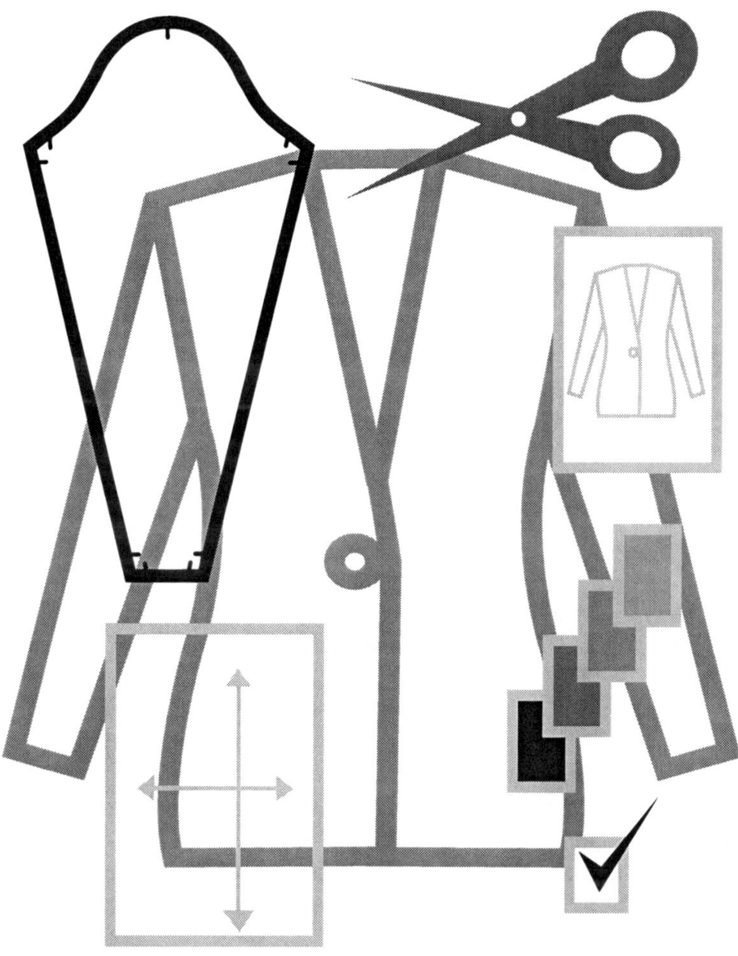

DEVELOPMENT STANDARDS

This chapter introduces standards and procedures for apparel samples and their development, including the fundamental specification package (tech package) and its components for all new works in development.

DEVELOPMENT STANDARDS

Producing a collection should be an exciting and exhilarating experience for designers and merchandisers alike. To make sure that the process is positive and productive, we have analyzed the steps that designers or merchandisers should take in producing their collections. After reading this chapter, you should be able to visualize the process and avoid some pitfalls.

Depending on the relationship and the level of trust you have with your vendor, some of the sampling processes can be disregarded. For example, you might go from proto/sample directly into sales sample/production, or you may avoid proto/sampling altogether and go from sales sample right into production. Of course, this will depend on your ability to provide your vendor/factory with the correct amount of information as well as where you are sourcing the contents. This chapter will provide you with a tech package to use as a guideline for the process.

SPECIFICATION/TECH PACKAGE

The Lead Sheets will be the first component of your tech package as you are putting together your collection. Having a lead sheet for every style and every color will allow you and your merchandiser to determine how many garments you have within the collection. This will help you create your own charts, determine how you will merchandise your collection, and decide if everything meets your budget constraints. You should consider attaching a swatch of each of the fabrics to the fabric information sheet. (Details will follow later in the chapter.)

When you have completed this part, you should simultaneously have a specification measurement sheet filled out with as many measurements as you can determine. This will help you fine-tune your garments after you receive your first proto. In some instances, you will leave measurements blank for the factory to provide. This does not mean that they will necessarily be correct or that you should follow them blindly, since they might be using someone else's pattern or measurements for your garment.

On the other hand, you should consider their suggestions, since an experienced factory or vendor will be able to guide you through your process. Always remember to question their reasoning so that you will understand it and consider it when developing your next collection.

CONSTRUCTION SHEET

This could be a multiple amount of sheets. The purpose is to show those details that make your collection special, as well as provide the factory with a precise guideline of what you are trying to accomplish.

SAMPLE APPROVAL AND TRACKING SHEET

This sheet is used mainly to keep everybody aware of the dates and comments, and to see the basic flow of the process that the particular garment took. There might be occasions in which you change the garment three times through the proto process. On the third garment, you might ask the factory to go back to the original garment/first comments. This will help you and them have a better flow of communication, and will help you accomplish your goals.

BILL OF MATERIALS (B.O.M.)

This chart is self-explanatory. If you don't know where something is coming from or where it is sourced from, you cannot expect the vendor or the factory to know either. They might do their best to provide you with alternatives, but they do not have all the resources that you assume they might have. It is up to you and your team to be resourceful and accurate in order to achieve the results.

COLORWAYS

This sheet will help you coordinate all of the color components of your garments to determine whether they will match or not. Many mills and suppliers use pantone colors; but depending on what part of the world you are in, asking for black does not mean that all the other black components will match! Try, if you can, to have a sample of each of the components that you feel is important to your collection in the correct color or finish. Otherwise, the factory or vendor will always choose what is readily available and most inexpensive.

COUNTER SAMPLE SPECIFICATION SHEET

This is just a continuation of your specification measurement sheet. At this point, you will probably have new measurement points. This gives you the opportunity to clean up your tech package and add all new points of measurement.

GRADE RULES

This sheet is used in order to grade your garment. As per the sample in the book that we are using, the sample size is M. The size will always depend on the company, who you are, and what you are trying to achieve. A size medium for an urban company will obviously not be the same for a sportswear company, nor will the grade. This, again, is just a guideline.

FABRIC INFORMATION SHEET

This sheet should always be accompanied by a header or a big enough swatch for you to always have for your records. This will enable you to go back to review the quality if there is ever a production issue. You should always make sure that the mill fills out the fabric sheet. This will help to eliminate future problems. Also make sure that you advise the factory in advance what side is the correct side of the fabric, or the side that you would like them to utilize for your garments.

TRIM INFORMATION SHEET

This sheet should be used in a very similar way as the fabric information sheet. Instead of a header or a swatch, you might want to ask your vendor for a gross or enough trims to meet your proto needs or sales samples needs. Always remember to keep one for your records.

COST BREAKDOWN WORKSHEET

This sheet will help you determine an approximate price per garment and will help you review costing from one factory or vendor to another. Remember this will always depend on your relationship with the factory or the vendor, and how much they are willing to share with you. As stated earlier, the more information you have in your hands, the easier it will be to negotiate price with your factory and vendors.

SAMPLE PROCEDURES

The following section details the procedure for sample garment submission. A sample is a model of a garment that comes from the factory or sewing room based on the specifications and design details that were sent from the designer. There are five types of samples:

SAMPLE DEFINITIONS

- **Prototype (Proto) Sample** - The initial sample of a style in a given season. This can be made in any available fabric/trim approved by the designer.
- **Counter Sample** - After the first prototype, submitted samples are called Counter Samples until approved for Sales Sample production.
- **Sales Sample** – This sample should be an exact replica of what will be purchased and shipped to the retailer. This will be used by the salesperson for that purpose.
- **Pre-Production (P/P) Sample** - Following the Sales Sample, submittals will be called Pre-Production (P/P) Samples until fit, construction, and all details are approved for bulk. Pre-Production Samples should be made in actual fabric and trims, and must be made in the factory where bulk production is being placed. Factory may not proceed with bulk until this sample is approved.
- **Top-of-Production (TOP)** - A Top-of-Production (TOP) Sample is a garment pulled from the 1st run of bulk production.

SPECIFICATION/TECH PACKAGE

When developing a new style, the designer first submits a **Tech Package** (also called a Specification or Spec Package) to the factory, of which the factory will use to make the Proto Sample. Each style number in your collection should be assigned to a **Tech Package**.

A full **Tech Package** consists of the following parts, however, depending on the nature of the individual company and style, some of the parts may be omitted:

1 Lead Sheet, also known as Sketch and Description Sheet
2 Specification Measurement Sheet
3 Construction Detail Sheet
4 Sample Approval Tracking Sheet
5 Bill of Materials (BOM)
6 Colorway Sheet
7 Counter Sample Specification Sheet
8 Grade Rule Sheet

For smaller companies, or for basic styles, a **Tech Package** may consist of only the following four parts:

1 Lead Sheet, also known as Sketch and Description Sheet
2 Specification Measurement Sheet
3 Construction Detail Sheet
4 Sample Approval Tracking Sheet

Samples are generally **sent within two weeks** from receipt of the initial **Tech Package** or Sample Review Comments (unless otherwise specified).

The following pages consist of a sample **Tech Package**. This is the basis of the package; it may vary from company to company and you can revise it and create your own depending on your company's needs.

Tech Package/Part 1: Lead Sheet or Sketch and Description Sheet

SPECIFICATIONS LEAD SHEET					
COMPANY NAME:			COMPANY ADDRESS:		
DATE:					
PROTO NO.:		SEASON:		MAIN LABEL:	
STYLE NO.:		DELIVERY:		CONTENT:	
PATTERN NO.:		CATEGORY:		CARE:	
SIZE RANGE:		DESCRIPTION:			
SAMPLE SIZE:					
front view sketch			back view sketch		
FABRIC 1:		SUPPLIER:			
FABRIC 2:		SUPPLIER:			
FABRIC 3:		SUPPLIER:			
LINING 1:		SUPPLIER:			
LINING 2:		SUPPLIER:			
POCKETS:		SUPPLIER:			
WAISTBAND:		SUPPLIER:			
BUTTON:		SUPPLIER:			
TRIM 1:		SUPPLIER:			
TRIM 2:		SUPPLIER:			
TRIM 3:		SUPPLIER:			
DETAILS:					

Tech Package/Part 2: Specification Measurement Sheet

SIZE SPECIFICATIONS - OUTERWEAR

SPECIFICATION MEASUREMENT SHEET (Garments Measured in Inches)									
Sample Size		**Proto No.**				**Style No.**			
SAMPLE STATUS		**ORIGINAL SAMPLE**		**PROTO SAMPLE**		**SALES SAMPLE**		**PRE-PRODUCTION SAMPLE**	
SAMPLE SIZE REQUEST									
MEASUREMENTS		**Actual**	**Request**	**Actual**	**Request**	**Actual**	**Request**	**Actual**	**Request**
1)	Center Back Length								
2)	Chest - 1" Below Armhole								
3a)	Bottom Opening - Relaxed								
3b)	Bottom Opening - Extended								
4)	Side Seam Length								
5)	Shoulder Point-to-Point								
6)	Shoulder Length - HSP to Armhole								
7)	Yoke Depth at CB								
8)	Armhole								
9)	Upper Arm - 1" Below Armhole								
10)	Elbow - 13" Down from Top of Arm								
11)	Sleeve Length from CB Neck								
12a)	Sleeve Length Long from Cap								
12b)	Sleeve Length Short from Cap								
12c)	Sleeve Cap Height								
13a)	Sleeve Placket Length								
13b)	Sleeve Placket Width								
14a)	Sleeve Cuff Opening - Relaxed								
14b)	Sleeve Cuff Opening - Extended								
15)	Cuff Width								
16)	Front Placket Width								
17)	Collar Height CB								
18)	Collar Length Top								
19)	Collar Point Front								
20)	Collar Spread								
21)	Collar Stand/Band Width CB								
22)	Neck Circumference								
23)	Front Neck Drop								
24)	Neck Width CB								
25)	Zipper Length CF								
26)	Collar Stand Length								
27)	Hood Length CB								
28)	Hood Width Horizontal								
29)	Hood Height CF								
30)	Difference Between CF and CB								

Bold writing = changed measurements

Tech Package/Part 3: Construction Detail Sheet

<table>
<tr><th colspan="6">CONSTRUCTION SHEET</th></tr>
<tr><td colspan="2">Sample Size:</td><td colspan="2">Proto No.:</td><td colspan="2">Style No.:</td></tr>
<tr><td colspan="3">Date:</td><td colspan="3">Description:</td></tr>
<tr><td colspan="3">Construction Detail: #__________</td><td colspan="3">Construction Detail: #__________</td></tr>
<tr><td colspan="3">sketch</td><td colspan="3">sketch</td></tr>
<tr><td colspan="3">Construction Detail: #__________</td><td colspan="3">Construction Detail: #__________</td></tr>
<tr><td colspan="3">sketch</td><td colspan="3">sketch</td></tr>
<tr><td colspan="6">Notes:</td></tr>
</table>

Tech Package/Part 4: Sample Approval Tracking Sheet

SAMPLE APPROVAL TRACKING			
Season:		Proto No.	Style No.
SALES SAMPLES			
APPROVED FOR FIT	DATE:		
APPROVED FOR CONSTRUCTION	DATE:		
APPROVED FOR FABRIC	DATE:		
APPROVED FOR EMBROIDERY	DATE:		
APPROVED FOR TRIMS	DATE:		
BULK			
APPROVED FOR FIT	DATE:		
APPROVED FOR CONSTRUCTION	DATE:		
APPROVED FOR FABRIC	DATE:		
APPROVED FOR EMBROIDERY	DATE:		
APPROVED FOR TRIMS	DATE:		
TEST REPORT SUBMITTED	DATE:		
CARE LABEL SUBMITTED	DATE:		

DATE	BY	SUBJECT	CHANGES/COMMENTS

Tech Package/Part 5: Bill of Materials (BOM)

BILL OF MATERIALS				Style No. Proto No.
MATERIALS	**DESCRIPTION**	**PLACEMENT**	**QUANTITY**	**SOURCE/ COUNTRY**
BUTTONS				
SNAPS				
ZIPPERS				
MAIN LABEL				
SECONDARY LABEL				
UPC TICKET				
UPC STICKER				
POCKET FLASHER				
JOKER TICKET				
COUNTRY OF ORIGIN LABEL				
SIZE TAB				
CARE/CONTENT LABEL				
HANGTAG				
HANGER				
POLY BAG				
BOX				
TISSUE				

Attach following:
***Packaging instructions**
***Label placement codes**
***Instructions for care/content labels**
***French translation for country of origin label**

Note: The vendor is responsible for accurate country of origin and care/content labels.

Tech Package/Part 6: Colorway Sheet

COLORWAYS					
STYLE NO:		DESIGNER:			
PROTO NO:		TECH DESIGN:			
SEASON:					
PATTERN	**DESCRIPTION**	**COLOR #**	**COLOR #**	**COLOR #**	**COLOR #**
Shell					
Lining 1					
Lining 2					
Thread Color 1					
Thread Color 2					
Thread Color 3					
Embroidery 1					
Embroidery 2					
Embroidery 3					
Trim 1					
Trim 2					
Trim 3					
Trim 4					
Trim 5					
Pocketing 1					
Pocketing 2					
Waistband					
Button 1					
Button 2					
Button 3					
Artwork					
Front					
Back					
Notes:					

Tech Package/Part 7: Counter Sample Specification Sheet

COUNTER SAMPLE SPECIFICATIONS (All Measurements in Inches)											
SAMPLE STATUS		ORIGINAL SAMPLE		FIRST SAMPLE		SECOND SAMPLE		THIRD SAMPLE		FINAL	
STYLE NO.	SIZE										
	DATE										
MEASUREMENTS		Actual	Request	Actual	Request	Actual	Request	Actual	Request	Actual	Request
1)	Center Back Length										
2)	Center Front Length										
3)	Chest - 1" Below Armhole										
4)	Waist - 8" Below Armhole										
5)	Bottom Opening										
6)	Side Seam Length										
7)	Shoulder - Point to Point										
8)	Shoulder Seam										
9)	Yoke Depth at CB										
10)	Armhole										
11)	Bicep - 1" Below Armhole										
12)	Elbow - 9 1/2" Above Cuff Seam										
13)	Sleeve Length CB										
14)	Sleeve Length from Shoulder Point										
15)	Cuff/Sleeve Opening										
16)	Cuff or Topstitching Width										
17)	Front Placket Width										
18)	Collar Width CB										
19)	Collar Length										
20)	Collar Point										
21)	Collar Spread - Buttoned and Folded										
22)	Tie Space - Buttoned and Folded										
23)	Collar Stand Width CB										
24)	Collar Stand Length/Neck Circumference										
25)	Sleeve Placket Length										
26)	Sleeve Placket Width										
27)	Pocket Length										
28)	Pocket Width										
29)	Pocket Placement from CF										
30)	Pocket Placement from Shoulder Seam at Neck										
31)	Pocket Flap Length/Depth										
32)	Pocket Flap Width										
33)	Front Neck Drop										
34)	Logo Placement - CF										

Tech Package/Part 8: Grade Rule Sheet

(An example from Men's Wear)

GRADE RULES (An Example From Men's Wear) Garment Measurements in Inches								**PROTO NO.** **STYLE NO.**
MEASUREMENTS				**SAMPLE SIZE**				
SIZE		**XS**	**S**	**M**	**L**	**XL**	**XXL**	**TOLERANCE**
Measurements taken on the flat								
1)	Center Back Length	-1	-1/2	0	1/2	1	1 1/2	1/2
2)	Center Front Length	-1	-1/2	0	1/2	1	1 1/2	1/2
3)	Chest 1" Below Armhole	-3	-1 1/2	0	1 1/2	3	4 1/2	1/2
4)	Waist 8" Below Armhole - Open Pleat	-3	-1 1/2	0	1 1/2	3	4 1/2	1/2
5)	Bottom Opening	-3	-1 1/2	0	1 1/2	3	4 1/2	1/2
6)	Side Seam Length	-1/2	-1/4	0	1/4	1/2	3/4	1/4
7)	Shoulder Point to Point	-1 1/2	-3/4	0	1 1/4	2 1/2	3 3/4	1/2
8)	Shoulder Seam	-1/2	-1/8	0	1/8	1/2	3/4	1/2
9)	Yoke Depth at CB	-1/2	0	0	0	1/2	1	1/4
10)	Armhole - Measured Straight	-2	-1	0	1 1/4	2 1/2	3 3/4	1/2
11)	Biceps - 1" Below Armhole	-2	-1	0	1	2	3	1/2
12)	Elbow - 9 1/2" Above Cuff Seam	-1	-1/2	0	1/2	1	1 3/4	1/2
13)	Sleeve Length CB	-2	-1	0	1	2	3	1/2
14)	Sleeve Length from Shoulder Point	-1 1/4	-5/8	0	3/4	1 1/2	2 1/4	1/2
15)	Cuff/Sleeve Opening	-1	-1/2	0	1/2	1	1 1/2	1/2
16)	Cuff or Topstitching Width	0	0	0	0	0	0	1/8
17)	Front Placket Width	0	0	0	0	0	0	1/8
18)	Collar Width CB	0	0	0	0	0	0	1/8
19)	Collar Length	-2	-1	0	1	2	3	3/8
20)	Collar Point	0	0	0	0	0	0	1/8
21)	Collar Spread - Buttoned and Folded	0	0	0	0	0	0	1/4
22)	Tie Space - Buttoned and Folded	0	0	0	0	0	0	1/8
23)	Collar Stand Width CB	0	0	0	0	0	0	1/8
24)	Collar Stand Length/Neck Circumference	-2	-1	0	1	2	3	3/8
25)	Sleeve Placket Length	0	0	0	0	0	0	1/4
26)	Sleeve Placket Width	0	0	0	0	0	0	1/8
27)	Pocket Length	0	0	0	0	0	0	1/8
28)	Pocket Width	0	0	0	0	0	0	1/8
29)	Pocket Placement from CF	-1/2	-1/4	0	1/4	1/2	3/4	1/8
30)	Pocket Placement from Shoulder Seam at Neck	-3/8	-1/8	0	1/8	3/8	1/2	1/8
31)	Pocket Flap Length (Depth)	0	0	0	0	0	0	1/8
32)	Pocket Flap Width	0	0	0	0	0	0	1/8
33)	Front Neck Drop	0	0	0	0	0	0	1/8
34)	Logo Placement-CF	-1/2	-1/4	0	1/4	1/2	3/4	1/8

Additionally, along with the **Tech Package**, all garments in development require the following three forms:

- Fabric Information Sheet
- Trim Information Sheet
- Cost Breakdown Sheet

Examples of these forms are on the following pages.

FABRIC INFORMATION SHEET

A **Fabric Information Sheet** should be completed for all fabrics used in each style. You, the customer or your agent, should send this sheet to the fabric mill. It should then be completed by the mill, and be returned to you or your agent with a swatch for your reference. The completed Fabric Information Sheet and swatch should be kept for documentation.

The **Fabric Information Sheet** outlines all pertinent information about any or all fabrics used within a particular style or SKU. This is particularly important if you are purchasing a "package" from the contractor. The term "package" is used when the contractor will be purchasing the fabrics, trims and findings on your behalf in order to complete your order. This information is vital in order to insure that the correct fabrics (construction, fiber content, pattern number, etc.) are delivered, with contracted delivery dates and prices. Care should be taken to include as much specific information as possible. Some of the information may include:

- **Customer Ref #** - The customer's proto, style or model number.
- **Mill Reference #** - The mill's specific number for a particular fabric, pattern or print.
- **Content** - The percentage breakdown of the fiber contents in the primary fabric (e.g. 60% Cotton/40% Polyester). This will affect duty rates on imported fabrics or garments.
- **Yarn Count** - Refers to the yarn size and plys used in constructing the fabric. This is an important factor in quality and costing.
- **Weight** - Fabric weight usually given in weight per sq. yard or sq. meter.
- **Width** - The "cuttable" width of a given fabric. This will affect the "yield" in cutting out the garment pieces.
- **Construction** - The specific construction and "set" of the yarns in woven fabrics. This is often combined with the yarn count and is expressed in form like an equation.
- **Country of Origin** - The country in which the final assembly (construction) of the garment takes place.
- **Gauge** - The relative fineness or coarseness of knitted fabrics.
- **Finish** - Refers to any special or customer-designated finishes or treatments.
- **Price** - **Proto**: Price for development or samples that are less than production minimums.
  Bulk: Price for production quantities.
- **Lead Time** - Projected delivery time after a production order is placed.
- **Care Instructions and Symbols** - Recommended care instructions provided by the mill. These may be modified for production depending on construction or end-use issues.

No Purchase Orders should be issued until all information on the **Fabric Information Sheet** is complete.

FABRIC INFORMATION SHEET

CUSTOMER:	SEASON:
CUSTOMER REFERENCE #:	

MILL:	AGENT INFO:

MILL REFERENCE #:	WEIGHT:
CONTENT:	WIDTH:
	CONSTRUCTION:
	COUNTRY OF ORIGIN:
YARN COUNT:	GAUGE:
	# OF ENDS:

MILL COLOR # AND DESCRIPTION:

FINISH:	

PRICE:

PROTO:	SAMPLE:
BULK:	

LEAD TIME: MINIMUMS:

SAMPLE:	
BULK:	

CARE INSTRUCTION AND SYMBOLS:

TRIM INFORMATION SHEET

A **Trim Information Sheet** should be completed for all trims used in each style. This sheet should be used for non-generic or specific trims. You, the customer, or your agent, should send this sheet to the trim company. It should then be completed by the trim company, and be returned to you or your agent with a sample for your reference. The completed **Trim Information Sheet** and sample should be kept for documentation.

The **Trim Information Sheet** outlines all pertinent information about any or all trims used within a particular style or SKU. This is particularly important if you are purchasing a "package" from the contractor. The term "package" is used when the contractor will be purchasing the fabrics and findings on your behalf in order to complete your order. This information is vital in order to insure that the correct trims are delivered, with contracted delivery dates and prices. Care should be taken to include as much specific information as possible on the Trim Sheet. Some of the information may include:

- **Customer Ref # -** The customer's proto, style or model number.
- **Reference # -** The trim manufacturer's specific number for a particular item.
- **Country of Origin -** The country in which the final assembly (construction) of the garment takes place.
- **Gauge -** The relative fineness or coarseness of the zipper.
- **Finish -** Refers to any special or customer-designated finishes or treatments.
- **Price -** **Proto**: Price for development or samples that are less than production minimums.
  Bulk: Price for production quantities.
- **Lead Time:** Projected delivery time after a production order is placed.

No Purchase Orders should be issued until all information on the **Trim Information Sheet** is complete.

TRIM INFORMATION SHEET

CUSTOMER:	SEASON:
CUSTOMER REFERENCE #:	

COMPANY NAME:	AGENT INFO:

REFERENCE #:	COUNTRY OF ORIGIN:
	GAUGE:

TRIM COMPANY COLOR # AND DESCRIPTION:

FINISH:	

PRICE:

PROTO:	SAMPLE:
BULK:	

LEAD TIME: MINIMUMS:

SAMPLE:	
BULK:	

COST BREAKDOWN WORKSHEET

PURPOSE

The purpose of the **Cost Breakdown Worksheet** (also called a Cost Calculation Sheet) is to provide you, as the customer, with a detailed cost breakdown for each garment in development. You will use this information to make decisions on whether any changes are needed to achieve your targeted cost.

PROCEDURE

- The customer provides the agent, manufacturer and/or contractor with the attached worksheet for cost breakdown quotations. This form should be sent with the initial prototype package or during the contractor's first development cycle, via fax or e-mail.
- At the start of each season the agent, manufacturer and/or contractor should submit ALL cost breakdown information on the worksheet.
- The agent, manufacturer and/or contractor should fill in all applicable areas in order to arrive at the total First Cost (the cost for all components must be included, such as: fabric, trim, etc.).
- CMT or CM must also be included in order to arrive at the total First Cost.
- All cost quotes should come to the customer via use of this form.

Purchase Orders should not be issued until the Cost Breakdown Worksheet is complete.

The following **Cost Breakdown Sheet** has been set up for an FOB contract. You can use this to calculate your total First Cost and target your Final Cost or Wholesale Price.

COST BREAKDOWN WORKSHEET/COST CALCULATION SHEET

COST CALCULATION SHEET	Date:		Style No.:	
	Label:		Size Range:	
	Season:		On Line: ______	Estimate: ____ ___

Category:	Description:	Yield/Style:	Cost/Yard:	Cost/Garment:	Total/Garment:
Fabric 1					
	Freight				
Fabric 2					
	Freight				
Fabric 3					
	Freight				
Trim 1					
	Freight				
Trim 2					
	Freight				
Notions 1					
Notions 2					
Notions 3					
Category:	**Direct Labor:**	**Mfg. Overhead:**	**Contract Wk.:**	**Excess:**	
Cutting					
Sewing					
Finishing					
Special Finish					
Special Finish					
Transportation					
Total Manufacturing Cost:					
Expense Category		**Total Manufacturing Cost x ____%**			
Administrative				10%	
Selling				4%	
Shipping				2%	
Insurance					
Close-Outs				1%	
Total Make and Sell Cost:					
Variable Marketing Expenses					
Total Make and Sell Cost:					
			A	B	C
Selling Price					
Net Profit (Selling Price less Make and Sell):					
Net Profit % (Net-Profit div. by Selling Price):					

RECEIVED SAMPLES

Once the sample is received, you, the customer, review the sample, and send your Sample Review Comments to the factory. Samples should be corrected and measurement and style corrections resubmitted until approval for Bulk Production is granted.

All samples submitted for review by the factory should have the following information attached:

1. Audit measurements

2. Completed **Sample Tag** (example on following page)

   The comments section of the **Sample Tag** should include:

   - Substitute trims
   - Status on correct trim
   - Construction issues
   - Factory limitations
   - Improvement/cost saving suggestions
   - Any details that differ from specs.

Hangtags are not required on Prototype or Counter Samples. They are required for the Sales Samples and Pre-Production Samples submitted for bulk approval. These hangtags will initially be provided by you, the customer.

Front side of tag:

To be filled in by factory:

Style#___________ CS#_____________

Description________________________

Season____________________________

Agent_____________________________

Factory____________________________

Date sent__________________________

Submitted for:

Fit/ Construction	Fabric	Trims	Embroidery

Outerwear/Wovens:

(Note: "S" for sub or "A" for actual)

Shell 1:	Shell 2:	Shell 3:
Lining 1:	Lining 2:	Lining 3:
Fill:	Embroid. 1:	Embroid. 2:

Comments:

Back side of tag:

Customer use only
Counter sample approval

Date received______________________

Date reviewed_____________________

Approved for _____________________

____

Fit/ Construction	Fabric	Trims	Embroidery

Fabric:
Yarn count:
Gauge:
Gm wt:

Comments:

CHAPTER 2

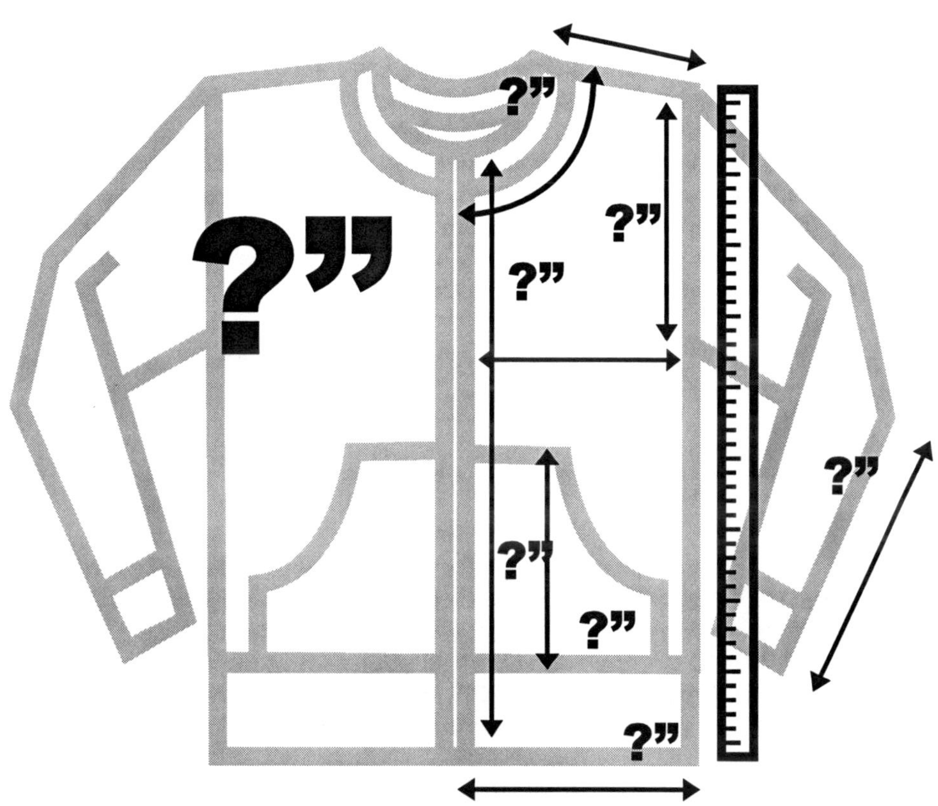

SPECIFICATIONS AND MEASUREMENTS

This chapter details the Specification Measurement Sheet, and offers examples of sheets for different product types. Additionally, Points of Measure are defined and illustrated, along with Construction Detail sketches that, utilized together, facilitate getting accurate sample garments back from the factory.

SAMPLE SPECIFICATION SHEETS

In the next few pages I will give you examples of different garments, spec measurement sheets. You will also see how to measure the garments and learn the steps to take from prototype to the final production package. These spec measurement sheets are given to you to create an overall idea of what a tech package together entails.

As described in Chapter 1, when creating a Spec Package (Tech Package) the **Specification Measurement Sheet** (Spec Sheet) is the second component of the packet. It is extremely important that this component be as meticulous as possible. The more measurements a designer adds to a Spec Sheet, the more likely the sample garment will arrive from the factory properly executed.

The following pages feature examples of Specification Measurement by various categories.
The following sheets can be used as templates and adapted to individual categories of product development. Please note that the following sheets are intended to track an individual style from prototype through to pre-production approval, taking into consideration changes and/or amendments made to each sample of the development and production processes.

Once the counter sample arrives, a designer can make revisions to the counter sample as necessary for fit and design and then proceed to Sales Samples (see Chapter 4.)

MEASUREMENTS AND SPECIFICATIONS

The following section details formats for specifying your measurements (points of measure) and guidelines for construction that are additionally used in the tech package. The examples given should encourage you to expand in detail all the various aspects of a particular style, when creating a Tech Package for a style. You can add more details to suit the framework of your own business. It is vitally important that all contracted items are as fully detailed in their specifications as possible to insure proper execution from the earliest product development stages through to final production.

SIZE SPECIFICATIONS - OUTERWEAR

SPECIFICATION MEASUREMENT SHEET (Garments Measured in Inches)									
Sample Size		Proto No.				Style No.			
SAMPLE STATUS		ORIGINAL SAMPLE		PROTO SAMPLE		SALES SAMPLE		PRE-PRODUCTION SAMPLE	
SAMPLE SIZE REQUEST									
MEASUREMENTS		Actual	Request	Actual	Request	Actual	Request	Actual	Request
1)	Center Back Length								
2)	Chest - 1" Below Armhole								
3a)	Bottom Opening - Relaxed								
3b)	Bottom Opening - Extended								
4)	Side Seam Length								
5)	Shoulder Point-to-Point								
6)	Shoulder Length - HSP to Armhole								
7)	Yoke Depth at CB								
8)	Armhole								
9)	Upper Arm - 1" Below Armhole								
10)	Elbow - 13" Down from Top of Arm								
11)	Sleeve Length from CB Neck								
12a)	Sleeve Length Long from Cap								
12b)	Sleeve Length Short from Cap								
12c)	Sleeve Cap Height								
13a)	Sleeve Placket Length								
13b)	Sleeve Placket Width								
14a)	Sleeve Cuff Opening - Relaxed								
14b)	Sleeve Cuff Opening - Extended								
15)	Cuff Width								
16)	Front Placket Width								
17)	Collar Height CB								
18)	Collar Length Top								
19)	Collar Point Front								
20)	Collar Spread								
21)	Collar Stand/Band Width CB								
22)	Neck Circumference								
23)	Front Neck Drop								
24)	Neck Width CB								
25)	Zipper Length CF								
26)	Collar Stand Length								
27)	Hood Length CB								
28)	Hood Width Horizontal								
29)	Hood Height CF								
30)	Difference Between CF and CB								

Bold writing = changed measurements

Figure 4.5 - Points of Measure

(An example from Outerwear)

No.	Point of Measure
1)	**Center Back Length** (Neck seam to bottom hem)
2)	**Chest 1" Below Armhole** (Double measurement)
3)	**Bottom Opening** (Double measurement)
4)	**Side Seam Length**
5)	**Shoulder Point to Point**
6)	**Shoulder Length**
7)	**Yoke Depth at CB**
8)	**Armhole Set-in** (Double measurement)
9)	**Upper Arm** (1" below armhole)
10)	**Elbow** (9 1/2" above cuff seam)
11)	**Sleeve Length from CB**
12)	**Sleeve Length Cap** (For set-in sleeve)
13)	**Sleeve Placket/Vent Length**
14)	**Sleeve/Cuff Opening** (Double measurement)
15)	**Cuff Width**
16)	**Front Placket Width**
17)	**Collar Width at CB**
18)	**Collar Length**
19)	**Collar Point**
20)	**Collar Spread** (Buttoned and folded)
21)	**Collar Stand/Collar Band Width at CB**
22)	**Neck Circumference**
23)	**Front Neck Drop**
24)	**Neck Width CB**
25)	**CF Zipper Length**
26)	**Collar Stand Length**
27)	**Hood Length CB**
28)	**Hood Width Horizontal** (Around to other side)
29)	**Hood Height CF**
30)	**Difference Between Center Front and Center Back**

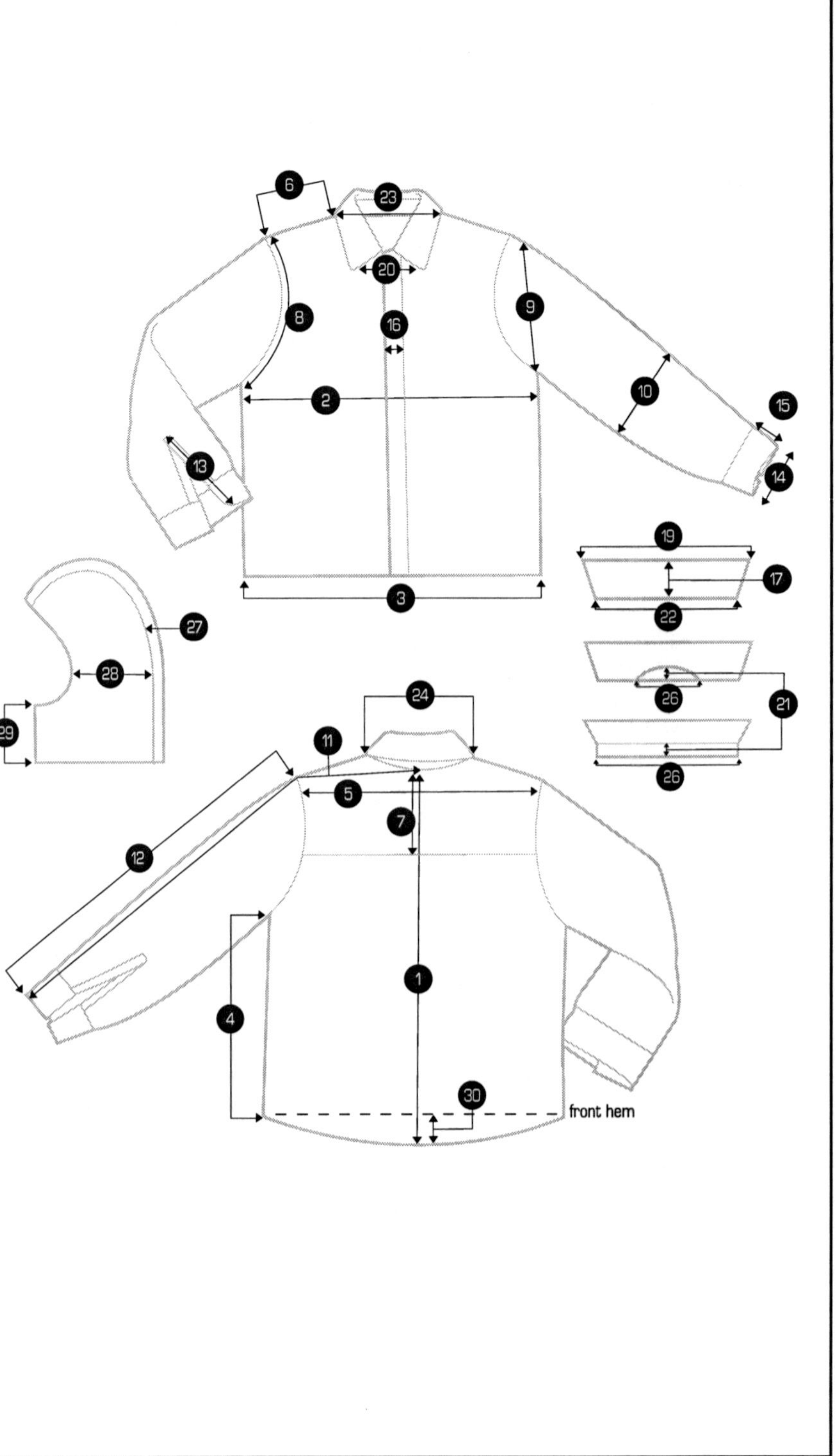

MEASUREMENT METHODOLOGY

The following measurement guidelines and standards for a men's sportswear company and can be adapted to any customer's unique product line. In communicating specific "points of measure" or "how to measure" guides, it is assured that the designers, product development staff, contractors, suppliers, and finally the customer's quality control staff will all adhere to the contracted specifications, by all using the same "points of measure," as stated in the Tech Package for each style.

See Figure 4.5 to follow with "points of measure" illustrations.

1) **Center Back Length:** Place garment flat with front facing down. Smooth all the wrinkles out of the back. Measure at the center back neckline seam, to the end of the garment hem.

2) **Chest 1" Below Armhole:** Place garment face up. Move sleeves to their natural extended position. Gently pull out extra fullness from any pleats. Smooth fabric flat. Measure 1" down from the very bottom of the armhole, across the chest, to the opposite side seam edge to edge. Double that measurement. For garments with box pleat, measure garment face down.

3) **Bottom Opening:** Lay garment face up. Smooth out extra fabric and wrinkles. Measure from the finished end of side seam across the garment to the opposite finished bottom end of side seam. Double that measurement. If garment has side vents or shirttails, measure across the top of the vent or shirttail.

4) **Side Seam Length:** Lay garment flat. Smooth out extra fabric on the body. Measure from the armhole seam intersection down to bottom finished edge of the side seam.

5) **Shoulder Point to Shoulder Point:** Place garment face down, put sleeves in their relaxed position and smooth out extra fabric. Place measuring tape at the natural fold point of the armhole seam. Measure across the garment to the opposite shoulder point.

6) **Shoulder Length:** Measure along shoulder seam from neckline to armhole.

7) **Yoke Depth at CB:** Measure from CB at neck seam vertically down to edge of yoke seam.

8) **Armhole Set-in:** Place garment front up. Align front and back armhole seams so that there are no wrinkles. Place measuring tape at the top of the shoulder point. Carefully follow contour of the sleeve seam and measure to the bottom of the armhole. Double that measurement.

9) **Upper Arm:** Smooth out extra fabric and wrinkles in sleeve. Starting at outer folded edge of sleeve, measure at a perpendicular angle down to seamed edge of sleeve 1" below armhole. Double that measurement.

10) **Elbow:** Smooth out extra fabric and wrinkles in sleeve. Measure 9 1/2" up from cuff seam. Starting at outer folded edge of sleeve, measure at a perpendicular angle down to seamed edge of sleeve. Double that measurement. If there is no cuff measure 9 1/2" up from hem edge.

11) **Sleeve Length from CB:** Measure from CB point of garment at neck seam of collar or collar stand. Measure to natural fold point of shoulder at armhole seam. Measure straight down fold of sleeve to top edge of cuff or sleeve opening.

12) **Sleeve Length Cap:** For set-in sleeve only. Measure from natural fold of shoulder at armhole seam to bottom of cuff opening along fold of sleeve to top of cuff or sleeve opening.

13) **Sleeve Placket/Vent Length:** Measure from the top point or edge of placket or vent to bottom of sleeve.

14) **Sleeve/Cuff Opening:** Open cuff and smooth flat. Measure from the center point of the button or snap to the buttonhole or the other snap.

15) **Cuff Width:** Measure from cuff set seam to the finished edge of the cuff.

16) **Front Placket Width:** Measure across the front placket from finished edge to finished edge.

17) **Collar Width at CB:** Turn collar up and place face up. Measure from the collar seam at CB up to the finished edge.

18) **Collar Length:** Open collar out straight. Measure straight across the top of the collar from point to point.

19) **Collar Point:** Measure along the outside edge of the collar set seam to the end of the collar point.

20) **Collar Spread:** Measure with garment buttoned or zipped and collar folded correctly. Measure distance between collar points.

21) **Collar Stand/Collar Band Width at CB:** Measure the center back of collar stand or band from neck seam to collar seam set.

22) **Neck Circumference:** Open garment and lay flat. Place tape on neckline and measure from center front to center front following the contour of the neckline. Include zipper if applicable.

23) **Front Neck Drop:** Measure down from neck seam at CB to neck seam at center front.

24) **Neck Width CB:** Measure back neck on seam from shoulder to shoulder.

25) **Center Front Zipper Length:** Measure from the top of the zipper to the bottom.

26) **Collar Stand Length:** Measure bottom edge of collar stand from edge to edge.

27) **Hood Length CB:** Measure from center front hood to CB neck seam at center of hood following the contour of the CB hood.

28) **Hood Width Horizontal:** Measure from the narrowest part of the front hood (eye level) around the back to the other front side.

29) **Hood Height CF:** Measure from the top of the hood at CF down to the neck seam at CF hood.

30) **Difference Between Center Front and Center Back:** Lay the garment flat, lining up side seams from armholes down. Flatten all wrinkles from the hem, and measure from CB hem to CF hem.

SIZE SPECIFICATIONS - DRESSES

SPECIFICATION MEASUREMENT SHEET (Garments Measured in Inches)									
Sample Size		Proto No.				Style No.			
SAMPLE STATUS		ORIGINAL SAMPLE		PROTO SAMPLE		SALES SAMPLE		PRE-PRODUCTION SAMPLE	
SAMPLE SIZE REQUEST									
MEASUREMENTS		Actual	Request	Actual	Request	Actual	Request	Actual	Request
1)	Body Length/High Point Shoulder to Hem								
2)	Body Length/High Point Shoulder to Finished Waist								
3)	Body Length Center Back to Hem								
4)	Body Length Center Back to Waist								
5)	Center Back Skirt Length								
6)	Shoulder to Shoulder								
7)	Shoulder Slope								
8)	Across Back 6" Down High Point Shoulder/Yoke								
9)	Back Yoke: Depth at Center Back								
10)	Body Width Flat 1"Down								
11)	Body Width Front: Seam to Seam								
12)	Waist: 17" Down From High Point of Shoulder								
13)	Waist Width at Seam								
14)	Waist Stretched								
15)	Waistband Width								
16)	Hip: 3" Down from Waist Seam								
17)	Hip: 7" Down from Waist Seam								
18)	Hip: 10" Down from Waist Seam								
19)	Hip: 23" Down from Waist Seam								
20)	Sweep at Edge								
21)	Bottom Hem								
22)	Across Front: 6" Down High Point Shoulder								
23)	Armhole Curve								
24)	Armhole Straight								
25)	Armhole Raglan: Front								
26)	Distance between Front Raglan Seams								
27)	Armhole Raglan: Back								
28)	Distance between Back Raglan Seams								
29)	Shoulder Seam								
30)	Sleeve Length/Shoulder Long								
31)	Sleeve Length/Shoulder Short								
32)	Sleeve Length/Neck Long								
Please add measurements as you need.									

Bold writing = changed measurements

Figure 4.6 - Points of Measure

(An example from Dresses)

1)	Body Length/High Point Shoulder to Hem
2)	Body Length/High Point Shoulder to Finished Waist
3)	Body Length Center Back to Hem
4)	Body Length Center Back to Waist
5)	Center Back Skirt Length
6)	Shoulder to Shoulder
7)	Shoulder Slope
8)	Across Back 6" Down High Point Shoulder/ Yoke
9)	Back Yoke
10)	Body Width Flat 1"Down
11)	Body Width Front
12)	Waist: 17" Down From High Point of Shoulder
13)	Waist Width at Seam
14)	Waist Stretched
15)	Waistband Width
16)	Hip: 3" Down from Waist Seam
17)	Hip: 7" Down from Waist Seam
18)	Hip: 10" Down from Waist Seam
19)	Hip: 23" Down from Waist Seam
20)	Sweep at Edge
21)	Bottom Hem
22)	Across Front: 6" Down High Point Shoulder
23)	Armhole Curve
24)	Armhole Straight
25)	Armhole Raglan
26)	Distance between Front Raglan Seams
27)	Armhole Raglan: Back
28)	Distance between Back Raglan Seams
29)	Shoulder Seam
30)	Sleeve Length/Shoulder Long

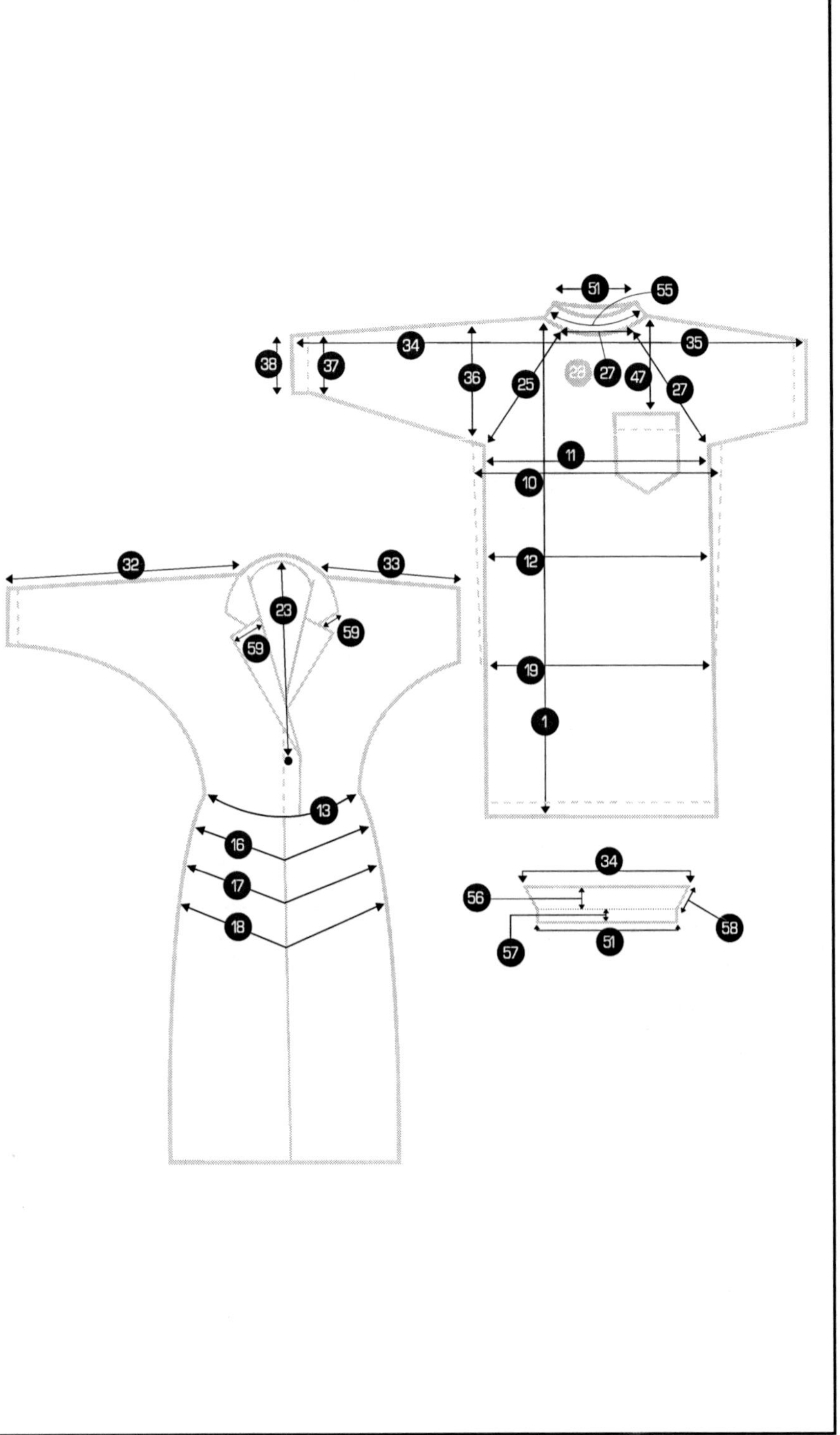

31)	Sleeve Length/Shoulder Short
32)	Sleeve length/Neck Long
33)	Sleeve length/Neck Short
34)	Sleeve Length/Center Back Long
35)	Sleeve Length/Center Back Short
36)	Sleeve Muscle 1" Down
37)	Sleeve 3" Above Cuff/ Edge
38)	Cuff Opening on Edge
39)	Cuff Width/Hem
40)	Sleeve Placket Length
41)	Sleeve Placket Width
42)	Front Placket Width
43)	Front Placket Length
44)	Pocket Length
45)	Pocket Width
46)	Pocket Trim Length/Hem
47)	Pocket Placement
48)	Pocket Placement
49)	Front Neck Drop
50)	Back Neck Drop
51)	Neck Opening Inside
52)	Neck Circumference to 19". Measure from button to end of button hole, along body join at neck
53)	Neck Circumference to 19" or more. For shape necklines
54)	Back Neck Seam to Seam
55)	Back Neck Seam High Point Shoulder to High Point of Shoulder
56)	Collar Back
57)	Collar Stand
58)	Collar Point
59)	Lapel Point
60)	Collar Point to Point
61)	Shoulder Pad Placement

MEASUREMENT METHODOLOGY

1) **Body Length/High Point Shoulder to Hem.** Measure from High Point of Shoulder to finished hem.

2) **Body Length/High Point Shoulder to Finished Waist.** Measure from High Point of Shoulder to finished waist seam.

3) **Body Length Center Back to Hem.** Measure from center back at neck seam, straight down to finished hem.

4) **Body Length Center Back to Waist.** Measure from center back at neck seam, straight down to finished waist seam or stitching.

5) **Center Back Skirt Length.** Measure from waist seam to finished hem.

6) **Shoulder to Shoulder.** Measure straight across back from end of shoulder seam to end of shoulder seam.

7) **Shoulder Slope.** Extend the imaginary line from the high points of shoulders. Measure the distance between the line and either the end of the shoulder seam or the finished edge of sleeve.

8) **Across Back 6" Down High Point Shoulder/Yoke.** 6" down from high point of shoulder or along yoke seam, measure across back from armhole to armhole.

9) **Back Yoke: Depth at Center Back.** Measure yoke depth at center back neck seam down to yoke seam.

10) **Body Width Flat 1"Down.** Lay garment completely flat (pleats open), measure 1" down from armhole straight across.

11) **Body Width Front: Seam to Seam.** Measure 1" down from armhole across front seam to seam.

12) **Waist: 17" Down From High Point of Shoulder.** 17" down from High Point of Shoulder, measure across waist.

13) **Waist Width at Seam.** Measurement taken across at waist seam.

14) **Waist Stretched.** Measure across garment at waist seam with garment stretched until fabric is flat.

15) **Waistband Width.** Measure from top edge of band or casing to seam.

16) **Hip: 3" Down from Waist Seam.** Measure 3" down from waist seam at sides and center front. Pivot tape measure between the 3 points across the hip.

17) **Hip: 7" Down from Waist Seam.** Measure 7" down from waist seam at sides and center front. Pivot tape measure between the 3 points across the hip.

18) **Hip: 10" Down from Waist Seam.** Measure 10" down from waist seam at sides and center front. Pivot tape measure between the 3 points across the hip.

19) **Hip: 23" Down from Waist Seam.** 23" down from High Point of Shoulder, measure across hip.

20) **Sweep at Edge.** Measure along finished edge.

21) **Bottom Hem.** Width of hem or stitching from edge.

22) **Across Front.** 6" Down High Point Shoulder. 6" down from the High Point Shoulder, measure across front from armhole to armhole seam.

23) **Armhole Curve.** Measure along curved seam of armhole, between side and shoulder seams with garment laying flat.

24) **Armhole Straight.** Measure straight from side seam to shoulder seam.

25) **Armhole Raglan: Front.** Measure on seam line from side seam to neck.

26) **Distance between Front Raglan Seams.** Measure straight across from raglan seam to raglan seam at neck.

27) **Armhole Raglan: Back.** Measure straight across at back neck depth point from seam to seam.

28) **Distance between Back Raglan Seams.** Measure straight across at back neck depth point from seam to seam.

29) **Shoulder Seam.** Measure from neck seam along top to finished edge of sleeve.

30) **Sleeve Length/Shoulder Long.** Measure from shoulder seam along top to finished edge of sleeve.

31) **Sleeve Length/Shoulder Short.** Measure from shoulder seam along top to finished edge of sleeve.

32) **Sleeve length/Neck Long.** Measure along shoulder seam from neck to finished edge of sleeve, including cuff.

33) **Sleeve length/Neck Short.** Measure along shoulder seam from neck to finished edge of sleeve, including cuff.

34) **Sleeve Length/Center Back Long.** Fold garment to establish center back. Measure from center back of garment to finished edge of sleeve/cuff.

35) **Sleeve Length/Center Back Short.** Fold garment to establish center back. Measure from center back of garment to finished edge of sleeve/cuff.

36) **Sleeve Muscle 1" Down.** Measure 1" down from armhole, straight across sleeve forming a perpendicular with grain.

37) **Sleeve 3" Above Cuff/Edge.** Measure 3" above cuff or finished edge straight across sleeve-with the pleats open perpendicular with grain.

38) **Cuff Opening on Edge.** Measure along finished edge of opening. Cuff closed.

39) **Cuff Width/Hem.** Finished width of cuff or depth of hem.

40) **Sleeve Placket Length.** Finished measurement.

41) **Sleeve Placket Width.** Finished measurement.

42) **Front Placket Width.** Finished width of Placket.

43) **Front Placket Length.** Finished measurement.

44) **Pocket Length.** Finished measurement.

45) **Pocket Width.** Finished measurement.

46) **Pocket Trim Length/Hem.** Measure from finished edge to stitching or depth of hem.

47) **Pocket Placement.** Down From High Point Shoulder. Measure from high point of shoulder to top edge of pocket.

48) **Pocket Placement.** Measure from center front to finished edge of pocket.

49) **Front Neck Drop.** Measure on front from center back neck straight down to bottom of front neck opening. If it has a lapel, measure down to center of first button.

50) **Back Neck Drop.** Measure from high point shoulder to center back of neckline on garment.

51) **Neck Opening Inside.** Measure along imaginary line inside neckline at finished edge or collar seam.

52) **Neck Circumference to 19".** Measure from button to end of button hole, along body join at neck. If no collar, measure finished edge center front to center front.

53) **Neck Circumference to 19" or more. For shape necklines.** Measure along edge of seam center front to center front.

54) **Back Neck Seam to Seam.** Measure along neck seam from shoulder seam to shoulder seam.

55) **Back Neck Seam High Point Shoulder to High Point of Shoulder.** Measure between high point of shoulder to High Point of shoulder along neckline.

56) **Collar Back.** Measure collar height at center back not including stand.

57) **Collar Stand.** Measure collar stand height at center back.

58) **Collar Point.** Measure notch to the point of collar.

59) **Lapel Point.** Measure from notch to the point of the lapel.

60) **Collar Point to Point.** Measure from point to point on the outer edge of collar.

61) **Shoulder Pad Placement.** Measure from high point of shoulder towards armhole.

SIZE SPECIFICATIONS - SKIRTS

SPECIFICATION MEASUREMENT SHEET (Garments Measured in Inches)									
Sample Size		**Proto No.**				**Style No.**			
SAMPLE STATUS		**ORIGINAL SAMPLE**		**PROTO SAMPLE**		**SALES SAMPLE**		**PRE-PRODUCTION SAMPLE**	
SAMPLE SIZE REQUEST									
MEASUREMENTS		**Actual**	**Request**	**Actual**	**Request**	**Actual**	**Request**	**Actual**	**Request**
1)	Waist (Closed) (Circumference measurement)								
2)	Waist Stretched (Circumference measurement)								
3)	Waistband width								
4)	Hip 3" Down From Waist Seam (Circumference measurement)								
5)	Hip 7" Down From Waist Seam (Circumference measurement)								
6)	Hip 10" Down From Waist Seam (Circumference measurement)								
7)	Sweep at Edge (Circumference measurement)								
8)	Length Center Front From Waist Seam								
9)	Waist at Top (Circumference measurement)								
10)	Hip 3" Down From Top (Circumference measurement)								
11)	Hip 7" Down From Top (Circumference measurement)								
12)	Hip 10" Down From Top (Circumference measurement)								
13)	Length From Top Edge								
14)	Hem Width								

Bold writing = changed measurements

Figure 4.7 - Points of Measure

(An example from Skirts)

1)	**Waist (Closed) Center of Waistband** (Circumference measurement) **Measure along center of waistband**
2)	**Waist Stretched** (Circumference measurement) **Stretch elastic waist until fabric is flat**
3)	**Waistband width**
4)	**Hip 3" Down From Waist Seam** (Circumference measurement)
5)	**Hip 7" Down From Waist Seam** (Circumference measurement)
6)	**Hip 10" Down From Waist Seam** (Circumference measurement)
7)	**Sweep at Edge** (Circumference measurement)
8)	**Length Center Front from Waist Seam**
9)	**Waist at Top** (Circumference measurement)
10)	**Hip 3" Down from Top** (Circumference measurement)
11)	**Hip 7" Down from Top** (Circumference measurement)
12)	**Hip 10" Down from Top** (Circumference measurement)
13)	**Length from Top Edge**
14)	**Hem Width**

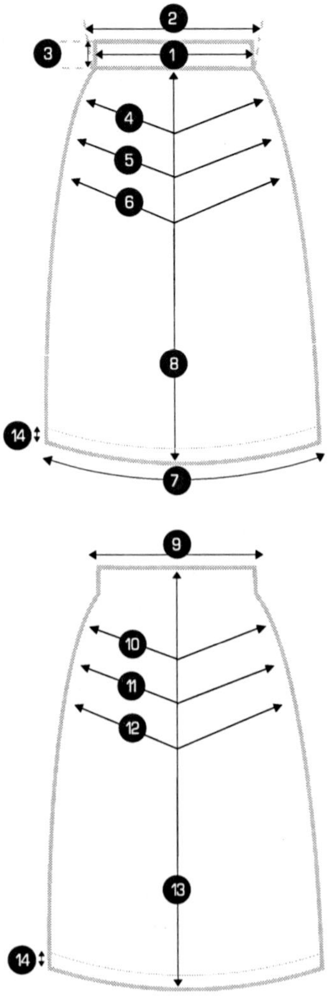

MEASUREMENT METHODOLOGY

1) **Waist (Closed) Center of Waistband (Circumference measurement).** Measure along center of waistband. Top edge of front and back waistband must be even. All closures must be fastened and button must be at end of button hole.

2) **Waist Stretched (Circumference measurement).** Stretch elastic waist until fabric is flat. Measure middle of band.

3) **Waistband width.** Measure from top edge of band to seam.

4) **Hip 3" Down From Waist Seam (Circumference measurement).** Measure 3" down from waist seam at sides and center front. Pivot tape measure between the three points across the hip, with pleats closed.

5) **Hip 7" Down From Waist Seam (Circumference measurement).** Measure 7" down from waist seam at sides and center front. Pivot tape measure between the three points across the hip, with pleats closed.

6) **Hip 10" Down From Waist Seam (Circumference measurement).** Measure 10" down from waist seam at sides and center front. Pivot tape measure between the three points across the hip, with pleats closed.

7) **Sweep at Edge (Circumference measurement).** Measure along edge of curve.

8) **Length Center Front from Waist Seam.** Measure at center front from waist seam to hem.

9) **Waist at Top (Circumference measurement).** Measure along top edge of waist, with top edges of waist even and all closures fastened.

10) **Hip 3" Down from Top (Circumference measurement).** Used when there is not a separate waistband. Measure down from top of skirt at sides and center front. Pivot tape measure between three points across hips.

11) **Hip 7" Down from Top (Circumference measurement).** Used when there is not a separate waistband. Measure down from top of skirt at sides and center front. Pivot tape measure between three points across hips.

12) **Hip 10" Down from Top (Circumference measurement).** Used when there is not a separate waistband. Measure down from top of skirt at sides and center front. Pivot tape measure between three points across hips.

13) **Length from Top Edge.** Measure at center front from top edge to hem.

14) **Hem Width.** Width of hem or stitching from edge.

SIZE SPECIFICATIONS - KNITS TOPS AND SWEATERS

SPECIFICATION MEASUREMENT SHEET (Garments Measured in Inches)									
Sample Size		**Proto No.**				**Style No.**			
SAMPLE STATUS		**ORIGINAL SAMPLE**		**PROTO SAMPLE**		**SALES SAMPLE**		**PRE-PRODUCTION SAMPLE**	
SAMPLE SIZE REQUEST									
MEASUREMENTS		**Actual**	**Request**	**Actual**	**Request**	**Actual**	**Request**	**Actual**	**Request**
1)	Shoulder - Point-to-Point								
2)	Chest/Bust - 1" Below Armhole								
3)	Shoulder - Point-to-Point								
4a)	Chest/Bust - 1" Below Armhole								
4b)	Across Chest - 5" Down from HPS								
5)	Bottom Opening								
6)	Sleeve Length								
8)	Armhole								
9)	Upper Arm - 1" Below Armhole								
10)	Cuff/Sleeve Opening								
11)	Cuff Height/Sleeve Hem Height								
12)	Neck Width – at Seam								
13)	Front Neck Drop - HPS to Seam								
14)	Back Neck Drop - HPS to Seam								
15)	Front Yoke Depth - HPS to Seam								
16)	Back Yoke Depth - CB Neck to Seam								
17)	Back Facing Depth at CB								
18)	CF Placket Width								
19)	CF Placket Length								
20)	Placket Box Height								
21)	Collar Height CF								
22)	Collar Height CB								
23)	Collar Stand Height CF								
24)	Collar Stand Height CB								
25)	Collar Spread								
26)	Pocket Width								
27)	Pocket Length								
28)	Pocket Placement- HPS to Top Edge								
29)	Pocket Placement from CF								
30)	Length of Side Vent								
31)	Bottom Hem Height								

Bold writing = changed measurements

Figure 4.9 - Points of Measure

(An example from Knit Tops and Sweaters)

All width measurements are on the 1/2

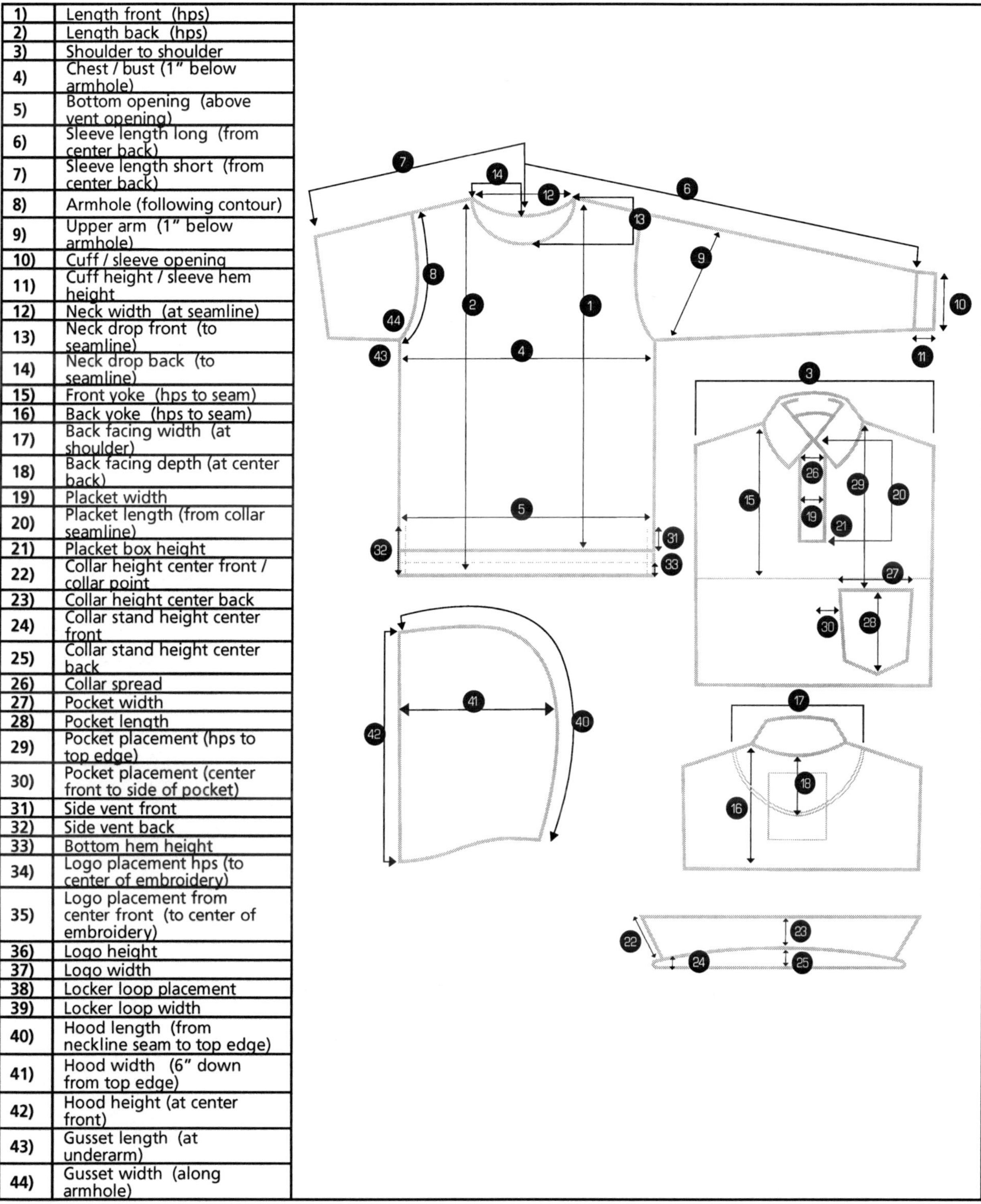

1)	Length front (hps)
2)	Length back (hps)
3)	Shoulder to shoulder
4)	Chest / bust (1" below armhole)
5)	Bottom opening (above vent opening)
6)	Sleeve length long (from center back)
7)	Sleeve length short (from center back)
8)	Armhole (following contour)
9)	Upper arm (1" below armhole)
10)	Cuff / sleeve opening
11)	Cuff height / sleeve hem height
12)	Neck width (at seamline)
13)	Neck drop front (to seamline)
14)	Neck drop back (to seamline)
15)	Front yoke (hps to seam)
16)	Back yoke (hps to seam)
17)	Back facing width (at shoulder)
18)	Back facing depth (at center back)
19)	Placket width
20)	Placket length (from collar seamline)
21)	Placket box height
22)	Collar height center front / collar point
23)	Collar height center back
24)	Collar stand height center front
25)	Collar stand height center back
26)	Collar spread
27)	Pocket width
28)	Pocket length
29)	Pocket placement (hps to top edge)
30)	Pocket placement (center front to side of pocket)
31)	Side vent front
32)	Side vent back
33)	Bottom hem height
34)	Logo placement hps (to center of embroidery)
35)	Logo placement from center front (to center of embroidery)
36)	Logo height
37)	Logo width
38)	Locker loop placement
39)	Locker loop width
40)	Hood length (from neckline seam to top edge)
41)	Hood width (6" down from top edge)
42)	Hood height (at center front)
43)	Gusset length (at underarm)
44)	Gusset width (along armhole)

MEASUREMENT METHODOLOGY – KNITS

1) & 2) Front & Back Length: Place garment flat with the back side down. Smooth all wrinkles out of the front of the garment. Measure from the high point of shoulder, to the end of the bottom garment hem.

3) Shoulder to Shoulder: Place garment face up, put sleeves in their relaxed position and smooth out extra fabric. Place measuring tape at the natural fold point of the armhole seam. Measure across the garment to the opposite point.

4) Chest / Bust: Place garment face up. Move sleeves to their natural extended position. Gently pull out extra fullness from pleats etc. Smooth fabric flat. Measure 1" down from the very bottom of armhole, across the chest, to the opposite side seam edge to edge. Double measurement. For garments with box pleat, measure garment face down.

5) Bottom Opening: Lay garment front up. Smooth out extra fabric and wrinkles. Measure from the finished bottom end of side seam across the garment to the opposite finished bottom end of side seam. Double measurement. If garment has side vents or shirt tails, measure across at top of vents or shirt tails.

6) & 7) Sleeve Length Long & Short: Measure from CB point of garment at neck seam of collar or collar stand. Measure to natural fold point of shoulder at armhole seam. Measure straight down fold of sleeve to top edge of cuff or sleeve opening.

8) Armhole: Place garment front up. Align front and back armhole seam so that it has no wrinkles. Place tape at the top of shoulder point and carefully follow contour of sleeve set seam with the measuring tape. Measure all the way to the bottom of armhole.

9) Upper Arm: Smooth out extra fabric and wrinkles in sleeve. Starting at outer folded edge of sleeve, measure at a perpendicular angle down to seamed edge of sleeve 1" below armhole.

10) Cuff / Sleeve Opening: Lay sleeve flat and measure from edge to edge along cuff opening.

11) Cuff Height / Sleeve Hem Height: Measure from cuff set seam to the finished edge of the cuff.

12) Neck Width: Measure from neckline seam and shoulder seam intersection, in a straight line from one side to the other.

13) & 14) Neck Drop Front & Back: Measure from high point of shoulder to back and front neckline seams.

15) & 16) Front & Back Yoke: Measure from high point of shoulder to front and back yoke seams.

17) Back Facing Width: Measure on back in a straight line from shoulder to shoulder.

18) Back Facing Depth: Measure from CB at neck seam vertically down to bottom row of topstitching.

19) Placket Width: Measure across placket from finished edge to finished edge.

20) Placket Length: Measure from neckline seam to bottom of placket.

21) **Placket Box Height:** Measure at base of placket from top of box stitch to bottom of box stitch.

22) **Collar Height Center Front / Collar Point:** Measure from the neckline seam to the top of the collar, or to the point of the collar.

23) **Collar Height CB:** Turn collar up and place face up. Measure from the center back collar set seam to finished edge of collar.

24) **Collar Stand Height CF:** Measure the center front of collar stand from neckline seam to the collar set seam.

25) **Collar Stand Height CB:** Measure the center back of collar stand from neckline seam to the collar set seam.

26) **Collar Spread:** Measure with garment buttoned and folded correctly. Measure distance between collar points.

27) **Pocket Width:** Measure horizontal distance from edge to edge at center of pocket.

28) **Pocket Length:** Measure vertical distance from top edge to bottom edge at center of pocket.

29) **Pocket Placement from Shoulder:** Measure down from finished shoulder seam at neck to top of pocket edge.

30) **Pocket Placement from CF Edge:** Measure from center front edge to top of pocket edge.

31) **Side Vent Front:** Measure from vent opening to bottom of front hem.

32) **Side Vent Back:** Measure from vent opening to bottom of back hem.

33) **Bottom Hem Height:** Measure inside garment from folded edge to top of hem.

34) **Logo Placement HPS:** Measure from high point of shoulder to center of embroidery.

35) **Logo Placement From CF:** Measure from center front of garment to center of embroidery.

36) **Logo Height:** Measure from top of logo to bottom.

37) **Logo Width:** Measure from one side of logo to the other side.

38) **Locker Loop Placement:** Measure at CB neck seam to top of loop.

39) **Locker Loop Width:** Measure from one end of the loop to the other.

40) **Hood Length:** Measure at center back neckline seam to top edge of hood.

41) **Hood Width:** Measure 6" down from center front to center back.

42) **Hood Height:** Measure at center front from neckline seam to top of hood.

43) **Gusset Length:** Measure from side seam and armhole intersection along underarm seam to the end of the gusset seam.

44) **Gusset Width:** Measure from side seam and armhole intersection along armhole seam to the end of the gusset seam.

MEASUREMENT METHODOLOGY – SWEATERS

1) & 2) **Front & Back Length:** Place garment flat with the back side down. Smooth all wrinkles out of the front of the garment. Measure from the high point of shoulder, to the end of the bottom garment hem.

3) **Shoulder to Shoulder:** Place garment face up, put sleeves in their relaxed position and smooth out extra fabric. Place measuring tape at the natural fold point of the armhole seam. Measure across the garment to the opposite point.

4) **Chest / Bust:** Place garment face up. Move sleeves to their natural extended position. Gently pull out extra fullness from pleats etc. Smooth fabric flat. Measure 1" down from the very bottom of armhole, across the chest, to the opposite side seam edge to edge. Double measurement. For garments with box pleat, measure garment face down.

5) **Bottom Opening:** Lay garment front up. Smooth out extra fabric and wrinkles. Measure from the finished bottom end of side seam across the garment to the opposite finished bottom end of side seam. Double measurement. If garment has side vents or shirt tails, measure across at top of vents or shirt tails.

6) & 7) **Sleeve Length Long & Short:** Measure from CB point of garment at neck seam of collar or collar stand. Measure to natural fold point of shoulder at armhole seam. Measure straight down fold of sleeve to top edge of cuff or sleeve opening.

8) **Armhole:** Place garment front up. Align front and back armhole seam so that it has no wrinkles. Place tape at the top of shoulder point and carefully follow contour of sleeve set seam with the measuring tape. Measure all the way to the bottom of armhole.

9) **Upper Arm:** Smooth out extra fabric and wrinkles in sleeve. Starting at outer folded edge of sleeve, measure at a perpendicular angle down to seamed edge of sleeve 1" below armhole.

10) **Cuff / Sleeve Opening:** Lay sleeve flat and measure from edge to edge along cuff opening.

11) **Cuff Height / Sleeve Hem Height:** Measure from cuff set seam to the finished edge of the cuff.

12) **Neck Width:** Measure from neckline seam and shoulder seam intersection, in a straight line from one side to the other.

13) & 14) **Neck Drop Front & Back:** Measure from high point of shoulder to back and front neckline seams.

15) & 16) **Front & Back Yoke:** Measure from high point of shoulder to front and back yoke seams.

17) **Back Facing Width:** Measure on back in a straight line from shoulder to shoulder.

18) **Back Facing Depth:** Measure from CB at neck seam vertically down to bottom row of topstitching.

19) **Placket Width:** Measure across placket from finished edge to finished edge.

20) **Placket Length:** Measure from neckline seam to bottom of placket.

21) **Placket Box Height:** Measure at base of placket from top of box stitch to bottom of box stitch.

22) **Collar Height Center Front / Collar Point:** Measure from the neckline seam to the top of the collar, or to the point of the collar.

23) **Collar Height CB:** Turn collar up and place face up. Measure from the center back collar set seam to finished edge of collar.

24) **Collar Stand Height CF:** Measure the center front of collar stand from neckline seam to the collar set seam.

25) **Collar Stand Height CB:** Measure the center back of collar stand from neckline seam to the collar set seam.

26) **Collar Spread:** Measure with garment buttoned and folded correctly. Measure distance between collar points.

27) **Pocket Width:** Measure horizontal distance from edge to edge at center of pocket.

28) **Pocket Length:** Measure vertical distance from top edge to bottom edge at center of pocket.

29) **Pocket Placement from Shoulder:** Measure down from finished shoulder seam at neck to top of pocket edge.

30) **Pocket Placement from CF Edge:** Measure from center front edge to top of pocket edge.

31) **Side Vent Front:** Measure from vent opening to bottom of front hem.

32) **Side Vent Back:** Measure from vent opening to bottom of back hem.

33) **Bottom Hem Height:** Measure inside garment from folded edge to top of hem.

34) **Logo Placement HPS:** Measure from high point of shoulder to center of embroidery.

35) **Logo Placement From CF:** Measure from center front of garment to center of embroidery.

36) **Logo Height:** Measure from top of logo to bottom.

37) **Logo Width:** Measure from one side of logo to the other side.

38) **Locker Loop Placement:** Measure at CB neck seam to top of loop.

39) **Locker Loop Width:** Measure from one end of the loop to the other.

40) **Hood Length:** Measure at center back neckline seam to top edge of hood.

41) **Hood Width:** Measure 6" down from center front to center back.

42) **Hood Height:** Measure at center front from neckline seam to top of hood.

43) **Gusset Length:** Measure from side seam and armhole intersection along underarm seam to the end of the gusset seam.

44) **Gusset Width:** Measure from side seam and armhole intersection along armhole seam to the end of the gusset seam.

SIZE SPECIFICATIONS - WOVEN SHIRTS AND BLOUSES

SPECIFICATION MEASUREMENT SHEET (Garments Measured in Inches)									
Sample Size		Proto No.				Style No.			
SAMPLE STATUS		ORIGINAL SAMPLE		PROTO SAMPLE		SALES SAMPLE		PRE-PRODUCTION SAMPLE	
SAMPLE SIZE REQUEST									
MEASUREMENTS		Actual	Request	Actual	Request	Actual	Request	Actual	Request
1)	Center Back Length								
2)	Center Front Length								
3a)	Chest - 1" Below Armhole								
3b)	Chest - 5" Down from HPS								
4)	Waist - 8" Below Armhole								
5)	Bottom Opening								
6)	Side Seam Length								
7)	Shoulder-to-Shoulder								
8)	Shoulder Seam								
9)	Yoke Depth at CB								
10)	Armhole								
11)	Biceps - 1" Below Armhole								
12)	Elbow - 9 " Above Cuff Seam								
13)	Sleeve Length CB								
14)	Sleeve Length Cap								
15)	Cuff/Sleeve Opening								
16)	Cuff/Topstitching Width								
17)	Front Placket Width								
18)	Collar Width CB								
19)	Collar Length								
20)	Collar Point								
21)	Collar Spread - Buttoned & Folded								
22)	Tie Space - Buttoned & Folded								
23)	Collar Stand Width CB								
24)	Collar Stand Length/Neck Circum.								
25)	Sleeve Placket Length								
26)	Sleeve Placket Width								
27)	Pocket Length								
28)	Pocket Width								
29)	Pocket Placement from CF								
30)	Pocket Placement from Shoulder Seam at Neck								
31)	Pocket Flap Length (Depth)								
32)	Pocket Flap Width								
33)	Neck Drop								

Bold writing = changed measurements

Figure 5.1 - Points of Measure

(An example from Woven Shirts and Blouses)

1)	Center back length
2)	Chest 1" below armhole - open pleat
3)	Bottom
4)	Side seam length
5)	Shoulder to shoulder
6)	Shoulder length
7)	Yoke depth at CB
8)	Armhole
9)	Upper arm 1" below armhole
10)	Elbow 9 1/2" above cuff seam
11)	Sleeve length CB
12)	Sleeve length cap
13)	Cuff/sleeve opening
14)	Cuff width
15)	Front placket width
16)	Collar width CB
17)	Collar length
18)	Collar point
19)	Collar spread - buttoned and folded
20)	Tie space - buttoned and folded
21)	Collar stand width CB
22)	Collar stand length/neck circumference
23)	Sleeve placket length
24)	Sleeve placket width
25)	Pocket length
26)	Pocket width
27)	Pocket placement from CF edge
28)	Pocket placement from shoulder at neck
29)	Flap depth
30)	Flat width
31)	Neck drop

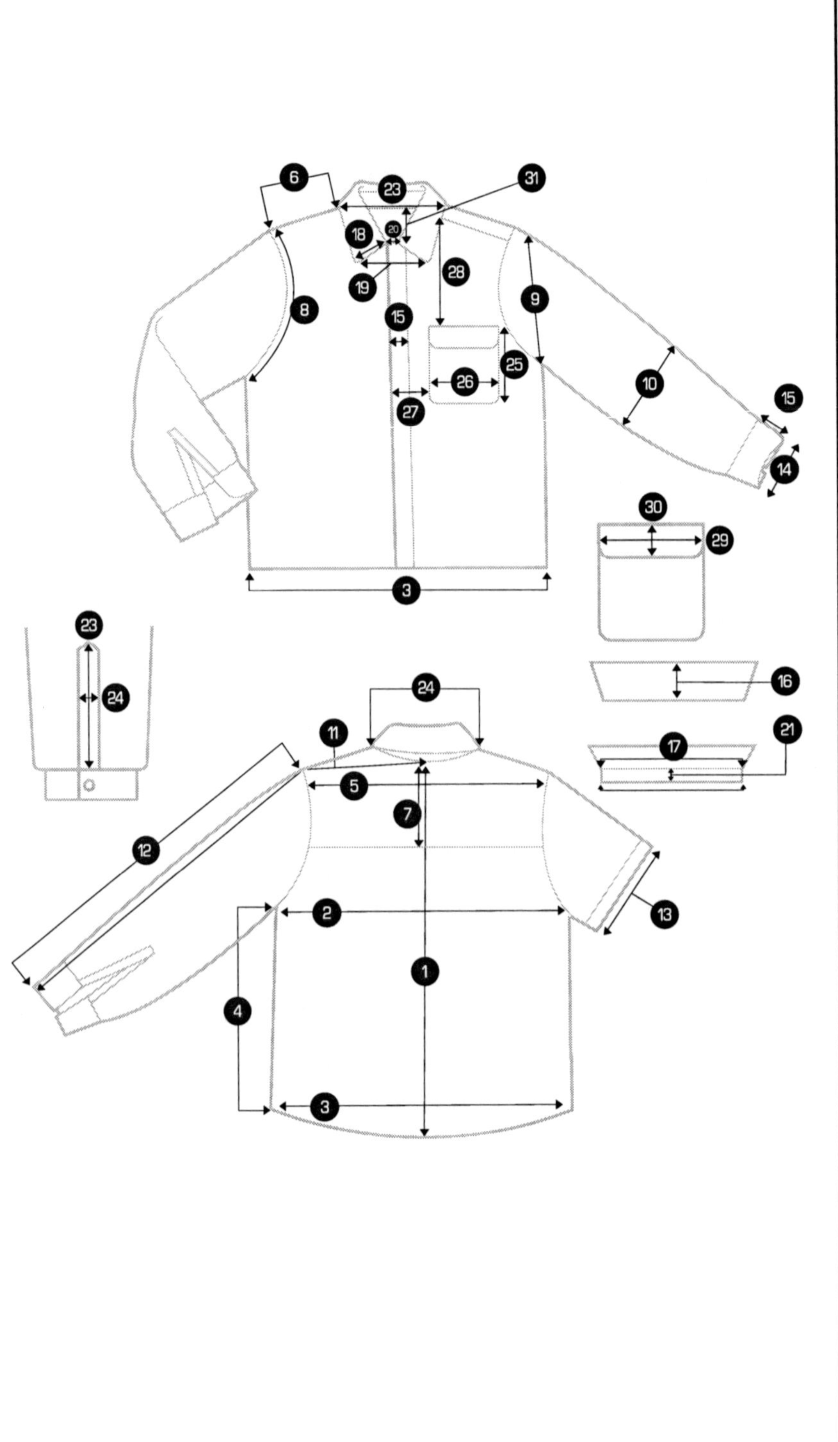

MEASUREMENT METHODOLOGY

1) **Center Back Length:** Place garment flat with the front facing down. Smooth all wrinkles out of the back of the garment. Measure from the center back neckline seam to the bottom edge of garment hem.

2) **Chest:** Place garment face up. Move sleeves to their natural extended position. Gently pull out extra fullness from pleats etc. Smooth fabric flat. Measure 1" down from the very bottom of armhole, across the chest, to the opposite side seam edge to edge. Double measurement. For garments with boxpleat, measure garment face down.

3) **Bottom Opening:** Lay garment front up. Smooth out extra fabric and wrinkles. Measure from the finished bottom end of side seam across the garment to the opposite finished bottom end of side seam. Double measurement. If garment has side vents or shirt tails, measure across at top of vents or shirt tails.

4) **Side Seam Length:** Lay garment flat. Smooth out extra fabric on the body of the garment. Measure from the armhole seam intersection down to bottom finished edge of the side seam.

5) **Shoulder to Shoulder:** Place garment face down, put sleeves in their relaxed position and smooth out extra fabric. Place measuring tape at the natural fold point of the armhole seam. Measure across the garment to the opposite point.

6) **Shoulder Length:** Measure along shoulder seam from neckline to armhole.

7) **Yoke Depth at CB:** Measure from CB at neck seam vertically down to edge of yoke seam.

8) **Armhole:** Place garment front up. Align front and back armhole seam so that it has no wrinkles. Place tape at the top of shoulder point and carefully follow contour of sleeve set seam with the measuring tape. Measure all the way to the bottom of armhole. Double measurement.

9) **Upper Arm:** Smooth out extra fabric and wrinkles in sleeve. Starting at outer folded edge of sleeve, measure at a perpendicular angle down to seamed edge of sleeve 1" below armhole. Double measurement.

10) **Elbow:** Smooth out extra fabric and wrinkles in sleeve. Measure 9 1⁄2" up from cuff set. Starting at outer folded edge of sleeve, measure at a perpendicular angle down to seamed edge of sleeve. Double measurement. If no cuff then measure 9 1/2" up from hem edge.

11) **Sleeve Length CB:** Measure from CB point of garment at neck seam of collar or collarstand. Measure to natural fold point of shoulder at armhole seam. Measure straight down fold of sleeve to top edge of cuff or sleeve opening.

12) **Sleeve Length Cap:** Measure from natural fold of shoulder at armhole seam to bottom of cuff opening along fold of sleeve to top of cuff or sleeve opening.

13) **Cuff / Sleeve Opening:** Long sleeved shirts: Open cuff and smooth flat. Measure from the center point of the button to the end of the buttonhole. Short sleeved shirts: Lay sleeve flat and measure from edge to edge along cuff opening. Double measurement.

14) **Cuff Width: Long sleeved shirts:** Measure from cuff set seam to the finished edge of the cuff. Short sleeved shirts: Measure from topstitched hem to the finished edge of the cuff.

15) **Front Placket Width:** Measure across placket from finished edge to finished edge.

16) **Collar Width CB:** Turn collar up and place face up. Measure from the center back collar set seam to finished edge of collar.

17) **Collar Length:** Open collar out straight. Measure straight from edge to edge of collar where collar is set into collarstand or neck hole.

18) **Collar Point:** Measure along the outside edge of collar from the collar set seam to the end of the collar point.

19) **Collar Spread:** Measure with garment buttoned and folded correctly. Measure distance between collar points.

20) **Tie Space:** Measure with garment buttoned and folded correctly. Measure distance between top edges of collar.

21) **Collar Stand Width CB:** Measure the center back of collar stand from neck seam to the collar set seam.

22) **Collar Stand Length/Neck Circumference:** Open collar stand and smooth out. Straight measure from center of button to inside edge of outside of buttonhole.

23) **Sleeve Placket Length:** Measure from top of point to cuff seam.

24) **Sleeve Placket Width:** Measure sleeve placket edge to edge.

25) **Pocket Length:** Measure vertical distance from top edge to bottom edge at center of pocket.

26) **Pocket Width:** Measure horizontal distance from edge to edge at center of pocket.

27) **Pocket Placement from CF:** Measure from center front to pocket edge.

28) **Pocket Placement from Shoulder:** Measure down from finished shoulder seam at neck to top of pocket edge.

29) **Flap Depth:** Measure vertical distance from edge to edge at center of flap.

30) **Flap Width:** Measure horizontal distance from edge to edge at center of flap.

31) **Neck Drop:** Measure seam to seam from bottom of collar/collar stand at CB to CF neck/collar stand.

SIZE SPECIFICATIONS - BOTTOMS AND TROUSERS

SPECIFICATION MEASUREMENT SHEET (Garments Measured in Inches)									
Sample Size		Proto No.				Style No.			
SAMPLE STATUS		ORIGINAL SAMPLE		PROTO SAMPLE		SALES SAMPLE		PRE-PRODUCTION SAMPLE	
SAMPLE SIZE REQUEST MEASUREMENTS		Actual	Request	Actual	Request	Actual	Request	Actual	Request
1)	Waist Relaxed								
2)	Waist Extended								
3)	Waistband Width								
4)	High Hip - 3" Down from Waist Seam								
5)	Hip - 7" Down from Waist Seam								
6)	Front Rise Not Including Waistband								
7)	Back Rise Not Including Waistband								
8)	Front Rise - From Top Edge of Waist								
9)	Back Rise - From Top Edge of Waist								
10)	Thigh - 1" Down from Crotch Seam								
11)	Knee - 13" Down from Crotch Seam								
12)	Leg Opening								
13)	Inseam								
14)	Hem Width								
15)	Cuff Width								
16)	Fly Length (To Outer Row of Topstitch)								
17)	Fly Width (To Outer Row of Topstitch)								
18)	Front Pocket Opening								
19)	Front Pocket Depth/Length								
20)	Coin Pocket from Side Seam								
21)	Coin Pocket from Waistband								
22)	Coin Pocket Opening								
23)	Back Pocket Opening								
24)	Back Pocket Depth/Length								
25)	Pocket Flap Depth/Length								
26)	Pocket Flap Width								
27)	Back Pocket from Side Seam								
28)	Back Pocket from Waistband								
29)	Belt Loop Length								
30)	Belt Loop Width								
SHORTS LINER:									
31)	Front Rise (Not Including Waistband)								
32)	Back Rise (Not Including Waistband)								
33)	Leg Opening Relaxed								
34)	Leg Opening Stretched								
35)	Outseam								
36)	Crotch Width								

Bold writing = changed measurements

Figure 5.2 - Points of Measure

(An example from Bottoms and Trousers)

1)	Waist relaxed
2)	Waist extended
3)	Waistband width
4)	High hip 3" down
5)	Regular hip 7" down
6)	Front rise (btm waist)
7)	Back rise (btm waist)
8)	Front rise (top waist)
9)	Back rise (top waist)
10)	Thigh
11)	Knee
12)	Leg opening
13)	Inseam
14)	Hem width
15)	Cuff
16)	Fly length
17)	Fly width
18)	Front pkt opening
19)	Front pkt depth/length
20)	Coin pkt from side seam
21)	Coin pkt from waistb
22)	Coin pocket opening
23)	Back pkt opening/flap width
24)	Back pkt length/depth
25)	Back pkt from side seam
26)	Back pkt from waistb
27)	Loop length
28)	Loop width
29)	Flap depth

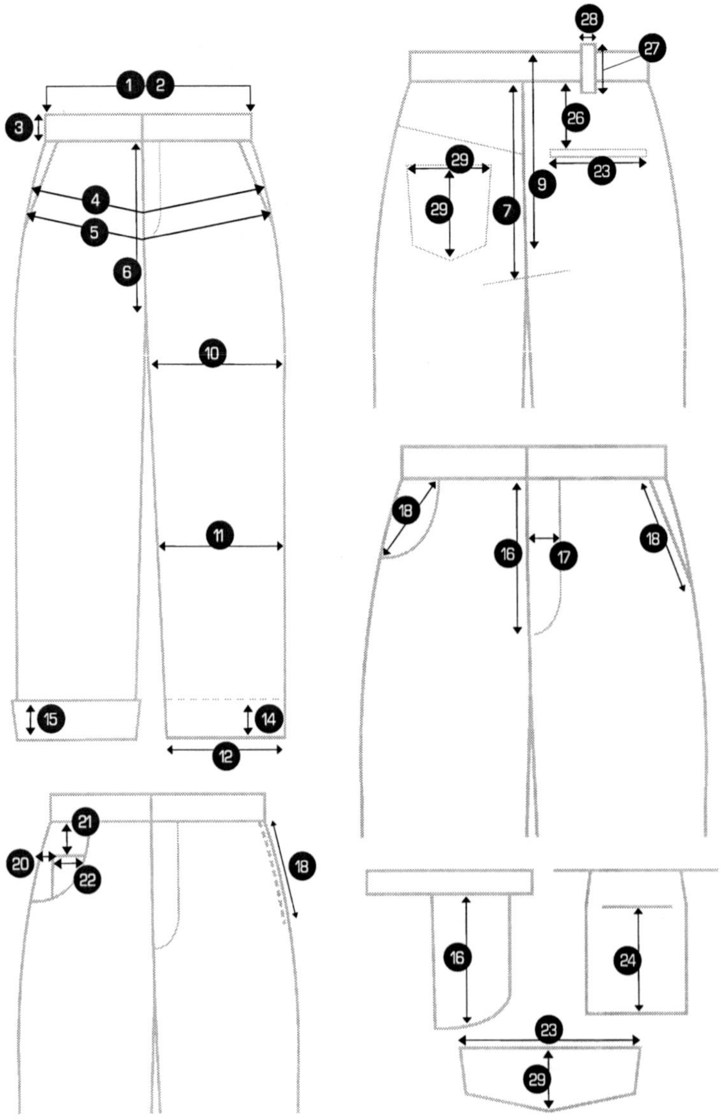

MEASUREMENT METHODOLOGY

1) **Waist Relaxed:** This measurement is taken from the top of the waistband seam. The garment should be placed on the measuring table front side up. The waist button and fly should be closed. The waistband should be smoothed flat with any belt loops rolled to the sides so they do not interfere with the measurement. No excessive pressure should be used to pull the waistband flat. The measurement taken should be doubled.

2) **Waist Extended:** This measurement is taken from the top of the waistband seam. This measurement should be used on elastic waist banded or stretched waist banded garments. The garment should be laid flat on the table. The waist button and fly should be closed. Belt loops should be rolled to the side. The elastic in the garment should be fully extended. The measurement taken should be doubled.

3) **Waistband Width:** Measure on the outside of the garment. Measure from the top of the waistband to the bottom of the waistband seam.

4) **High Hip 3" Down (Open Pleat):** Place garment front facing up with front and back bands even. Smooth out any fullness in garment. If the garment is pleated, open them and smooth out the extra material. Do not tilt the legs in or out to an unnatural position. Measure 3" down from the bottom of the waistband seam, and pin the spot. Repeat on the outside seams and pin. Measure following the contour across the front of the garment using the pins as markers. Double the measurement taken. For garment without waistband measure 4 1/2" down from top of the waistband.

5) **Regular Hip 7" Down (Open Pleat):** Place garment front facing up with front & back waistband even. Smooth out any fullness in garment. If the garment is pleated, open them and smooth out the extra material. Do not tilt the leg in or out to an unnatural position. Measure 7" down from the bottom of the waistband seam, and pin the spot. Repeat on the outside seams and pin. Measure following the contour across the front of the garment using the pins as markers. Double the measurement taken. For garments without waistband, measure 8 1/2" down from top of the waistband.

6) **Front Rise:** With the front of the pant facing you, gently smooth out all of the wrinkles in the crotch area so that the rise seam is flat and straight from the bottom of the waistband to the crotch seam intersection. Measure from the bottom of the waistband to the crotch seam intersection. Do not stretch.

7) **Back Rise:** With the back of the pant facing you, gently smooth out all of the wrinkles in the crotch area so that the rise seam is flat and straight from the bottom of the waist to the crotch seam intersection. Measure from the bottom of the waistband to the crotch seam intersection. Do not stretch.

8) **Front Rise From Top Of The Waistband:** With the front of the pant facing you, gently smooth out all of the wrinkles in the crotch area so that the rise seam is flat and straight from the top of the waistband to the crotch seam intersection. Measure from the top of the waistband to the crotch seam intersection. Do not stretch.

9) **Back Rise From Top Of The Waistband:** With the back of the pant facing you, gently smooth out all of the wrinkles in the crotch area so that the rise seam is flat and straight from the top of the waist to the crotch seam intersection. Measure from the top of the waistband to the crotch seam intersection. Do not stretch.

10) **Thigh:** With the front of the pant facing you, measure 1" down from the crotch seam intersection. Smooth out any extra material and take the measurement from that point. Double your measurement. Measure perpendicular to vertical.

11) **Knee:** With the front of the pant facing you, measure 13" down from the crotch seam intersection. Smooth out any extra material and take the measurement from that point. Double your measurement.

12) **Leg Opening:** Measure straight across the bottom opening, outside, from edge to edge. Double the measurement.

13) **Inseam Length:** Lay pant legs flat matching inseams to side seams, fold one leg from crotch seam over the top of waist exposing the inseam of the bottom leg. Smooth out any wrinkles, and measure from the crotch seam intersection to the bottom of the cuff. Do not stretch.

14) **Hem Width:** Measure from the bottom of the leg opening to the top of the hem. Hem for cuffed garment is from bottom of leg opening before garment is cuffed.

15) **Cuff Width:** Measure from the bottom of the leg opening to the edge of the cuff.

16) **Fly Length:** Measure from the bartack to the bottom of the waistband.

17) **Fly Width:** Measure from the edge of the fly opening across to outside topstitching of the J Stitch.

18) **Front Pocket Opening:**

Quarter top pockets: measure from the bartack on the side seam, along the slant of the pocket opening to the bottom of the waistband or top of bartack.

Side Seam Pockets: measure from the bottom bartack/ pocket opening to the top bartack at the bottom of the waistband.

Scoop Pockets: measure straight along angle from the point at which the pocket meets the waistband to the point the pocket meets the sideseam (rivet to rivet on jeans).

19) **Front Pocket Depth:** Measure pocket bag at deepest point from bottom of bag to bottom of waistband seam.

20) **Coin Pocket From Side Seam:** Measure from top left edge of pocket horizontal to waistband seam.

21) **Coin Pocket Front Waistband:** Measure from center of top edge pocket

22) **Coin Pocket Opening:** At top of pocket measure horizontal from edge to edge.

23) **Back Pocket Opening:** Measure from edge to edge at top of the pocket horizontal.

24) **Back Pocket Depth/Patch Pocket:** Measure vertical distance from center of edge of top of pocket topstitch to bottom edge of pocket. Measure from inside garment measure from top of pocket topstitch to bottom edge of pocket bag.

25) **Back Pocket From Side Seam:** Measure horizontal distance from side seam to top edge of pocket closest to side seam.

26) **Back Pocket From Waistband:** Measure vertical distance from center top of pocket opening to edge of waistband.

27) **Loop Length:** Measure vertical distance from top center edge to bottom edge of loop.

28) **Loop Width:** Measure horizontal at center of loop edge to edge.

29) **Flap Depth:** Vertical distance of center of flap from bottom to top of flap.

CHAPTER 3

ACTION AND PROGRESS REPORTS

This chapter introduces the Work-in-Progress Report and the Time and Action Calendar. Both of which are vital tools in keeping the design and production departments, along with the factory management up-to-date and on track. Report and calendar schedules must be adhered to in order to deliver garments on time to the retailers.

WORK-IN-PROGRESS (WIP) REPORTS

ACTION AND PROGRESS REPORTS

This, again, is just a way for you to track each step of your process. This is separate from your tech package. It is condensed and it should be separated either by group, delivery, or vendor. The work-in-progress report (WIP) is generally driven by your merchandiser or production person from your team. This will help you and your designers create checks and balances among the factory, design, merchandising, and production.

You can add and delete as many components as you see fit in order to give you a better grasp of the day-to-day of your garments. Depending on the information, you might (and I suggest you do) send this to the vendor or factory on a weekly basis for them to fill out regardless of whether there is a change in the process or not. This will give you a sense of security that everything is working. If you perceive a problem, you will be able to correct it before it affects your bottom line.

TIME AND ACTION CALENDAR

The time and action calendar in this book requires every department to work together in order to give you realistic dates, so you can all accomplish your collection/line and meet the required delivery dates. This will help you avoid chargeback's and chasing orders within your season. For example, your factory, at times, is more than willing to make you sales samples or even tell you that there are no problems; but if a larger customer comes in, they will put you on the back burner to make room for the larger customer's sales samples. You should make yourself aware of when the peak times of the factory are and when their downtimes are. This will alleviate a lot of issues in your sampling process.

Once you have this information from your factory, you should ask your sales and marketing team when they will need sales samples for market (selling time). You should also get the delivery windows from them in order to begin putting this calendar together. With this information, your production and planning department will be able to determine lead times (depending on what mill and what country you are working in) for each item. This should give you the time when the design department should accomplish its tasks.

Please keep in mind that things do not always happen in the above-mentioned order. Most likely, you will need to start with your sales and marketing team and work from there.To track the progress of the many styles each season, a company needs a **Work-in-Progress (WIP) Report**. There are two types of **Work-in-Progress Reports**. The first is the **Development Work-in-Progress Report**, and is for all styles in sample development; the second is the **Production Work-in-Progress Report**, and is utilized to track each step for all styles that are selected for production.

DEVELOPMENT WORK-IN-PROGRESS (WIP) REPORT GUIDELINES

Every development style in the collection should be included in the **Development Work-in-Progress Report**.

- All components should be included in the report i.e.: trims, labels etc.
- The product development team of each factory should submit the report on a weekly basis to the designer. Marking each change in the process.

The following is a **Development Work-in-Progress Report**, the example is on two pages for formatting purposes only.

Depending on your company's needs, you can add and delete columns for steps that are, or are not, needed. Definitions of the abbreviations at the head of each column follow the chart.

DEVELOPMENT WORK-IN-PROGRESS (WIP) REPORT

To be used for Fabric, Trims, Protos, and Samples

CATEGORY:					SEASON:				
STYLE #	PROTO #	DESCRIPTION	FABRIC	FACTORY	PRICE	APRVL FAB	APRVL L/DIP	APRVL TRIM	APRVL EMB

UPDATED:

PROTO DLVY	1ST SMPL DLVY	2ND SMPL DLVY	S/SMPL PO #	S/SMPL COLOR	S/SMPL FAB DLVY	S/SMPL DLVY	EX-FTY DATE	AWB or BL #	REMARKS COMMENTS

DEFINITION OF EACH DEVELOPMENT WIP REPORT COLUMN:

STYLE # - Customer's style number.

PROTO # - Customer's first assigned number to a style.

DESCRIPTION - Basic depiction of what garment is, i.e., women's trouser.

FABRIC - What garment is made of.

FACTORY - Factory or agent name.

PRICE - Price quoted by factory or agent.

APRVL FAB - Date fabric is approved.

APRVL L/DIP - Date lab-dip(s) are approved.

APRVL TRIM - Date trim(s) are approved.

APRVL EMB - Date embroidery is approved.

PROTO DLVY - Delivery date of first prototype.

1ST SMPL DLVY - Delivery date of first sample with all correct components.

2ND SMPL DLVY - Delivery date of second sample after correction from first sample.

S/SMPL PO # - Purchase Order number for sales samples.

S/SMPL COLOR - Colors per style that are issued under Sales Sample PO.

S/S SMPL FAB DLVY - Date that sales sample fabric will be available to cut sales samples.

S/SMPL DLVY - Date that sales samples will be delivered.

EX-FTY DATE - Actual date that sales samples depart factory.

AWB OR BL # - Tracking number of sales samples.

REMARK/COMMENTS - Additional information on this style.

PRODUCTION WORK-IN-PROGRESS (WIP) REPORT GUIDELINES

A **Production Work-in-Progress (WIP) Report** should be required from each contractor producing the customer's product. This report should be submitted on a weekly basis once a PO has been issued.

- One report should be submitted for each season in process.
- Individual seasons should be represented on separate WIP Reports.
- Every style/PO must remain documented on the WIP Report even if the style/PO has shipped complete. Styles/PO's should not be removed from the WIP Report after shipping.
- Each PO should be detailed on individual lines of the WIP Report at the style/destination level.
- Each WIP Report should include status of all Customer and Distribution PO's.

PROCEDURE FOR SUBMISSION

- The WIP Report may be submitted by e-mail (this is the preferred method).

  NOTE: The agent and/or contractor should have compatible interface (i.e.: Word or Excel) with what your company has, in order to generate the WIP Report.

- Do not send or fax hard copies of the WIP Report. The WIP Report must be submitted to the customer electronically for easy updating and tracking.
- The report should be sent once a week (or as agreed upon) on a scheduled day determined by the customer's production manager responsible for that product category.
- WIP Reports should be sent to the customer's production manager and/or a designated agent/ representative.

The following is a Production Work-in-Progress Report, the example is on two pages for formatting purposes only.

Depending on your company's needs, you can add and delete columns for steps that are, or are not, needed. Definitions of the abbreviations at the head of each column follow the chart.

PRODUCTION WIP REPORT

For Production Styles

AGENT: SEASON:

CATEGORY: UPDATED:

STYLE #	CUST. PO #	DEST.	PO QTY	FTY	COUNTRY OF ORIGIN	FOB	DATE PO ISSUED	PO CNFRM EX-FTY	REVISE EX-FTY DATE	SCHED FABRIC ETA FTY	ACTUAL FABRIC ETA FTY	SCHED TRIMS ETA FTY	ACTUAL TRIMS ETA FTY	SCHED CUT DATE FABRIC	ACTUAL CUT DATE FABRIC	CUT QTY	SCHED START SEW DATE

ACTUAL START SEW DATE	SCHED FINISH SEW DATE	ACTUAL FINISH SEW DATE	FINISH SEWING QTY	START WASH DATE	SCHED FINISH PACK DATE	SCHED FINAL AUDIT DATE	PASS / FAIL	SHIPPED QTY	SCHED EX-FTY DATE	ACTUAL EX-FTY DATE	AIR/ OCEAN/ SURFACE	SHIPPING DOCS SENT	COMMENTS

NOTE: The WIP Report should be on legal size paper. This example is on two pages for formatting purposes only.

DEFINITION OF EACH PRODUCTION WIP REPORT COLUMN:

AGENT - Agent name or "Direct" if not applicable. (You to the factory.)

CATEGORY - Product group category, i.e., woven bottoms, knits, etc.

SEASON - Season that is represented on the WIP Report. Each season should be detailed on a separate WIP Report.

UPDATED - Date WIP Report was last updated. This should be weekly.

STYLE # - Customer's style number.

CUST. PO # - Purchase Order number.

DEST. - End destination for each Purchase Order.

PO QTY - Purchase Order quantity as originally ordered. This column should remain unchanged.

FTY - Factory name.

COUNTRY OF ORIGIN - Country of production.

FOB - Country of shipment embarkation.

DATE PO ISSUED - Issue date of Purchase Order to agent or contractor.

PO CNFRM EX-FTY - Original agreed ex-factory date. This date should remain unchanged on WIP Report.

REVISE EX-FTY - Revised ex-factory date as needed.

SCHED FABRIC ETA FTY - Date when fabric is scheduled to arrive at the factory.

ACTUAL FABRIC ETA FTY – Actual date fabric arrives at the factory.

SCHED TRIMS ETA FTY - Date when trims are scheduled to arrive at the factory.

ACTUAL TRIMS ETA FTY – Actual date when trims arrive at the factory.

SCHED CUT DATE FABRIC - Scheduled date of production cutting.

ACTUAL CUT DATE FABRIC – Actual date of production cutting.

CUT QTY - Actual number of units cut.

SCHED START SEW DATE - Scheduled date to begin sewing.

ACTUAL START SEW DATE - Actual date sewing starts.

SCHED FINISH SEW DATE - Scheduled date to finish sewing.

ACTUAL FINISH SEW DATE - Actual date sewing is finished.

FINISH SEWING QTY - Actual number of units sewn.

START WASH DATE - Actual date to begin special wash finishes, if applicable.

SCHED FINISH PACK DATE - Expected date when units will be completed in packing.

SCHED FINAL AUDIT DATE - Expected date when shipment will be audited.

PASS/FAIL - Results of audit.

SHIPPED QTY - Actual number of units shipped.

SCHED EX-FTY DATE - Expected date goods will ex-factory.

ACTUAL EX-FTY DATE - Actual date shipment exits factory.

AIR/OCEAN/SURFACE - Mode of transportation.

SHIPPING DOCS SENT - Column must be completed after the shipping documents have been sent to the customer and must include how the documents were sent (i.e. by fax, courier or both) and the date documents were sent. All shipping documents should be faxed to the attention of the appropriate individual in the Traffic or logistic Department. Under certain circumstances, factories may also be required to send documents via overnight courier. If sent via overnight courier, include AWB #.

COMMENTS - Any pertinent comment regarding production and shipment status. Once the style/PO has shipped complete, the word "COMPLETE" should be noted in this column.

TIME AND ACTION CALENDAR

Before and during the development and production of a season, in addition to Work-in-Progress Reports, it is strongly recommended to follow a pre-determined **Time and Action Calendar,** which specifies when each step of development and production should be completed by each department. A **Time and Action Calendar** should be followed for each season. These seasonal calendars will overlap, as future seasonal development begins, so that as you may be discussing Product Review for one season, you may also be Approving Samples for the previous season.

The following is an example of a Time and Action Calendar for a FALL I Line: In store and on the floor 7/15:

SAMPLE PLAN AND ACTION CALENDAR

MONTH	WEEK #	DESIGN DEPARTMENT	PRODUCTION PLANNING	SALES AND MARKETING	FACTORIES
JULY	1	Product Discussion and Review.	Product Discussion and Review.	Product Discussion and Review.	
	2	Receive Line Plan.	Line Plan Distributed. Sales Budget.	Sales Budget.	
	3				
	4				
AUGUST	1	Review theme boards, colors, concepts.			
	2	Designs to factories. Prototypes in work.			Factories receive designs and tech packages.
	3	Color palette set.			
	4	Designs to factories. Prototypes in work.			Factories receive designs and tech packages.
SEPTEMBER	1				
	2	All sample yarn placed. 80% P/G placed.			
	3		Sample yarn and fabric orders completed.		
	4	Spec sheets finalized. All lab dips, knitdowns, strike-offs approved.	Receive finalized spec sheets.		Receive finalized spec sheets. All lab dips, knitdowns, strike-offs approved. Initial price quotes forwarded.
OCTOBER	1		All sample and finding's PO's completed and placed.		Begin receiving completed sample PO's.
	2	Submit final changes to prints, all information is to be completed. Piece goods placed.	Receive initial price quotes.		
	3	Fit comments for sales samples.	Swatch card layout completed by end of week.		Protos approved.
	4	Sample yarn and fabric ex-mill. 1st line review meeting.	Sample yarn and fabric ex-mill. 1st line review meeting.	1st line review meeting.	Sample yarn and fabric ex-mill. Receive balance of any outstanding sample PO's completed.
NOVEMBER	1				
	2				
	3				

	4	Line sheet.		Line sheet.	
DECEMBER	1	Descriptions for price list to Production completed.	Receive finalized descriptions for Price List.		Final pricing issued by all vendors.
	2	Samples ex-factory.	Samples ex-factory. Create calendar for commitments. Create costing file for 1st delivery production orders, F/G's placed. Last date for late samples to ship, drop all others.	Review and commit to 1st delivery pc gds.	Samples to ex-mill.
	3		1st delivery production orders.		1st delivery production orders.
	4		Sample allocation completed. Swatching completed.		
JANUARY	1	Line finalization/pricing meeting.	Line finalization/pricing meeting. Pricelist completed.		
	1	Pre-editing.	Prepare for pre-editing.		
	1	Pricing meeting.	Pricing meeting.	Pricing meeting.	
	2		Last date for late samples to ship, drop all others. Finalize sales plan with Sales and Marketing.	Finalize sales plan with Production Planning.	Last date for late samples to ship, drop all others.
	2	Pre-editing.			
	2	Pricing meeting.	Pricing meeting.	Pricing meeting.	
	3	Sales meeting, hand off notes to Production Planning Department.	Sales meeting. Receive all notes on changes from designs. All samples shipped for sales force. Cut 1st delivery Production Projection PO's.	Sales meeting.	Sales meeting. Receive 1st group of PO's for production.
	4				
FEBRUARY	2		2nd delivery production orders.		2nd delivery production orders.
	4				
MARCH	1				
	2		1st delivery pc gds ex-mill.		1st delivery pc gds ex-mill.
	3		1st delivery pc gds ex-mill.		1st delivery pc gds ex-mill.
	4				
APRIL	1				
	2		2nd delivery pc gds ex-mill.		2nd delivery pc gds ex-mill.
	3				
	4		2nd delivery pc gds ex-mill.		2nd delivery pc gds ex-mill.
MAY	1				
	2				
	3				
	4				
JUNE	1		1st delivery ex-factory, 95% to be shipped.		1st delivery ex-factory, beginning of week, 95% complete.
	2				
	3				
	4				
JULY	1		2nd delivery ex-factory.		2nd delivery ex-factory, beginning of week.
*	JULY 12		95% production received in system.		
*	JULY 15		Customer start ship.	Customer start ship.	Start ship finished product begins to customers.

DEFINITION OF EACH TIME AND ACTION CALENDAR COLUMN

:

1ST / 2ND DELIVERY EX-FACTORY - Finished garments exit factory.

1ST / 2ND DELIVERY PC GDS EX-MILL - Piece goods exit mill.

1ST / 2ND DELIVERY PRODUCTION ORDERS - Production orders placed.

1ST LINE REVIEW MEETING - Meeting for design, production and sales to look at each item on line, review costs, fabric, etc.

95% PRODUCTION RECEIVED IN SYSTEM - Bulk production received at warehouse/distribution center.

ALL LAB DIPS, KNITDOWNS, STRIKE-OFFS APPROVED - Date final correction comments/approvals items must be sent in to mill.

ALL SAMPLE AND FINDING'S PO'S COMPLETED AND PLACED - Sales samples and fabric and trim orders placed.

ALL SAMPLE YARN PLACED - Yarn order completed and sent for Sales Samples.

ALL SAMPLES SHIPPED FOR SALES FORCE - Sales samples shipped from design company.

BEGIN RECEIVING COMPLETED SAMPLE PO'S - Sales samples start arriving from factory.

COLOR PALETTE SET - Color range and standards for fabric, yarn, trims, collection in place.

CREATE CALENDAR FOR COMMITMENTS - Orchestrate 1st and 2nd deliveries and coordinate all materials and production accordingly.

CREATE COSTING FILE FOR 1ST DELIVERY PRODUCTION ORDERS - Complete Cost Calculation sheets for bulk styles.

CUSTOMER START SHIP - Begin shipping completed bulk productions from warehouse/distribution center.

CUT 1ST DELIVERY PRODUCTION PROJECTION PO'S - Purchase orders for 1st delivery completed.

DESCRIPTIONS FOR PRICE LIST TO PRODUCTION COMPLETED - Style sketches and descriptions for price list and line list completed.

DESIGNS TO FACTORIES - Tech packages completed.

F/G PLACED - Purchase orders for bulk placed.

FACTORIES RECEIVE DESIGNS AND TECH PACKAGES - Confirm receipt and start of tech packages.

FINAL PRICING ISSUED BY ALL VENDORS - Factories submit price quotes for all sales samples.

FINALIZE SALES PLAN WITH PRODUCTION PLANNING - Sales and production depts. confirm prices, ship dates and in-store deliveries.

FINALIZE SALES PLAN WITH SALES AND MARKETING - Design and sales depts. confirm design and production details for selected bulk styles and revise details for targeted costs.

FIT COMMENTS FOR SALES SAMPLES - Prototypes fit and all comments/corrections sent out.

HAND OFF NOTES TO PRODUCTION PLANNING DEPARTMENT - Tech packages for styles selected for bulk passed to production.

INITIAL PRICE QUOTES FORWARDED - Factories submit price quotes for styles based on tech packages.

LAST DATE FOR LATE SAMPLES TO SHIP, DROP ALL OTHERS - Sales samples out-by date, firm.

LINE FINALIZATION - Styles/colors adapted for production confirmed.

LINE PLAN DISTRIBUTED - Action/plan passed to all departments with schedule for started season.

LINE SHEET COMPLETED - Sketches, style numbers, details for each line created.

P/G / PIECE GOODS PLACED - Fabric orders sent.

PRE-EDITING - 1st edit based on styles that are unsuitable due to style/cost/etc.

PRICE LIST COMPLETED - Bulk prices complete.

PRICING MEETING - Review factory price quotes/actual sample/final costs/targeted selling price.

PRODUCT DISCUSSION AND REVIEW - Meeting on proto samples and direction of collection.

PROTOS APPROVE - Fit/sample comments out for counter/sales samples.

PROTOTYPES IN WORK - Factory working on protos after receiving tech packages.

RECEIVE 1ST GROUP OF PO'S FOR PRODUCTION - Production Purchase Orders placed for early styles.

RECEIVE ALL NOTES ON CHANGES FROM DESIGNS - Production receives revised tech packages and confirmations on dropped samples.

RECEIVE BALANCE OF ANY OUTSTANDING SAMPLE PO'S COMPLETED - Last of sales samples delivered.

RECEIVE FINALIZED DESCRIPTIONS FOR PRICE LIST - All revised descriptions/style detail changes confirmed.

RECEIVE FINALIZED SPEC SHEETS - Tech packages sent from design department.

RECEIVE INITIAL PRICE QUOTES - From factories.

RECEIVE LINE PLAN - Starting season plan and Action Calendar completed.

REVIEW AND COMMIT TO 1ST DELIVERY PC GDS - Fabric orders placed.

REVIEW THEME BOARDS, COLORS, CONCEPTS - Collection mood/direction presented/discussed.

SALES BUDGET - Projections for sales quantities/dollars made.

SALES MEETING - Samples/initial prices/targeted prices/merchandising discussed.

SAMPLE ALLOCATION COMPLETED - Styles/colors for sales samples complete.

SAMPLE YARN AND FABRIC EX-MILL - Fabric/yarn shipped to factory for sales samples.

SAMPLE YARN AND FABRIC ORDERS COMPLETED - Fabric/yarn complete for sales samples.

SAMPLES EX-FACTORY - Sales samples shipped.

SPEC SHEETS FINALIZED - Fit/Sample comments recorded and confirmed styles complete.

SUBMIT FINAL CHANGES TO PRINTS, ALL INFORMATION IS TO BE COMPLETED - Review and complete corrections/approvals of textile design/colorways/etc.

SWATCH CARD LAYOUT COMPLETED BY END OF WEEK - Fabrics in each color of bulk palette laid out.

SWATCHING COMPLETED - Fabrics in each color of bulk palette cut, mounted and distributed.

CHAPTER 4

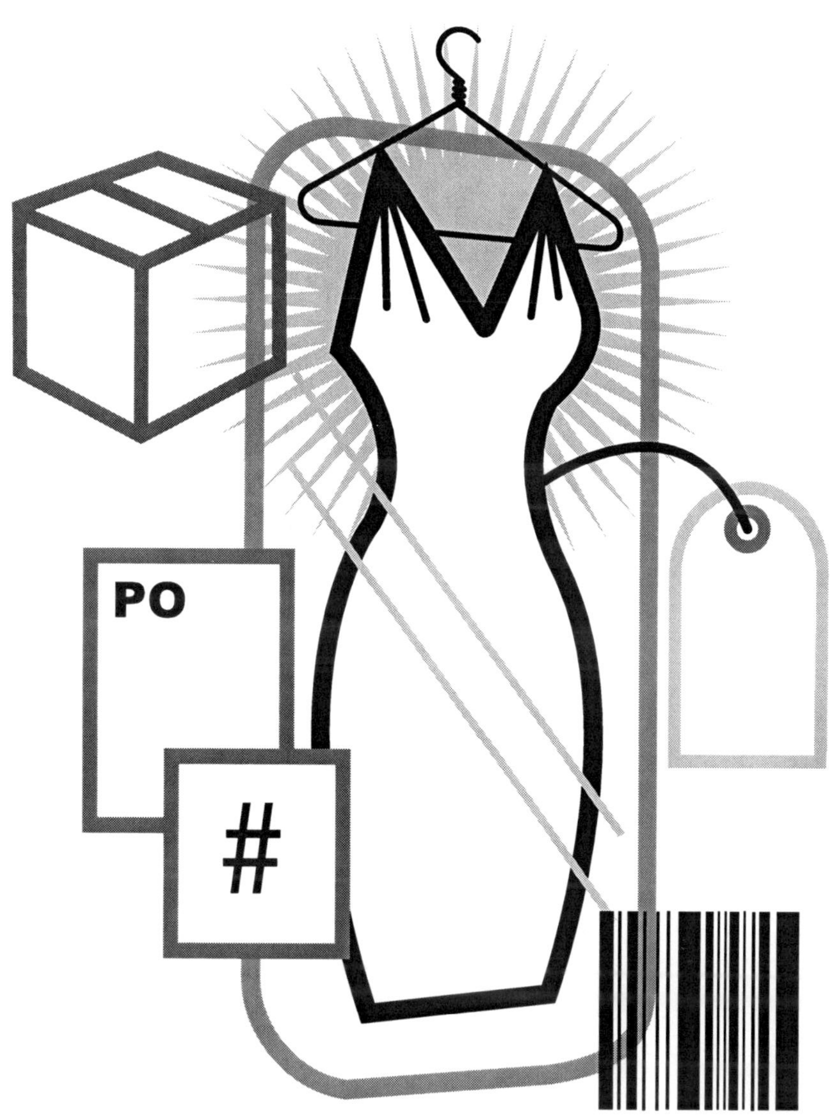

SALES SAMPLE PROCEDURES

This chapter describes the Sales Sample (historically called Salesman's Samples). Sales Samples are produced seasonally and used as actual samples to be shown to buyers during the selling season. They are the development samples in which production orders are, or are not, placed depending on the orders made when the buyers review the Sales Samples. The shipped production garments must look as good or better than your Sales Samples.

SALES SAMPLE PROCEDURES

Please make sure you discuss sales sample costs with your suppliers, and what this entails. Be sure to ask: If a production order is given to them, will they discount this amount from the bulk production order? This is also the time when all minimums, prices, and deliveries should be discussed with the factory or vendors. Also find out what the surcharges will be if minimums are not met. You want to make sure that you are not losing money. You also want to give your sales team the right price for selling.

Sales Samples are currently the most common selling tools in the apparel and accessories industries. Customers (buyers) expect to see an example of a given item or style (SKU), in order to make certain its overall appearance, stylishness and quality of workmanship. The number and assortment of samples vary, based on the way each company chooses to market its merchandise. A company with a large, widespread sales force will have to provide its sales people with a meaningful representation of each style in each collection. These sales sample requirements can be quite extensive and costly. With the growth of digital and computer-generated imaging, it has become easier and highly cost-effective to represent some styles and colorways without producing a physical facsimile of every item for each showroom, salesperson or representative. Still, it is customary to represent each item or style within the collection by at least one or more samples. Sales samples can also perform the role of preproduction samples, since they are often made on the factory's production line and should accurately represent the specified "make," "size spec" and quality for final production. Correct and timely sales sample delivery is vital to every company for its merchandising and marketing calendar.

DESTINATION / QUANTITY / SIZE BREAKDOWN

DESTINATIONS

Each sample season will vary in the destination breakdown of samples. In most cases, the majority of sales samples should be sent to the customer's offices or warehouse (as stipulated in the Sales Sample PO). There may be other destinations that can vary from season to season. When the contractor is advised of the sales sample quantities, the destination should also be included.

QUANTITY

At the beginning of a season, the customer's production department should provide a total sales sample quantity by category to the contractor. These quantities should be broken down by styles, color and destination. The customer bases these quantities on showroom requirements, size of sales force, photo and publicity samples and quality control.

SIZE

The customer should stipulate the sales sample size in the PO. Sales sample sizes usually reflect industry standards for sizing in that category, i.e.: Size M (Medium), Misses Size 8, Men's Size 40 Jacket, etc.

SALES SAMPLE PURCHASE ORDER

The individual responsible for sales samples issues the **Sales Sample Purchase Orders** (PO) in the form attached after the quantities and destinations are advised.

PURCHASE ORDER NUMBER

The PO number is in the upper-right-hand corner of the purchase order. This PO number should be referenced on all paperwork sent regarding a sales sample shipment.

DESTINATIONS

The destination should be listed under "WHSE." Each destination is listed on a separate page on the PO. Refer to the definitions of the abbreviations below:

AMMENDMENTS TO PO

- When Sales Sample POs are passed, the contractor and/or agent should carefully review the POs. If any discrepancies are discovered in price, quantity, or color breakdown, the contractor and/or agent must immediately notify the individual coordinating sales samples so the PO can be amended.

- The customer should not pay for samples shipped that exceed the quantity stated on the PO, unless written authorization has been received from the customer.

- The sales sample coordinator and production manager must be notified if a shortage is expected in order for allocation to be modified.

SALES SAMPLE PURCHASE ORDER:

YOUR COMPANY LLC		
ADDRESS:		
CITY, STATE:		
TEL:	FAX:	EMAIL:

SALES SAMPLE PURCHASE ORDER			
PO NUMBER:		DATE:	
TO:			
ATTN:		FAX:	
FROM:		TEL:	

We confirm having ordered from you the following:

ITEM CODE	ITEM / DESCRIPTION	QUANTITY (YDS)	UNIT PRICE (USD)	AMOUNT (USD)

INVOICE INSTRUCTIONS AND DOCUMENTATIONS:		ADDRESSED TO:
		YOUR COMPANY
TOTAL ORDER VALUE:		
DELIVERY:		
TERMS OF PAYMENT:		
OTHER TERMS:		
REMARKS:		
ACCEPTED BY:		
SELLER'S SIGNATURE:		

NAME ______________________ YOUR COMPANY, LLC

SALES SAMPLE PACKAGING, SHIPPING AND DOCUMENTATION

Special handling is required for shipping sales samples to the customer's warehouse or offices. A PO must be completed detailing the items and quantities required for each new style to be produced.

Refer to later chapter on Packaging and Shipping for packaging, invoicing and packing list guidelines. In addition to these, the following guidelines must also be adhered to, and non-compliance should result in a charge back to the contractor and/or agent.

PACKAGING

- **Do Not Mutilate Sales Samples (for samples imported <u>into</u> the U.S.A.)**
    - If garments are mutilated or stamped "**Sample**" (for U.S. Customs purposes) without authorization, the customer should not pay for the samples.
    - If samples are mutilated or stamped, the invoice must clearly state how the garment has been mutilated and where the mutilation is located on the garment.

- **Garment Tagging**

  The customer's sales sample tag should be attached to each sales sample. The customer should provide an initial quantity of this tag to the contractor and/or agent. The tag must be sourced locally by the contractor, and then submitted to the appropriate party for approval.

- **Poly-Bag Requirements**

  Each sample garment or article should be individually poly-bagged for shipment. Each poly-bag **must** have a visible sticker indicating the customer's style number, color name, color number and size. The sticker should be placed on the lower-right-hand corner of the poly-bag. The poly-bag sticker must also state that it is a "Factory Sample."

- **Carton Markings**
    - An approved bulk-shipping carton should be used for sales samples.
    - Carton markings must reflect the PO Number(s).
    - Style number/color number/size and PO number and quantity should be indicated.
    - Carton number sequence noted.
    - Carton with copy of Packing List should be marked for quick access.
    - Carton weight must be noted.
    - Exterior of the shipping carton must be clearly marked "**Samples**" and must include the season code (e.g. "S 08" for Spring 2008) using a label with lettering no smaller than 1" in height. Handwritten markings are acceptable.

  The corrugated shipping container must only have labels that pertain to that shipment.

  Cartons should contain only one style and color. The exception to this policy is the use of mixed cartons when there is not enough of one SKU to fill a carton.

DOCUMENTATION

Documentation requirements for shipping sales samples are listed below. In order to avoid delays it is important to include all pertinent paperwork when shipping the sales samples. If a shipment from an offshore contractor does not include all the necessary paperwork, it may result in a delay with U.S. Customs, causing the Sales Samples to arrive past the due date. The customer should not accept any such oversight. The customer is entitled to withhold payment or issue a chargeback.

Shipping Documentation

I. Samples to Customer's Office or Warehouse (SS)

1. Commercial invoice (inside and outside of package)
2. Packing list (inside and outside of package)
3. Visa (when coming from outside the US)
4. Textile declaration (when coming from outside the US).

II. Samples to Customer Affiliates

1. Commercial invoice (inside and outside of package)
2. Packing List (inside and outside of package)
3. Export license (when required)
4. Certificate of origin (when required).

Note: Please check with custom officials before you start your season in order to assure yourself no policies have been changed.

DOCUMENTATION RECAP

Below is a suggested customer policy for sending shipping details to individuals coordinating sale samples. This policy, in combination with the documentation already stated, is necessary for shipping all sales samples.

DAILY RECAP

On the day of actual shipment, the contractor and/or agent must fax or e-mail a daily recap to the sales sample coordinator. This recap must include:

Style #
Color #
Quantity
Shipped
Destination
Tracking or AWB #

This recap should be sent the day that the samples are shipped.

ORIGINAL INVOICES

After a shipment has been sent, the original invoices should be sent to the customer's offices, ATTN: ACCOUNTS PAYABLE. Copies of the Invoices, Packing Lists, and AWB's must be sent concurrently to the sales sample coordinator. Original invoices submitted for payment should not be sent to the sales sample coordinator. Copies of the invoices and packing lists should be sent no later than 5 days after the shipment has been sent.

INVOICES/PACKING LISTS

- All invoices and packing lists must reference the PO number clearly. They also should include the style, color, quantity, and destination.
- The packing list is the customer's proof of shipment. To ensure prompt payment of invoices, packing lists should be sent to the sales sample coordinator in a timely manner.
- All packing lists and invoices should indicate **"Samples."**
- All documents required for shipment should identify the shipment as **"Samples."**

CHAPTER 5

MANAGEMENT, EVALUATION AND COMPLIANCE FORMS

This chapter introduces production and evaluation forms and certificates to use for apparel production orders and manufacturing factories. Included are Purchase Orders and Purchase Order Confirmations, Contractor Evaluations, and Contractor/Vendor Compliance Certifications.

PRODUCTION MANAGEMENT FORMS

MANAGEMENT EVALUATION AND COMPLIANCE FORM

This chapter gives you an overall view of the production forms that you may or may not choose to use. A purchase order is a must, since many vendors will not work with you unless they have a PO number to ensure they will eventually be able to collect their funds.

PURCHASE ORDER CONFIRMATION

This was mentioned in the previous chapter. When the vendor or factory certifies the price, delivery, and quantity for each style, it provides you with some security, knowing that this is the price he will keep for production. You need to have this secured for each style before beginning production.

CONTRACTOR INFORMATION SHEET

Please make sure that you have this sheet completed before you begin working with any vendor. Generally, a vendor might have three different names within the same factory because there are three types of garments being produced there. By utilizing this sheet, we try to avoid having your garment subcontracted unless you are first told. You will not be able to avoid being subcontracted all of the time, but this will help you hold your original vendor or factory accountable.

CONTRACTOR ASSESSMENT AND EVALUATION

This will help you obtain a thorough understanding of who you are working with. Please make sure you review this carefully so you know beforehand if they can manufacture your product. If the factory is desperate for work, they will all say, "Yes, we can do it." You need to know if this is a reality.

VENDOR COMPLIANCE CERTIFICATION

This sheet is generally completed by a third party quality and assurance company. You can search for these companies on the Web or you can ask your vendor or factory if they will share this information with you from past customers. Most likely they will tell you that they cannot provide this information to you. This is common practice. If they do share this with you, it will give you an assurance that they are aware of the process and know what it entails, and you'll know how they where evaluated. If they do not, you have a choice of hiring one of these companies, which is an expensive process, or trusting your agent or your gut. It's all about relationships in this industry.

PURCHASE ORDER AND PURCHASE ORDER CONFIRMATION SHEET

The **Purchase Order** confirms what is being ordered from the factory, and upon receipt of a customer's Purchase Order, the agent and/or contractor must sign and return a **Purchase Order Confirmation Sheet**. The signed form signifies that the agent and/or contractor agree to the terms and conditions of the Purchase Order and the customer's Contractor Compliance Manual. Once signed, the Purchase Order Confirmation Sheet should be returned to the customer's production or accounting departments. In addition, you, the customer should not be held liable for any excess raw material.

LETTER OF CREDIT/SHIPPING INFORMATION FORM

The opening and use of Letters of Credit will be discussed further in Chapter 6. However, Letters of Credit are the most common method of transferring money to an offshore manufacturer in payment for services in the future, upon compliance with a Purchase Order. This **Shipping Information Form** should provide all pertinent information necessary for opening Letters of Credit for a specific contractor or manufacturer.

The **Letter of Credit/Shipping Information Form** must be completed, where applicable, for Purchase Orders and returned to the customer's production or accounting departments as indicated. Letters of Credit will not be opened until the form has been returned. Please see the example of this form in Chapter 6.

Before a Purchase Order is completed, there are three forms regarding the contractor(s) that must be fulfilled:

CONTRACTOR INFORMATION SHEET

This form is provided to give key information for setting up communication and doing business with a given contractor. It is, in effect, a contractor profile for your records.

The **Contractor Information Sheet** must be completed before a Purchase Order (PO) can be issued.

CONTRACTOR ASSESSMENT AND EVALUATION

The **contractor assessment and evaluation** is completed on a form titled the Customer's Appraisal of Manufacturing Resource Form. This form is an evaluation of a contractor's facility, and is used when visiting and assessing a factory on the products they manufacture, their working standards, and the factory management. It will be completed before the Contractor Information Sheet, and the information from it is used for the Vendor Compliance Certificate (to follow).

VENDOR COMPLIANCE CERTIFICATION

Additionally, the **Customer/Vendor Compliance Certification** form, which states that a factory upholds good labor practices with respect to human rights, and is therefore equipped to carry out the company's production, must be completed prior to issuing a Purchase Order.

EXAMPLE OF A PURCHASE ORDER

YOUR COMPANY LLC		
ADDRESS:		
CITY, STATE :		
TEL:	FAX:	EMAIL:

PURCHASE ORDER

PO NUMBER:		DATE:	
TO:			
ATTN:		FAX:	
FROM:		TEL:	

We confirm having ordered from you the following:

ITEM CODE	ITEM / DESCRIPTION	QUANTITY (YDS)	UNIT PRICE (USD)	AMOUNT (USD)

INVOICE INSTRUCTIONS AND DOCUMENTATIONS:		ADDRESSED TO:
		YOUR COMPANY
TOTAL ORDER VALUE:		
DELIVERY:		
TERMS OF PAYMENT:		
OTHER TERMS:		
REMARKS:		
ACCEPTED BY:		

SELLER'S SIGNATURE:

NAME

YOUR COMPANY, LLC

PURCHASE ORDER CONFIRMATION
PURCHASE ORDER #:
STYLE:
QUANTITY:
EX-MAKER DATE:
CANCELLATION DATE:
PRICE:
VENDOR NAME:
Signature and return by fax from Contractor acknowledges: **Receipt, Review and Agreement to Price, Quantity** by **Style / Color / Size** and **Delivery Date**, and receipt and understanding of the Customer's Contractor Compliance Manual.
signed / date Response and confirmation is anticipated within 48 hours of receipt. Date sent by customer is:
Return To:

CONTRACTOR INFORMATION SHEET

Contractor Name: ______________________________
(as appears on Purchase Order)
____

Contractor Address: ______________________________
(as appears on Purchase Order)
____
____
Country ______________________________

Mailing Address:
(if different than PO address)
Name ______________________________
Address ______________________________
____
Country ______________________________

Contractor Point of Contact:
Name ______________________________
Telephone ______________________________
Fax ______________________________

Product Origin: ______________________________

Payment Terms (e.g. Net 30, L/C): ______________________________

FOB Terms (e.g. FOB HK): ______________________________

Buying Agent: ______________________________

CONTRACTOR ASSESSMENT AND EVALUATION

PURPOSE:
The Contractor Assessment and Evaluation process identifies potential contractors and measures the performance of current ones. The contractor's facilities, which meet the customer's assessment procedures, may be placed on their vendor matrix or list. Only those factories, which are listed, would be used for production of the customer's product.

The contractor assessment and evaluation process assures:

- Product integrity.
- Environmental and social integrity standards consistent with customer's current policies.
- Consistent and reliable contractor performance (delivery, quality, pricing).

PROCEDURES:
These critical components are incorporated into a five-step assessment and evaluation procedure:

1. CONTRACTOR OR FACILITY VISIT
The customer, customer production manager, agent or customer's representative visits the contractor to confirm current physical operations and observe the quality of product.

2. CUSTOMER ASSESSMENT
The customer or representative prepares and provides a Contractor and Resource Assessment Form to the appropriate customer production manager (a copy of the Contractor and Resource Assessment Form will be supplied to each representative). The assessment evaluates:

- Physical structure
- Capacity
- Management
- Quality and competency aspects of the contractor

The assessment also includes a review of environmental and social integrity standards employed by the contractor.

3. PRODUCTION OR QC VISIT
Members of customer's production or quality control department may also visit the contractor to confirm the agent's assessment.

4. ADDITION TO VENDOR MATRIX/LIST
If the contractor receives a favorable assessment, the customer and the contractor may enter into a manufacturing agreement. The contractor may be utilized for production for one season and will be added to the vendor matrix or list for a "trial." At that time, the contractor will file a Contractor Compliance Certification. If the contractor performs to a satisfactory level during the "trial" period, the contractor may be considered an "acceptable" resource for further production. While the designation "acceptable" does not guarantee the customer will utilize the contractor for future production, it allows the customer to price and sample garments for overall quality and performance.

5. CONTRACTOR EVALUATION

The contractor will be evaluated after each season it produces the customer's product. The evaluation measures sales sample delivery, pricing, quality, bulk delivery, communication and other pertinent criteria. If the contractor continues satisfactory performance, the Manufacturing Agreement will be renewed and the contractor will remain on the matrix or list. If the contractor does not perform to a standard acceptable to the customer, the Manufacturing Agreement will not be renewed and the vendor will be removed from the matrix/list. If appropriate, the Manufacturing Agreement will be renewed but the contractor will need to perform an additional "trial" season before the possibility of returning to the matrix is considered.

THE CUSTOMER'S PRODUCTION MANAGER WILL PROVIDE THE CONTRACTOR ASSESSMENT FORM.

CUSTOMER'S APPRAISAL OF MANUFACTURING RESOURCE	
DATE:	
REVIEWED BY:	
FACTORY NAME:	
ADDRESS:	
COUNTRY:	
TELEPHONE:	
FAX:	
CONTACT NAME:	

PRODUCT TYPES:	
YEAR ESTABLISHED:	
EXPORT MARKET:	
OTHER CUSTOMERS:	
TERMS OF PAYMENT:	
ANNUAL VOLUME:	
MONTHLY CAPACITY:	
FABRIC AFFILIATION:	
PRODUCTION LEAD TIME:	
MINIMUM QTY/STYLE:	
PATTERNMAKING ABILITY:	
# OF SEWING MACHINES:	
# OF EMPLOYEES:	
LAUNDRY AFFILIATIONS:	
TYPES OF WASHES:	
COMMENTS/EQUIPMENT:	

FACILITY DESCRIPTION:

1. UNSATISFACTORY	2. MARGINAL	3. ACCEPTABLE	4. COMMENDABLE
Dirty, poorly lit, disorganized layout.	Crowded w/ poor work flow and little organization.	Work flow is steady with adequate facilities.	Well run with good supervision.
REMARKS:			

FABRIC PRODUCTION:

1. UNSATISFACTORY	2. MARGINAL	3. ACCEPTABLE	4. COMMENDABLE
No safeguards or quality checks.	Haphazard supervision and quality procedures.	Adequate machinery with regular quality checks.	Strong quality control program w/ modern equipment.

REMARKS:

SUPERVISION:

1. UNSATISFACTORY	2. MARGINAL	3. ACCEPTABLE	4. COMMENDABLE
Little or no supervision of workers and product.	Some random supervision.	Regular supervision over major areas w/ 25:1 ratio.	Strong supervisory staff and separate quality auditing.

REMARKS:

CUTTING:

1. UNSATISFACTORY	2. MARGINAL	3. ACCEPTABLE	4. COMMENDABLE
Messy area w/little or no control over cut parts.	Cut parts are not well identified or protected from soiling.	Cuts flow in an orderly manner directly to the sewing sections.	Ply identification maintained throughout cutting and always protected from soiling.
REMARKS:			

GARMENT PRODUCTION:

1. UNSATISFACTORY	2. MARGINAL	3. ACCEPTABLE	4. COMMENDABLE
Various levels of production quality w/no repairs/audits.	Random audits, no formal final inspection, minimal repairs.	In-process checks and final audit with strong repair program.	Documented in-process inspection and final audits w/ rework systems for all repairable items.

REMARKS:

PRESSING AND FINISHING:			
1. UNSATISFACTORY	**2. MARGINAL**	**3. ACCEPTABLE**	**4. COMMENDABLE**
Little or no facilities for pressing and finishing.	Product is often poorly pressed and finished.	Product is generally acceptable in appearance.	Crisp, neat finished product w/very few packing errors.
Pressing equipment (circle as applicable) Hand / Steam / Vacuum Exhaust / Press Form / Tunnel			
REMARKS:			

PACKING / SHIPPING:			
1. UNSATISFACTORY	**2. MARGINAL**	**3. ACCEPTABLE**	**4. COMMENDABLE**
Haphazard system in an inadequate space.	Little assurance of accuracy in content and count.	Organized area with checks for correct packing.	Generally accurate packing.
REMARKS:			

PAPERWORK:			
1. UNSATISFACTORY	**2. MARGINAL**	**3. ACCEPTABLE**	**4. COMMENDABLE**
Haphazard system w/ little accuracy on packing slips.	Often makes packing slip errors.	Packing slip generally accurate and complete.	Shipping info correct and prior to shipment.
REMARKS:			

COMMUNICATION:			
1. UNSATISFACTORY	**2. MARGINAL**	**3. ACCEPTABLE**	**4. COMMENDABLE**
Difficult to contact and slow in responding.	Haphazard responses to production inquiries.	Provides generally reliable answers within a reasonable time frame.	Provides accurate and timely information.
REMARKS:			

SUBCONTRACTING:			
1. UNSATISFACTORY	**2. MARGINAL**	**3. ACCEPTABLE**	**4. COMMENDABLE**
Most or all of work given out with little or no supervision.	Some contact with sub-contractors.	Performs regular quality checks.	Subcontractors are selected and reliable.
REMARKS:			

MANAGEMENT'S ABILITY:			
JUDGMENT: Thinks situations through clearly, making sound business decisions.			
1. UNSATISFACTORY	**2. MARGINAL**	**3. ACCEPTABLE**	**4. COMMENDABLE**
REMARKS:			

ATTITUDE: Demonstrates willingness to work hard and is accommodating.			
1. UNSATISFACTORY	2. MARGINAL	3. ACCEPTABLE	4. COMMENDABLE

FLEXIBILITY: Adjusts readily to changes, updates and revisions. Accepts challenges readily.			
1. UNSATISFACTORY	2. MARGINAL	3. ACCEPTABLE	4. COMMENDABLE

COMMUNICATIONS: Responds readily to queries promptly and honestly, open and accurate with information.			
1. UNSATISFACTORY	2. MARGINAL	3. ACCEPTABLE	4. COMMENDABLE

STABILITY: Has history of fulfilling commitments and meeting deadlines. Financing is not a problem affecting production.			
1. UNSATISFACTORY	2. MARGINAL	3. ACCEPTABLE	4. COMMENDABLE

MANAGEMENT'S OPERATING SKILLS:

PRODUCT KNOWLEDGE: Possesses technical knowledge and equipment to produce the garment.			
1. UNSATISFACTORY	2. MARGINAL	3. ACCEPTABLE	4. COMMENDABLE

PLANNING: Has control over production, flow and factory loading. Does not merely react to problems.			
1. UNSATISFACTORY	2. MARGINAL	3. ACCEPTABLE	4. COMMENDABLE

ORGANIZATION: Defines functions and responsibilities within own organization.			
1. UNSATISFACTORY	2. MARGINAL	3. ACCEPTABLE	4. COMMENDABLE

FOLLOW-UP: Responds to instructions and successfully completes them.			
1. UNSATISFACTORY	2. MARGINAL	3. ACCEPTABLE	4. COMMENDABLE

CREATIVITY: Demonstrates innovative techniques and originality, seeking new and better ways of doing things.			
1. UNSATISFACTORY	2. MARGINAL	3. ACCEPTABLE	4. COMMENDABLE

SUGGESTED IMPROVEMENTS:

BASIC HUMAN RIGHTS ISSUES:

CHILD LABOR: Factory does not employ any person under the age of 14 or younger than the local compulsory age for school attendance.

1. UNSATISFACTORY Does not subscribe to this policy.	**2. ACCEPTABLE** States to be in compliance.	**3. COMMENDABLE** Proven record of adherence and proactive programs in place.	

PRISON LABOR: Factory does not employ any prison labor or forced labor.

1. UNSATISFACTORY Does not subscribe to this Policy.	**2. ACCEPTABLE** States to be in compliance.	**3. COMMENDABLE** Proven record of adherence and proactive programs in place.	

FREEDOM OF ASSOCIATION: Employees are free to join organizations.

1. UNSATISFACTORY Does not subscribe to this Policy.	**2. ACCEPTABLE** States to be in compliance.	**3. COMMENDABLE** Proven record of adherence and proactive programs in place.	

MINIMUM WAGE: Factory pays at least local minimum wage.

1. UNSATISFACTORY Does not subscribe to this Policy.	**2. ACCEPTABLE** States to be in compliance.	**3. COMMENDABLE** Proven record of adherence and proactive programs in place.	

OVERTIME: Factory **does not** require employees to work overtime and employees are compensated for any overtime hours worked.

1. UNSATISFACTORY Does not subscribe to this Policy.	**2. ACCEPTABLE** States to be in compliance.	**3. COMMENDABLE** Proven record of adherence and proactive programs in place.	

WORKING CONDITIONS: Factory provides safe and healthy work environment.

1. UNSATISFACTORY Does not subscribe to this Policy.	**2. ACCEPTABLE** States to be in compliance.	**3. COMMENDABLE** Proven record of adherence and proactive programs in place.	

ENVIRONMENTAL ISSUES:

WATER WASTE: Factory meets legal requirement for water waste management.

1. UNSATISFACTORY Does not subscribe to this policy.	2. ACCEPTABLE States to be in compliance.	3. COMMENDABLE Proven record of adherence and proactive programs in place.	

AIR / LAND WASTE: Factory meets legal requirements for disposal of air and land waste.

1. UNSATISFACTORY Does not subscribe to this Policy.	2. ACCEPTABLE States to be in compliance.	3. COMMENDABLE Proven record of adherence and proactive programs in place.	

COUNTRY OF ORIGIN ISSUES: Factory complies with customs regulations pertaining to the country of origin requirements.

1. UNSATISFACTORY Does not subscribe to this Policy.	2. ACCEPTABLE States to be in compliance.	3. COMMENDABLE Proven record of adherence and proactive programs in place.	

SUBCONTRACTING:

Factory agrees not to subcontract production or parts thereof without prior approval from the customer. The customer may require special visit to subcontractor for additional evaluation.

1. UNSATISFACTORY Does not subscribe to this Policy.	2. ACCEPTABLE States to be in compliance.	3. COMMENDABLE Proven record of adherence and proactive programs in place.	

ASSESSMENT OF OVERALL APPRAISAL*:

Check the one statement below that most accurately reflects your overall appraisal of this resource.
In selecting a rating for the resource, please keep in mind that:

_ All elements of the resource's capabilities should be considered.

_ This rating should **not** be determined by finding an average of the ratings given in the preceding sections.

_ Varying degrees of importance you may place on those factors can make averaging them inappropriate.

_ The assessment should represent a composite of your thoughts and impressions of the source's overall performance and capabilities.

1. UNSATISFACTORY	2. AUTHORIZED	3. ACCEPTABLE	4. COMMENDABLE
Not acceptable to produce for customer at this time.	Authorized for trial period.	Has proven acceptable during trial period.	Has proven consistently to meet or exceed customer's standards.
X	X	X	X

***Please sign in the appropriate box for the overall rating suggested for this resource.**

VENDOR COMPLIANCE CERTIFICATION

Following is the Customer Vendor Compliance Certification, which must be completed prior to issuing a Purchase Order.

CUSTOMER – VENDOR COMPLIANCE CERTIFICATION

(The contractor agrees to restrict circulation of any information provided by the customer to the contractor's personnel who have need for such information in development and production.)

A. OVERVIEW

1. Contract Manufacturer/Contractor Name or Facility Name:

   ____

2. Address:

   ____

   ____

3. Please list other companies currently contracting products from this facility:

   ______________ ______________

   ______________ ______________

   ______________ ______________

4. Please list any primary subcontractors who will be directly involved in the customer's production:

CONFIDENTIAL

Component	Supplier	Location(s)

B. VALUE OF DIVERSITY/HUMAN RIGHTS

1. Please provide available documentation of actual practices and/or written policies verifying the protection and insurance of basic human rights and non-discrimination in this facility (or related subcontractors): ______________________________

C. ENVIRONMENTAL STEWARDSHIP

1. Please indicate if this facility (or related subcontractors) has been cited for non-compliance with any local laws governing environmental management:

   YES ☐ **NO** ☐

   If yes, please provide available documentation explaining such citing.

2. Please indicate if this facility (and related subcontractors) takes measures to control pollution of land, water and air:

YES ☐ **NO** ☐

D. COMMUNITY BUILDING/CORPORATE CITIZENSHIP

1. Please provide information regarding any community involvement or support activities in place at this facility (and related subcontractors), or any product/facility contributions made to the local community through this facility (or related subcontractors):____________________

E. COMPENSATION

1. Please indicate the following:

	Local Currency	US Dollars
Minimum hourly wage required by law		
Prevailing hourly wage of workers		
Average hourly wage paid this facility		
Lowest hourly wage paid this facility		

2. Please indicate if wages are held back from workers for any reason:

____

____

____

3. Please indicate any and all benefits paid to workers at this facility (e.g. Medical, Education, Leave / Vacation, Housing, etc.):

____

____

____

F. WORKING HOURS

1. Please indicate the following:

	Your Facility	Related Subcontractors
Scheduled hours per day / week	/	/
Average number of overtime hours per week		

2. Please indicate the process for assigning overtime at this facility (i.e. equal access, right of refusal):

____

____

G. VOLUNTARY EMPLOYMENT

1. Please indicate if there are any workers in this facility (or related subcontractors) present on less than a voluntary basis. If yes, please provide documentation regarding the circumstances of their employment:

YES ☐ **NO** ☐

H. CHILD LABOR

1. Please indicate if there are workers younger than 14 years of age in this facility (or related subcontractors):

YES ☐ **NO** ☐

2. Please indicate the following:

Facility Name / Location	Age of Youngest Employee

3. Please indicate the minimum age for working in this locale / country: ______________
4. Please indicate the minimum age for required school attendance: ______________

I. HEALTH AND SAFETY

1. Please indicate if this facility (or related subcontractors) has been cited for non-compliance with local laws governing health and safety:

YES ☐ **NO** ☐

If yes, please provide an explanation of the circumstances.

2. Please provide any documentation and/or written policies governing health and safety procedures, equipment and training available at this facility (or related subcontractors): ____

J. MANUFACTURE

1. Subcontractor shall only produce the specific number of products ordered by the customer and at no time shall intentionally produce excess goods or overruns. Manufacturer shall not sell any products bearing the customer's trademarks to any third parties without the express written consent of the Customer: ____

K. RESTRICTIONS

1. Subcontractors shall be bound by all terms and conditions of the Manufacturing Agreement between customer and manufacturer/contractor:

Facility Name: ______________________________

Facility Location: ______________________________

Signature: ______________________________

Name Printed: ______________________________

Title: ______________________________

Date: ______________________________

CHAPTER 6

LETTERS OF CREDIT PAYMENT TERMS

This chapter discusses Letters of Credit, which are used extensively in the apparel production industry today. A Letter of Credit is a transfer of payment to an offshore manufacturer, upon completion of a Purchase Order/Production order. Letters of Credit are not opened until the Purchase Order Confirmation and the Letter of Credit Shipping Information Form are received.

LETTERS OF CREDIT PAYMENT TERMS

LETTERS OF CREDIT PAYMENT TERMS

This chapter will take you through a letter of credit procedure. Don't be surprised if you encounter different payment terms from you to the factory or from you to the retailers. The latter term is the one you should try to negotiate immediately after writing the order.

Be very cautious not to let the excitement of an order distract you from paying careful attention to all the details. Many times, you or your sales team will be so excited by the fact that a retailer liked your line, placed an order, and will be sending you a PO, that you can neglect to discuss in length such important details as the method of payment or shipping terms.

Before including this order into your projections, you should try to find out through a credit company, like D&B, whether this company pays on time and has credit worthiness. You do not want to project your sales on retailers who are inconsistent, late, or cancel orders at the last minute. This will make your life with the factory and the production team a nightmare.

When dealing with small boutique stores or the "mom and pop" stores, your best option is to try to get 50 percent upfront and the balance upon delivery of the goods. (Make sure the retailers are not planning to sell your merchandise on a consignment basis.) If you still need to negotiate terms with these types of stores, you should consider asking them to ship two entire seasons before allowing them credit. There are advantages and disadvantages to dealing with smaller retailers. They will not help you meet the minimums of the factory. On the upside, however, you have better management of your projections and your cash flow for each season.

Large retailers are generally difficult to work with, especially if you are a start-up. They often want long payment terms of 120 days or more if your sell throughs are not somewhere around 80 percent. With these accounts, you run a high risk of getting chargeback's for discounted merchandise (markdowns), or they might just pack up everything not sold and mark it as a "return to vendor" (RTV). You can imagine the consequences if you don't conform to their requests of RTV's or mark down money—the likelihood of them purchasing from you in seasons to come are slim to none.

There is an upside to dealing with retailers of this magnitude, since their sales will ensure you have leverage when determining your prices. The downside is you minimize your account list to only a few stores

No matter whom you decide to accept orders from, as excited as you are, you should always remember to discuss the important payment and shipping details to avoid being left with unpaid or returned orders, because these will come out of your bottom line.

When negotiating with your factories, keep in mind that unless you are a large corporation that has been in business for several years, they will not manufacture anything for you unless you wire money to them for prototypes and sales samples, or open a letter of credit for production.

Always try to negotiate with the factories about minimums, prototypes, and development. Attempt to get them to agree that if minimums are met, all monies that have been spent on prototypes and development (not including sales samples) will be deducted from the production order. This, again, will help you manage your cash flow.

Once your relationship with the factory has grown over two seasons, try to negotiate the proto development cost to avoid a huge overhead.

In the following pages, you will see how a letter of credit works. This chapter is one of the key elements to your business. This will help you with your cash flow and help you avoid costly mistakes. Remember: Always try to negotiate with all your suppliers or vendors.

Letters of Credit are one of the most common methods of securing payment for goods and services to an offshore manufacturer for imports into the United States today. With the Letter of Credit, a company can transfer money, at a designated date in the future, once the product is in compliance with the contract or purchase order. In effect, the customer (applicant), as the importer of contracted goods, applies to a commercial lending institution (bank) to assure payment to the individual or company (beneficiary) responsible for full and proper completion of the designated imported product.

A **Letter of Credit** is also know as LOC or L/C, and is a document issued by a financial institution, such as a commercial bank, and acts as an irrevocable form of payment to the designated beneficiary, even if the applicant has failed to perform his obligations. The Letter of Credit can also be drawn up to provide payment for a business transaction, such as a foreign manufacturer or supplier being paid for delivery of goods or services, by redeeming the Letter of Credit upon proof of compliance with its conditions.

Today, **Letters of Credit** are used extensively in international trade and commerce because they have the advantage of providing a guarantee of payment to the beneficiary regardless of such variables as local trade regulations, fluctuating currency rates or political instability. Simply put, an importer applies (as the applicant) to a financial institution (the issuing bank) to transfer funds or payment to the manufacturer/supplier/exporter (the beneficiary) for goods or services in compliance with the terms of the L/C. Usually, the applicant is a client of the issuing bank and the beneficiary is a client of the advising bank. The advising bank is customarily located in the country of the beneficiary. The issuing bank and the advising bank may be part of a larger international banking organization, but not necessarily.

Importing Goods through Letters of Credit

The applicant has four primary objectives in using Letters of Credit for international trade transactions:

- To obtain assurance that they will receive the correct quality and quantity of goods as stated in the contract.

- To have the contracted goods delivered on a timely basis and by the method(s) of delivery outlined.

- To manage cash flow by postponing or extending payment(s) or by the issuing bank to arrange financing to pay for the goods.

- To provide assurance that the payment actually reaches the beneficiary and is credited toward the contracted merchandise.

In order to expedite opening a **Letter of Credit**, the following points should be considered at the outset. Details on the following points may be confirmed with the U.S. Department of Commerce or through a Customs Broker.

- **Licenses and permit -** Required for imported goods under government authorization.
- **Customs clearance -** Depends on the nature of the product, the country of import, regulations, restrictions, etc. A customs broker is usually engaged to help in this process.
- **Standard documentation -** Varies from country to country, but generally includes an application for entry (a visa), a commercial invoice, a title document (ocean bill of lading or air-way bill), a packing list, appropriate declarations and certificates.
- **Product compliance -** Completed by U.S. Customs officials as per current U.S. import laws.
- **Import duties and customs fees -** As appropriate, and as required by the U.S. Government.

POSSIBLE RISK FACTORS

There are several "risk factors" that the advising bank will consider in an international transaction.

- Financial soundness of the beneficiary
- Buyer's and seller's reputations in the business community
- Seller/buyer relationship
- Type of merchandise
- The relative value of the merchandise or services vs. fees and cost of doing business with the beneficiary.

There may also be "risk factors" concerning the country of origin, including:

- Political situations, like wars, revolutions, trade embargos and the general fluctuations of that country's economy.
- Customs regulations and embargoes
- Availability and valuation of foreign currency.

There are advantages to opening Letters or Credit with a new supplier, but there are some disadvantages that the applicant must also consider. The applicant's capitol will be tied up until receipt or release of the goods. The applicant bears the greatest financial risk since there is no assurance that: the goods will be received at all; the goods will be received in the correct quality or specified quantity; or the goods will be received within the specified time period.

TYPICAL DOCUMENTATION REQUIRED OF THE BENEFICIARY

- Bill of Lading (a.k.a. title document, since possession of an original Bill of Lading is equivalent to having the title of the goods in possession of the holder).
- Commercial Invoice
- Consular Invoice
- Certificate Country of Origin
- Draft (a.k.a. Bill of Exchange)
- Other documents may include an Inspection Certificate and advice from the shipper regarding shipment information.

IRREVOCABLE CREDITS

Documentary, or Trade Letters of Credit are usually irrevocable credits. The credit can be confirmed or unconfirmed, depending on the:

- Accepted payment terms in the applicant's country
- Amount of the goods covered by the L/C
- Demand for the goods
- Degree of country risk the exporter is willing to take.

LETTER OF CREDIT APPLICATION

To apply for opening a Letter of Credit, the importer will need to have a credit line with a bank and complete a **Letter of Credit Application**. The information required for a Letter of Credit Application is fairly straight forward and reflects the information that will appear on the final Letter of Credit.

The Letter of Credit application usually contains the following information:

- **Applicant** - The name(s) of the applicant or the applicant's business.
- **Beneficiary** - ("In favor of") - The company name and complete address of the exporter.
- **Advising Bank or Beneficiary's Bank** - ("To be advised through") - This is optional and indicates the beneficiary's bank. This may be left blank so that the issuing bank is free to select an advising bank. If the exporter has specified a particular advising bank, it is customary for the applicant to list this bank on the Letter of Credit application.
- **Amount** - The amount of the credit, including any freight, insurance or other costs agreed upon by the applicant and beneficiary. "Approximate" or "about" amounts indicate an acceptable level of 10%—plus-or-minus—of the stated amount. If the amount is to be in a currency other than U.S. dollars, this should be indicated.
- **Validity or Expiry Date** - The time period or deadline required of the beneficiary to prepare the shipment and the necessary documents for presentation to the advising bank.

- **Tenure or Payment Availability** – The tenure of the credit determines when the payment is available and for how long. Sight Drafts call for "Payment-upon-Shipment" with appropriate documentation. "Time Drafts" or "Deferred Payments" may be used by agreement between the applicant and beneficiary to allow for a specified period between the time of shipment and payment.
- **Required Documents** - Documents required of the beneficiary in order to confirm compliance and in order to receive payment.
- **Description of Goods** — A short description of the goods being shipped, including the quantity. If the L/C allows for an "Approximate Amount," it is acceptable for the goods shipped to be 10%—plus-or-minus—the stated quantity.
- **Other Conditions** - Additional conditions required of the beneficiary. For instance, if the credit is transferable, it will be indicated in this section of the Letter of Credit application.

When opening a **Letter of Credit**, the wording should be specific, but not overly detailed. An overly detailed Letter of Credit is likely to be rejected by the beneficiary, as the terms may be too difficult to meet. The applicant should define exactly what is being purchased and shipped. When specifying the documents required of the Beneficiary/Exporter, it is important to indicate those required for Customs Clearance, and those that correspond to the agreement, purchase order, or sales contract as agreed to by the applicant and beneficiary.

The balance of the **Letter of Credit Application** will contain specific instructions and extensive information on the legal points of Payment Terms and Obligations, Amendments, Liabilities, Defaults, etc. The application will conclude with the applicant's business name, business address, the authorized representative of the applicant, a signature and date.

Special Purpose Letters of Credit

There are three types of **Special Purpose Letters of Credit**:

- **Standby Letters of Credit**
- **Transferable Letters of Credit**
- **Revolving Letters of Credit**

STANDBY LETTERS OF CREDIT

A **Standby Letter of Credit** indicates the issuing bank's responsibility to the beneficiary to:

- Repay money borrowed by the applicant (or advanced to the account of the applicant).
- Make payment because of any indebtedness undertaken by the applicant.
- Make payment because of any default by the applicant in the performance of an obligation.

The **Standby Letter of Credit** supports the beneficiary in the event of a default by the applicant. Although it is recognized as a primary obligation of the issuing bank, it serves as a backup or secondary means of payment.

TRANSFERABLE LETTERS OF CREDIT

In the **Transferable Letter of Credit**, the beneficiary (first beneficiary) may request the advising bank make the credit available in whole or in part to one or more other beneficiaries (second beneficiary).

REVOLVING LETTERS OF CREDIT

Revolving Letters of Credit allow applicant/importers to maintain an ongoing financial relationship with a beneficiary/supplier.

- The L/C may be revocable or irrevocable.
- To provide for the renewal of contracts by reinstating a time limitation or availability of a set dollar amount.
- To allow a fixed limit to be set for the amount to be shipped and for drafts drawn in specified time frames.

For instance, when a beneficiary receives a **Revolving Letter of Credit**, they will make shipments within the time allowed and up to the amount of the credit in compliance with the conditions. When the amount of the credit is exhausted, the credit is automatically renewed. If the credit is cumulative, the unused balance accrues to the next period. If non-cumulative, the unused portion credit is canceled.

LETTER OF CREDIT/SHIPPING INFORMATION FORM

The **Letter of Credit/Shipping Information Form** should provide all pertinent information necessary for opening Letters of Credit for a specific contractor or manufacturer. It must be completed, where applicable, for POs and returned to the customer's production or accounting departments as indicated. Letters of Credit will not be opened until the form has been returned. See actual Shipping Information Form on next page.

A sample of a **Letter of Credit** follows the Shipping Information Form, along with the terminology typically used in a Letter of Credit.

LETTER OF CREDIT/SHIPPING INFORMATION

THIS FORM PERTAINS TO THE FOLLOWING STYLES: ______________________

____

L/C BENEFICIARY
NAME ______________________
ADDRESS ______________________
____
____
COUNTRY ______________________

ADVISING BANK *
NAME ______________________
ADDRESS ______________________
____
____
COUNTRY ______________________

* **Beneficiary and Advising Bank Should Be in the Same Country.**

COUNTRY OF ORIGIN/MANUFACTURE ______________________
(If Different Than Beneficiary, Provide Factory Address)
NAME ______________________
ADDRESS ______________________
____
____
COUNTRY ______________________

SHIPPING TERMS (i.e. FOB Hong Kong) ______________________

AGENT ______________________
If No Agent, Who Signs Inspection Certificate? ______________________

IF L/C IS TO BE TRANSFERRED COMPLETE NAME AND ADDRESS OF TRANSFEREE COMPANY
NAME ______________________
ADDRESS ______________________
____
____
COUNTRY ______________________

VENDOR/CONTRACTOR NUMBER (Provided by customer) ______________________
SHIPPING CARTON DIMENSIONS ______________________
ACTUAL WEIGHT OF EACH SIZE CARTON ______________________
GARMENT WEIGHT ______________________
NUMBER OF PIECES PER CARTON ______________________

SPECIAL REQUIREMENTS ______________________
____
____

NATIONAL BANK NEW YORK, NY - U.S.A	**LETTER OF CREDIT**	
Applicant John Doe Fashions 400 East 40th Street New York, NY - USA	**Beneficiary** Kowloon Knitting Consortium 4 Pedder Street - Suite 2904 Tsim Sha Shui, Kowloon - Hong Kong	**Advising Bank** Bank of Kowloon Kowloon, Hong Kong
Reference Number ILCBLN40000231	**Date and Place of Issue** May 30, 2004, New York, NY, USA	**Date and Place of Expiry** Aug. 15 2004, New York, NY, USA
Transshipment [ ] Allowed [ ] Not Allowed **Partial Shipment** [ ] Allowed [X] Not Allowed	**Amount** USD 25,400.00 Twenty-five thousand, four hundred US Dollars **Credit available with** Bank of Kowloon, Hong Kong by ~~*PAYMENT / ACCEPTANCE*~~ /***NEGOTIATION*** against the documents detailed herein and beneficiary's draft 60 days sight drawn on National Bank of New York, USA	
Shipment / dispatch / taking in charge from/at Kowloon	**For transportation to** San Diego	**Not later than** Aug. 1, 2004

Documents to be presented
One signed original commercial invoice and four copies evidencing dispatch of 1,600 dolman sleeve sweaters, Syle 257099 @ USD 15.89, CIF Kowloon, Hong Kong.

Full set of blank endorsed Bills of Lading marked "Freight Paid" + Notify "Joe Doe Fashions, 400 East 40th Street, New York, NY USA"

DOCUMENTS PRESENTED 7 AUGUST 2004

One original blank endorsed insurance certificate covering all risks as per Institute Cargo Clauses "A" + strikes

One certificate of origin issued by American Chamber of Commerce

These documents to be presented within . . . . Days of the issue of the transport document(s) but within the validity of the credit.

Instructions for Advising Bank

Please advise beneficiaries of opening of the credit ~~adding/~~without adding your confirmation.

Method of reimbursement
At maturity we will reimburse you according to your instructions

Documents should be forwarded to us by air mail

We hereby agree with the drawers, endorsers and bona fide holders that drafts drawn and negotiated in conformity with the terms of this credit will be duly honored upon presentation and that drafts accepted within the terms of this credit will be accepted at maturity. This credit is subject to Uniform Customs and Practice for documentary credits (1993 revision) International Chamber of Commerce publication no. 500.

for **NATIONAL BANK**

Glossary of Terms used in Letters of Credit

Acceptance Commission: The fee that is usually paid by the applicant to the issuing bank to compensate for drafting the Letter of Credit.

Advising Bank: The beneficiary's (exporter's) local bank that: takes responsibility, advises of the opening of the Letter of Credit and communicates its conditions.

Airway Bill (AWB): A non-negotiable contract covering domestic and international flights, used for the transportation of freight including shipping instructions, description of shipment and transportation charges.

Analysis Certificate: A document that confirms the goods have been analyzed for quality, composition, etc.

Applicant: The individual or company applying for a Letter of Credit; a.k.a. the importer, buyer or account party.

Beneficiary: The individual or company to whom a Letter of Credit is issued, or who is entitled to draw or demand payment, a.k.a. the exporter, vendor, shipper or seller.

Bill of Exchange: Used interchangeably with the word "Draft." It is a written order from one person (the drawer) to another (the drawee) and specifies the terms (time and amount) when payment is due.

Bill of Lading (B/L): A document that lists and acknowledges receipt of goods for transport. It serves as a document of title and a contract of carriage.

C&I (Cost and Insurance): (...port of destination). Shipping term included in a Contract of Sale where the seller agrees to arrange and pay for transportation and cargo insurance over the goods to the named destination. Such costs are included in the price of the goods. The buyer is responsible for the cost of the ocean freight and arranging the transportation from the port of discharge.

Certificate of Origin (CO): A document that certifies a specific country as the origin of specific goods. The U.S. and certain other countries require this certificate for tariff purposes.

Commercial Invoice: A document that generally contains the name and address of the seller and buyer, date of the sale, a description of the goods, quantity, unit price, terms of sale, amount due under the Letter of Credit and type of currency.

Consignor: The exporter that delivers the merchandise; also referred to as the shipper on a Bill of Lading.

C&F (Cost and Freight): (...port of destination). The seller pays the costs and freight of the goods to the port of destination, with the risk of loss of or damage to the goods, as well as additional costs occurring after the time the goods are delivered on board the vessel. Responsibility is transferred from the seller to the buyer when the goods pass the ship's rail in the port of shipment. The seller usually chooses the forwarder.

CIF (Cost, Insurance and Freight): (...port of destination). The seller has the same obligations as under C&F, but must also pay for marine insurance against loss or damage to the goods during transport. The seller pays for the insurance but only is required to obtain minimum coverage. Again, the seller usually chooses the freight forwarder. Delivery is made at the port of destination.

Discount Charges: The interest or fee charged by a bank that discounts the draft to the beneficiary. Discount charges are usually calculated based on the amount of the draft, an interest rate and the number of days prior to maturity of the draft. The beneficiary can choose to receive immediate payment by having the draft discounted for early shipment.

Draft: A written order from one person (the drawer) to another (the drawee) specifying the terms (time and amount) when payment for the shipment is due (also referred to as Bill of Exchange).

Drawn On: Refers to the party on whom the draft is drawn or who has the obligation to pay the holder of the draft when due.

Expiry (Expiration Date): The last date by which the beneficiary/seller can present documents to the advising bank for payment in compliance with terms of the Letter of Credit.

Ex-Works (Ex-factory): (...port of loading). A shipping arrangement that places a minimum responsibility on the seller. In an Ex-Works transaction, goods are made available for pickup at the beneficiary/seller's factory or warehouse and delivered to the buyer's freight forwarder. The buyer is responsible for making arrangements for insurance, export clearance and handling all other paperwork. Simply, the buyer takes possession (ownership) of goods as soon as it leaves the seller's facility.

FAS (Free Alongside Ship): (...port of loading). The buyer bears all the transportation costs and the risk of loss of goods. Normally, buyers use their freight forwarder to clear the goods for export. Delivery is completed when the goods are turned over to the buyer's forwarder for insurance and transportation.

FOB (Free on Board): (...port of loading). A price quoted based on inclusion of the cost of transporting merchandise from a seller's facility and loading onto the approved method of transport.

Inspection Certificate: A document that certifies that merchandise was in good condition and as specified in a contract prior to shipment. Often obtained from an independent testing organization.

Insurance Certificate: A document required under a Letter of Credit as proof that insurance has been secured against loss or damage of the goods.

International Commercial Terms (Incoterms): International terms of sale published by the International Chamber of Commerce that define the buyer's and seller's obligations in a transaction.

Issue Method: The method by which the Letter of Credit will be transmitted overseas.

Latest Shipping Date: The last date that the exporter can ship the merchandise and comply with the terms of the Letter of Credit, usually stated on the Shipment Transport Document.

Letter of Credit (L/C), Commercial: A bank-issued document (requested by the customer/applicant) to a specified beneficiary by which the bank substitutes its credit for that of the applicant. The bank makes payments to the beneficiary under conditions specified in the L/C.

Letter of Credit, Sight: A Letter of Credit, payable immediately upon shipment of the merchandise or on demand with accompanying documents of compliance (compare Letter of Credit, Usance).

Letter of Credit, Usance: A Letter of Credit payable at some future date, also called a Timed Letter of Credit because it allows the buyer a certain period of time to pay all drawings under the Letter of Credit (compare Letter of Credit, Sight). The bank accepts a draft and payment is made at a future point in time.

Multimodal Transport: Transportation that includes at least two modes of transport, such as shipping by rail and by sea.

Packing List: A list prepared by the shipper that lists the quantity and kinds of items being shipped.

Partial Shipment: A shipment under a Letter of Credit representing only part of the goods covered by the Letter of Credit.

Reimbursement and Security Agreement: Document required by the issuing bank, signed by the applicant authorizing the bank to issue credit with the specified terms and conditions; includes the applicant's legal promise to reimburse the issuing bank for all drawings and payments made under the Letter of Credit.

Swift/Telex: Electronic communication method used between banks to transmit information related to Letters of Credit.

Terms, Shipping: Terms outlining the buyer's and seller's responsibility with regard to shipping the merchandise and other associated charges (e.g. FAS, FOB, C&F, CIF). (See Incoterms)

Time Draft: A draft that is payable at a fixed or determinable future date.

Timed Letter of Credit: See Letter of Credit, Usance.

Transferable: Allows the beneficiary of the Letter of Credit to transfer the entire transaction to a third party, usually when the first beneficiary is an intermediary between the importer and the bank applicant and the ultimate shipper of the merchandise.

Transport Document: Any document that indicates accepting, receiving and shipping of goods.

Transshipment: When products manufactured in one country, commercially enter another country, and are then exported for sale in a third country.

Uniform Customs and Practice for Documentary Credits (UCP): International standards of Letter of Credit practice established for bankers by the International Chamber of Commerce. The UCP is revised about every ten years to keep apace with changing practices. The most recent revision, UCP500, was completed in 1993. Although the UCP defines rights and obligations of the various parties in a Letter of Credit transaction, it is not law and any Letter of Credit is subject only to the extent indicated in the Letter of Credit itself.

Weight List: A document prepared by the shipper that typically indicates the exact weight of the individual cartons, containers or pieces being shipped, as well as the total weight.

CHAPTER 7

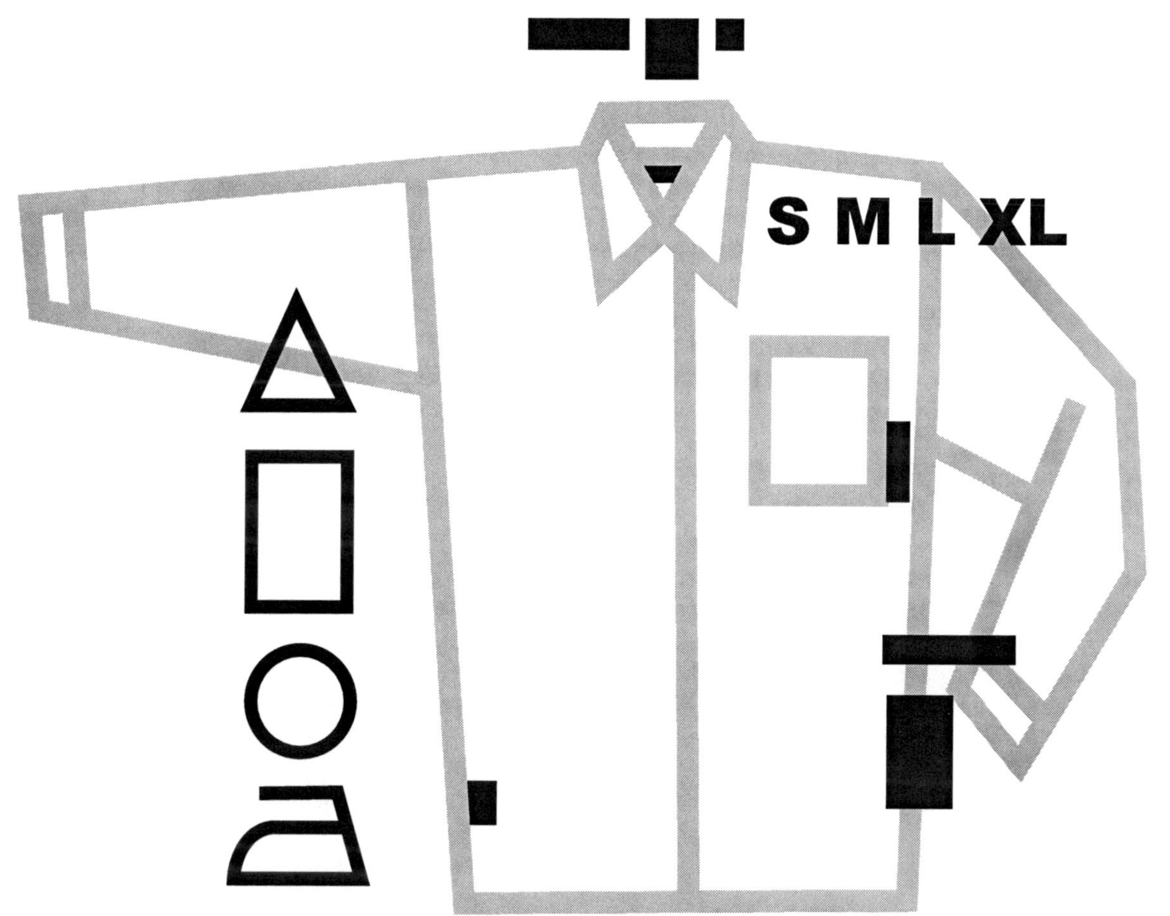

LABELING

This chapter discusses the different types of labels used for apparel and accessories, and their placements within the products. From the Main Brand-Name Label to the Country-of-Origin, Size, and Care Labels, all must be in compliance for acceptance at the retail level.

LABELS

LABELING

How important is labeling? It may seem like a small item, but its impact can be enormous. You can use labeling to highlight the different aspects of your collection and make it identifiable by utilizing a bold color, prints, embroidery, or just plain labels.

Labeling is not only important to highlight the details of your garments, it also serves other purposes: It is a requirement for customs; it indicates where a garment was made; and it gives everyone the ability to identify the fabric contents.

This chapter will give you examples of label placement used throughout the industry for different garments. The variation is huge. Among other important considerations, however, is that the labeling should be visible, identify the country of origin, tell if the garment was made overseas, and name the contents of the fabric. All other labels could be inserted at your discretion - size, tabs, main labels, etc.

Always keep in mind to whom you are selling your goods and how they will be merchandised in the store. Your goal is to make your sizing visible and easy to read for your end customer. The customer should always know who is the designer and they should be able to locate their size in a timely manner.

ORDERING PROCEDURE FOR WOVEN OR PRINTED LABELS

The following describes how to order labels for the customer's production:

- The customer advises the label maker a projected number of labels needed for each season and provides a list of factories that are authorized to purchase the customer's labels for that season.

- The label maker produces all labels required. Quantities for each season are based on projections. Certain labels should be produced in advance, such as main labels and size tags, to ensure immediate needs are fulfilled.

- Each contractor and/or agent is responsible for contacting the label maker and placing a label order.

- The label maker should ship and bill each contractor and/or agent directly for labels ordered.

Many label makers have facilities in the U.S., as well as in Europe and Asia, and should advise which facility offshore manufacturers should utilize.

The contractor and/or agent is responsible for using labels that are to the customer's quality, color, and size specification for both the country-of-origin label and the care content label. The contractor and/or agent is responsible for ensuring the correct wording on these labels and in compliance with country-of-origin laws. The layout with correct wording of country-of-origin label and the care/content label must be submitted to the customer for approval prior to production.

LABEL APPLICATION

- All labels must be attached securely and neatly.

- All the customer's logo rivets, snaps, and buttons (or other trims bearing their logo) must have the logo pointing up.

LABEL DEFINITIONS

The labels can be identified as follows:

Label Identified on Sketch	Corresponding Customer Label
Label **A**	Main Label
Label **B**	Secondary Label
Label **C**	Country-of-Origin Label
Label **D**	Size Tab
Label **E**	Care/Content Label

Label A: Main Label

The **main label** is the woven label identifying the garment as the customer's garment. This label normally includes the customer's registration number.

Label B: Secondary Label

The **secondary label** may be an additional woven label identifying the garment as the customer's garment. The location for this label may include shirt plackets, side pockets, below the main label or as designated in the spec package.

Reference samples of Labels A and B

The specific labels and the appropriate source for the labels should be identified in each specification package.

Label C: Country-of-Origin Label

The **country-of-origin label** identifies the country of origin of a garment as well as CA number and fabric/fiber components.

EXAMPLE:

This example is set up for a garment to be sold in a French-speaking country.

CA #19792
MADE IN *(insert country of origin)*
FABRIQUE *(insert country of origin in French)*
SHELL: *(insert shell fabric content)*
VESTE: *(insert shell fabric content in French)*
LINING: *(insert lining fabric content)*
DOUBLURE: *(insert lining fabric content in French)*

Lining or significant trims (with a fabric content that is different from main shell fabric) must also be indicated on this label.

Label D: Size Tab

The **size tab** identifies the size of a garment.

Label E: Content/Care Label

The **content/care label** identifies the fabric/fiber content of the major components as well as care instructions for the garment. This label is usually white with black printed lettering.

EXAMPLE:

SEASON/STYLE#:
RN #76382
MADE IN (*insert country of origin*)
SHELL: (*insert shell fabric content*)
LINING: (*insert lining fabric content*)
CARE (*insert approved care instructions*)
CARE SYMBOLS (*insert corresponding care symbols*)

***FOLD*--**
FOLD

CA #19792
COUNTRY OF ORIGIN: (*insert country of origin in Italian language*)
CONTENT: (*insert fabric content for shell and lining in Italian language*)
COUNTRY OF ORIGIN: (*insert country of origin in Spanish language*)
CONTENT: (*insert fabric content for shell and lining in Spanish language*)
COUNTRY OF ORIGIN: (*insert country of origin in Dutch language*)
CONTENT: (*insert fabric content for shell and lining in Dutch language*)
COUNTRY OF ORIGIN: (*insert country of origin in German*)
CONTENT:(*insert fabric content for shell and lining in German*)
COUNTRY OF ORIGIN: (*insert country of origin in Portuguese*)
CONTENT: (*insert fabric content for shell and lining in Portuguese*)

S98/3866
RN# 76382
Made in Hong Kong
100% Cotton
Machine Wash Cold
Do Not Bleach
Tumble Dry Low
Warm Iron When Needed
Wash Dark Colors Separately
Do Not Dry Clean

***FOLD*--**
FOLD

CA# 19792
Fabbricato in Hong Kong
100% Cotone
Fabricado en Hong Kong
100% Algodón
Gefabriceerd in Hong Kong
100% Katoen
Hergestellt in Hongkong
100% Baumwolle
Fabricado em Hong Kong
100% Algodão

See table on the following page for a key to care label reference codes and corresponding care symbols.

A GUIDE TO CARE SYMBOLS

This illustrates the symbols used for laundering and drycleaning instructions. Laundering instructions include, in order, four symbols: washing, bleaching, drying and ironing; drycleaning instructions include the one symbol. Additional words or symbols may be used for clarification.

Wash

Machine Wash Cycles: normal; permanent press; delicate / gentle; hand wash

Water Temperatures (Maximum) Symbol (s)

(140F)	(120F)	(105F)	(65F-85F)
60C	50C	40C	30C
••••	•••	••	•

* 50C ••• normal

*Temperature should be shown within the Wash Cycle Symbol

Bleach

any bleach when needed; only non-chlorine bleach when needed

Dry

Tumble Dry Cycles: normal; permanent press; delicate / gentle

line dry / hang to dry; drip dry; dry flat

Tumble Dry Heat Settings: any heat; high; medium; low; no heat / air

Iron

Iron Temp.- Dry or Steam

maximum temperature	200 C (390 F) high	150 C (300F) medium	110 C (230 F) low

Dryclean

Dryclean

(A) normal cycle any solvent

Professionally Dryclean --requires modified drycleaning

reduce moisture; no steam finishing; short cycle; low heat

(P) any solvent except trichloroethylene

(F) petroleum solvent only

Warning Symbols for Laundering

do not wash

do not bleach

do not dry (used with do not wash)

do not iron

Additional Instructions in Symbols & Words

do not wring

do not tumble dry

in the shade (added to line dry, drip dry, or dry flat)

no steam (added to iron)

Warning Symbol

do not dryclean

LABEL TRANSLATION GRIDS

The following are a series of grids containing common country-of-origin, fabric/fiber and garmnet location translations required on the customer's woven labels.

COUNTRY OF ORIGIN – LABEL TRANSLATIONS						
ENGLISH	**FRENCH**	**SPANISH**	**PORTUGUESE**	**ITALIAN**	**DUTCH**	**GERMAN**
in Bulgaria	en Bulgarie	en Bulgaria	na Bulgária	in Bulgaria	in Bulgarije	in Bulgarien
in Canada	au Canada	en Canadá	no Canadá	in Canada	in Canada	in Kanada
in China	en Chine	en China	na China	in Cina	in China	in China
in England	en Angleterre	en Inglaterra	na Inglaterra	in Inghilterra	in Engeland	in England
in Hong Kong	à Hong Kong	en Hong Kong	em Hong Kong	in Hong Kong	in Hong Kong	in Hongkong
in Hungary	en Hongrie	en Hungría	na Hungria	in Ungheria	in Hongarije	in Ungarn
in India	en Inde	en India	na Índia	in India	in India	in Indien
in Indonesia	en Indonesie	en Indonesia	na Indonésia	in Indonesia	in Indonesië	in Indonesien
in Ireland	en Irlande	en Irlanda	na Irlanda	in Irlanda	in Ierland	in Irland
in Italy	en Italie	en Italia	na Itália	in Italia	in Italië	in Italien
in Korea	en Corée	en Corea	na Coréia	in Corea	in Zuid-Korea	in Korea
in Macau	à Macao	en Macao	em Macau	in Macao	in Macao	in Macao
in Malaysia	en Malaisie	en Malasia	na Malásia	in Malesia	in Maleisië	in Malaysia
in Mexico	au Mexique	en México	no México	in Messico	in Mexico	in Mexiko
in Peru	au Pérou	en Perú	no Peru	in Peru	in Peru	in Peru
in Portugal	au Portugal	en Portugal	em Portugal	in Portogallo	in Portugal	in Portugal
in Scotland	en Ecosse	en Escocia	na Escócia	in Scozia	in Schotland	in Schottland
in Singapore	à Singapour	en Singapur	em Singapura	in Singapore	in Singapore	in Singapur
in Sri Lanka	au Sri Lanka	en Sri Lanka	em Sri Lanka	in Sri Lanka	in Sri Lanka	in Sri Lanka
in Taiwan	a Taiwan	en Taiwan	em Taiwan	in Taiwan	in Taiwan	in Taiwan
in Thailand	en Thaïland	en Tailandia	na Tailândia	in Thailandia	in Thailand	in Thailand
in Turkey	en Turquie	en Turquía	em Turquia	in Turchia	in Turkije	in Türkei
in the Philippines	aux Philippines	en Filipinas	nas Filipinas	nelle Filippine	in de Filipijnen	auf den Philippinen
in United States	aux Etats-Unis	en Estados Unidos	nos E.U.A.	negli Stati Uniti	in de Verenigde Staten	in USA
in Uruguay	en Uruguay	en Uruguay	no Uruguai	in Uruguay	in Uruguay	in Uruguay
with USA components	avec des composants fabriqués aux Etats-Unis	con componentes fabricados en Estados Unidos	com componentes fabricados nos E.U.A.	con Materiale fabbricato negli Stati Uniti	met materialen uit de V.S.	mit in USA hergestellten Teilen
Made in	Fabriqué en (F) Fabriqué au (M)	Fabricado en	Fabricado em	Prodotto manifatturato	Gefabriceerd in	Hergestellt in
Assembled in	Assemblé en (F) Assemblé au (M)	Montado en	Peça montada em	Assemblato in	Geassembleerd in	Zusammengesetzt in

FABRIC / FIBER CONTENT – LABEL TRANSLATIONS

ENGLISH	FRENCH	SPANISH	PORTUGUESE	ITALIAN	DUTCH	GERMAN
Acetate	Acétate	Acetato	Acetato	Acetato	Acetaat	Acetat
Acrylic	Acrylique	Acrílico	Acrílico	Acrilico	Acryl	Acryl
Cashmere	Cachemire	Cachemir	Cachmere	Cachemire	Cashmere	Cashmere
Cotton	Coton	Algodón	Algodão	Cotone	Katoen	Baumwolle
Feathers	Plumes	Plumas	Penas	Piuma	pluimen	Federn
Genuine Cowhide Leather	Peau de vache véritable imperméable	Piel legítima de bovino	Pele de couro # bovino	Vera pelle bovina	Echt rundleer	Echtes Rindsleder
Genuine Lambskin Leather	Peau d'agneau véritable imperméable	Piel legítima de ovino	Pele de carneiro genuína	Vera pelle d'agnello	Echt lamsleer	Echtes Lammleder
Genuine Leather	Cuir véritable	Piel legítima	couro genuíno	Vera pelle	Echt leder	echtes Leder
Goose Down	Duvet	Pluma de Oca	Penas de ganso	Piuma d'oca	Dons	Gänsedaunen
Linen	Lin	Lino	Linho	Lino	Linnen	Leinen
Nylon	Nylon	Nylon or Nailon	Nylon	Nylon	Nylon	Nylon
Other Fibers	Autre fibres	Otras fibras	Outras fibras	Altre Fibre	Andere vezels	Andere Fasern
Polyester	Polyester	Poliester	Poliéster	Poliestere	Polyester	Polyester
Ramie	Ramie	Ramio	Rami	Ramie	Ramie	Ramie
Polyurethane	Polyurethanne	Poliuretano	Poliuretano	Poliuretano	Polyurethaan	Polyurethan
Rayon	Rayonne	Rayón	Seda artificial	Rayon	Rayon	Rayon
Recycled Wool	Laine recyclée	Lana reciclada	Lã reciclada	Lana reciclata	Hergebruikte wol	wiederverwertete Wolle
Suede	Daim	Ante	camurça	Crosta	Suède	Veloursleder
Ultra Suede	Daim Ultra	Ante	Ultra camurça	Crosta fine	Ultra-Suède	sehr hochwertiges Veloursleder
Wool	Laine	Lana	Lã	Lana	Wol	Wolle

CONTENT LOCATION – LABEL TRANSLATIONS

ENGLISH	FRENCH	SPANISH	PORTUGUESE	ITALIAN	DUTCH	GERMAN
Excluding Trim	A l'exception des bordures	Excepto bordes	Exceto debrum	Esclusa rifinitura	Met uizondering van de boord	Ausgenommen Verzierung
Fill	Matelassage	Relleno	Enchimento	Imbottitura	Vulling	Füllung
Inner Jacket Fill	Matelassage intérieur de la veste	Relleno interior	Enchimento interior da peça	Imbottitura interna del capo	Vulling binnenjas	Innere Jackenfüllung
Inner Jacket Lining	Intérieur de la veste	Forro interior	Interior da peça	Fodera interna capo	Binnenvoering	Inneres Jackenfutter
Inner Jacket Shell	Veste intérieure	Prenda interior	Revestimento interior	Interno giacca	Binnenjack	Innere Jackenschicht
Lining	Doublure	Forro	Forro	Talsia	Voering	Futter
Lower Lining	Bas de la doublure	Forro inferior	Forro inferior	Fodera della parte inferiore	Ondervoering	Unteres Futter
Mesh	Maille	Redecilla	Malha	Maglia	Mesh	Masche
Outer Shell	Veste extérieure	Chaqueta exterior	Revestimento exterior	Parte Esterna	Buitenlaag	Außenschicht
Outer Shell Lining	Doublure de la veste extérieure	Forro de la chaqueta exterior	Revestimento do forro exterior	Rivestimento fodera esterna	Voering van de buitenlaag	Futter der Außenschicht
Resin	Résine	Resina	Resina	Resina	Coating	Harz
Shell	Veste	Chaqueta	Revestimento	Fodera	Jack	Aussenmaterial
Sleeves	manches	mangas	Mangas	Maniche	mouwen	Ärmel
Trim	Garnitures	Bordes	Debrum	Rifinitura	Boord	Verzierung
Upper Lining	Haut de la doublure	Forro superior	Forro superior	Fodera della parte superiore	Bovenvoering	Oberes Futter
Waterproof Outer Shell	Veste extérieure imperméable	Chaqueta exterior impermeable	Revestimento exterior á prova D' água	Parte esterna impermeabile	Waterbestendige buitenjack	Wasserfeste Außenschicht
Waterproof Interlining	Doublure intermédiaire	Forro interior impermeable	Forro áprova D' água	Fodera interna impermeabile	Waterbestendige tussenvoering	Wasserfestes Zwischenfutter
Waterproof Shell	Veste imperméable	Chaqueta impermeable	Revestimento á prova D' água	Capo impermeabile	Waterbestendig jack	Wasserfeste Aussenmaterial

Label Placement Sketches

Label placement sketches are referenced in the specification package (tech package). The designer, production department, agent, and factory should all have a copy of all of the label placement sketches that a company uses. The factory can match the label sketch number in the specification package to the number located in the column to the left of the sketch in the label placement sketches.

Example: The specification package indicates I.D.#____ as the correct label placement for a particular style.

Label Placement I.D.# _______	LABEL

LABEL PLACEMENT SKETCHES - NECK LABELS

Label Placement # ________

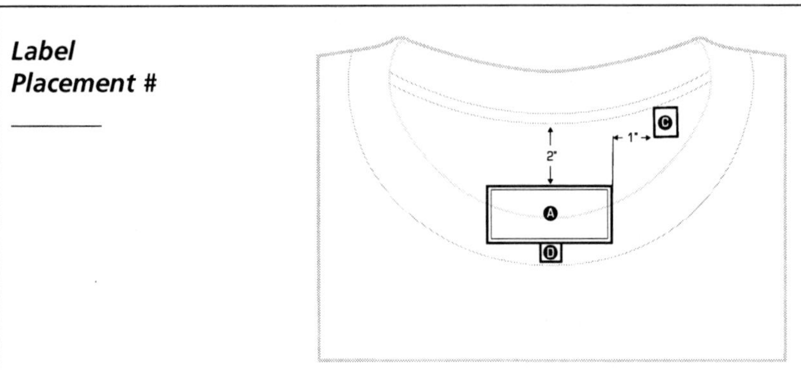

Label A:
Boxstitch through one layer of self.

Label C:
Set label in between layers of fabric at neck.

Label D:
Center label under "A" label.

Label Placement # ________

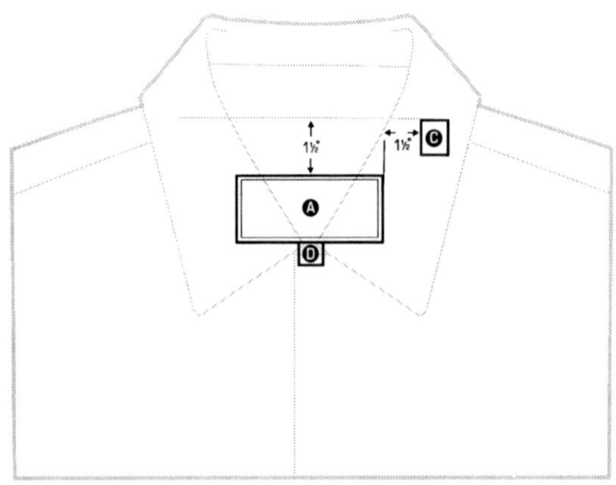

Label Holder:
Boxstitch through one layer of fabric.

Label A:
Boxstitch through one layer of self.

Label C:
Set label in between layers of fabric at neck.

Label D:
Center label under "A" label.

Label Placement # ________

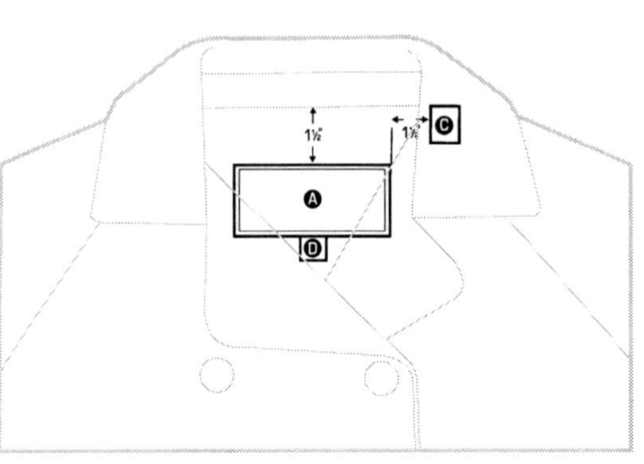

Label Holder:
Boxstitch through one layer of fabric.

Label A:
Boxstitch through one layer of self.

Label C:
Set label in between layers of fabric at neck.

Label D:
Center label under "A" label.

Label Placement # ________

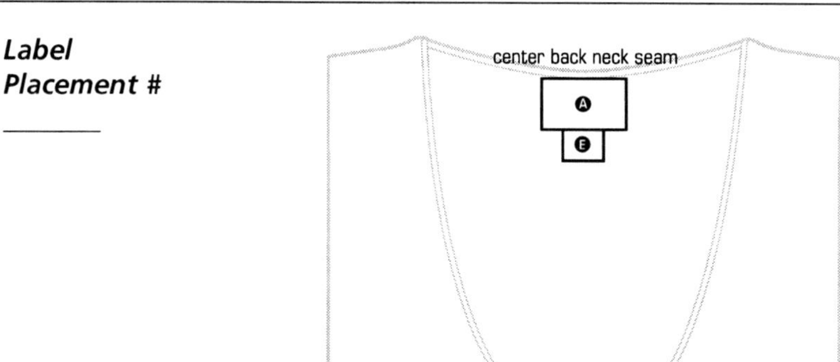

Label A:
Set label underneath seams at neckline.

Label E:
Set label underneath label A and topstitch at top.

Label Placement # ________

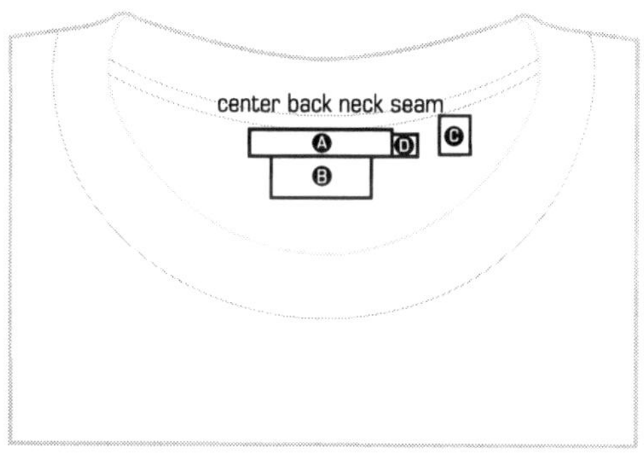

Label A:
Set label in between layers of fabric at neck.

Label B:
Set label underneath Label A.

Label C:
Set label in between layers of fabric at neck.

Label D:
Set label on right side of label "A."

LABEL PLACEMENT SKETCHES - BOTTOM LABELS

Label Placement #

____

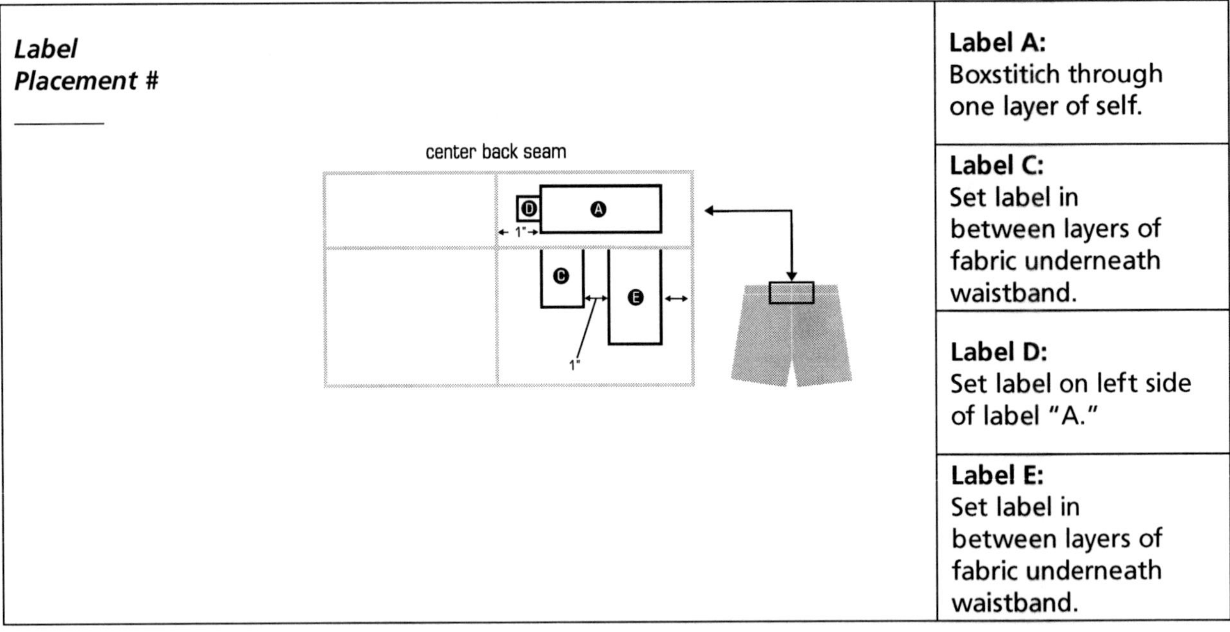

center back seam
D
A
1"
C
E
1"

Label A:
Boxstitich through one layer of self.

Label C:
Set label in between layers of fabric underneath waistband.

Label D:
Set label on left side of label "A."

Label E:
Set label in between layers of fabric underneath waistband.

Label Placement #

____

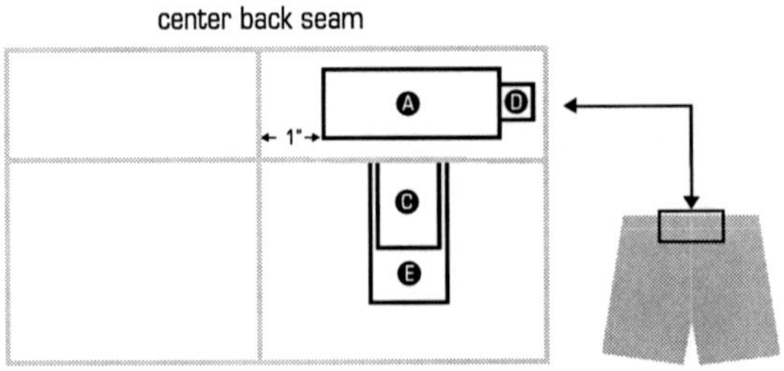

center back seam
A
D
1"
C
E

Label A:
Boxstitich through one layer of self.

Label C:
On top of label "E," set label in between layers of fabric underneath waistband.

Label D:
Centered at right side of label "A."

Label E:
Set label in between layers of fabric underneath waistband.

Label Placement # ________

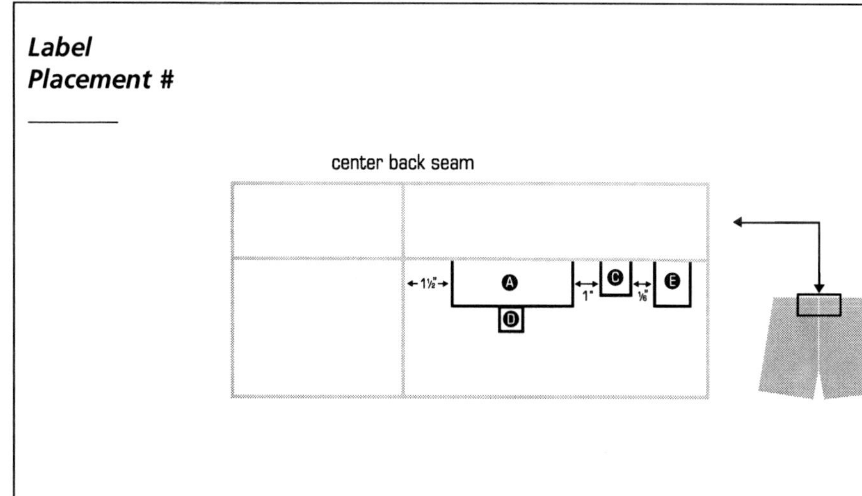

Label A: Set label underneath seam at waistband.
Label C: Set label in between layers of fabric underneath waistband.
Label D: Centered underneath label "A."
Label E: Set label in between layers of fabric underneath waistband.

Label Placement # ________

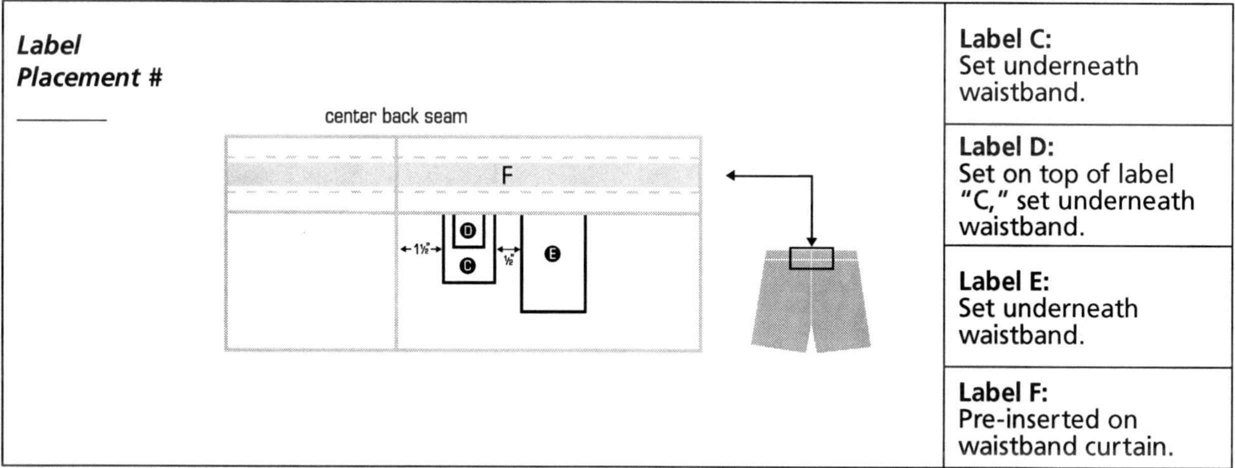

Label C: Set underneath waistband.
Label D: Set on top of label "C," set underneath waistband.
Label E: Set underneath waistband.
Label F: Pre-inserted on waistband curtain.

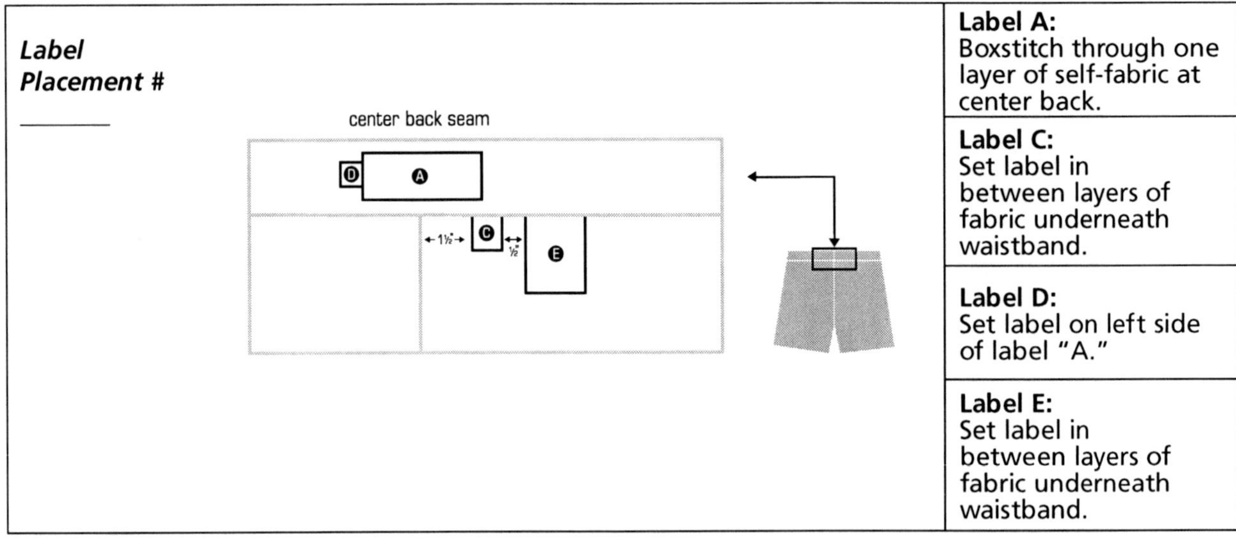

Label Placement # ________

Label A: Boxstitch through one layer of self-fabric at center back.

Label C: Set label in between layers of fabric underneath waistband.

Label D: Set label on left side of label "A."

Label E: Set label in between layers of fabric underneath waistband.

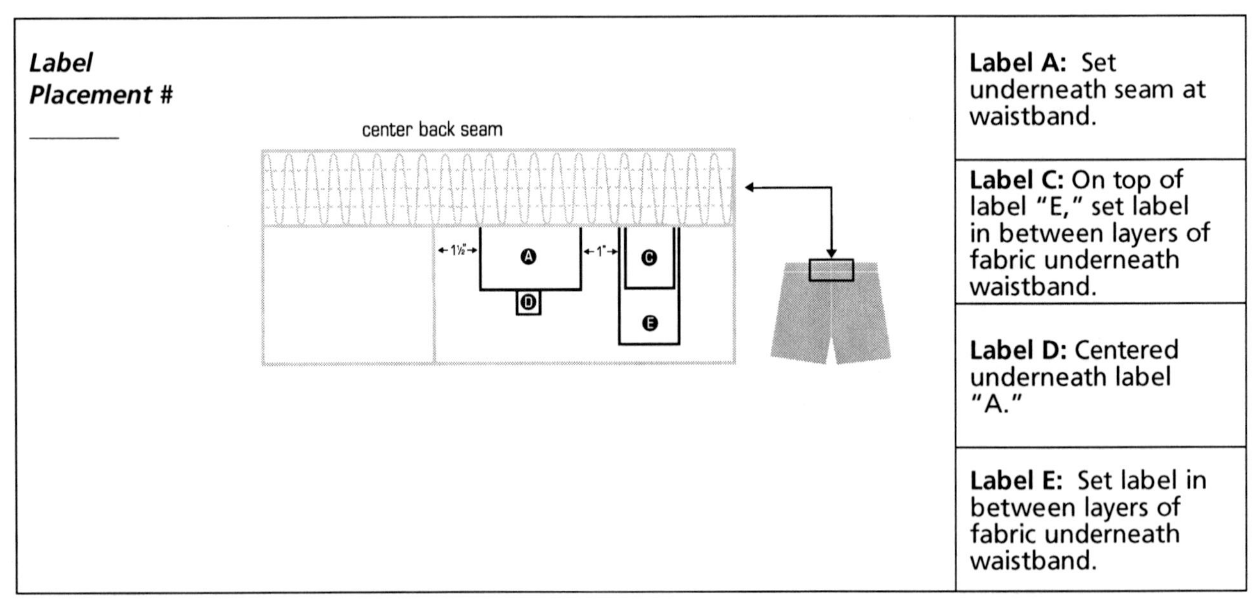

Label Placement # ________

Label A: Set underneath seam at waistband.

Label C: On top of label "E," set label in between layers of fabric underneath waistband.

Label D: Centered underneath label "A."

Label E: Set label in between layers of fabric underneath waistband.

LABEL PLACEMENT SKETCHES - SECONDARY LABELS

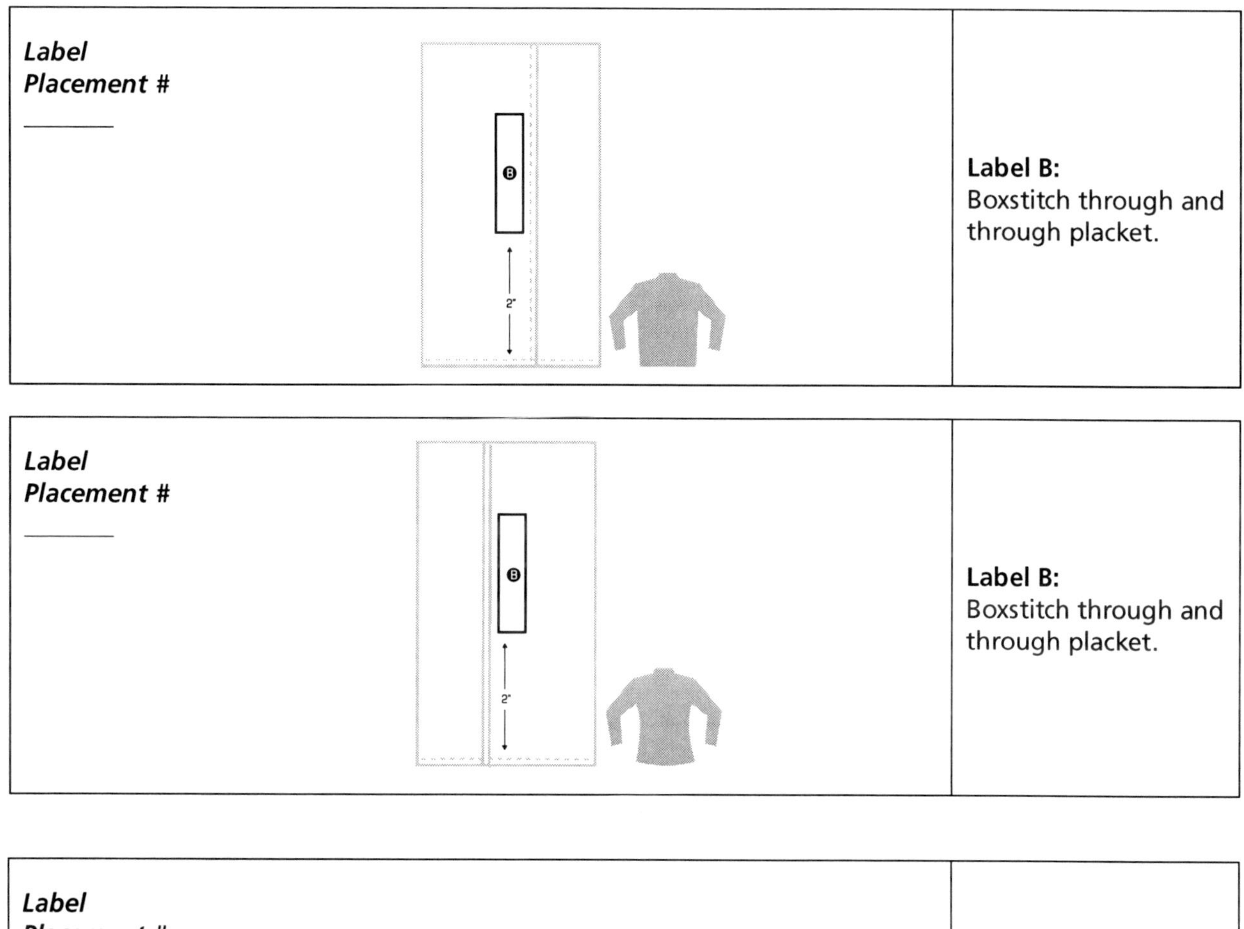

Label Placement # ________

Label B:
Boxstitch through and through placket.

Label Placement # ________

Label B:
Boxstitch through and through placket.

Label Placement # ________

4"
B2

Label B2:
Set in at side pocket.

LABEL PLACEMENT SKETCHES - CARE/CONTENT LABELS

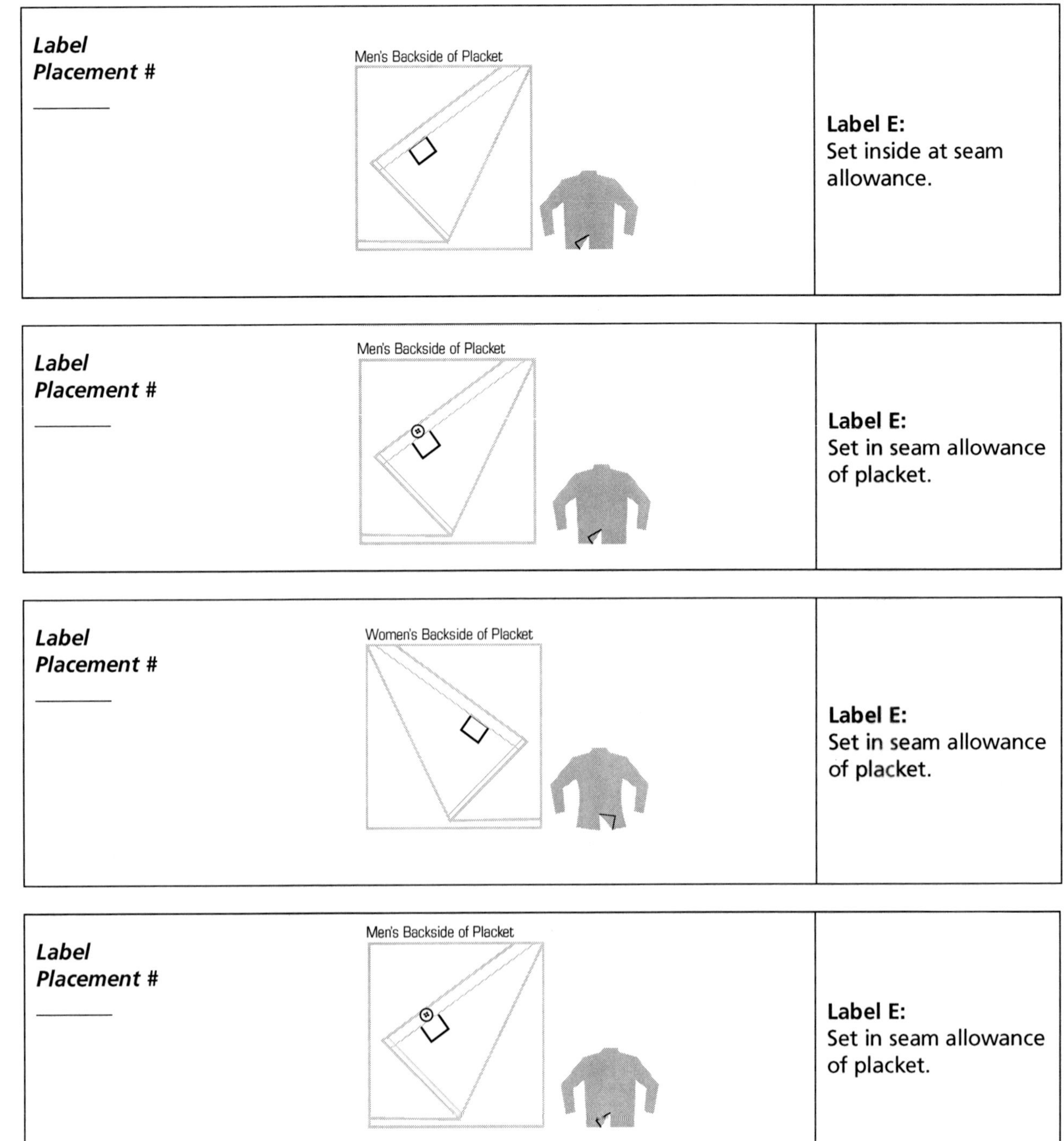

CHAPTER 8

TESTING AND FABRIC STANDARDS

This chapter details the Specification Measurement Sheet, and offers examples of sheets for different product types. Additionally, Points of Measure are defined and illustrated, along with Construction Detail sketches that, utilized together, facilitate getting accurate sample garments back from the factory.

TESTING

TESTING AND FABRIC SAMPLES

Many of the people involved in the development of your collection will become resources for you. When placing an order, whether it is a full-package order or one in which you are individually picking all the components, you should try to ask the vendor (mill, trim company, thread company, or supplier) of any of your components (thread, fabric) to provide you with any specifications (testing done) that they are aware of for this product. This will help you if you are a small company that cannot afford to do testing to determine potential problems. Having this information gives you the option to look for substitutions for your components.

Below, you will find a few examples. Keep in mind, as per the other chapters, that there is a huge variety within each product range.

Example 1—Children's trousers that include a belt: Generally the fabric from the trousers and the material for the belt will be from different sources. If you are asking your end consumer to wash the garment, you are most likely following specifications from your fabric vendor. Because you do not know how your belt fabric was dyed or the quality of the material, it could bleed into your trousers, dissolve etc....Or suppose there is shrinkage in the belt loops. Imagine trying to put the belt back through the pants after they were washed. To avoid this problem, always try to have the shrinkage as close as possible or leave enough allowance in the belt loop.

Example 2—A cloth jacket that has leather trims: The effects of cleaning non-treated leather can be disastrous. Take into consideration bleeding, and whether you will dry-clean this garment or wash it in a washing machine.

The following pages will give you examples of testing and standards that larger operations would put in place to ensure quality standards.

PURPOSE

The contractor is responsible for ensuring that all materials used for the customer's products meet the customer's quality requirements. The contractor must communicate the customer's fabric quality requirements to all mills prior to fabric selection.

The following steps and procedures would particularly apply to apparel considered "high-performance level," "active," or "hard-wearing." They are intended to give you the full scope of Quality Assurance and Quality Control standards in the apparel industry that you are entitled to expect. Smaller companies (or in cases where smaller quantities and reduced orders are desirable) can reduce the stringency of these guidelines to fit the customer's particular needs.

PROCEDURE

Each season, the contractor is responsible for completing the following three steps to ensure that materials used in the garments meet the customer's quality requirements.

STEP ONE - FABRIC AND TRIMS

Upon confirmation of a style within a season:

- Ensure each fabric and trim meets all requirements of customer's fabric and garment inspection standards.
- Report test results to you, your production department or manager.

STEP TWO – GARMENTS

- One garment per style in actual fabric, trims and any special finishing should be tested for correct care instructions.
- Test results should be sent to you, your production department or manager.
- The contractor should recommend the care instructions and submit completed care label information for the customer's approval and records.

STEP THREE - BULK FABRIC/GARMENTS

When bulk fabric is ready at the mill:

- Test one garment in high contrast or dark color for all quality requirements.
- Test each color for color properties (colorfastness, wet and dry crocking).
- Report testing to you, your production department or manager.
- The customer's production department may also request a test garment.

FABRIC STANDARDS

The following standards and tests were devised and utilized by a high-performance outerwear and sportswear company and may exceed some ordinary applications. These should function as guidelines for the optimum in garment and textile inspection standards and procedures. As the customer, you should review this with your contractors or agents to determine which are appropriate and to what extent.

SHADE RANGE STANDARDS

Shade range standards should be established and agreed upon by both the customer and the contractor and/or agent. Each party should have a Shade Range Standard approved by the customer.

An example Shade Range Standard would be: The light box set on D65 "daylight" with an "ultra violet" check to verify shade ranges. A secondary check may be done under cool white to approximate store lighting.

FABRIC HAND STANDARDS

The **fabric hand** (feel) of all fabrics used for the customer's production should be maintained consistently within a shipment and from shipment to shipment.

Hand standards should be established at the time of shade approvals and all parties should retain a standard for hand verification.

FIBER COMPOSITION

The **fiber composition** should be established during development. The contractor must ensure that fiber composition remains consistent to the standard. This is very important for imported garments or textiles and pertains to duty rates and charges.

FABRIC WEIGHT (YIELD) AND STITCH COUNT

The **fabric weight (yield) and stitch count** should be established and agreed on by the customer and the contractor, mill or agents. It is the contractor's responsibility to ensure that fabric weight (yield) and stitch count are consistent within a shipment and from shipment to shipment. The yield and stitch count affect the weight and quality of the garment or textile.

PHYSICAL TESTING AND FABRIC PERFORMANCE

- No fabric shipment should be accepted as first quality that does not meet all of the customer-specified Fabric/Leather/Material Performance Requirements.
- The contractor should examine a minimum of 10% of all fabric receipts using the AQL (Acceptable Quality Level). See more on AQL in Chapter 10: Inspection Standards.
- Simulation testing must occur prior to any production to determine if the fabrics, trims, and/or components used in a given garment function adequately together. Fabrics, linings, etc. must be tested for compatible shrinkage, colorfastness, crocking, as well as the ability to withstand wash treatments (i.e. stone wash, garment wash, enzyme wash, etc.). In addition, all care instructions must be verified.

THE FOLLOWING TESTS WERE DEVISED AND UTILIZED FOR HIGH-PERFORMANCE QUALITY OUTERWEAR AND SPORTSWEAR (Test definitions follow tables)

TESTS FOR LEATHER	
Crocking AATCC	
Wet	3
Dry	3
Colorfastness AATCC 61	
Minimum result	4
Waterproof Leather	
Water Repellency AATCC 22	80
Oil Repellency AATCC 118	4
Alcohol Repellency AATCC 118	6
Abrasion Resistance (Oil)	3
Abrasion Resistance (Alcohol)	5
AZO Dyestuff - MAK II A1 and MAK III A2	
Maximum detection limit	30ppm

Due to the nature of leather, random tests must be performed every 10,000 square feet at the tannery and at the factory.

TESTS FOR WOVENS		
Breaking Strength ASTM D5034 (Grab Method)		
Minimum for non-outerwear: Less than 5 oz	32 lbs	
Minimum for non-outerwear: 5 oz or greater	40 lbs	
Minimum for outerwear	55 lbs	
Seam Strength ASTM D1683		
Minimum for non-outerwear	22 lbs	
Seam Slippage Strength ASTM D434-75		
Minimum for non-outerwear	25 lbs	
Minimum for outerwear	35 lbs	
Tear Resistance ASTM D1424-83		
Less than 5 oz	1.5 lbs	
Greater than 5 oz and less than 8 oz	2.5 lbs	
Greater than 8 oz	3.0 lbs	
Crocking AATCC 8		
Specialty fabrics (Pigment-dye, Over-dye and Garment-dye, Sulfur, Black, Madras):	Wet	2
	Dry	3
All other woven fabrics:	Wet	3
	Dry	4
Colorfastness AATCC 61 Scale 1-5		
Minimum result	4	
Light Resistance AATCC16E		
20 hours	4.0	
Pilling ASTM D3512 (30 minutes)		
Minimum	3	
Flammability Title 16 CFR 1610		
All fabrics	Class 1	
Dimensional Change AATCC 135-1987 Maximum acceptable change after three washes (*Warp x Fill*):		
Nylon/Blends	2% x 2%	
Cotton/Blends, Flannel, Twill and Denim	3% x 3%	
Corduroy, Madras	4% x 4%	
Linen/Blends	5% x 5%	
Linings (all fibers) must be compatible with shell	+/- 1%	
Dry-Cleaning Dimensional Change AATCC 158		
Maximum acceptable change after three cycles: Warp	2%	
Maximum acceptable change after three cycles: Fill	2%	
AZO Dyestuff - MAK II A1 and MAK III A2		
Maximum detection limit	30ppm	

TESTS FOR KNITS			
Burst Strength ASTM D3787-89			
Minimum for sweaters/outerwear		55 lbs	
Minimum for sportswear		55 lbs	
Bowing and Skewing			
Solids:	Bowing / Skewing may not exceed 5% of the cuttable width. Any yardage containing bias or bowing in excess of the limits shall be considered unacceptable.		
Plaid and Stripes:	Bowing / Skewing may not exceed 2.5% of the cuttable width. Any yardage containing bias or bowing in excess of the limits shall be considered unacceptable.		
Crocking AATCC 8			
Specialty Fabrics (Pigment dye, Overdue and Garment dye, Sulfur, Black, Madras):		Wet	2
		Dry	3
All other knit fabrics		Wet	3
		Dry	4
Colorfastness to Bleach STR TP 80			
Chlorine minimum		4	
Non-chlorine minimum		4	
Colorfastness AATCC 61 scale 1-5			
Minimum result		4	
Light Resistance AATCC16E			
20 hours		4.0	
Pilling ASTM D3512 (30 Minutes)			
Minimum		3	
Flammability Title 16 CFR 1610			
All fabrics		Class 1	
Dimensional Change AATCC 135-1987 (3 Launderings)			
Maximum acceptable change after washes	Length	-6%	+2%
	Width	-6%	+2%
Dry-Cleaning Dimensional Change AATCC 158			
Maximum acceptable change after three cycles	Length	-4%	+2%
	Fill	-4%	+2%
AZO Dyestuff **MAK II A1 and MAK III A2**			
Maximum detection limit		30ppm	

TESTS FOR WOVEN OUTERWEAR In addition to the above "WOVEN" testing, the following must be performed for outerwear applications:	
Water Resistance AATCC 35 (Rain Test Method)	
Woven technical outerwear with a coating	< 1.0 gram absorbed
Perspiration AATCC 15 (Colorfastness to Perspiration)	
Color change maximum	Grade 4
Color stain maximum	Grade 3

FABRIC PERFORMANCE TEST DEFINITIONS

Abbreviated Test Name	Official Test Name	Test # to Follow
Azo Dyestuff	AZO Dyestuffs MAK II A1 and MAK III A2	16
Breaking Strength	Standard Test Method for Breaking Strength and Elongation of Textile Fabrics (Grab Test) ASTM Designation: 5034-95	15
Burst Strength	Standard Test Method for Bursting Strength of Knitted Goods—Constant-Rate-of-Traverse (CRT) Ball Burst Test ASTM Designation: D3787-89	14
Colorfastness	Colorfastness to Laundering, Home and Commercial: Accelerated AATCC Test Method 61-1996	6
Colorfastness to Bleach	Colorfastness to Chlorine Bleach, Specialized Technology Resources, Inc. TP 80	17
Crocking	Colorfastness to Crocking AATCC Test Method 8-1996	1
Dimensional Change	Dimensional Change in Automatic Home Laundering of Woven and Knit Fabrics AATCC Test Method 135-1995	8
Dry-Cleaning Dimensional Change	Dimensional Change on Dry-cleaning in Perchloroethylene: Machine Method AATCC Test Method 158-1995	9
Flammability	Flammability of General Wearing Apparel Title 16 CFR 1610	18
Light Resistance	Colorfastness to Light AATCC Test Method 16E-1993 (Water-Cooled Arc Lamp, Continuous Light)	3
Oil Repellency	Oil Repellancy: Hydrocarbon Resistance Test AATCC Test Method 118-1997	7
Perspiration	AATCC Test Method 15-1997	2
Pilling	Standard Test for Pilling Resistance and Other Related Surface Changes of Textile Fabrics: Random Tumble Pilling Tester ASTM Designation: D3512-96	13
Seam Slippage Strength	Standard Test Method for Resistance to Slippage of Yarns in Woven Fabrics Using a Standard Seam ASTM Designation: D434-75	10
Seam Strength	Standard Test Method for Failure in Sewn Seams of Woven Fabrics ASTM Designation: D1683-90a	12
Tear Resistance	Standard Test Method for Tearing Strength of Fabric by Falling-Pendulum Type (Elmendorf) Apparatus ASTM Designation: D1424-96	11
Water Repellency	Water Repellancy: Spray Test AATCC Test Method 22-1996	4
Water Resistance	Water Resistance: Rain Test AATCC Test Method 35-1994	5

FABRIC PERFORMANCE TEST DETAILS

Note on following tests:

Gray Scale is a scale that measures colorfastness of textile dyes. **Gray Scale** shows the amount of staining of adjacent materials that happens with washing of a sample.

AATCC stands for the **American Association of Textile Chemists and Colorists.** The AATCC is the worldwide association of professionals active in textile wet processing. AATCC provides the textile wet processing industry with a communication center and a clearinghouse for new ideas and innovation in textile chemistry and color science. AATCC has published more than 175 test methods addressing such topics as colorfastness, staining, laundering, and electrostatics.

FABRIC PERFORMANCE TEST EVALUATIONS

1. **Colorfastness to Crocking AATCC Test Method 8-1996**

   Evaluation:

   - **Grade 5** Negligible or no color transfer.
   - **Grade 4.5** Color transfer equivalent to Step 4-5 on the Gray Scale for Staining.
   - **Grade 4** Color transfer equivalent to Row 4 on the Chromatic Transference Scale or Step 4 on the Gray Scale for Staining.
   - **Grade 3.5** Color transfer equivalent to Step 3-4 on the Gray Scale for Staining.
   - **Grade 3** Color transfer equivalent to Row 3 on the Chromatic Transference Scale or Step 3 on the Gray Scale for Staining.
   - **Grade 2.5** Color transfer equivalent to Step 2-3 on the Gray Scale for Staining.
   - **Grade 2** Color transfer equivalent to Row 2 on the Chromatic Transference Scale or Step 2 on the Gray Scale for Staining.
   - **Grade 1.5** Color transfer equivalent to Step 1-2 on the Gray Scale for Staining.
   - **Grade 1** Color transfer equivalent to Row 1 on the Chromatic Transference Scale or Step 1 on the Gray Scale for Staining.

2. **Perspiration AATCC Test Method 15-1997**

   Evaluation:

   - **Grade 5** Negligible or no change as shown in Gray Scale Step 5.
   - **Grade 4.5** A change in color equivalent to Gray Scale Step 4.5.
   - **Grade 4** A change in color equivalent to Gray Scale Step 4.
   - **Grade 3.5** A change in color equivalent to Gray Scale Step 3.5.
   - **Grade 3** A change in color equivalent to Gray Scale Step 3.
   - **Grade 2.5** A change in color equivalent to Gray Scale Step 2.5.
   - **Grade 2** A change in color equivalent to Gray Scale Step 2.
   - **Grade 1.5** A change in color equivalent to Gray Scale Step 1.5.
   - **Grade 1** A change in color equivalent to Gray Scale Step 1.

3. **Colorfastness to Light AATCC Test Method 16E-1993 (Water-Cooled Arc Lamp, Continuous Light)**

Evaluation:

Color change is quantified using either the AATCC Gray Scale for Color Change (preferred), or by colorimetric measurement of color difference at the specified exposure level whether in AATCC Fading Units, kilojoules of radiant energy, or compared to a reference standard.

4. **Water Repellancy: Spray Test AATCC Test Method 22-1996**

Evaluation:

Immediately after tapping, the wet or spotted pattern is compared with the rating chart. The side of the fabric impacted by the water is rated. The test specimen is assigned a rating corresponding to the nearest standard in the rating chart. Intermediate ratings can be used for ratings of 50 or higher. In rating loosely woven or porous fabrics, such as voile, any passage of water through the openings of the fabrics is disregarded.

5. **Water Resistance: Rain Test AATCC Test Method 35-1994**

Evaluation:

Water penetration as indicated by the increase in weight of the blotter during the five-minute test period is calculated, and the average for at least three test specimens is reported. Individual determinations or average values of over 5.0 grams may be simply reported to 5 + grams or > 5 g.

In order to obtain a complete overall picture of the penetration resistance of a fabric or fabric combination, the average penetrations with different pressure heads on the nozzle should be obtained. The pressure head should be varied by one-foot increments in order to determine (a) the maximum head at which no penetration occurs, (b) the change in penetration with increasing head, and (c) the minimum head required to cause "breakdown" or the penetration of more than five grams of water. At each pressure head a minimum of three specimens should be tested in order to obtain the average penetration for that head.

6. **Colorfastness to Laundering, Home and Commercial: Accelerated AATCC Test Method 61-1996**

Evaluation:

- **Grade 5** Negligible or no change as shown in Gray Scale Step 5.
- **Grade 4.5** A change in color equivalent to Gray Scale Step 4.5.
- **Grade 4** A change in color equivalent to Gray Scale Step 4.
- **Grade 3.5** A change in color equivalent to Gray Scale Step 3.5.
- **Grade 3** A change in color equivalent to Gray Scale Step 3.
- **Grade 2.5** A change in color equivalent to Gray Scale Step 2.5.
- **Grade 2** A change in color equivalent to Gray Scale Step 2.
- **Grade 1.5** A change in color equivalent to Gray Scale Step 1.5.
- **Grade 1** A change in color equivalent to Gray Scale Step 1.

7. Oil Repellancy: Hydrocarbon Resistance Test AATCC Test Method 118-1997

Evaluation:

The AATCC Oil Repellancy Grade of a fabric is the numerical value of the highest-numbered test liquid which will not wet the fabric within a period of 30 ± 2 sec. Listed in the following table are standard test liquids for this test.

AATCC Oil Repellancy Grade Number	Composition
0	None (Fails Kaydol)
1	Kaydol
2	65:35 Kaydol: n-hexadecane by volume
3	n-hexadecane
4	n-tetradecane
5	n-dodecane
6	n-decane
7	n-octane
8	n-heptane

A failure occurs when three (or more) of the five drops applied from a given test liquid show complete wetting or wicking with loss of contact angle. A pass occurs if three or more of the five drops applied show clear, well-rounded appearance with high contact angle. The grade is expressed as the integer value of the pass test liquid immediately prior to the fail test liquid. A borderline pass occurs if three (or more) of the five drops applied show the rounded drop with partial darkening of the test specimen.

8. Dimensional Change in Automatic Home Laundering of Woven and Knit Fabrics AATCC Test Method 135-1995

Measurement:

After conditioning, lay each test specimen without tension on a flat, smooth, and horizontal surface. Measure and record the distance between each pair of bench marks to the nearest millimeter, tenth of an inch, or smaller increment. This is measurement B. If using a scale calibrated in percent dimensional change, measure to the nearest 0.5% or smaller increment and record the percent dimensional change directly.

The wrinkles in most fabrics flatten sufficiently under pressure of a measuring instrument at the time of measurement not to cause measurement bias.

Calculation and Interpretation:

If measurements were made directly in percent dimensional change, average the measurements in each direction made on the three specimens after the first and, if completed, the fifth or other specified number of washing and drying cycles. Calculate length and width averages separately to the nearest 0.1%.

If measurements were made to the nearest millimeter or 0.1 inch or smaller, calculate the dimensional change after the first and, if completed, the fifth or other specified washing and drying cycle as follows:

$$\% DC = 100 (B-A) / A$$

Where DC = Dimensional Change
A = Original dimension
B = Dimension after laundering

Both original and final dimensions are the averages of the measurements in each direction made on the three test specimens. Calculate length and width averages separately to the nearest 0.1%.

A final measurement smaller than the original measurement results in a negative dimensional change, which is shrinkage. A final measurement larger than the original measurement results in a positive dimensional change, which is growth or negative shrinkage.

If the dimensional change after one washing, drying, and, if used, restoration cycle as calculated is within a specification previously agreed on, continue the test procedures as directed until an agreed upon number of cycles has been completed. If the dimensional change exceeds a specification previously agreed on, terminate the test.

9. Dimensional Change on Dry-cleaning in Perchloroethylene: Machine Method AATCC Test Method 158-1995

Calculation and Expression of Results:
Calculate the dimensional change in the length and width directions of each fabric specimen or in the principal dimensions of a garment. Express as average percentage dimensional change, rounded to the nearest 0.2%, using a minus sign to indicate shrinkage and a plus sign to indicate an increase in dimensions.

10. Standard Test Method for Resistance to Slippage of Yarns in Woven Fabrics Using a Standard Seam ASTM Designation: D434-75

Evaluation:
Resistance to slippage should be measured to the nearest 0.5 lb. (2 N) or other end point such as fabric breaks, thread breaks, or exceeds capacity of testing machine.

11. Standard Test Method for Tearing Strength of Fabric by Falling-Pendulum Type (Elmendorf) Apparatus ASTM Designation: D1424-96

Evaluation:
Tearing force for individual specimens is measured to the nearest 1% of full-scale test instrument range.

12. Standard Test Method for Failure in Sewn Seams of Woven Fabrics ASTM Designation: D1683-90a

Evaluation:
Calculate the maximum sewn seam strength of individual specimens having a like seam assembly; that is, maximum force in newtons per meter to cause a specimen to rupture as read directly from the testing instrument.

13. **Standard Test for Pilling Resistance and Other Related Surface Changes of Textile Fabrics: Random Tumble Pilling Tester ASTM Designation: D3512-96**

Evaluation:

- **5** No pilling
- **4** Slight pilling
- **3** Moderate pilling
- **2** Severe pilling
- **1** Very severe pilling

When the appearance of a test specimen falls between that of two rating standards, assign the half value, for example, 3.5 or 2.5.

14. **Standard Test for Bursting Strength of Knitted Goods: Constant-Rate-of-Traverse (CRT) Ball Burst Test ASTM Designation: D3787-89**

Evaluation:

Report the bursting strength of each specimen and the average bursting strength of the five specimens from each laboratory sample to the nearest 0.1 lb. (0.5 N).

15. **Standard Test Method for Breaking Strength and Elongation of Textile Fabrics (Grab Test) ASTM Designation: 5034-95**

Evaluation:

For each laboratory sample and testing condition, calculate the average of the breaking force observed for all acceptable specimens; that is, the maximum force exerted on the specimen as read directly from the testing machine indicating mechanism.

16. **AZO Dyestuffs MAK II A1 and MAK III A2**

Evaluation:

Test method according to section 35 of the Foods and Commodities Act: treatment with a citrate buffer, reductive cleavage with sodium dithionite, extraction with ether. Analysis is performed with GS-MSD. Method for leather: DIN 53316E 04/1996.

Amines as per German law, detection limit 5 ppm.

MAK III A1

Benzidin
4-Chlor-o-toluidin
2-Naphthylamin
4-Aminodiphenyl

MAK III A2

p-Chloranilin
2,4-Diaminoanisol
4,4'-Diaminodiphenylmethan
3,3'-Dimethoxybenzidin
4,4'Methylen-bis-(2-chloranilin)
2,4-Toluylendiamin

4,4'-Thiodainilin
2,4,5-Trimethylanilin
3,3'-Dimethyl-4,4'-diaminodiphenylmethan
3,3'-Dichlorbenzidin
p-Kresidin
4,4'-Oxydianilin
o-Toluidin

The amines o-aminoazotoluene and 2-amino-4-nitrotoluene are detected by means of their degradation products o-toluidine or 2,4 tolyenediamine.

17. Colorfastness to Chlorine Bleach, Specialized Technology Resources, Inc. TP 80

Evaluation:
A drop of diluted chlorine bleach is applied to the fabric and the color fading is evaluated using the AATCC Gray Scale.

- **Grade 5** Negligible or no change as shown in Gray Scale Step 5.
- **Grade 4.5** A change in color equivalent to Gray Scale Step 4.5.
- **Grade 4** A change in color equivalent to Gray Scale Step 4.
- **Grade 3.5** A change in color equivalent to Gray Scale Step 3.5.
- **Grade 3** A change in color equivalent to Gray Scale Step 3.
- **Grade 2.5** A change in color equivalent to Gray Scale Step 2.5.
- **Grade 2** A change in color equivalent to Gray Scale Step 2.
- **Grade 1.5** A change in color equivalent to Gray Scale Step 1.5.
- **Grade 1** A change in color equivalent to Gray Scale Step 1.

18. Flammability of General Wearing Apparel Title 16 CFR 1610

Evaluation:

- **Class 1** **Normal Flammability**
  Plain Surface Fabrics: Time of flame spread is 3.5 seconds or more.
  Raised Surface Fabrics: Time of flame spread is more than 7 seconds or when the surface burns with a rapid surface flash provided the intensity of the flame is so low as not to ignite or fuse the base fabric.

- **Class 2** **Intermediate Flammability**
  Raised Surface Fabrics: Time of flame spread is from 4 to 7 seconds (both inclusive) and the base fabric ignites or fuses.

- **Class 3** **Rapid and Intense Burning**
  Plain Surface Fabrics: Time of flame spread is less than 3.5 seconds.
  Raised Surface Fabrics: Time of flame spread is less than 4 seconds and the intensity of the flame is such that it ignites or fuses the base fabric.

Exemptions:

Plain surface fabrics, regardless of fiber content, weighing 2.6 ounces per square yard and all fabrics (both plain and raised surface), regardless of weight, made entirely from any of the following fibers or entirely from a combination of the following fibers: acrylic, modacrylic, nylon, olefin, polyester, and wool.

CHAPTER 9

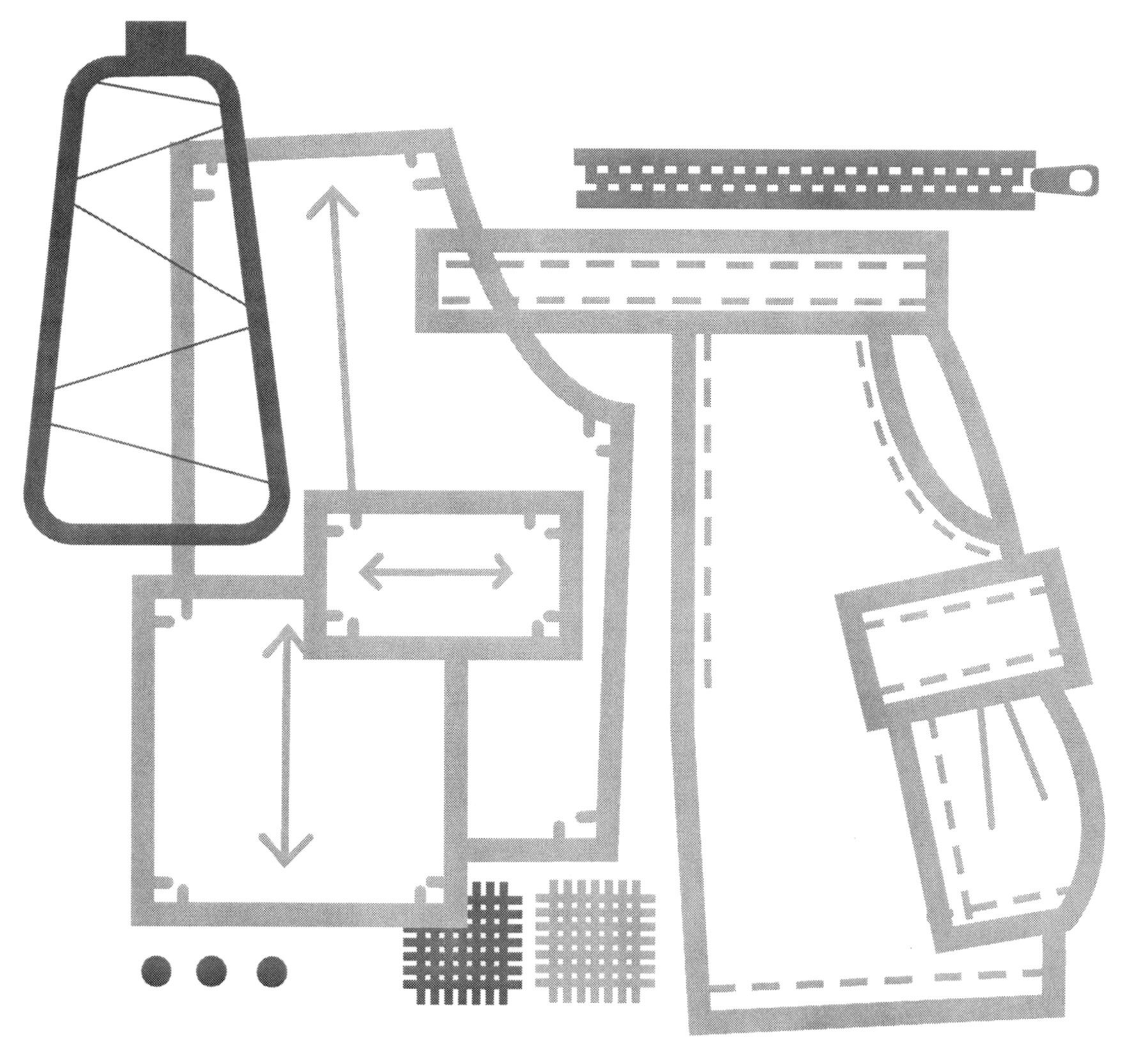

WORKMANSHIP STANDARDS

This chapter provides construction and workmanship guidelines that you should require and standardize in your relationship with contractors, factories and agents. All details need to be cut, placed, and knitted or sewn properly to pass quality control standards and to be acceptable to retailers. Garments with poor workmanship standards are not considered to be First Quality.

WORKMANSHIP STANDARDS

STANDARDS OF WORKMANSHIP

Please keep in mind that these are suggested standards. You should try to come up with your own set of standards for workmanship that work for you and all your suppliers.

You will see a sample set of grade rules on a few garments. As stated earlier in this book, the grade always depends on what you are trying to achieve. Try to work with your factory's patternmaker to ensure the best results for all sizes, as what applies to one size is not always consistent with all other sizes.

Workmanship is the principal benchmark for quality, performance, and care in the apparel arts. There are demonstrable standards for proper preparation, construction, and finishing to be applied throughout the manufacturing process. Each item, style, or fabrication may require its own special applications and handling. Much of this can be indicated in the individual tech package/spec package and through regular communication with your suppliers. Counter samples and sales samples should reflect these consensual standards, even prior to bulk production.

WORKMANSHIP STANDARDS

All garments manufactured for the customer should meet the following workmanship standards in order to be considered first quality merchandise. All parts of the garment should be fully operative and function in the manner intended.

STITCHING, SEAMS, AND EMBROIDERY

STITCHING

- The number of stitches per inch should conform to those indicated on the specification sheet. The following are some possible guidelines. Individual fiber contents, fabric constructions, type and end use of the garment, and the contractor or factory's machinery and capabilities, should also be taken into consideration. It is recommended that the contractor test seams, topstitching, etc., on each fabrication and submit these to the customer. Keep in mind that certain sections of a single garment may require different types and different stitch counts, i.e.: armholes, crotch seams, special stress points or decorative effects based on thread size, etc.

Garment Type	Stitches per inch
Knits (serged and overlock seams)	10, 12
Woven Shirts (for denim)	10, 12
Woven Shirts and Blouses (seams)	16, 18

- With bottoms, outerwear, leather, water-resistant, and rugged or luxury items, the variations in fabric and function are too great to generalize. Stitches per inch should be determined per design (or parts thereof) in the specification package.
- Darts and pleats should be uniform in shape and length.
- Darts should not bubble or pucker at ends.

SEAMS

- All exposed seams should be finished and back-tacked (backstitched) at ends.
- All exterior threads should be trimmed to within 1/16".
- All interior threads should be trimmed to within 1/4".
- All seams should lie flat and smooth.

EMBROIDERY

- There should be no broken stitches or thread tails on embroidery.
- It is recommended that all embroidery should have non-fusible interfacing backing unless otherwise specified.
- Embroidery should not pucker.
- Embroidery should be straight (registered properly).
- Underlying fabric should be *completely* covered by the embroidery or as approved design.
- Trim non-fusible interfacing precisely.

SNAPS, GROMMETS, DRAWSTRINGS, AND ZIPPERS

SNAPS

- All snaps and metal shank buttons should be non-rusting, non-corroding and non-toxic, with finishes that do not chip.
- All snaps and metal shank buttons should be reinforced with a backing, suitable interfacing or two-ply self-fabric.
- All snaps and metal shank buttons bearing the customer's logo or a special design should have them correctly oriented.

GROMMETS

- All grommets should be reinforced with a backing material or two-ply self-fabric.
- Grommets should meet the customer's standards as indicated in the spec sheet.

DRAWSTRINGS

- Ends of drawstring tunnel should either have a clean finished end, stitched eyelet, buttonhole or securely placed grommet.
- All drawstrings should hang 4" below grommet or tunnel opening on each side when in a relaxed state (unless otherwise noted on the specification sheet).
- All drawstring ends should be clean finished with a plastic shoe tip, knot, or heat set.
- Finished diameter of grommet opening should allow drawstring to move freely, without stress or binding.
- Punch holes should be no larger than necessary to accommodate diameter of grommet.
- An extra layer of shell fabric should be used for reinforcement behind all drawstring grommets. Reinforcement piece should be centered at grommet placement, directly between shell and washer. Raw edges should be caught on at least 3 sides by tunnel topstitch.
- Drawcords should fit the garment. When loosely extended, there should be no more than 1 1/2" extending out of tunnel.
- 3 mm shockcord at hood.
- 4 mm shockcord at waist and hem draws.

ZIPPERS

- Should be fully functional and locking.
- Should not bulge or appear wavy when sewn into garment.
- All center-front zipper sliders should be locking.
- All pocket zipper sliders should be the "floating" type.
- Zipper pull should correspond to the hole in the zipper slider.
- Parka-length jackets and longer (generally those with a center back length of 32" or longer) generally require 2-way zippers at center front.
- Zipper slider placement requirement: Men's and women's CF zipper slider should be on the right side of the garment (U.S. method).

BUTTONS, BUTTONHOLES, THREAD, AND NEEDLE QUALITY

BUTTONS

- All buttons should be securely fastened.
- All external buttons should be sewn through all layers of garment.
- All buttons on outerwear garments should have button stays at center front and cuffs unless otherwise specified (button stay should be applied simultaneously with button).
- 4-hole buttons should be cross-stitched if possible – contractor's equipment permitting.
- Automated equipment: Lock stitch preferred. Tails should be pulled through to back and knotted securely.
- Hand-sewn buttons: Wrap thread around button stand at least 3-4 passes before tying off.
- All buttons having the customer logo should have the logo pointing up.
- Shirt-collar buttons or buttons on single-plys of fabric should be reinforced with non-fusible interfacing or suitable fabric circles or fine button stay.
- All buttons should be able to withstand appropriate garment wash or appropriate method of cleaning unless otherwise specified.
- The customer should require one extra button (or as specified) per ligne size used on the garment. The spec sheet should indicate correct extra button placement.

BUTTONHOLES

- Buttonholes should be stitched around completely with clean, finished edge.
- Buttonholes should not fray (should be cut with a sharp knife).
- All machine buttonholes on jackets, trousers, outerwear and skirts should be keyhole type whenever possible (or as specified).
- Leather or cloth-bound buttonholes should measure 1/4" longer than diameter of button (3/16" wide for each welt). Machine buttonhole (if placed on underside of garment) should be as long as and centered over bound buttonhole.

THREAD

- Wrapped polyester core threads are preferred in all button applications.
- Thread should be colorfast.
- Should be dyed to match ground fabric unless otherwise specified.

NEEDLE

- The correct needle size should be used for all applications.
- Ballpoint needles should be used for cut-and-sew knits.
- Triangular point needles should be used on all leathers.

LINING AND FILL

- All linings (and shell fabrics on washed outerwear) should be serged.
- Linings should have adequate ease to allow for movement and durability (cut larger than garment unless specially used to stay a portion of the garment).
- Linings should not hang below hem.
- Fill should not migrate.

FUSIBLE AND INTERLINING

- It is the manufacturer's responsibility to test each fabric for fusible or interlining compatibility (before and after washing or dry cleaning) and to provide the customer with the test results.
- Fusible should not show through.
- Should lie flat and not bubble or delaminate in pressing or cleaning.

POCKETS

- All pocket bags should conform to the customer's size specifications.
- All pocket bags may be clean finished (serged then turned and/or stitched with 1/4" topstitch) unless otherwise specified.
- All pocket facings should be clean finished (by turn and topstitch or serge or coverstitch).
- All pockets should be evenly aligned (registered).
- Drill holes should be covered.
- All jackets and coats should have an inside left chest pocket or as specified. It is often customary for the customer to provide a "Lining and Inside Pocket Specification Package" for jackets, performance wear and outerwear.
- All pockets should follow specified dimensions (H x W) and placement.

WELT POCKET

- Pocket should be rectangular (true squared) unless otherwise specified as a design element.

PATCH POCKET

- Pockets should cover punch holes by 1/4" (width and length).
- Leather patch pockets should be reinforced with 1 1/2" fusing (or twill) where stitched to shell (note: this also applies to woven fabrics that tear or shift easily).

POCKET FLAPS

- Should be uniform in size, smooth-edged and possess no points (unless specified as a design element).
- Raw edge of flap should be set 3/8" above finished top pocket edge unless otherwise specified.

ZIPPER POCKETS

- Pockets should close with the pull at top for vertical pockets (unless otherwise specified).
- Pockets should close with pull toward side seam for horizontal pockets unless otherwise specified.

INSIDE WELT POCKET

- Set on inside left front lining.

BELT LOOP STANDARDS

- Should be clean finished at ends.
- Should be set as indicated on Construction Sheet in Spec Package.
- Should be securely tacked.
- Should be uniform in width and length.
- Should be equal distance from left side to right side.
- May be fused or parasealed (as specified).

PLAID STANDARDS

- BALANCE = mirrored image from left to right, side to side.
- MATCH = something exactly corresponding to another.

WOVEN SHIRTS AND OUTERWEAR/PLAID STANDARDS

Garment pieces that must be balanced:

- Sleeves

Garment pieces that must be balanced on a predominant stripe of the plaid*:

- Collar
- Cuffs

Garment pieces that must match:

- Left and right front - horizontally
- Pockets and pocket flaps - horizontally and vertically

BOTTOMS/PLAID STANDARDS

Garment pieces that must be balanced on a predominant stripe of the plaid*:

- Waistband
- Left and right front leg - horizontal and vertical

Garment pieces that must match:

- Left and right front leg - horizontal and vertical
- Left and right back leg - horizontal and vertical
- Waistband - horizontal

* Predominant stripe of each plaid should be chosen by the customer and should be noted in each specification package.

STRIPE STANDARDS

WOVEN SHIRTS, JACKETS AND OUTERWEAR/STRIPE STANDARDS

Garment pieces that must be balanced:

- Sleeves
- Collar
- Cuffs

Garments that must match:

- Left and right fronts
- Pockets and pocket flaps

BOTTOMS/STRIPE STANDARDS

Garment pieces that must be balanced:

- Left and right front leg - vertically
- Left and right back leg - vertically

Garment pieces that must match:

- Waistband – horizontally
- Left and right front at CF
- Left and right back at CB
- Front and back outseam below hip curve

ELASTIC AND RIBBING

- Should extend to the fullest width of the body without breaking stitches, or binding.
- Elastic within casings should be stitched down or tacked to avoid rollover or twisting.

FINISHING

BAR TACKS AND OTHER REINFORCEMENTS

- All pocket openings should be bartacked or understitched.
- Base of fly should be bartacked.
- All other stress points should be bartacked.
- Other types of reinforcements are acceptable only if listed in the customer specification package.

HEMS

- Should be even with no raw edges exposed.
- Should not rope.
- Pant hems should start and finish on inseam of leg (1" overlap).

SHOULDER SEAMS

- All cut-and-sew knits and sweaters should have twill tape, self or elastic material reinforcement at shoulder (or as indicated in the customer specification package).

SHOULDER PADS

- Should lie smooth and be securely fastened.
- Should be applied to shell fabric at seam allowances (except leather, which may be applied to lining).

SWEATERS

- All yarn ends should be tied and clipped.

TRIM STANDARDS

TRIM SOURCE

- Refer to trim chart for the list of approved vendors.
- All trims sourced by the contractor need to be submitted for the customer's approval.

RIB TRIM

- Tubular rib at sleeve cuff and collar should have 1-2% spandex for stability.
- Rib trim should be submitted for approval of color and quality.

INTERFACING

- Best/better quality fusible used for:
- Woven top collar
- Self top collar
- Self-placket facing.

TWILL TAPE

- 3/8" twill tape is used to clean finish side vents unless otherwise indicated on specs.
- 1 1/2" twill tape is used for placket facing unless otherwise indicated on specs.

CONSTRUCTION DETAILS AND STANDARDS

For specific construction methods, detailed illustrations and supplemental written information assures that all uniquely-constructed details and elements of a style are executed as the designer and product development staff intend. This third component of the specifications (tech) package is increasingly more important, as customers are often dealing with multiple contractors and suppliers, often involved in producing the same item in different locations. The customer may also wish to standardize some of these details and standards for use in future product development. Companies often maintain an extensive library of these details, in order to maintain a continuity of quality and design. This is particularly useful with standards concerning fancy lining construction, special details, unique closures, and similar things. Here are a few examples of Construction Detail diagrams. Construction Detail diagrams go directly onto the Construction Detail Sheet in your Tech Package:

OUTERWEAR WORKMANSHIP STANDARDS

Outerwear Piece: Front and Back

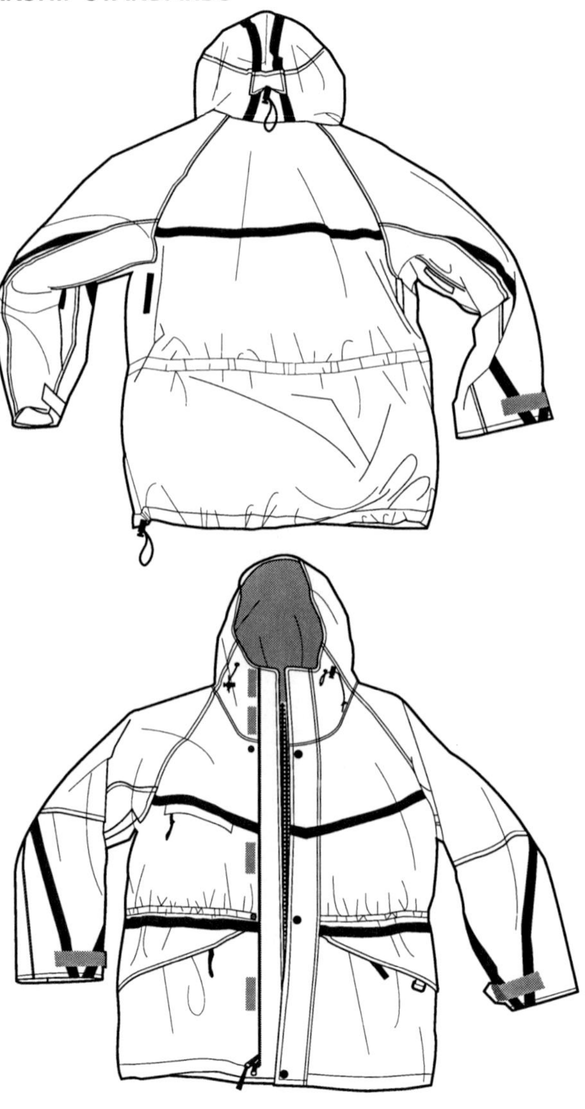

Windskirt: Inside lining of outerwear jacket to prevent water infiltration with elastic

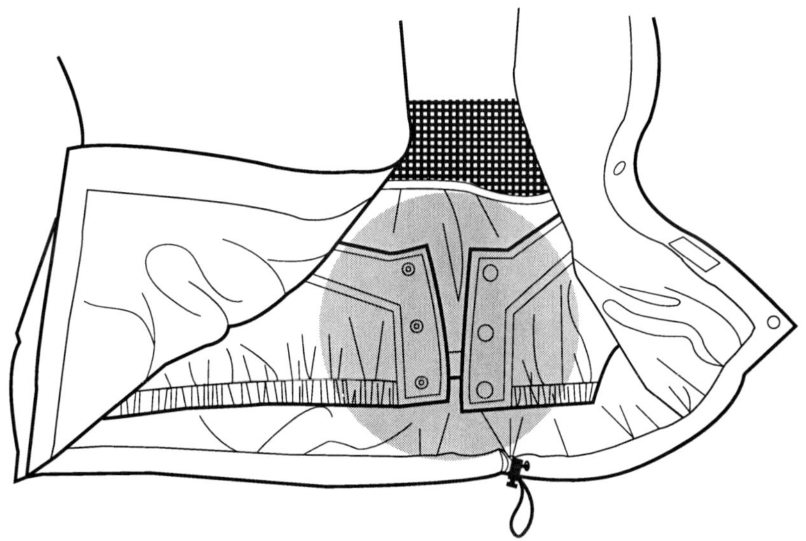

Cuffs: Opening

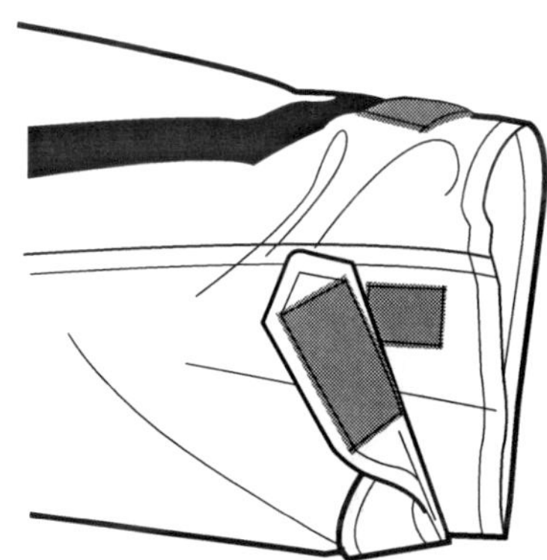

Hood Construction: Details may vary from design

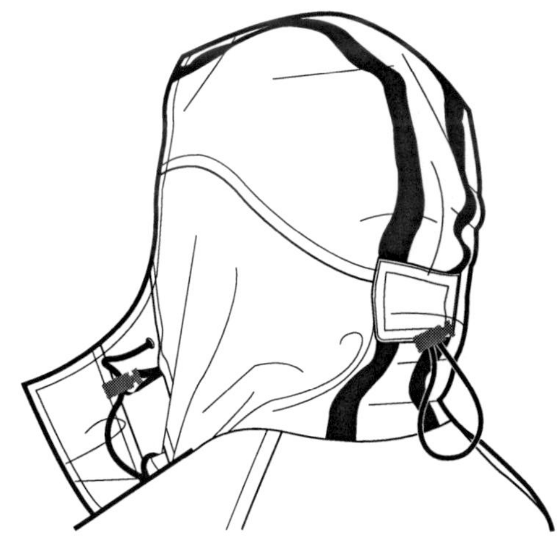

Gussets: Underneath sleeve at underarm

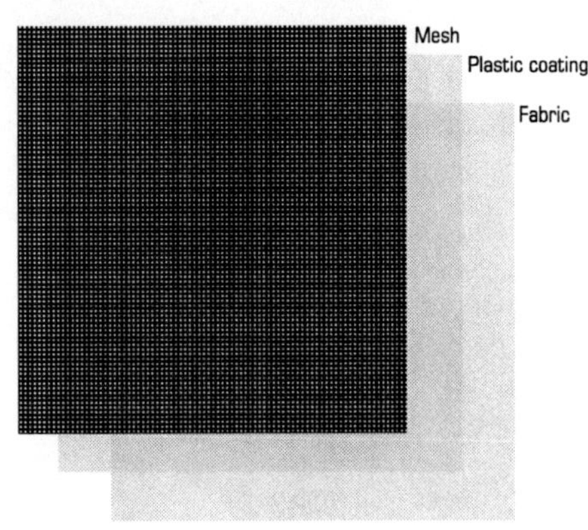

Pockets:

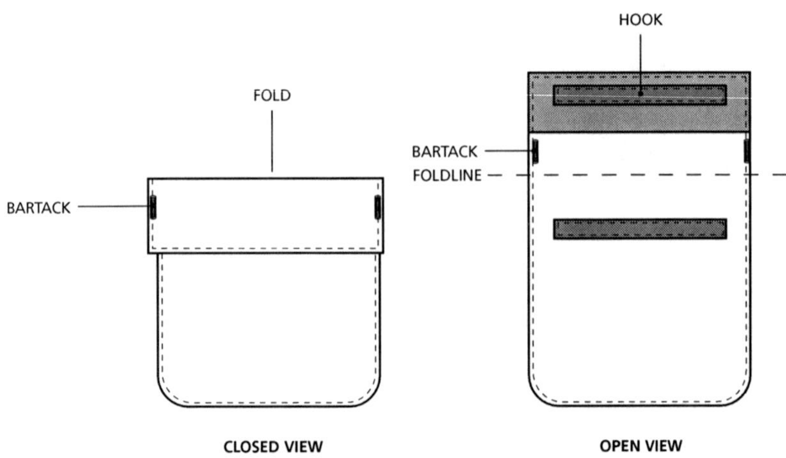

One hole cordlock: Grossgrain ribbon threading through side loop of cordlock

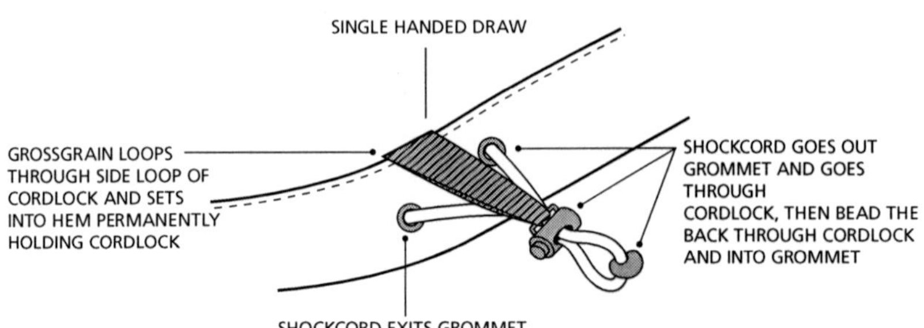

One hole cordlock: Inside view

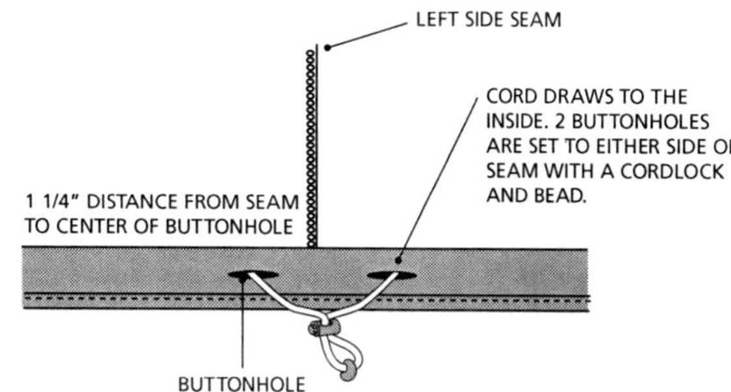

One hole cordlock: View of back collar and closeup of how grossgrain is attached

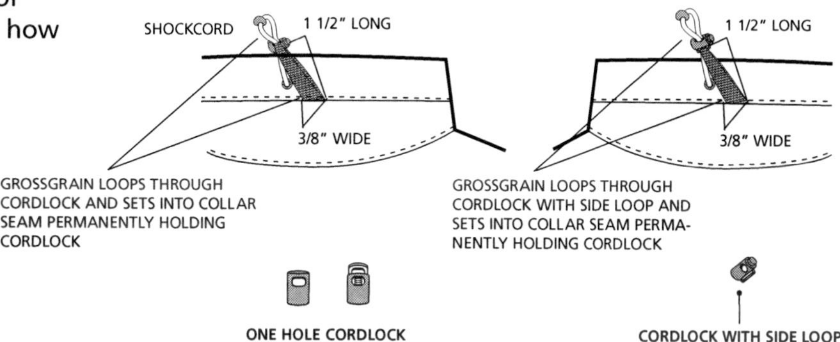

One hole cordlock: Single handed

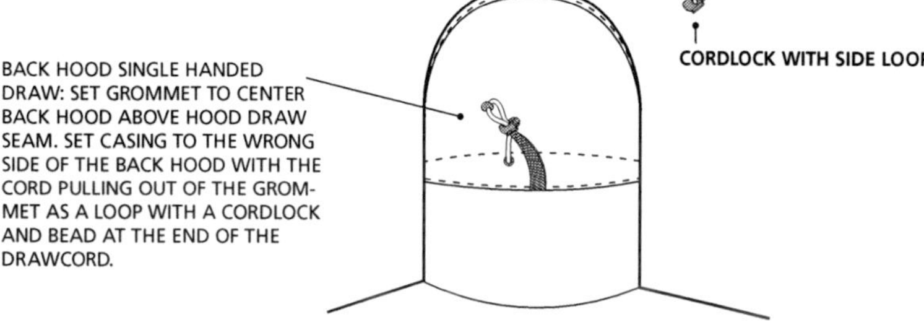

One hole cordlock:

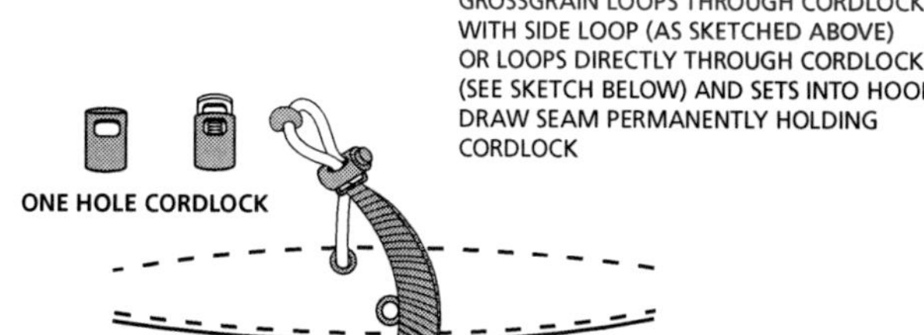

Hood down: Front view

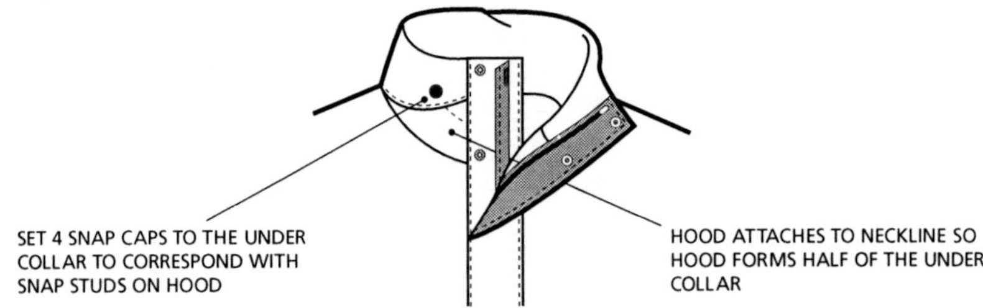

Hood down: Hood before rolling into collar

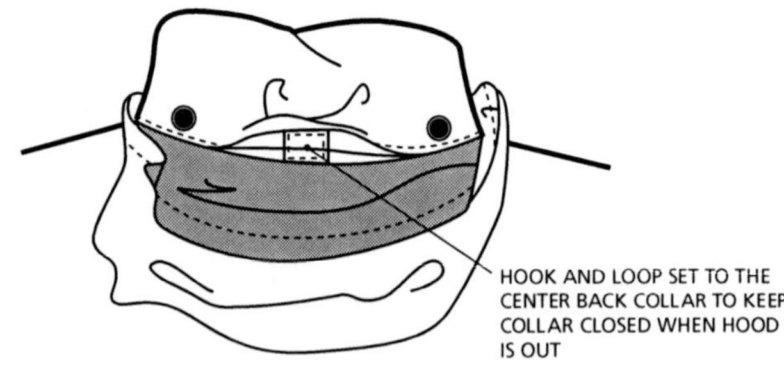

Hood down: Hood rolled into collar

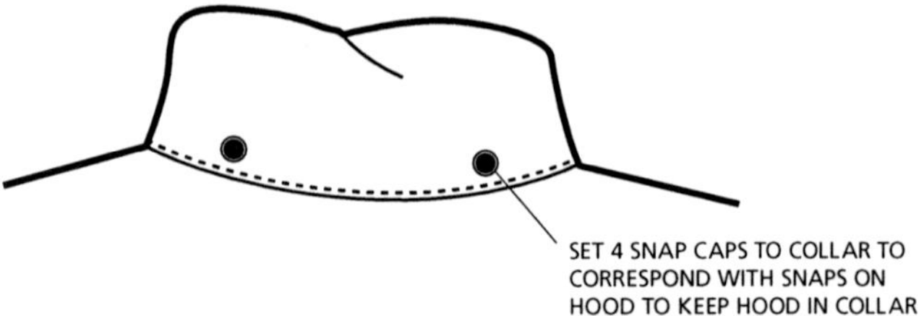

Hood down: Front view

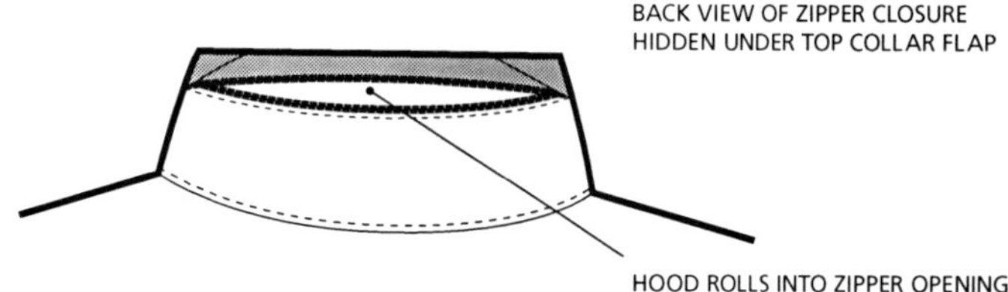

Hood down: Hood rolled into collar

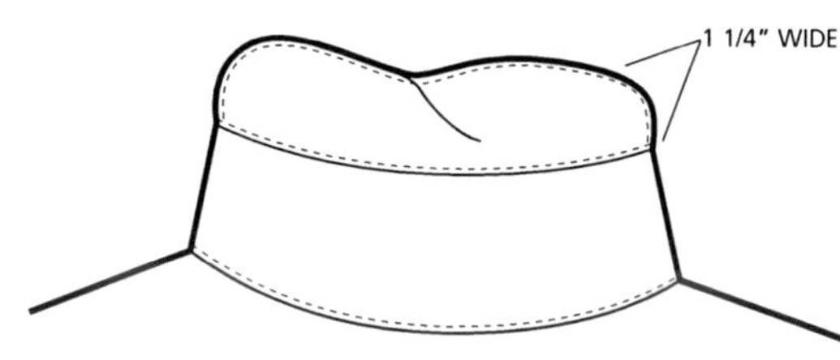

Hood tunnel: Front view

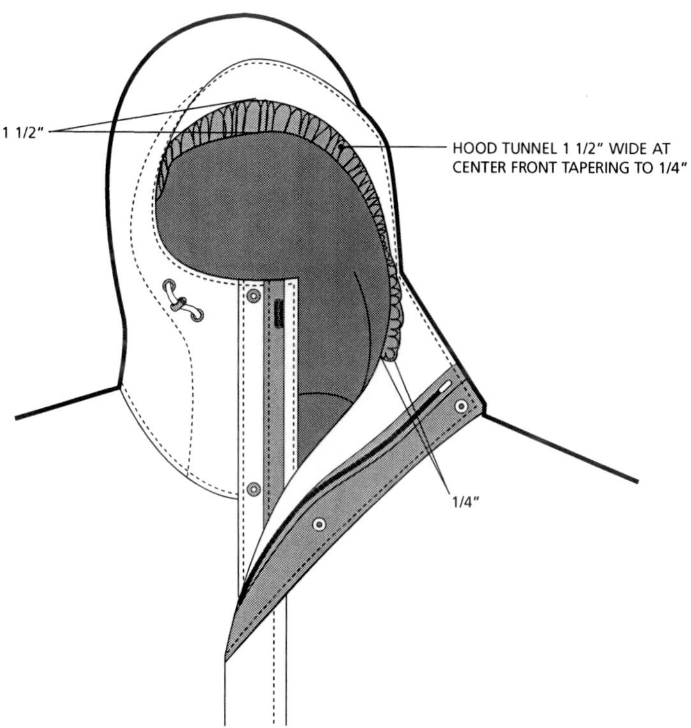

Zipper Pulls: Locking zipper head with cording and clip

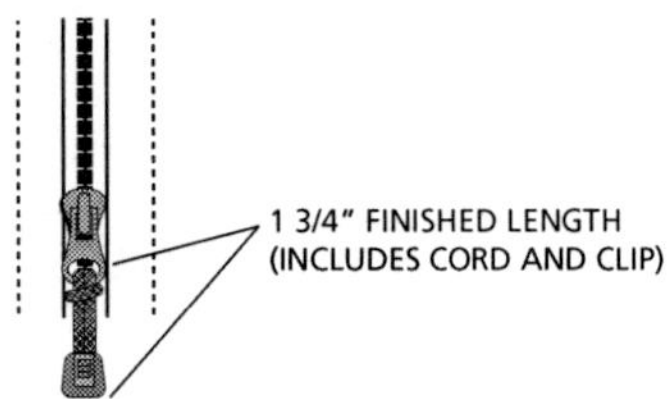

Zipper Pulls: Floating zipper head with cording and clip

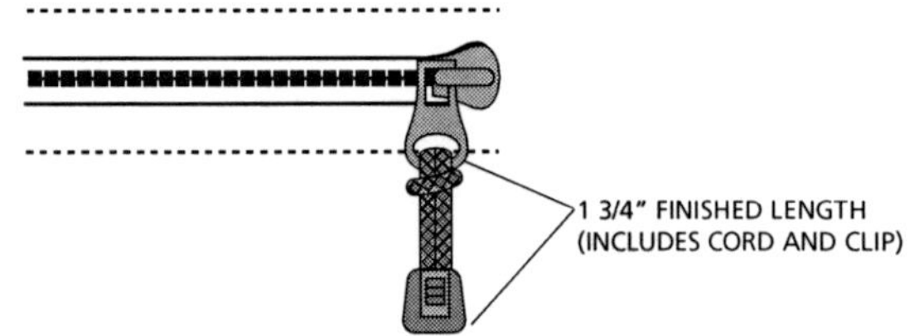

Zipper Pulls: Extension with knotted cord

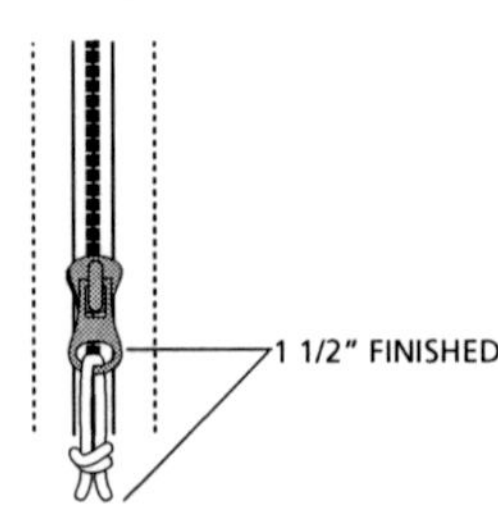

Zipper Pulls: Floating zipper head with knotted cord

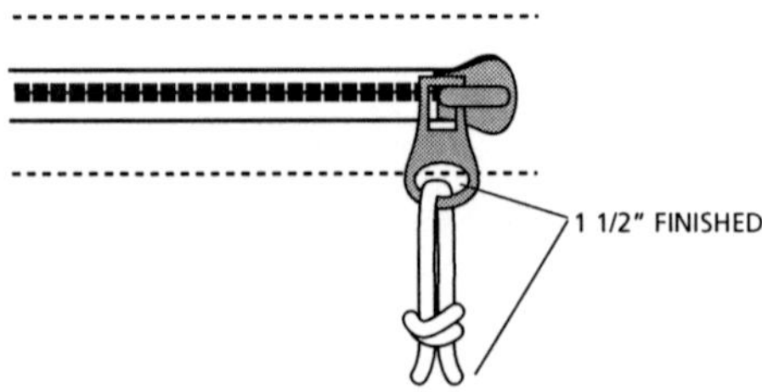

Zipper Pulls:

LOCKED ZIPPER SLIDER WITH NON-STRETCH CORDING AND CLIP

FLOATING ZIPPER SLIDER WITH NON-STRETCH CORDING AND CLIP

Zipper Pulls:

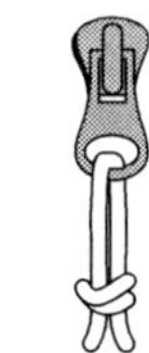
LOCKED ZIPPER SLIDER WITH NON-STRETCH CORDING KNOTTED AND HEAD CUT

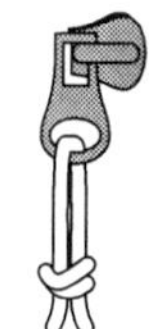
FLOATING ZIPPER SLIDER WITH NON-STRETCH CORDING KNOTTED AND HEAD CUT

Zipper Pulls:

LOCKING ZIPPER SLIDER AT CENTER FRONT

FLOATING ZIPPER SLIDER AT POCKETS AND PIT ZIPPERS

Cordlock with side loop:

LOCKED SLIDER WITH RUBBER TREE LOGO FOR #5 COIL ZIPPERS

LOCKED SLIDER WITH NO LOGO FOR #3 COIL ZIPPERS

Cordlock:

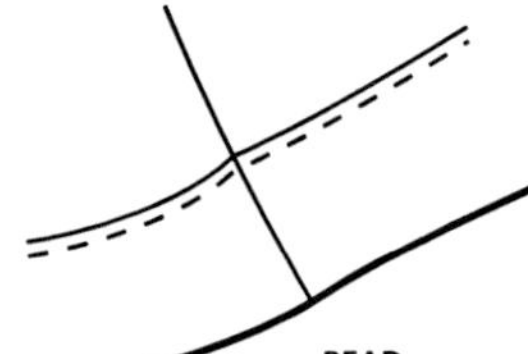

Rubber cordlock bead:

RUBBER CORDLOCK BEAD FOR LIGHTWEIGHT FABRICS AT HOODS/ SEAMS/WAIST DRAWS

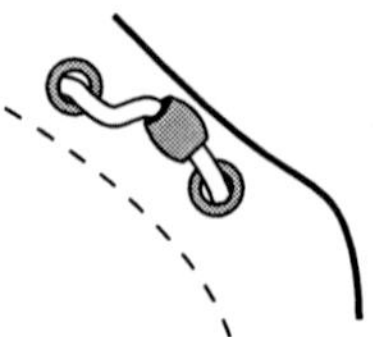

Rubber softlock:

RUBBER SOFTLOCK FOR LIGHT-WEIGHT FABRICS AT HOODS/ SEAMS/WAIST DRAWS

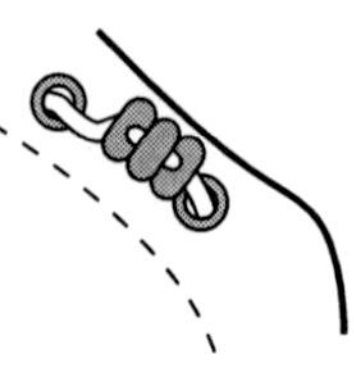

Rubber softlock: Outside view

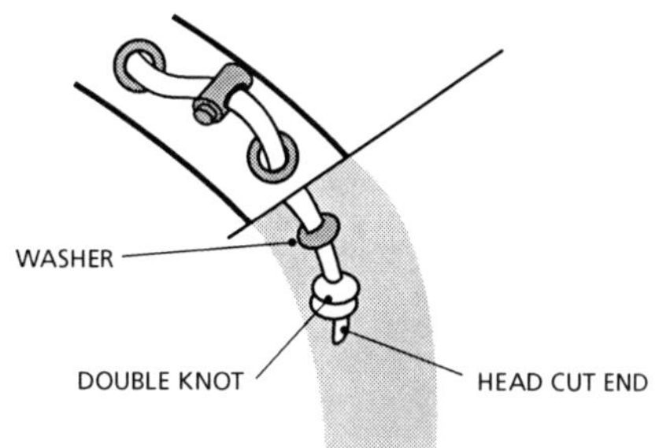

Trims - Grommets:

OVAL LOGO GROMMET

SCREENED GROMMET

UNSCREENED GROMMET

SKIRTS WORKMANSHIP STANDARDS

Skirt:

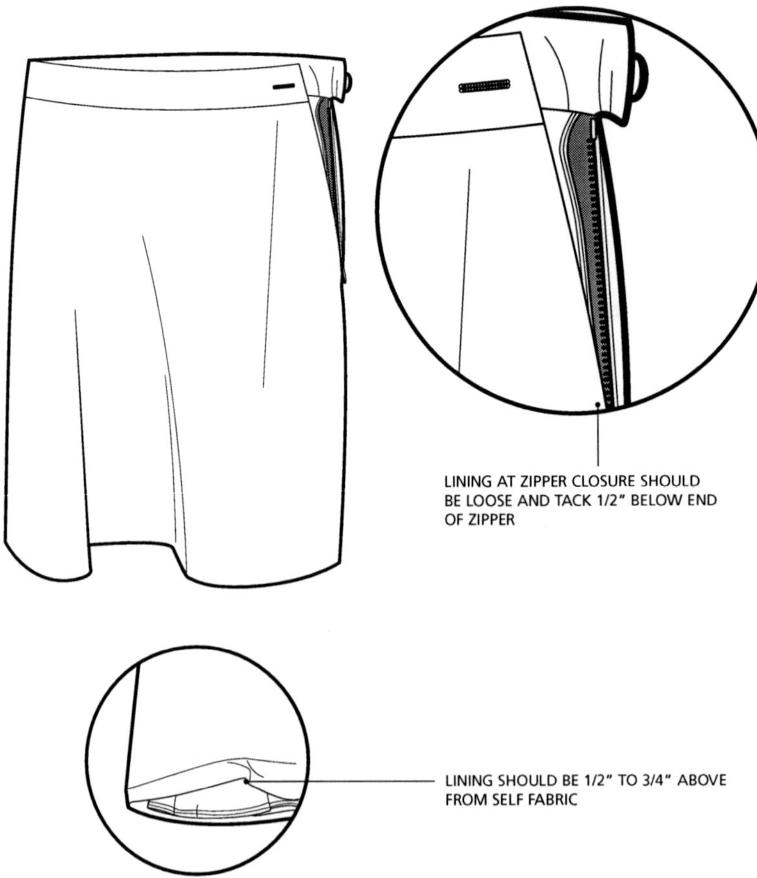

KNIT TOPS AND SWEATERS WORKMANSHIP STANDARDS

Sweater:

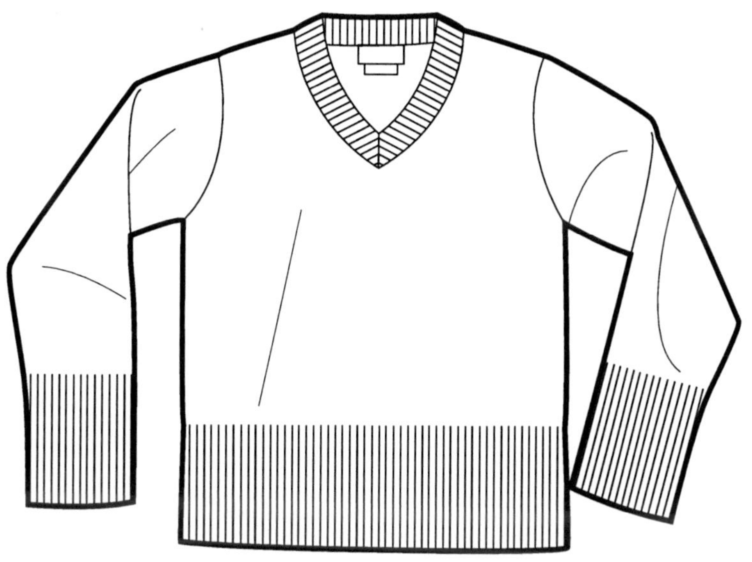

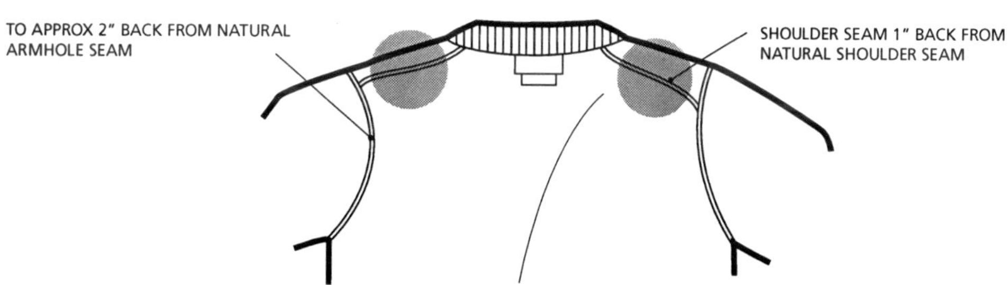

Side vents:
Side vents must be clean finished with 3/8" twill tape, unless otherwise indicated on specs.

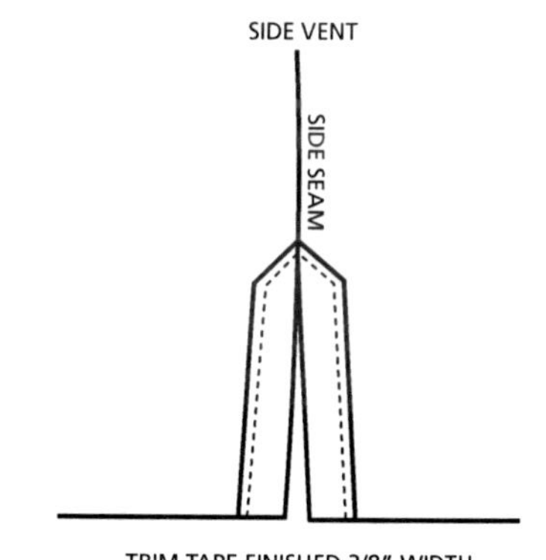

Embroideries:
Embroideries must have a high density stitch count.
Embroideries must be straight and centered.
Backing must be trimmed off to minimum.

Placket:
Self placket must be clean finished.
Twill placket must be sewn with edgestitching, exception for hidden placket.

Button/Button Loop:
Standard rugby shirts have double placket facings as construction below.

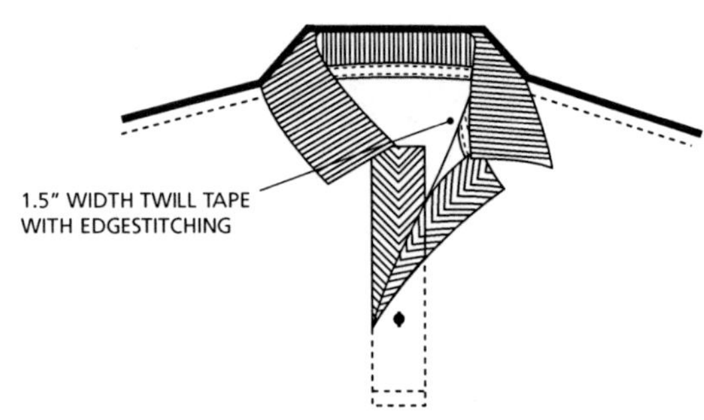

Button/Button Loop:
Placement

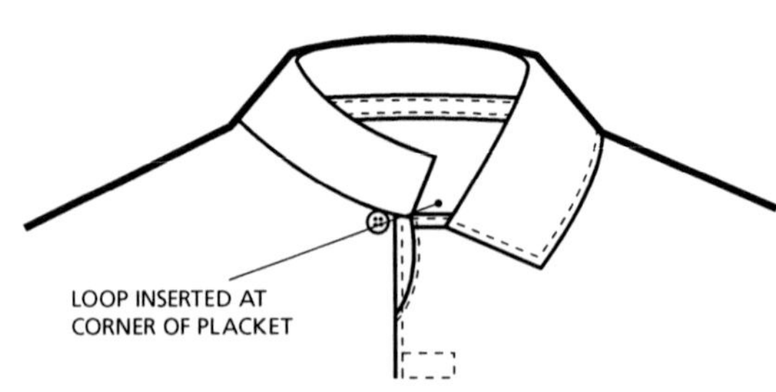

Button/Button Loop:
Placement

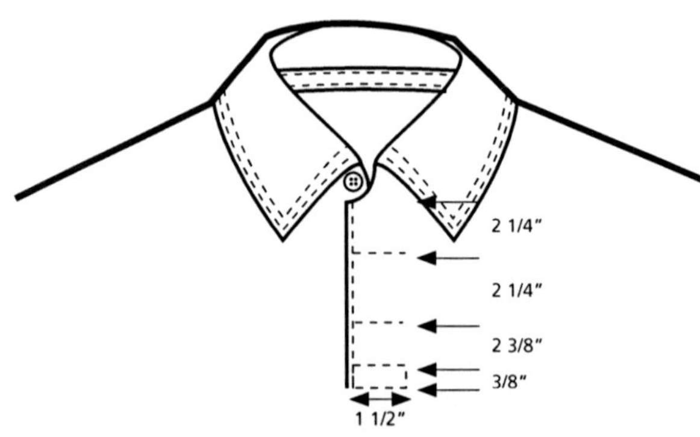

Neck Finishing:
Polo shirts with rib collar should have twill tape to cover full circumference of inside back neck seam.
Crew shirts have twill tape or jersey cover only on inside back neck seam.
V-neck with tubular rib: mitered at center front.
V-neck bound with self or rib: make a tuck at center front to form the "v" shape.

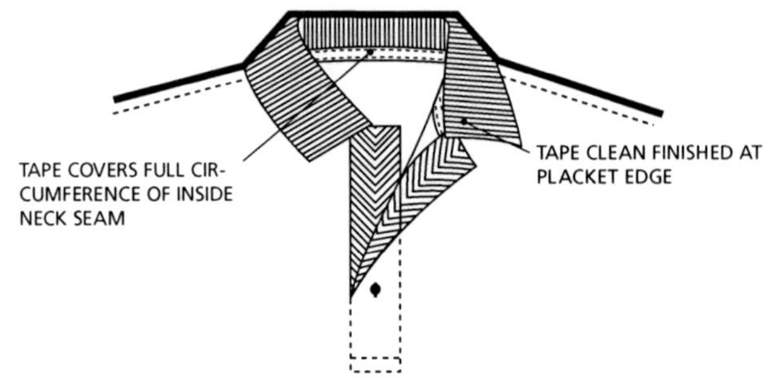

Zip Front:
Zip front must be finished with front facing, unless otherwise indicated on specs.

Polo Collar Standards:

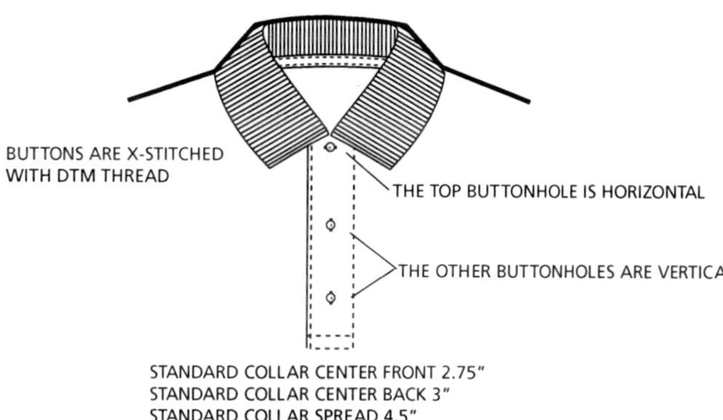

WOVEN SHIRTS AND BLOUSES WORKMANSHIP STANDARDS

PLAID MATCH STANDARDS

- Center lines on button front, buttonhole front, and top center must be positioned on the goods to produce an exact match both horizontally and vertically.

- Pockets and pocket flaps must match both horizontally and vertically to the specified location on shirt front. In case of large plaids: Horizontal match only on plaids with repeats of 12" and over; must be approved by the customer.

- Top cuffs are not positioned on center lines of piece goods; however, they must match each other horizontally (as set on shirt).

- Top collars are cut with center lines running through center of collar points. Collar points are balanced so that the color block of plaid appears the same on each collar point. Top collar and outside collar stand to be balanced horizontally and vertically to center back within each piece.

- Shirt back must be balanced vertically from center back.

- Outside yoke must be balanced horizontally and vertically from center back.

- Sleeves, facings, and sleeve plackets are to be balanced vertically, within each pair.

- Inside yoke, inside collar stand, bottom collar, and bottom cuffs are not matched.

- All plaid patterns need to be submitted in actual samples and approved.

STRIPE MATCH STANDARDS

- Center lines on button front, buttonhole front, and top center must be positioned on the goods to produce an exact match in stripe direction.

- Pockets and pocket flaps must match stripe direction to the specified location on shirt front.

- Top cuffs are not positioned on center line of piece goods; however, cuff must match each other as set on shirt and should be balanced from center point of pattern piece.

- Top collars are cut with center lines running through center of collar points. Top collars and outside collar stands should be balanced from center point of each pattern piece.

- Inside yoke, inside collar stand, bottom collar, and bottom cuffs are not matched.

- Shirt back and outside yoke to be balanced from center point of each pattern piece.

- Sleeves, sleeve plackets, and facings to be balanced within each pair.

SEAM REQUIREMENTS: Standard stitches per inch is 10 for denim, 12 on all other fabrics.

A. FELL (1/4″ between needles) - side and underarm seams (front over back), sleeve set.

B. FELL (1/4″ between needles) - side and underarm seams (front over back).
FELL (1/4″ single needle) - sleeve set.

C. FELL (1/4″ between needles) - side and underarm seams (front over back).
FELL (1/16″ edgestitch) - sleeve set.

D. SAFETY STITCH - all seams.

E. SAFETY STITCH - side and underarm seams.
SAFETY STITCH with 1⁄4″ TOPSTITCH - sleeve set.

F. SAFETY STITCH - side and underarm seams.

G. SAFETY STITCH with 1/16″ TOPSTITCH - sleeve set.

BUTTON APPLICATION:

A. Stitch first button 3 1/8″ down from collar stand at center front to center of button. Space remaining buttons 3 3/4″ apart, from center of button to center of button. (Measurements noted are suggested for men's shirt.)

B. Set 1st buttonhole horizontally; 3/8″ down from finished top edge to buttonhole center and 3/8″ in from finished center front edge to buttonhole edge. Vertically set remaining buttons with 3 3/4″ spacing, center of button to center of button. (Measurements noted are suggested for men's shirt.)

- Shirts with full length center front placket: Extra button is set to inside of right front placket 3″ up from hem.
- Shirts with partial length or no center front placket: Extra button is set to inside of left side seam 4″ up from hem.
- Thread used to apply buttons should match button color.
- If extra button is set to inside left side seam, the thread used to apply the extra button should be DTM garment shell.

SLEEVE/CUFF:

1. LONG SLEEVE - Two pleats at front sleeve bottom, first pleat is 2″ from cuff/placket edge. Second pleat is 1″ from first pleat (3″ from cuff/placket edge) and both are 3⁄4″ deep. Sleeve placket is 6″ long to point by 1″ wide, with one button/buttonhole centered. Edgestitch around placket and single needle topstitch across width at 1 3/8″ down from point; see diagram: Cuff has two buttons with one horizontal buttonhole; adjustment button set 1″ away from first button. Cuff edges are rounded.

Cuff topstitching choices:

a. 1⁄4″ single needle topstitch cuff; 5/16″ double needle topstitch cuff set.
b. 1⁄4″ double needle topstitch cuff and cuff set.
c. 1⁄4″ double needle topstitch cuff; 5/16″ double needle topstitch cuff set.
d. 1/16″ edgestitch cuff and cuff set.
e. 1/16″ edgestitch cuff; 5/16″ double needle topstitch cuff set.

2. SHORT SLEEVE - 1 3/8″ turn, clean finish and topstitch at 1″. Stitch sleeve seam before hemming.

3. LONG SPLIT SLEEVE - Split seam lines up with back yoke seam and continue into sleeve vent. 1/4″ double needle topstitch split seam on front. Sleeve vent is a continuation of the split seam. Vent opening is 3″ long; horizontal topstitch across end of vent. 3/8″ double turn and 1/4″ double needle topstitch vent to clean finish. Two pleats at front sleeve bottom: 1″ apart finished and 3/4″ deep. Cuff has two buttons with one horizontal buttonhole; adjustment button set 1″ away from first button. Cuff edges are rounded.

Cuff topstitching choices:

a. 1/4″ single needle topstitch cuff; 5/16″ double needle topstitch cuff set.
b. 1/4″ double needle topstitch cuff and cuff set.
c. 1/4″ double needle topstitch cuff; 5/16″ double needle topstitch cuff set.
d. 1/16″ edgestitch cuff and cuff set.
e. 1/16″ edgestitch cuff; 5/16″ double needle topstitch cuff set.

Performance Shirt:

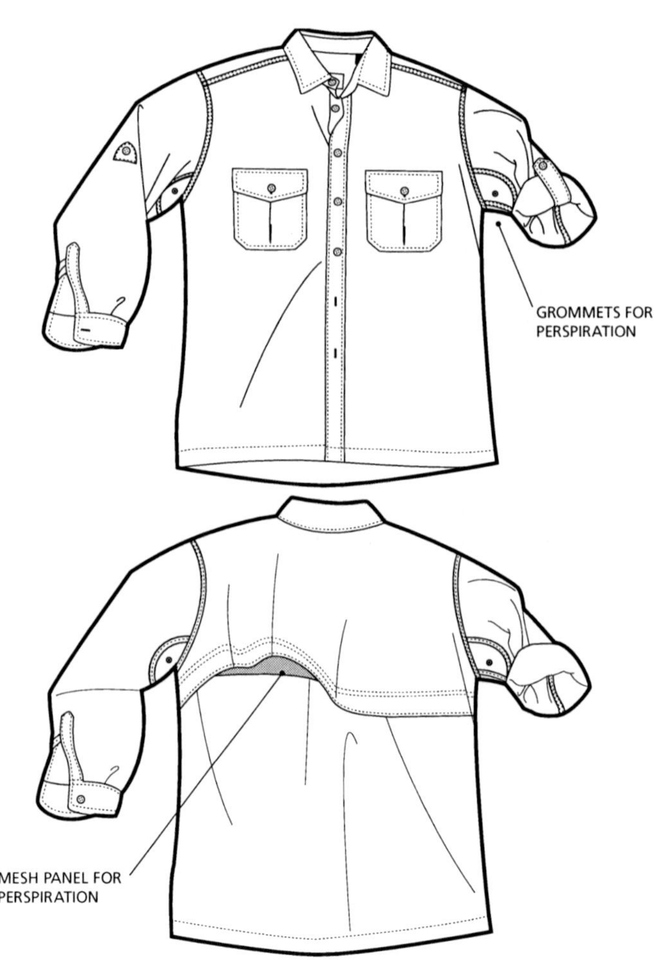

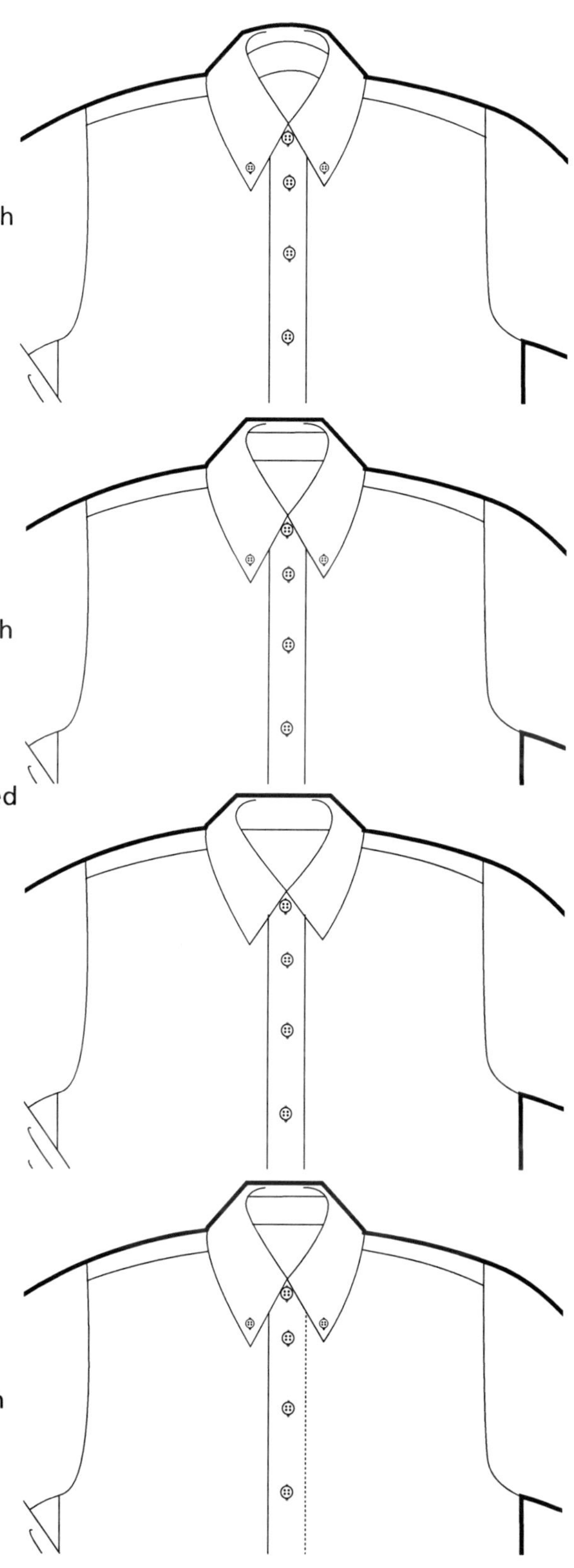

True Top Center (topped on placket)

Topstiching choices for CF Placket:
a. 1/16" edgestitch both sides
b. 1/4" single needle topstitch both sides.
c. 1/4" double needle topstitch both sides.
Right Front: 1 3/8" fused turn, clean finish and topstitch at 1".

Simulated Top Center (extension from CF and folded back)

Topstitching choices for CF Placket:
a. 1/16" edgestitch both sides.
b. 1/4" single needle topstitch both sides.
c. 1/4" double needle topstitch both sides.
Right Front: 1 3/8" fused turn, clean finish and topstitch at 1".

Self faced: Left and right front edges are clean finished with self facings. Facing edge should be clean finished with a 3/8" serged turn and 1/4" topstitch. Clean finish edge at shoulder by stitching into seam. Placket allowance for button placement is 1 1/4".

Topstitching choices for CF edge:
a. none
b. 1/16" edgestitch
c. 1/4" single needle topstitch
d. 1/4" double needle topstitch

Extended CF: Extension from left front; clean finish inside edge with a turn and topstitch.

Topstitching choices for CF edge:
a. none
b. 1/16" edgestitch
c. 1/4" double needle topstitch both sides
Right Front: 1 3/8"fused turn, clean finish and topstitch at 1".

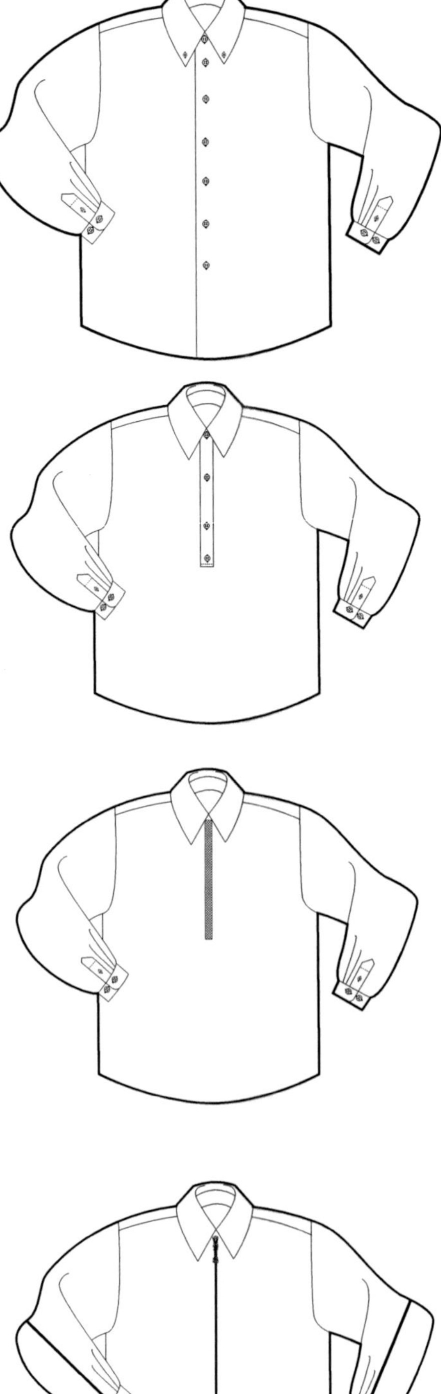

Extended CF: Extension from left front; double turn to clean finish.

Topstitching choices for CF Placket:
a. No topstitch at CF edge
b. 1/16"edgestitch at CF edge
c. 1/4" single needle topstitch at CF edge

Partial Pocket: – Placket with mitered bottom: X-box topstitch at bottom end.

Topstitching choices for CF placket:
a. No topstitch at CF edge: 1/16" at inner edge
b. 1/16" edgestitch both edges
c. 1/4" double needle topstitch both edges

Partial Length Zip Front:
A. Exposed zipper front at CF; clean finish and set zipper.
B. Exposed zipper at CF; clean finish inside zipper set with a facing.
Facing should be clean finished into shoulder/yoke seam; free edge should be 5/16" double turned with 1/4" topstitch.

Topstitching choices for CF placket:
a. 1/16" edgestitch both sides
b. 1/4"single needle topstitch both sides
c. 1/4" double needle topstitch both sides
d. Topstitched X-box at zipper base

Full Length Zip Front: Exposed zipper front; clean finish and topstitch zipper set. Topstitched X-box at zipper base. Box is 1" long by 1 1/2" wide, with stitching centered.

Topstitching choices for CF:
a. 1/16" edgestitch both sides
b. 1/4" single needle topstitch both sides
c. 1/4" double needle topstitch both sides

COLLAR WORKMANSHIP STANDARDS

Spread Collar:
The Spread Collar is a rolled collar attached to a straight or shaped collar stand. Variations can be made to the collar by adding shaping and changing the point and spread. Also called a Straight Collar or Shirtwaist.

1/16 " edgestitch collar stand through and through; double needle topstitch inside collarstand at neckline, 3/16 " between needles. One button and horizontal machine buttonhole set to collar stand.

Topstitching choices for collar:
a. 1/16" edgestitch
b. 1/8" single needle topstitch
c. 1/4" single needle topstitch
d. 1/4" double needle topstitch
e. Triple needle topstitch, 1/8" between needles.

Button-Down Collar:
A variation of the Spread Collar (above). The Button-Down Collar has a vertical buttonhole set to each collar point and a button set accordingly on the shirt. Generally used on more "dressy" shirts and on shirts that could be worn with a tie.

Standard collar point button placement is 1 3/8" over from CF to button center and 1 3/8" down from collar stand set to button center. Reinforce inside button set with a small circle of interfacing. 1/16" edgestitch collar stand through and through; double needle topstitch inside collarstand at neckline 3/16" between needles. One button and horizontal machine buttonhole set to collar stand.

Topstitching choices for collar:
a. 1/16" edgestitch
b. 1/8" single needle topstitch
c. 1/4" single needle topstitch
d. 1/4" double needle topstitch
e. Triple needle topstitch, 1/8" between needles.

Convertible Collar:
The Convertible Collar is a rolled collar and can be worn open or closed. Generally the collar stand is built into the collar piece on both top and under collars. Also called a Camp Collar.

Collarstand is built into pattern piece for collar. Edgestitch to set.

Topstitching choices for collar:
a. 1/16″ edgestitch
b. 1/8″ single needle topstitch
c. 1/4″ single needle topstitch
d. 1/4″ double needle topstitch
e. Triple needle topstitch, 1/8″ between needles.

Banded Collar:
The Banded Collar is a standing band that extends up from the neckline; it has no roll back. It may be set to the normal neckline or to a scooped neckline. Also called a Mandarin Collar, Coolie, Chinese, Military, Nehru, or Stand-Up Collar.

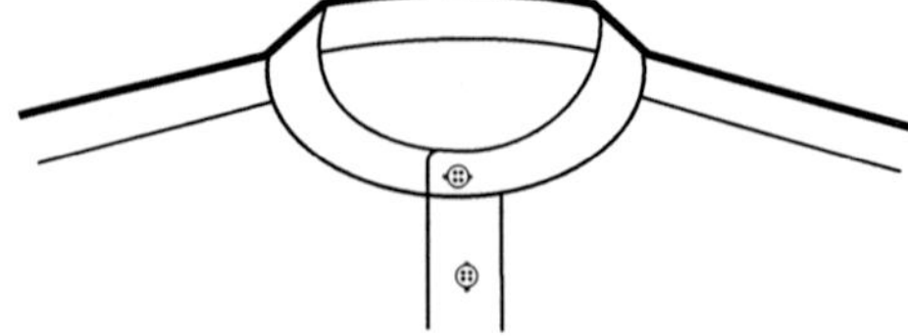

Edgestitch to set; 3/16″ double needle topstitch at inside set.

Topstitching choices for Collar:
a. None
b. 1/16″ edgestitch
c. 1/8″ single needle topstitch
d. 1/4″ single needle topstitch
e. 1/4″ double needle topstitch.

POCKET WORKMANSHIP STANDARDS

1. Patch pocket with machine buttonhole

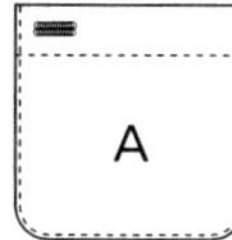

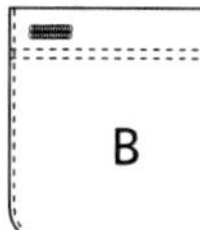

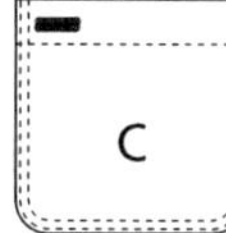

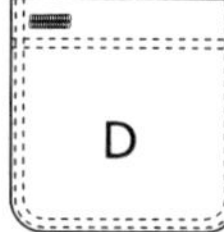

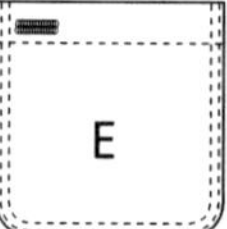

Topstitching choices for pocket:

a. 1/16″ edgestitch set and bendback, single needle topstitch pencil pocket.
b. 1/16″ edgestitch set, 1/4″ double needle topstitch bendback and pencil pocket.
c. 1/4″ double needle topstitch set, single needle topstitch pencil pocket, edgestitch bendback.
d. 1/4″ double needle topstitch set, bendback, and pencil pocket.
e. 1/4″ double needle topstitch set and pencil pocket, edgestitch bendback.

Construction Details:

- Pocket bendback is a clean finished turn. Topstitch at 1″ for single needle detail, or at 1″ and 1 1/4″ for double needle detail.
- Versions a and b: 3/16″ angled corner reinforcement stitching at bendback.
- Pencil pocket is topstitched 1 3/4′″in from edge for single needle detail. Topstitch at 1 1/2″ and 1 /34″ in from edge for double needle detail.
- 3/4″ long horizontal machine buttonhole centered on pencil pocket.
- Pocket bottom corners are rounded.

2. Plain patch pocket

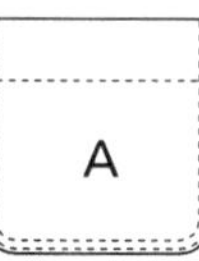

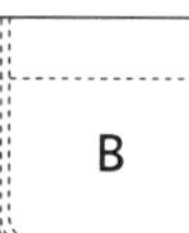

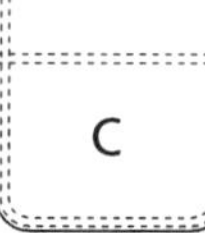

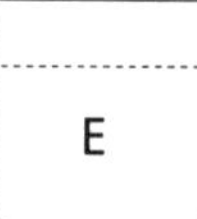

Topstitching choices for pocket:

a. 1/4″ double needle topstitch set, edgestitch bendback, single needle topstitch pencil pocket.
b. 1/4″ double needle topstitch set and pencil pocket, edgestitch bendback.
c. 1/4″ double needle topstitch set, pencil pocket and bendback.
d. 1/16″ edgestitch set and bendback, 1/4″ double needle topstitch pencil pocket.
e. 1/16″ edgestitch set and bendback, single needle topstitch pencil pocket.

Construction Details:

- Pocket bendback is a clean finished turn. Topstitch at 1″ for single needle detail, or at 1″and 1 1/4″ for double needle detail.
- Versions d and e: 3/16″ angled corner reinforcement stitching at bendback.
- Pencil pocket is topstitched 1 3/4″ in from edge for single needle detail.
- 1″ long by 1/8″ wide (each welt) bound buttonhole centered at pencil pocket. Topstitch at 1 1/2″ and 1 3/4″ in from edge for double needle detail.
- Pocket bottom corners are rounded.

3. Button-through patch pocket

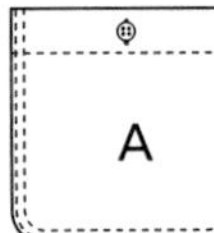

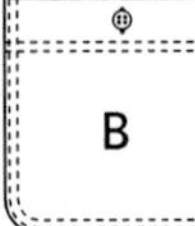

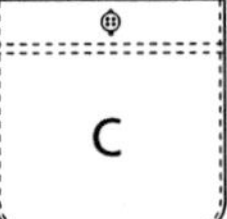

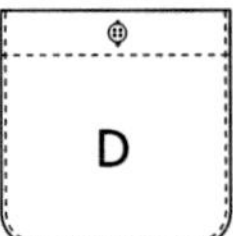

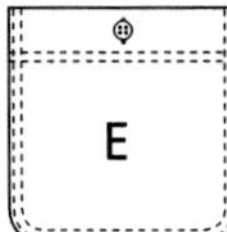

Topstitching choices for pocket:
a. 1/4" double needle topstitch set, edgestitch bendback – vertical buttonhole.
b. 1/4" double needle topstitch set and bendback.
c. 1/16" edgestitch set, 1/4'"double needle topstitch bendback.
d. 1/16" edgestitch set and bendback.
e. 1/4" double needle topstitch set and bendback – horizontal buttonhole.

Construction Details:
- Pocket bendback is a clean finished turn. Topstitch at 1" for single needle detail, or at 1" and 1 1/4" for double needle detail.
- Machine buttonhole centered on bendback.
- Reinforce inside button set with interfacing circles.
- Pocket bottom corners are rounded.

4. Flap pocket

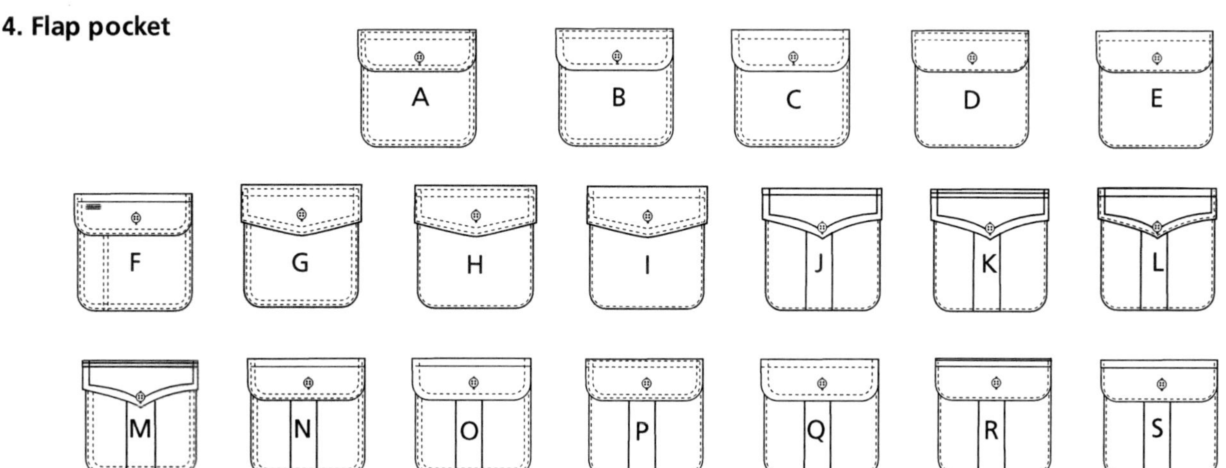

Topstitching choices for pocket:
a. 1/4″ double needle topstitch patch set, flap, and flap set.
b. 1/4″ double needle topstitch patch set and flap set, 1/4″ single needle topstitch flap.
c. 1/4″ double needle topstitch patch set, 1/4″ single needle topstitch flap and flap set.
d. 1/16″ edgestitch patch set and flap, 1/4″ double needle topstitch flap se.
e. 1/16″ edgestitch patch set and flap, 1/4″ single needle topstitch flap set.
f. 1/4″ double needle topstitch patch set, flap set, and pencil pocket, 1/4″ single needle topstitch flap.
g. 1/4″ double needle topstitch patch set and flap set, 1/4″ single needle topstitch flap.
h. 1/16″ edgestitch patch set, 1/4″ single needle topstitch flap, 1/4″ double needle topstitch flap.
i. 1/16″ edgestitch patch set and flap, 1/4″ single needle topstitch flap set.
j. 1/16″ edgestitch patch set, 1/4″ single needle topstitch flap and flap set.
k. 1/16″ edgestitch patch set, 1/4″ single needle topstitch flap, 1/4″ double needle topstitch flap set.
l. 1/16″ edgestitch patch set and flap, 1/4″ single needle topstitch flap set.
m. 1/4″ double needle topstitch patch set and flap set, 1/4″ single needle topstitch flap.
n. 1/4″ double needle topstitch patch set, flap, and flap set.
o. 1/4″ double needle topstitch patch set and flap set, 1/4″ single needle topstitch flap.
p. 1/16″ edgestitch patch set, 1/4″ double needle topstitch flap and flap set.
q. 1/16″ edgestitch patch set, 1/4″ singe needle topstitch flap and flap set.
r. 1/16″ edgestitch patch set and flap, 1/4′″double needle topstitch flap set.
s. 1/16″ edgestitch patch set and flap, 1/4″ single needle topstitch flap set.

Construction Details:
• Pocket bendback is 1″ wide clean finished with button centered.
• Pocket bottom corners are rounded.
• Pocket flap is set 1/4″ up from top edge of pocket (finished distance).
• Vertical machine buttonhole is centered on flap width.

Pocket version F:
• Pencil pocket is topstitched 1 1/2″ and 1 3/4″ in from pocket edge.
• Pocket flap has a 3/4″ long horizontal buttonhole for pencil pocket opening. Buttonhole is set 1/2″down from top edge of flap to buttonhole center, and 7/8″ in from CF edge of flap to buttonhole center.

Pocket versions J to S:
• 1″ wide box pleat centered on pocket. Pleat depth is 1/2″ each side.

5. Guide shirt pocket

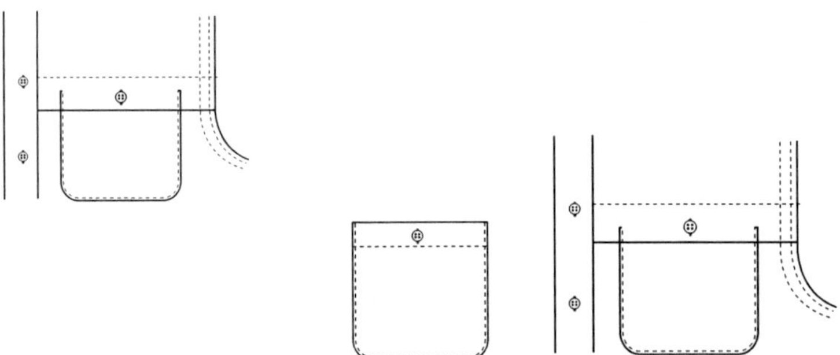

Construction Details:
Shirt front has a mock yoke (fold over) which serves as a pocket flap. Mock yoke is 1 1/4" wide with a centered vertical machine buttonhole. Pocket is set 1/4" below pocket flap seam/stitch line. 1/16" edgestitch patch pocket to set. Pocket bendback is 3/4" wide clean finished with 3/16" angled corner reinforcement stitching. Center button to bendback. Pocket bottom corners are rounded.

6. Patch pocket with clean finished pencil pocket

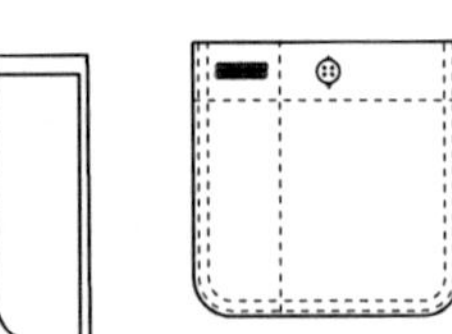

Construction Details:
1/4" double needle topstitch patch pocket to set. Pocket bendback is clean finished and topstitched at 1". One button/vertical buttonhole centered on bendback. Reinforce inside button set with a small circle of interfacing. Pencil pocket is a separate piece stitched to inside of patch pocket; turn edges under to clean finish and edgestitch to set. Pencil pocket is 1 3/4" wide finished. 3/4" horizontal machine buttonhole centered on pencil pocket bendback. Pocket bottom corners are rounded.

7. Angled bottom patch pocket

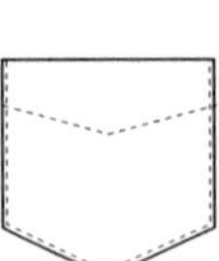

Construction Details:
Set pocket with an edgestitch. Pocket bendback is clean finished and edgestitched. Reinforce bendback at corners with 3/16" angled topstitching. Pocket bottom corners and bendback shape are angled.

Bound Buttonhole Construction

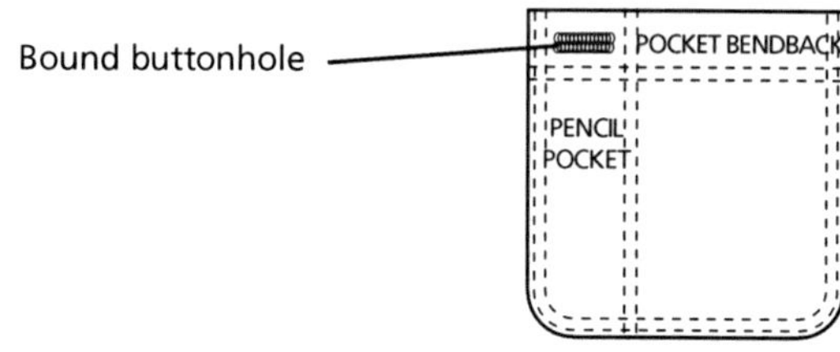

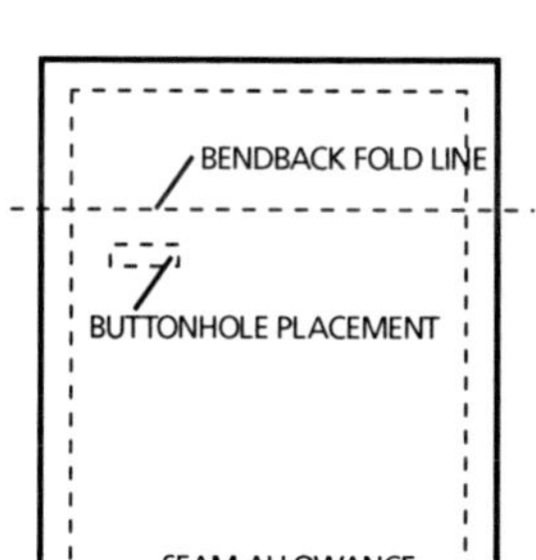

Pocket pattern piece with buttonhole placement

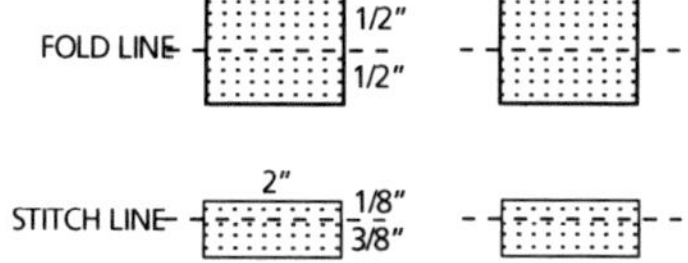

Cut 2 rectangles of self-fabric or other desired button-hole material– 2" long by 1" wide. This measurement allows 1/2" seam allowance on each end and 3/8" to set. Fold in half lengthwise.

Rectangles folded in half. Portion above the dotted line represents the 1/8" welt, and the portion below the dotted line represents the seam allowance.

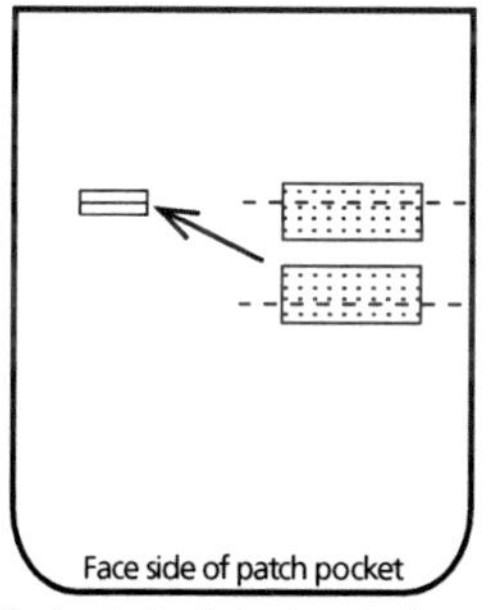

Set the two buttonhole pieces to the pocket, making sure to line up correctly over marked placement.

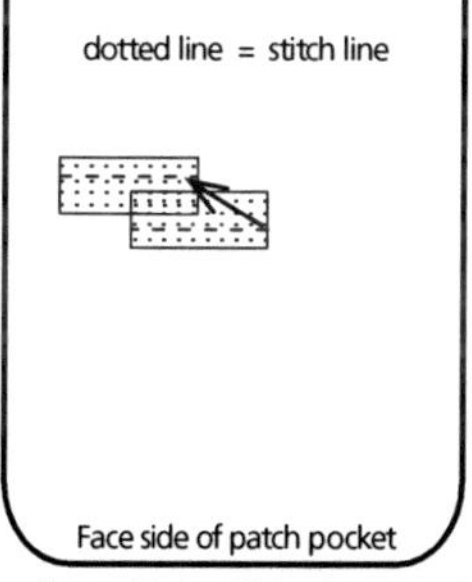

Pieces will need to be stitched on one at a time and they will overlap at the center.

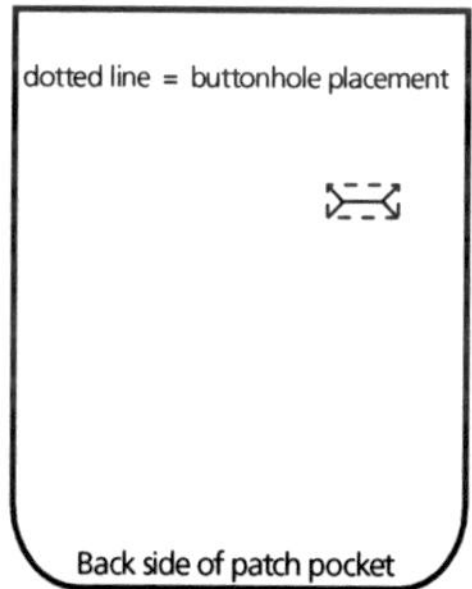

Turn pocket over and clip buttonhole. Be sure to clip right to the corners.

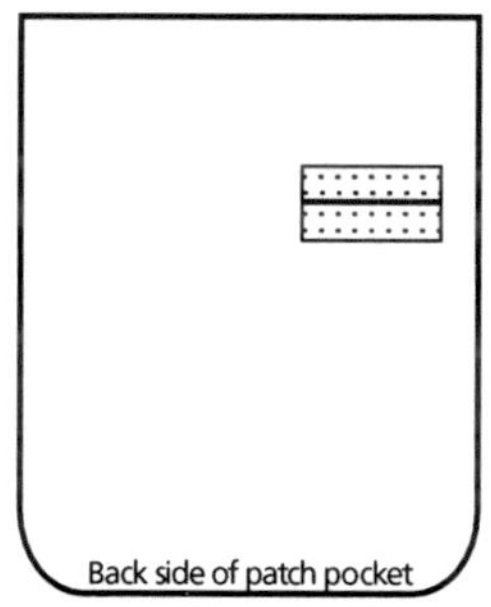

Push seam allowance of both rectangles through the center opening to the back side of the pocket.
(Optional: Stitch the triangle shaped clipped ends to the end of each seam allowance.)

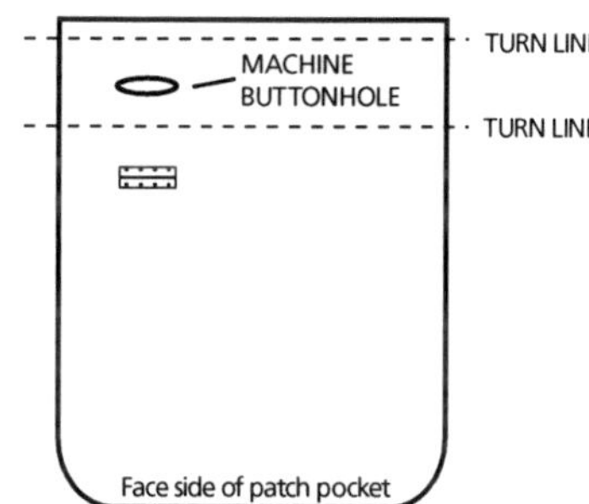

Stitch a 1" long horizontal machine buttonhole to pocket bendback, making sure its center will line up with the center of the bound buttonhole after the pocket bendback is turned.

Finished view of pocket

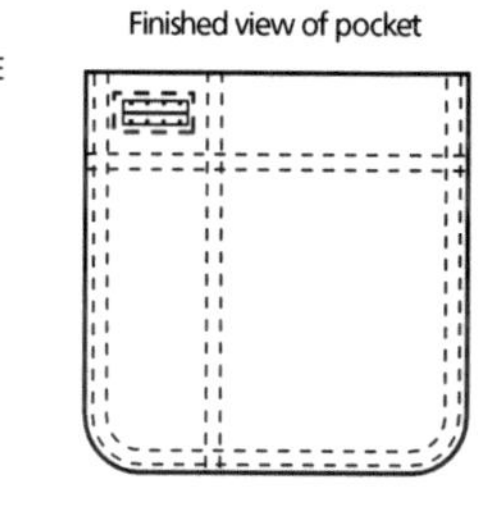

-Turn and topstitch pocket bendback
- 1/16" edgestitch a box around finished bound buttonhole through both layers of pocket bendback.
- Do not topstitch across top edge of pencil pocket.
- Set pocket to shirt.

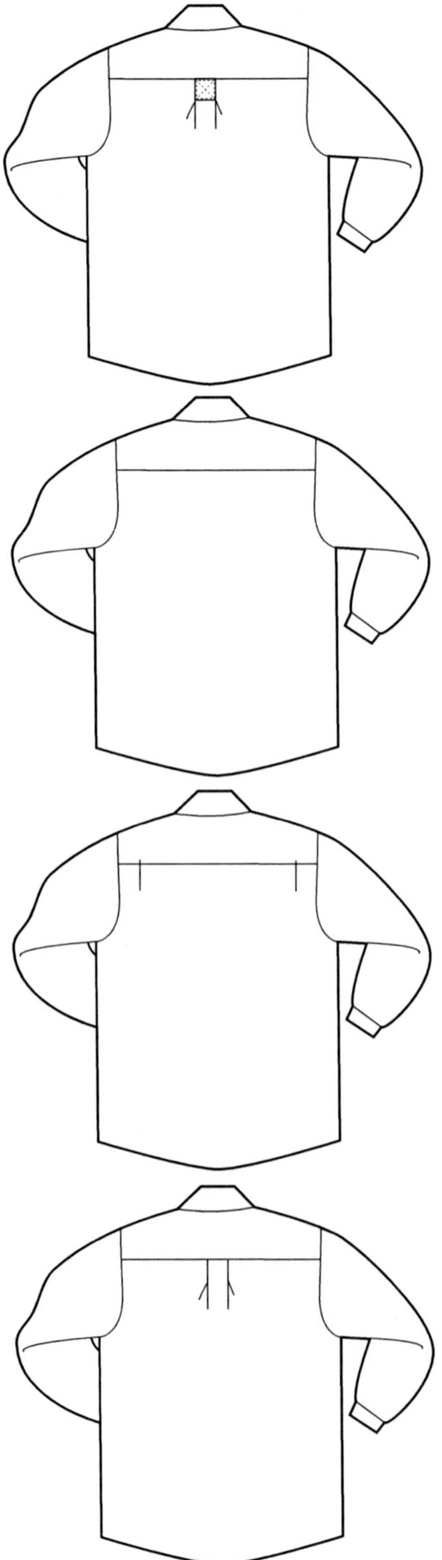

Center back:

Center back has a 1 1/2" x 1 1/2" box pleat; topstitch box at 1 3/8" by 1 3/8" and "X" topstitch inside of box.

Topstitching choices for yoke at shoulder and back:
a. 1/16" edgestitch
b. 1/4" single needle topstitch
c. 1/4" double needle topstitch
d. Triple needle topstitch, 1/8" between needles.

Plain shirt back:

Topstitching choices for yoke at shoulder and back:
a. 1/16" edgestitch
b. 1/4" single needle topstitch
c. 1/4" double needle topstitch
d. Triple needle topstitch, 1/8" between needles.

Shirt back has one pleat each side:

Shirt back has one pleat each side. Pleat is 3 1/2" in from finished armhole, 3/4" deep, and opens toward armhole.

Topstitching choices for yoke at shoulder and back:
a. 1/16" edgestitch
b. 1/4" single needle topstitch
c. 1/4" double needle topstitch
d. Triple needle topstitch, 1/8" between needles.

Center back has 1 1/2" wide box pleat:

Center back is a 1 1/2" wide box pleat; do not topstitch. (released pleat)

Topstitching choices for yoke at shoulder and back:
a. 1/16" edgestitch
b. 1/4" single needle topstitch
c. 1/4" double needle topstitch
d. Triple needle topstitch, 1/8" between needles.

Side Seam and Hem Details

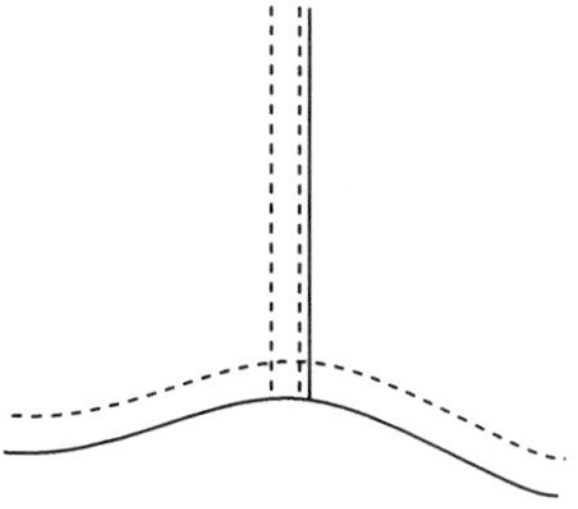

Standard side seam; hem shaped with shirt tails. 5/16" double turn with 1/4" single needle topstitch.

Side seam with vent, hem is straight/squared.

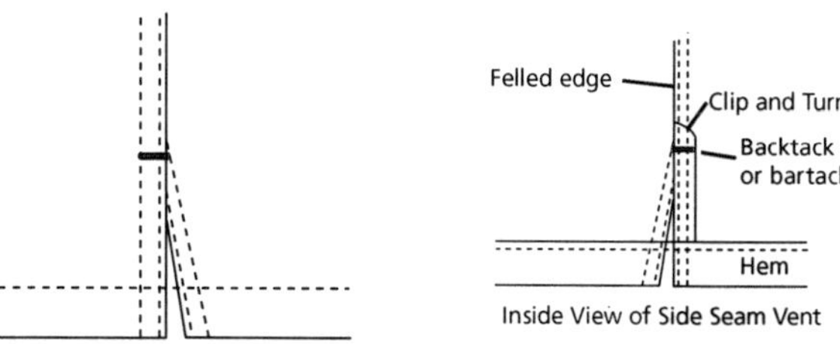

Inside View of Side Seam Vent

Slit choices:
a. 2" long slit
b. 3" long slit
Hem choices:
1. Clean finished turn with 1/4" topstitch
2. Clean finished turn with 1/2" topstitch
3. Clean finished turn with 1" topstitch.

Side seam with slit, hem is straight/squared.

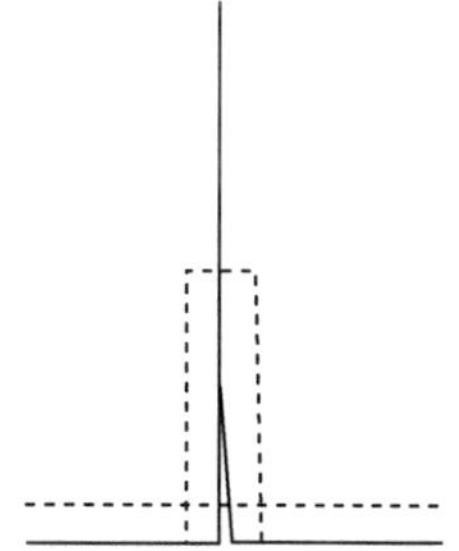

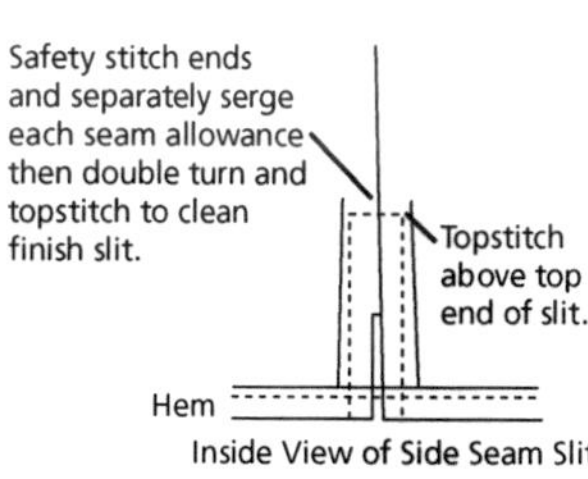

Inside View of Side Seam Slit

Slit choices:
a. 2" long slit – clean finished turn with 1/4" topstitch
b. 2" long slit – clean finished turn with 1/2" topstitch
c. 3" long slit – clean finished turn with 1/4" topstitch
d. 3" long slit – clean finished turn with 1/2" topstitch

Hem choices:
1. Clean finished turn with 1/4" topstitch
2. Clean finished turn with 1/2" topstitch
3. Clean finished turn with 1" topstitch
4. Serged turn with 1" topstitch

Side seam with slit, hem is straight/squared.

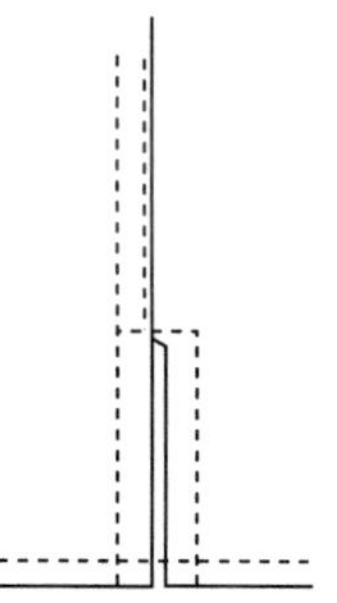

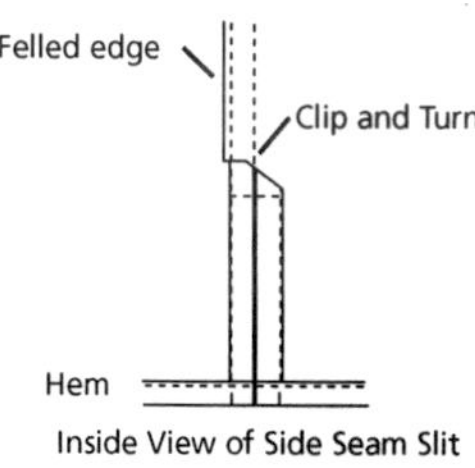

Inside View of Side Seam Slit

Slit choices:
a. 2" long slit – clean finished turn with 1/4" topstitch
b. 2" long slit – clean finished turn with 1/2" topstitch
c. 3" long slit – clean finished turn with 1/4" topstitch
d. 3" long slit – clean finished turn with 1/2" topstitch

Hem choices:
1. Clean finished turn with 1/4" topstitch
2. Clean finished turn with 1/2" topstitch
3. Clean finished turn with 1" topstitch
4. Serged turn with 1" topstitch

Hang Loop Details

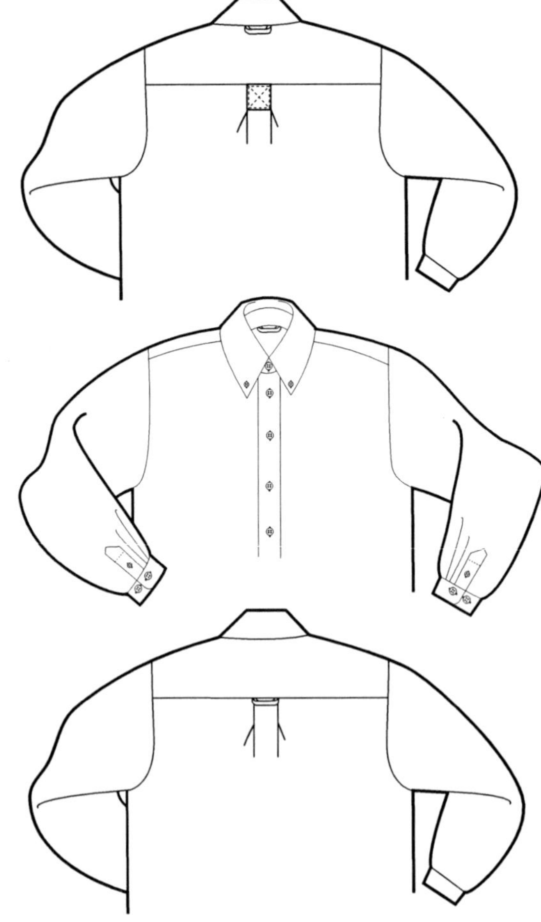

1. Hang loop is set to outside back neck.

- Center loop at CB.
- Loop is set when stitching the collar stand/back yoke seam.

2. Hang loop is set to inside back neck.

- Center loop at CB.
- Loop is set when stitching the collar stand/back yoke seam.

3. Hang loop is set to outside back.

- Center loop at CB.
-Loop is set when stitching the back yoke/shirt back seam.

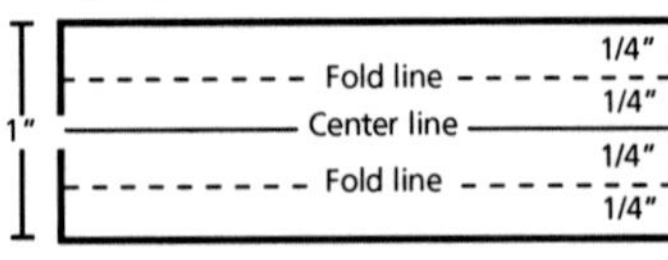

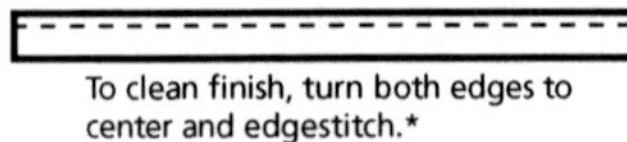

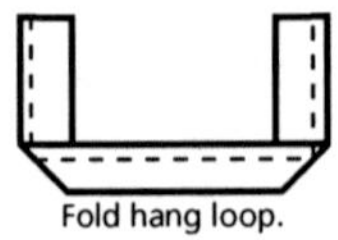

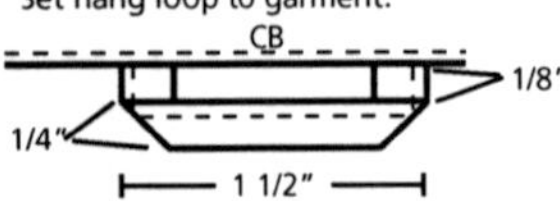

*These steps are necessary for hang loops made of shell fabric. If using twill tape, etc, can just fold and set to garment.

BOTTOMS AND TROUSERS WORKMANSHIP STANDARDS

Cargo Pants

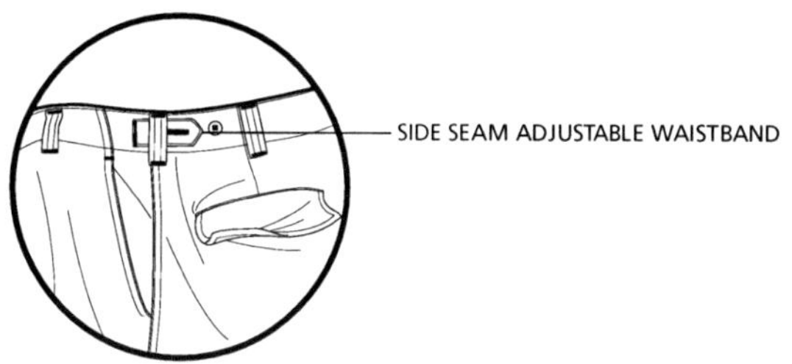

Trousers

INSIDE MEN'S/WOMEN'S TROUSER
WITH 1/2 LINING. LINING SHOULD
ALWAYS GO ON TOP OF POCKETS
EDGE OF LINING HAS RAW FINISH.

INSIDE WAIST FOR FORMAL MEN'S
TROUSER
PRE-MADE WAISTBAND

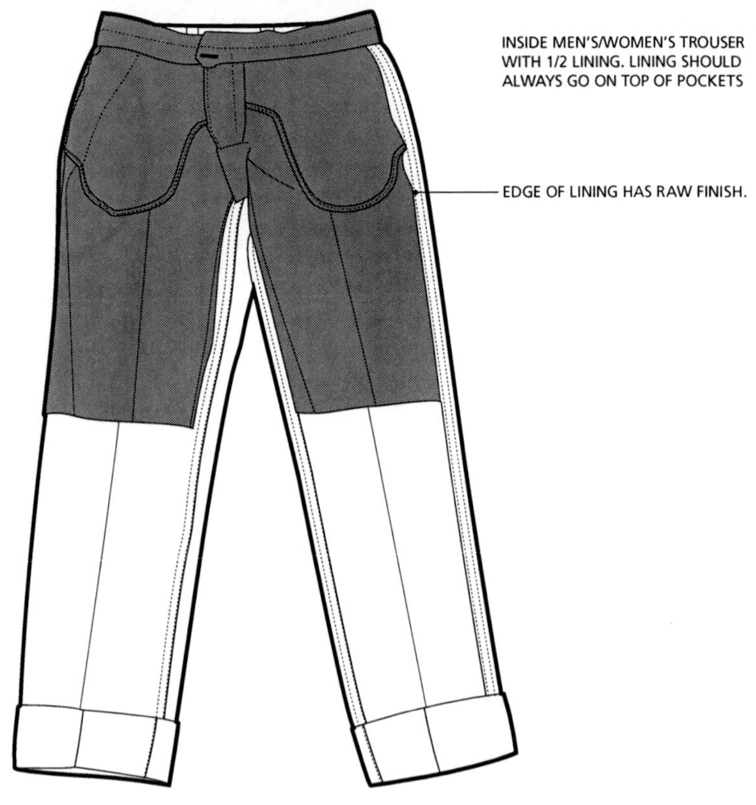

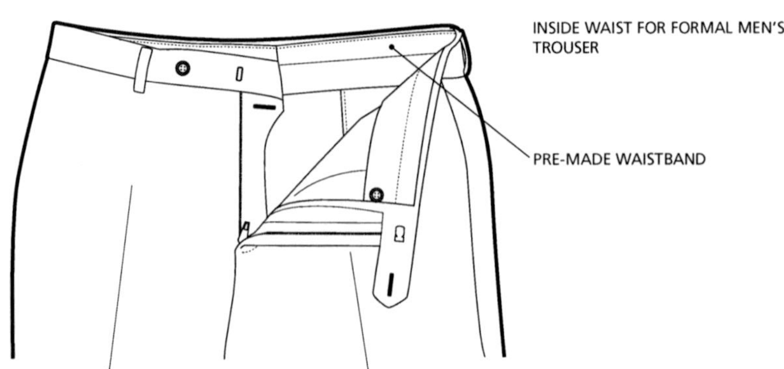

Waistbands:

A) Hollywood Waistband:
Waistband has self-fabric separate piece inside waistband facing, clean finished.

Buttonhole: Keyhole buttonhole on left front set 1⁄2″ from edge (opening should be 3⁄4″).

Button placement: Set on right above fly seam.

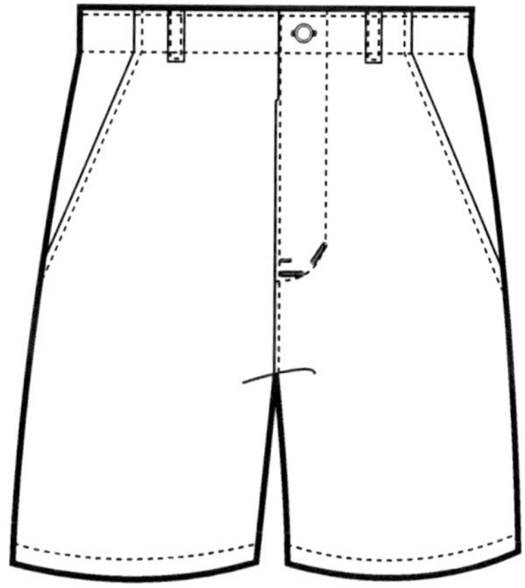

B) Reverse Hollywood Waistband:
All same piece, no separate waistband. Waistband has self-fabric facing, width as specified, sewn to outside of panel at waistband. Clean finished.

Buttonhole: Keyhole buttonhole on left front set 1⁄2″ from edge (opening should be 3⁄4″).

Button placement set on right above fly seam.

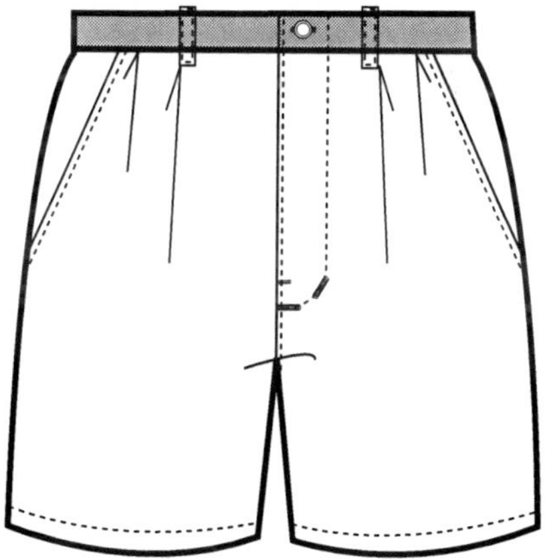

C) Standard One-Piece Waistband:
One piece finished width as specified. Bendback is clean finished all around, with top stitching as specified in construction details (as per spec).

Buttonhole: Keyhole buttonhole on left front set 1⁄2″ from edge (opening should be 3⁄4″).

Button placement set on right above fly seam.

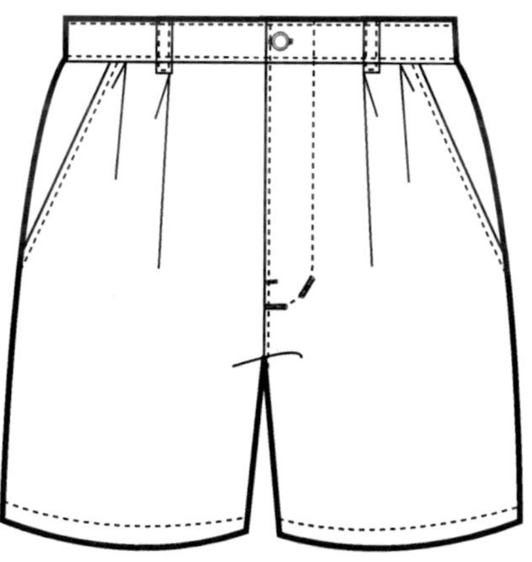

Waistbands:

D) Standard Two-Piece Waistband:
Two pieces finished width as specified. Waistband is split at centerback for tailoring, otherwise same construction as one-piece. Bendback is clean finished all around, top stitching as specified in construction details.

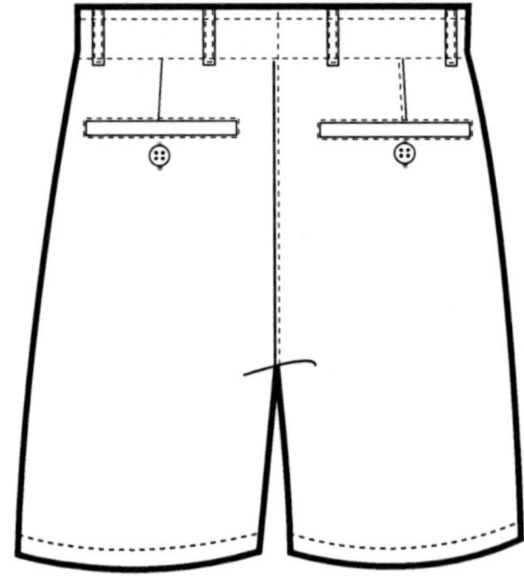

Buttonhole: Keyhole buttonhole on left front set 1/2" from edge (opening should be 3/4").

Button placement: Set on right above fly seam.

E) Classic Curtain Waistband:
One- or two-piece waistband* finished width as specified. Inside bendback extends 3/8" below waistband length to form curtain. Bottom edge of facing is bound with 1/4" bias binding.

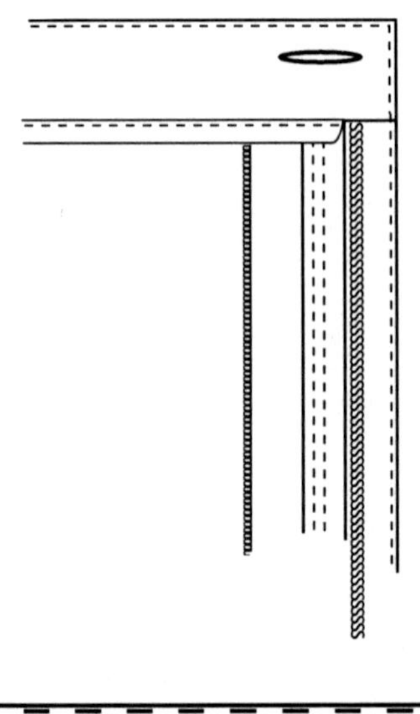

Buttonhole: Keyhole buttonhole on left front set 1/2" from edge (opening should be 3/4").

Button placement: Set on right above fly seam. See sketch.

*Two-piece classic construction is exactly the same as above, with a split seam in the back for tailoring.

F) Trouser Curtain Waistband:
Two- or three-piece waistband* finished width as specified, clean finished. Separate piece of self-fabric is edgestitched to inside waistband only, extending 3/8" below finished waistband to form inside curtain. Edge of facing is bound with 1/4" bias binding.

* Three-piece trouser construction is exactly the same as above, except with a seam in the back for tailoring.

Waistbands:

G) Standard Formal Separate Facing Waistband:
Two-piece waistband finished width as specified. Inside facing is separate piece stripping (as specified in spec sheet), which is clean finished to the customer's logo tape. Total width of inside curtain as specified in spec sheet.
Waistband is finished with stitching as specified in construction details (on spec).

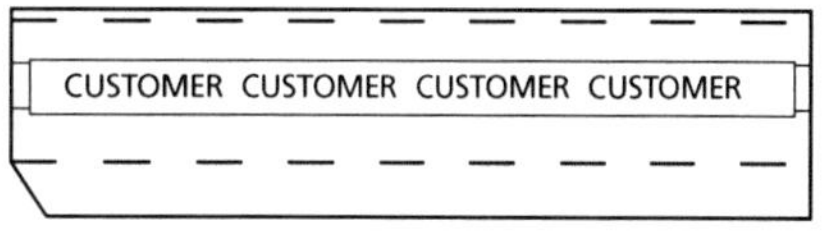

Buttonhole: Keyhole buttonhole on left front set 1⁄2" from edge (opening should be 3⁄4").

Button placement: Set on right above fly seam.

H) Premium Formal Separate Facing Waistband:
Two-piece waistband finished width as specified. Inside waistband consists of herringbone (do same for pocketing) cut in strips and edgestitched to the customer's logo ribbon on both sides forming waistband facing. Facing is 2" wide finished. Outside waistband is finished as specified in construction details (on spec).

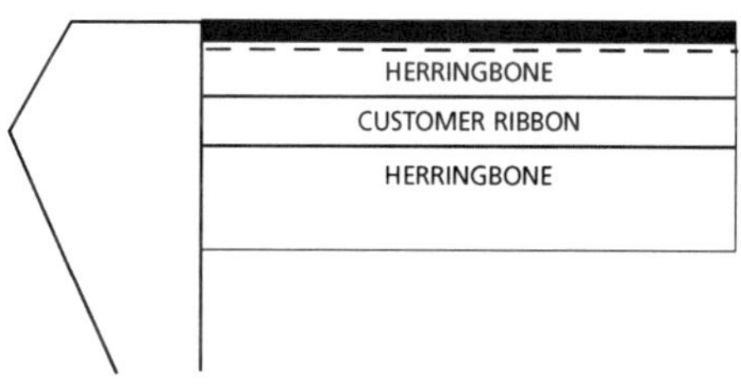

Buttonhole: Keyhole buttonhole on left front set 1⁄2" from edge (opening should be 3⁄4").

Button placement: Set on right above fly seam.

I) Waistband with Twill Facing:
Two-piece waistband. Inside piece is faced with 100% cotton twill. Pieces are clean finished and edgestitched all around.

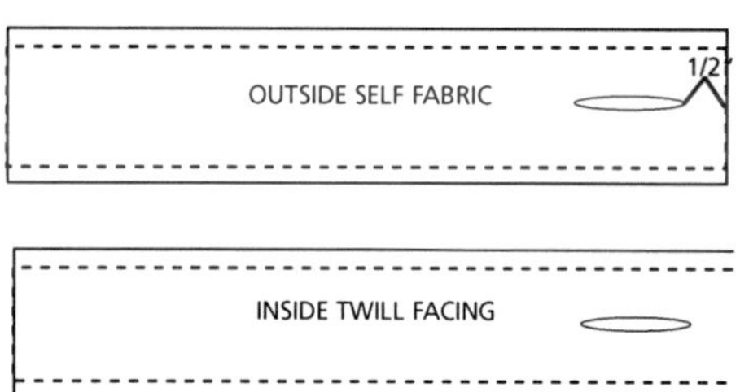

Buttonhole: Keyhole buttonhole on left front set 1⁄2" from edge (opening should be 3⁄4").

Button placement: Set on right above fly seam.

Waistbands:

J) Elastic Waistband:

Full elastic waistband. Waistband should be all one piece (inside is bendback, rather than separate piece). Waistband has either three or four rows of topstitching placed as specified in construction details. Do not edgestitch along the top edge of Waistband. Inside waistband has 1⁄2" vertical buttonholes placed 3⁄4" from center front seam for drawcord (if applicable).

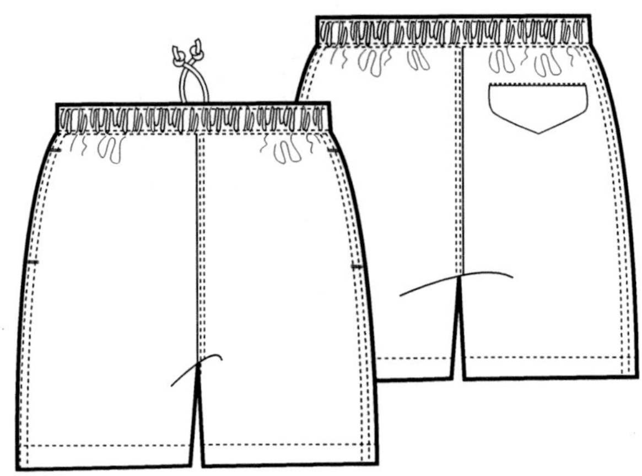

K) Half-Elastic Waistband:

One-piece outside waistband with 5 piece inside self facing, pieced to encase elastic on sides only. Back and front are plain. Specify details for size of waistband and elastic. Waistband is edgestitched at bottom to set, and 1⁄4" double needle topstitched at center of waistband on back and sides only. (Front pieces are open). Other waistband finishing is as specified in construction details.

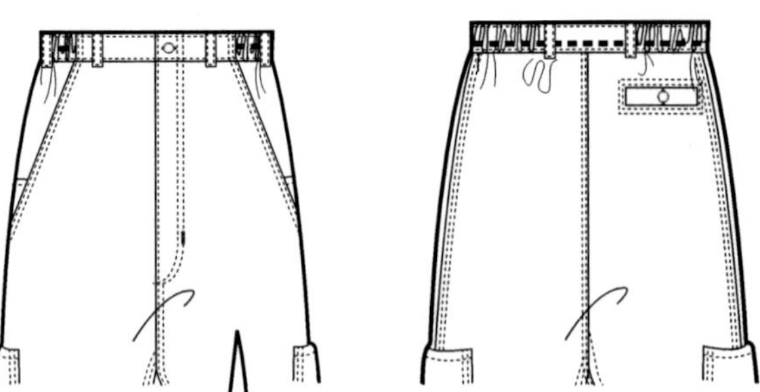

Belt Loops:

A) Standard:

Specify placement and dimensions. Bottom of loops are sewn into waistband. Top and bottom of belt loops are bartacked. Raw edges should be trimmed to eliminate fraying. Specification for finishing: see F "Finishing details" below.

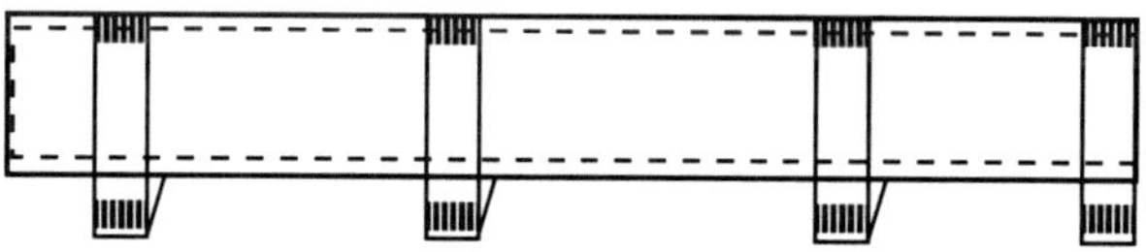

B) Rugged:

Specify placement and dimensions. Top and bottom loops are bartacked. Raw edges should be trimmed to eliminate fraying. See specification for finishing: see F "Finishing details" below.

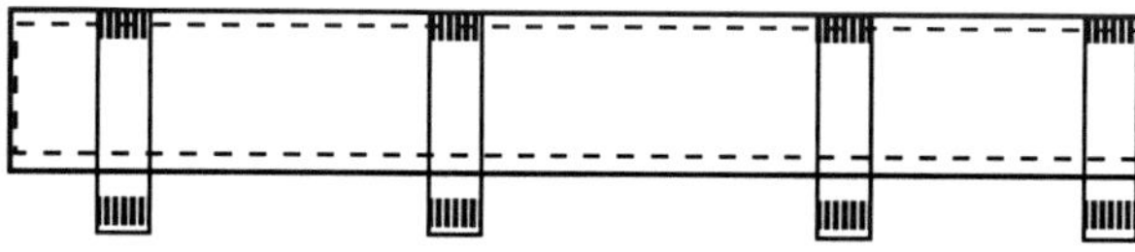

C) Classic:

Specify placement and dimensions. Bottom of loops are sewn into waistband. Top and bottom of belt loops are bartacked. Bottom bartack is hidden. Raw edges should be trimmed to eliminate fraying. See specification for finishing: see F "Finishing details" below.

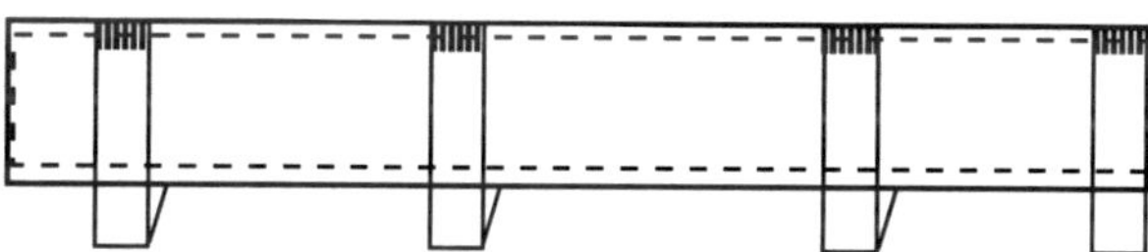

D) Wide:

Specify placement and dimensions. 1/4" horizontal bartack at all four corners. Raw edges should be trimmed to eliminate excessive fraying. See specification for finishing: see F "Finishing details" below.

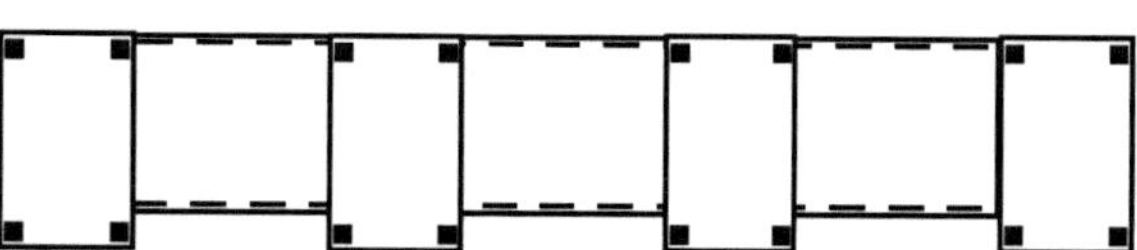

E) Leather Patch:

Placed on back waistband on wearer's right. Specify placement. Patch is edgestitched on top and bottom, which forms functional belt loop. Bartack on all four corners. Patch is washed separately and then placed on garment.

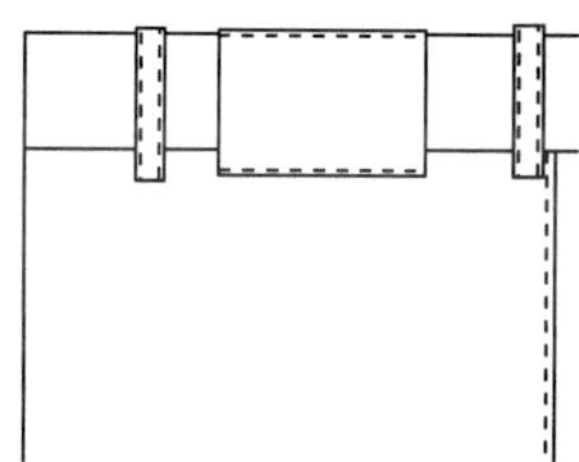

F) Finishing Details:

- Edgestitching: Belt loops are 2-ply and edgestitched.
- Topstitching: Belt loops are 2-ply and 1/4" double needle topstitched.

Coverstitching: Single piece, belt loop raw edges are caught in coverstitching (merrowed). 1/4" double needle finished.

Pockets:

A) Box Pleat Cargo Pocket

- Cargo pocket with flap. Placement as specified, centered on side seam.
- Size should be as specified on measurement sheets. (Total measurements will include flap measurements.)
- 1 1⁄2" bellows on front and back of pocket.
- Pocket has 1 1⁄2" box pleat down centered. Pleat is 3⁄4" deep. (1 1⁄2" total).
- Pocket is 1⁄4" double needle topstitched all around. Pleat may or may not be topstitched on sides. If so, pleat must not be stitched down.
- 1⁄4" angled bartack extending from each bottom corner.
- If snaps: Hidden at bottom flap corner edges (3⁄4" from edge) with 1⁄4" single needle topstitch entire flap with 1⁄2" vertical bartack extending from top flap corner edges.
- If buttons: Top Flap: Top flap piece with hidden under flap. Set flap with 1⁄4" double needle topstitch along top. 1⁄4" horizontal bartacks at corners. 1⁄4" single needle topstitch at side and bottom of flap.
- Hidden flap: 1⁄4" single needle topstitch at sides and edge stitch at bottom edge. Two 1" vertical buttonholes placed 1 1⁄4" from each side and 1⁄2" above bottom edge.

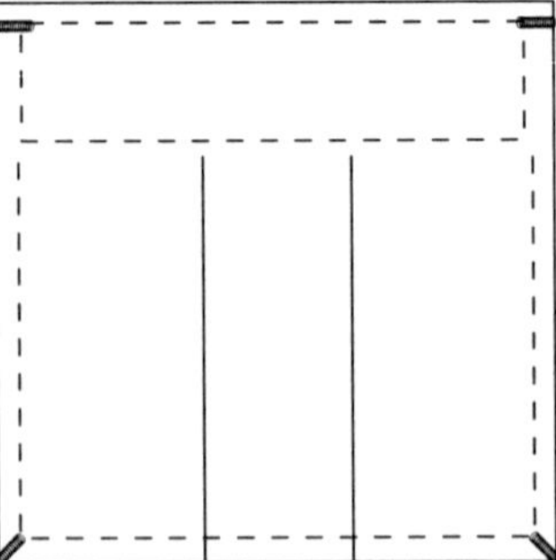

B) Asparated Cargo Pocket:

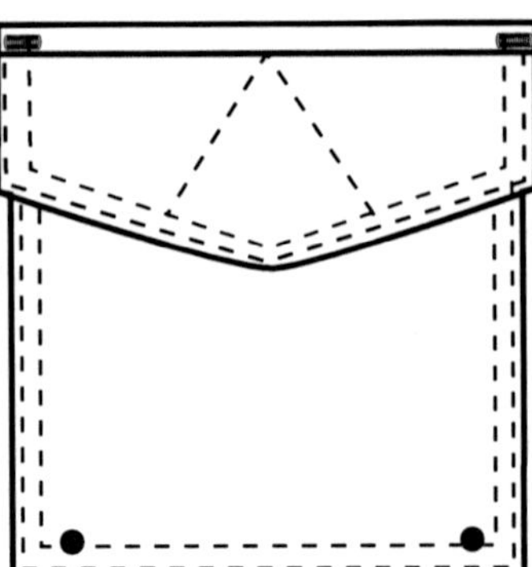

- Placed as specified on measurements sheet.
- Flap set above pocket with closure (hook and loop fastener tab, X-stitched. Set hook to flap, loop to pocket, or button or snap).
- 1" inverted box pleat at center of pocket. Pleat is not stitched down. Bottom dissipates into pocket (but adds extra fullness). Pleat depth 1⁄2".
- Double needle topstitch around flap except at top. Please use 1⁄4" topstitch at top flap edge.
- Some pockets will ask for grommets at corners of pocket (as sketch). These should be whip-stitched grommets, not metal.

See specification package for other details.

Pockets:

C) Jean Patch Pocket (Work Jean Type):

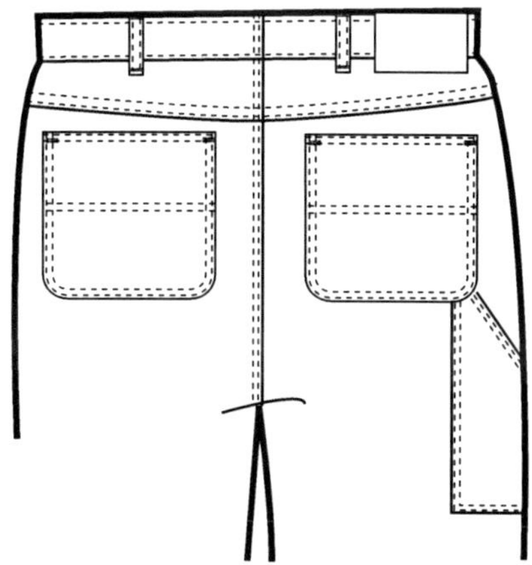

- One squared patch pocket with rounded bottom edges at each back leg panel.
- Actual pocket dimensions must be indicated in specification package.
- 1/4" double needle entire pocket, with 3/8" angular bar tacks extending from top pocket corner edges.
- 1/4" horizontal double needle topstitch placed 3" below pocket opening.

D) Standard Patch Pocket (Standard Five-Pocket Jean/Twill Type):

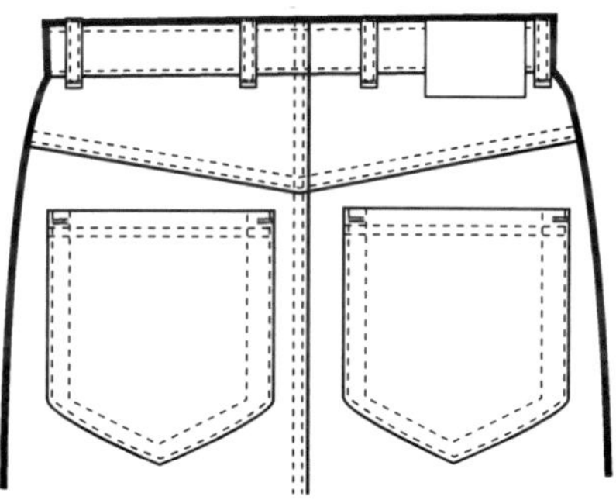

- One patch pocket at each back leg panel.
- Actual pocket dimensions must be indicated in specification package.
- 1/4" double needle topstitch at top opening with 5/8" topstitching at sides tapering to 1/4" double needle along sides. 1/4" double needle at bottom pocket.
- 3/4" horizontal bartack at top corners. Pocket placement should be specified on measurement sheet.

E) Besom (Double Welt) Pocket:

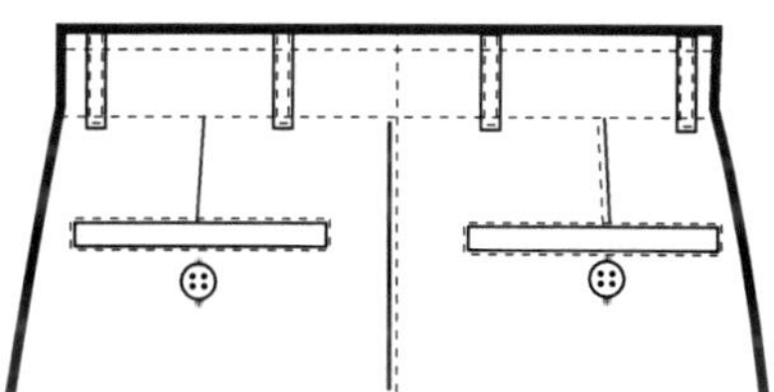

- See specification package for dimensions, placements.
- Facings can be clean finished with edge stitching or serge and single needle coverstitched.
- Edgestitch entire welt pocket.
- Pocket bags are safety stitched, turned, and 1/4" topstitched.
- 1" vertical keyhole buttonhole placed 3/8" under bottom welt and centered.
- Button is placed to correspond.

Pockets:

F) Single Welt Pocket:

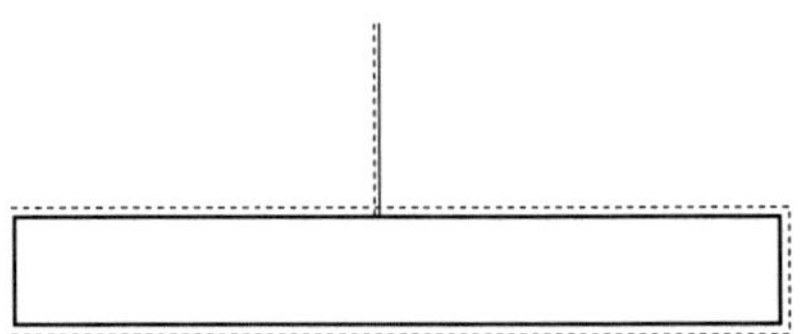

- See specification package for opening measurement.
- Edgestitch entire welt.
- Pocket has 1⁄2" vertical bartack at each side.
- Welt height is 1⁄2".
- 3⁄4" buttonhole placed 3/8" below welt pocket and centered.
- Button set to correspond 3/8" below edge.
- Back pocket is placed as specified.

G) Reverse Quarter Top Pocket:

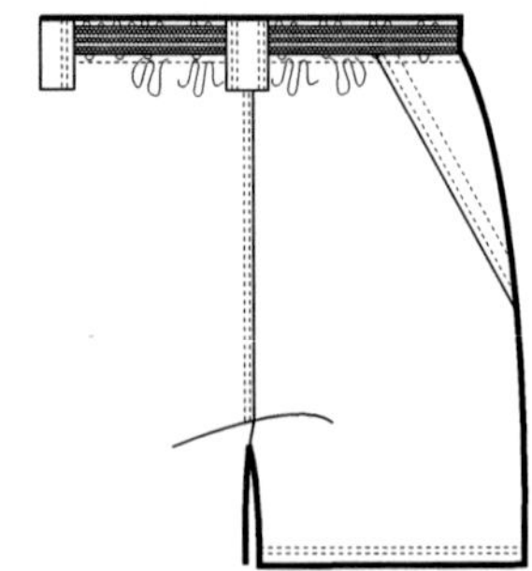

- Reverse 1⁄4 top pocket with hidden zipper.
- See specification package for pocket dimensions.
- Top of pocket is flap (to cover zipper). Flap is edgestitched and single needle topstitched at 5/8".
- Zipper is set beneath, and is edgestitched and serged to top pocket opening and facing, and edgestitched and serged to bottom pocket opening.
- Zipper head is at the bottom when closed.
- Inside of pocket has 2" self-fabric facing.
- Pocket bag is mesh or other specified fabric. Seams are overlocked.

H) On-Seam Pocket:

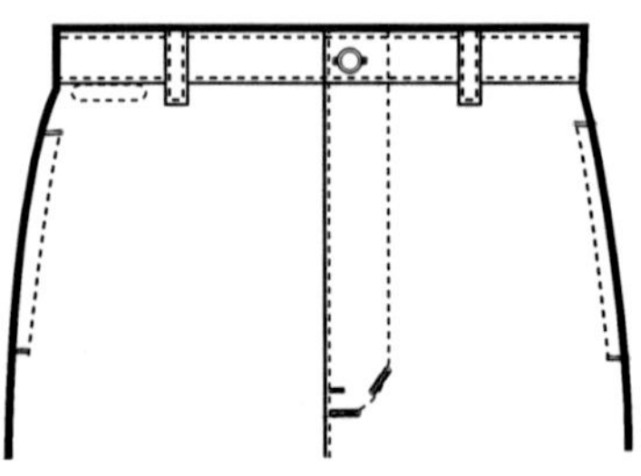

- On-seam pocket. See specification package for actual dimensions.
- 1⁄4" single needle topstitch with 1⁄4" horizontal bar tack at top and bottom pocket opening.
- Top bartacking is 1 1⁄4" below waistband.
- Facing should be clean finished with edge stitching.

I) Standard Coin Pocket:

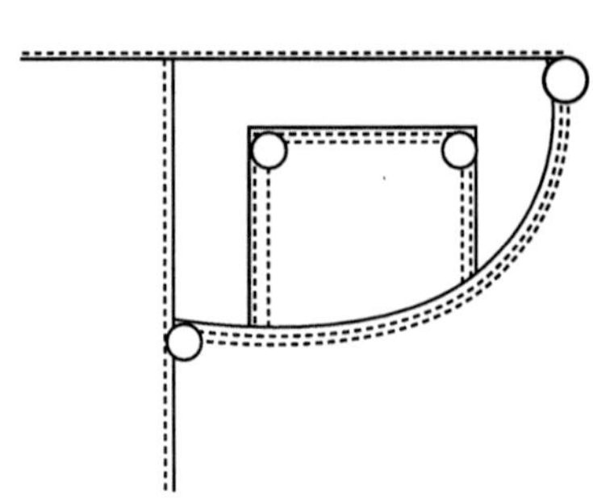

- Hem: double needle topstitch, double needle set pocket.
- Position: 1 1⁄4" from bottom of the waistband, 1 1⁄4" over from side seam.
- Label set 1⁄2" below coin pocket opening.
- Pocket opening: 3".
- Rivets at top pocket corners.

Pockets:

J) Designer Coin Pocket:

- See specification for dimensions.
- Hem is 1⁄4" double needle edgestitched.
- Pocket is 1 1⁄4" from bottom of waistband and 1 1⁄4" from side seam.
- Rivet placed at top left corner only.
- Inside edge of coin pocket is invisible and attaches to inside facing of scoop pocket with single needle topstitching. Whole edge (all pieces of facing are serged).

If pocket calls for label, it will placed 1⁄2" below waistband.

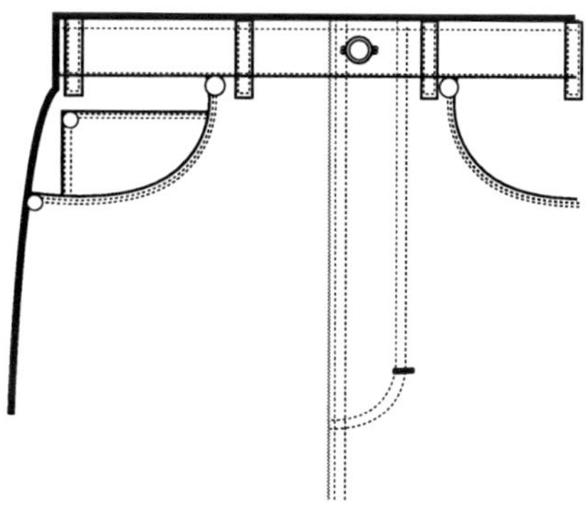

K) Besom Coin Pocket:

- Double-welt coin pocket (for non-scoop pockets). See specification for dimensions.
- Vertical bartack at sides.
- Edgestitch at top and bottom.
- Placement is 1 3⁄4" from top waistband edge and 1 3⁄4" from side seam.

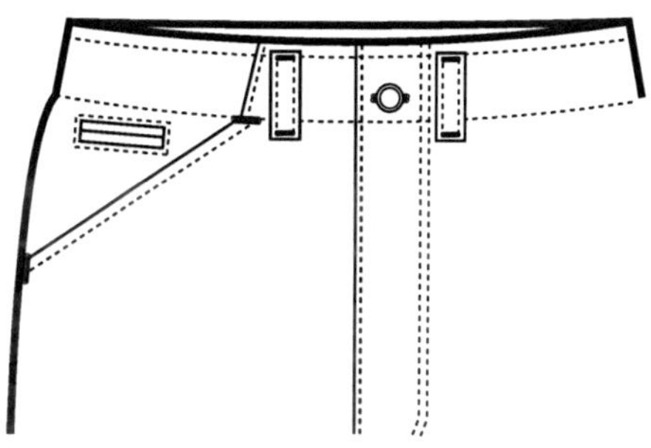

L) Watch Pocket:

- Single welt, placed on waistband seam. See specification for dimensions.
- Pocket is placed 2" from side seam (for men's size 34 or M, or as specified in your specification package).
- Vertical bartacks at each side.
- Edgestitch sides and bottom of pocket.

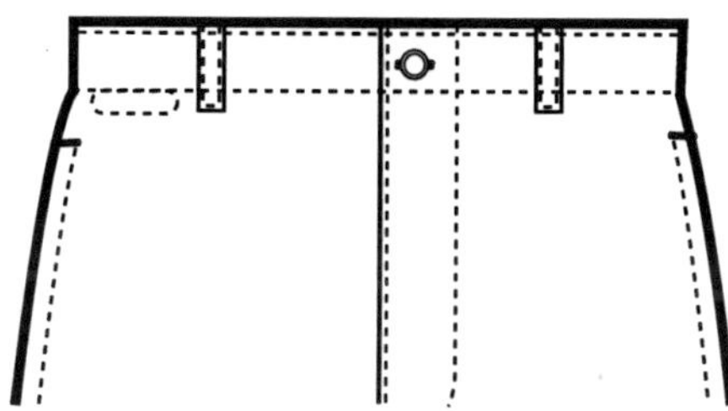

M) Utility Pocket:

- Placed at the back right corner of wearer's back right pocket.
- See specification package for dimensions.
- 1⁄4" double needle topstitch entire pocket with 3/8" angular bartacks extending from bottom corner (side closest to inseam).

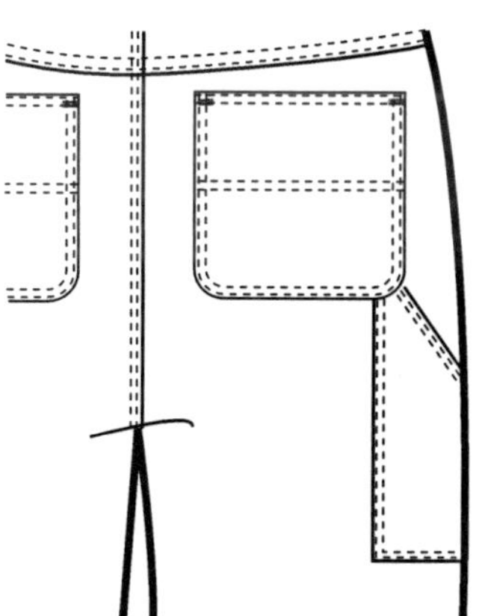

Notes on Pocket Flaps:

- Placements are as follows*:

a) Welt Pockets: directly above top of pocket.
b) Besom Pockets: under top welt (tuxedo style).
c) Patch and Cargo Pockets: 1/2" above top of pocket for buttons, 7/8" above top of pocket for snaps.

* Unless otherwise specified on specification.

Fly Closures:

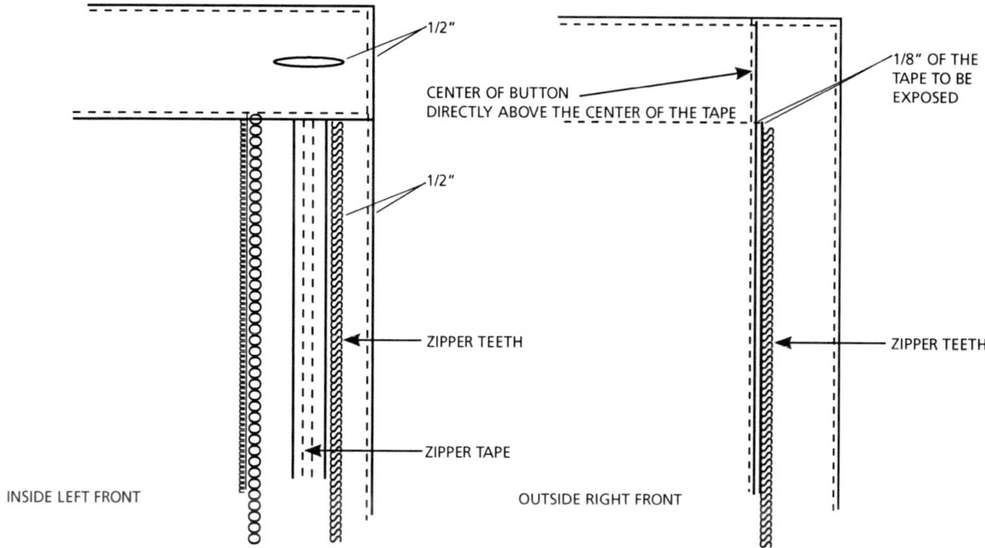

A) Standard Zip Fly:

- Center front zipper.
- See specification for length. Zipper will be 1⁄2" shorter than finished fly length.
- Left Fly: "J" stitch, single needle topstitch and edge stitch at center front edge.
- Horizontal bartack at "J" stitch base and 6 1⁄2" below waistband along "J" stitch.
- Right Fly: Edge stitch and serged.

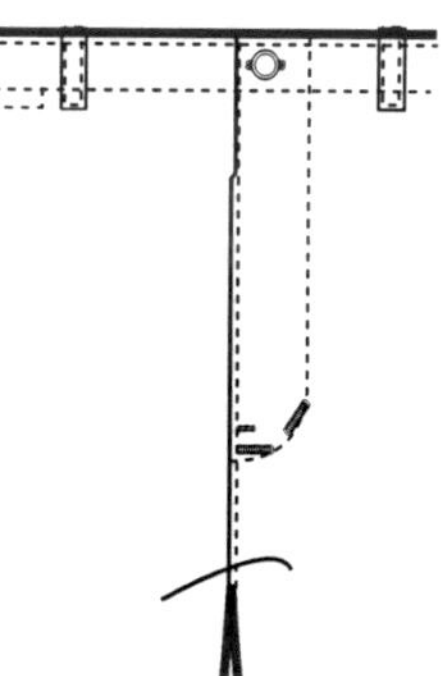

B) Casual Zip Fly:

- Center front zipper.
- See specification for length. Zipper will be 1⁄2" shorter than finished fly length.
- Left Fly: "J" stitch, 1⁄4" double needle topstitch and edge stitch at center front edge.
- Horizontal bartack at "J" stitch base and on inside "J" stitch 6 1⁄2" below waistband.
- Right Fly: Edgestitch and serged.

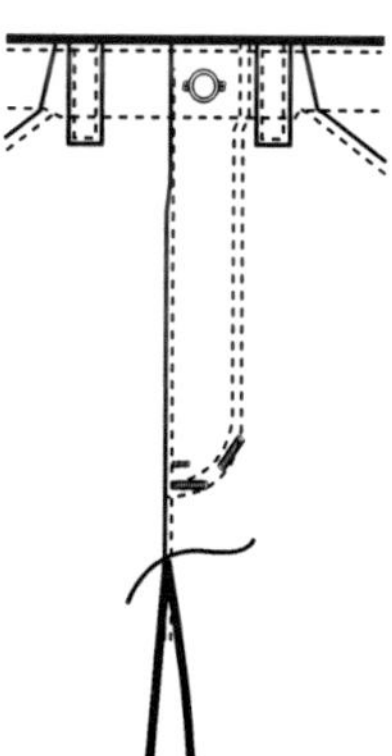

Fly Closures:

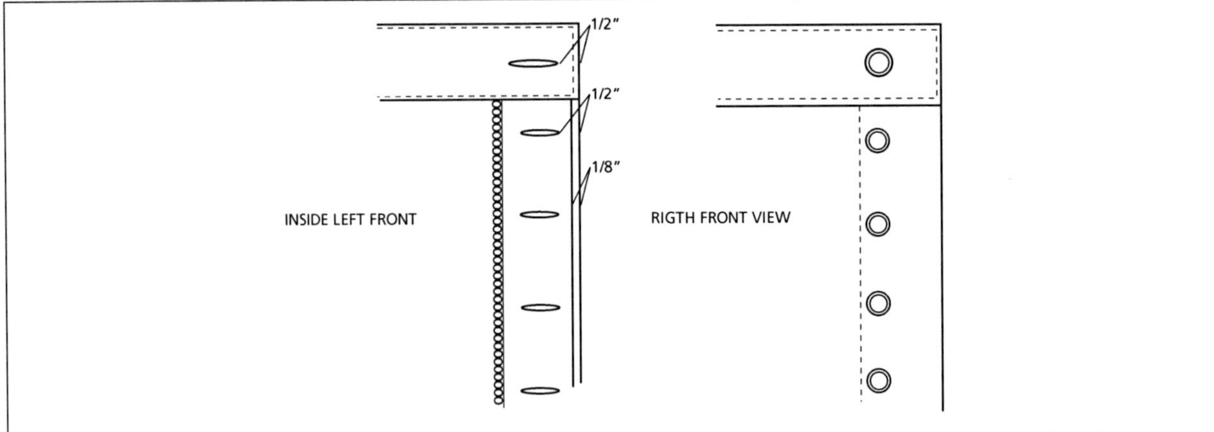

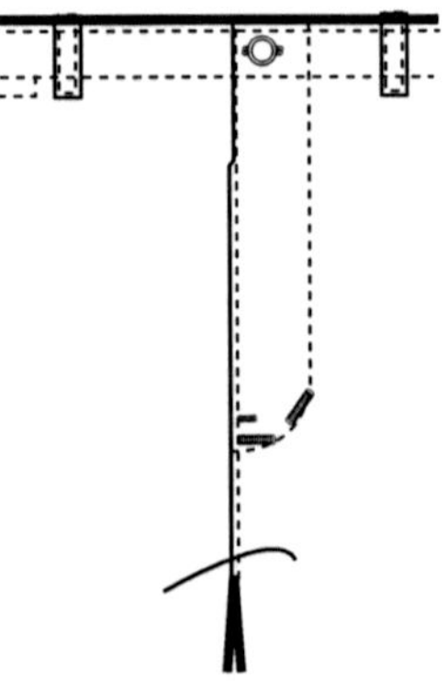

C) Standard Button Fly:

- See specification for measurements.
- Right Fly:
  - a) Facing is 1⁄2" longer than finished fly length.
  - b) Serged and edgestitched.
  - c) 24L button placed 1" below waistband on facing.
  - e) Remaining buttons evenly spaced 13⁄4" apart, or as measurement specified.
- Left Fly (2 pieces):

  Top fly:

  a) Edgestitched with 1 1⁄2" single needle "J" stitch.

  b) 1⁄4" horizontal bartack at base of fly and on "J" stitch 6 1⁄2" below waistband.

  Bottom:

  a) 2" facing placed 1/8" from top fly edge, and serged.

  b) 7/8" horizontal buttonhole placed 1" below waistband.

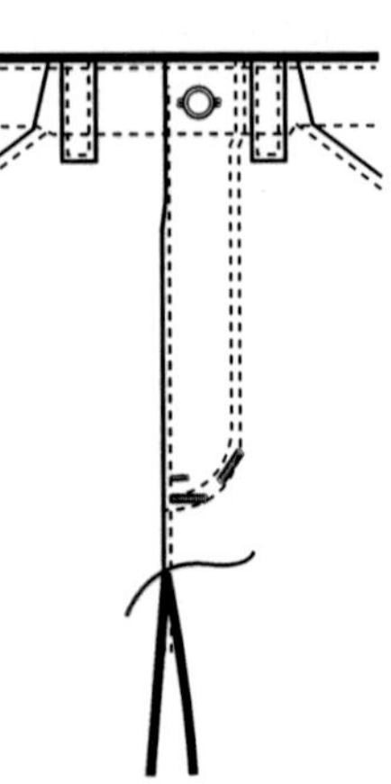

D) Casual Button Fly:

- See specification for measurements.
- Right Fly:
  - a) Facing is 1⁄2" longer than finished fly length.
  - b) Serged and edgestitched.
  - c) 24L button placed 1" below waistband on facing.
  - d) Remaining buttons evenly spaced 13⁄4" apart, or as measurement specified.
- Left Fly (2 pieces) :

  Top fly:

  a) Edgestitched with 1⁄4" double needle "J" stitch at 1 3⁄4".

  b) 1⁄4" horizontal bartack at base of fly and on inside "J" stitch 6 1⁄2" below waistband.

  Bottom:

  a) 2" facing placed 1/8" from top fly edge and serged.

Fly Closures:

E) New French Fly (Extended Fly Facing):

- Waistband extends 2 1⁄2″ along top. Facing extends as well and is sewn to fly and waistband extension.
- 3⁄4″ horizontal buttonhole placed 3/8″ from waistband edge and centered.
- Stay button at inside waistband, placed to correspond with buttonhole. See sketch.

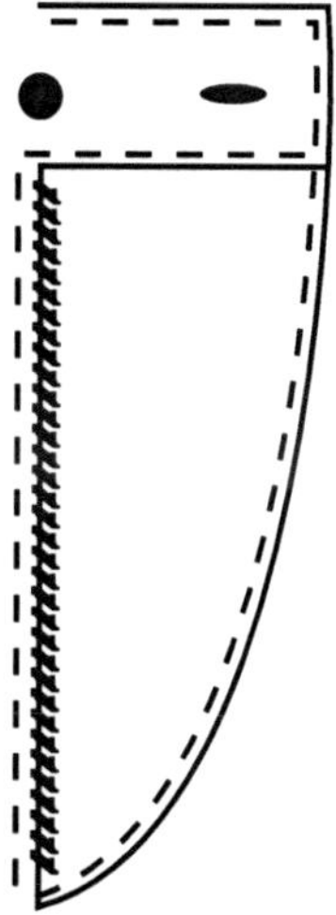

Hems:

A) Standard Hem:

- 1 1⁄2″ turn with 1⁄2″ turn under.
  Single needle topstitch at 1″.

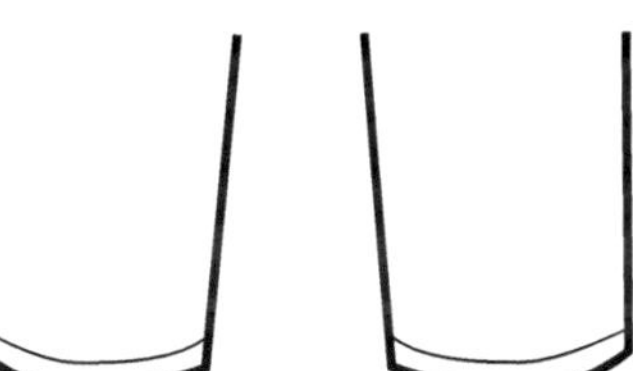

B) Jean Hem:

- 5/8″ fold and turn back.
  1⁄2″ single needle topstitch.

C) Cuffed Hem:

- 21⁄4″ double turn under and single needle topstitch at 2″.
- 5/8″ (from seam) fold to form 1 1⁄4″ cuff.
  Stitch sides down along side seam.

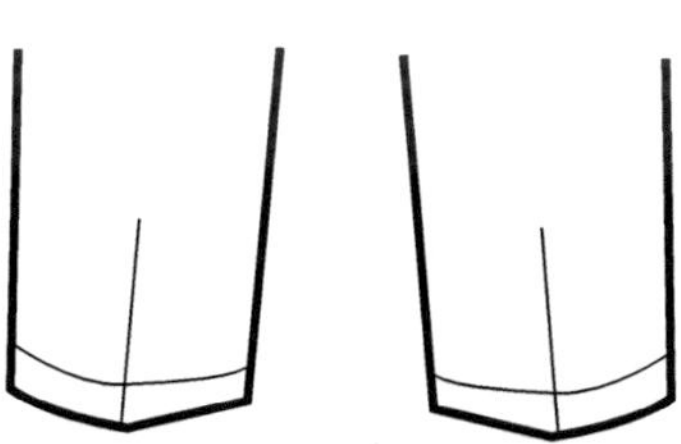

MISCELLANEOUS WORKMANSHIP STANDARDS

Maternity Shirt:

SHOULD ALWAYS BE 3/4" TO 1" LOWER AT THE FRONT TO COVER BELLY*

* ON FIT MODEL, DRESS FORM OR BODICE

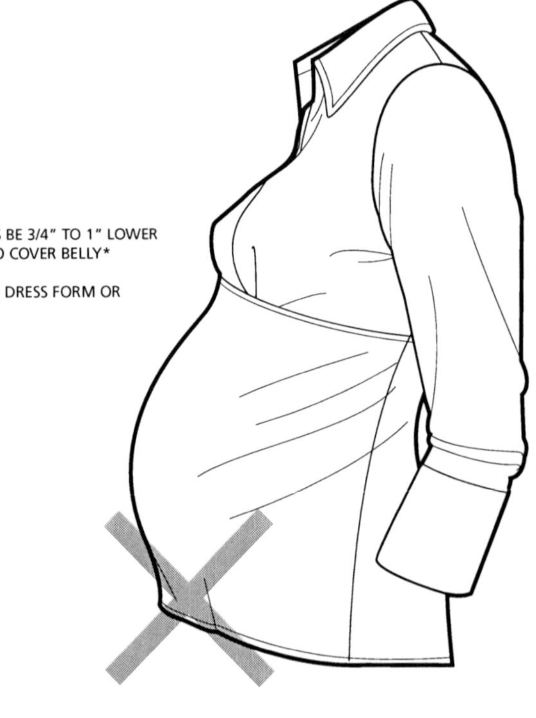

INCORRECT

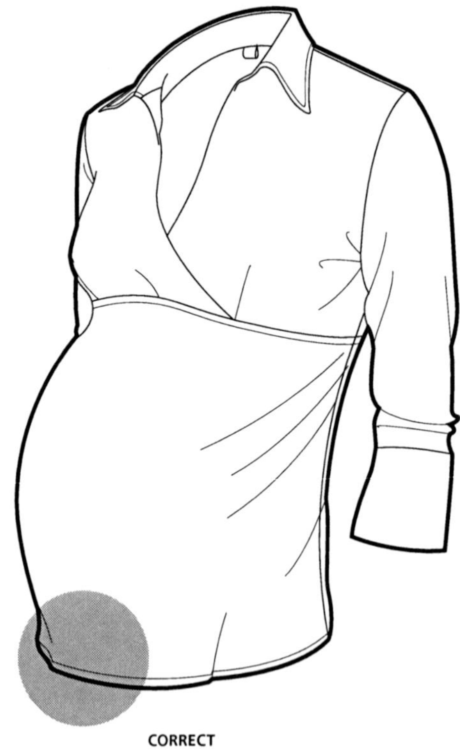

CORRECT

Maternity Bottoms:

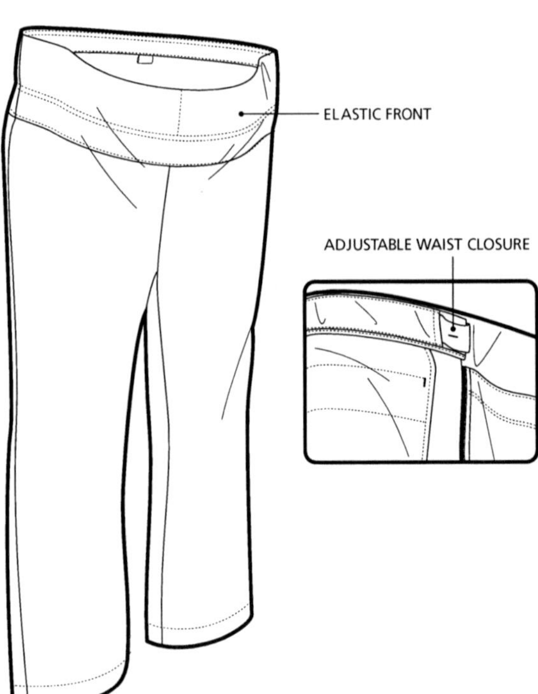

Men's Suit Jacket Fully-Lined:

Men's Suit Jacket Fully-Lined:

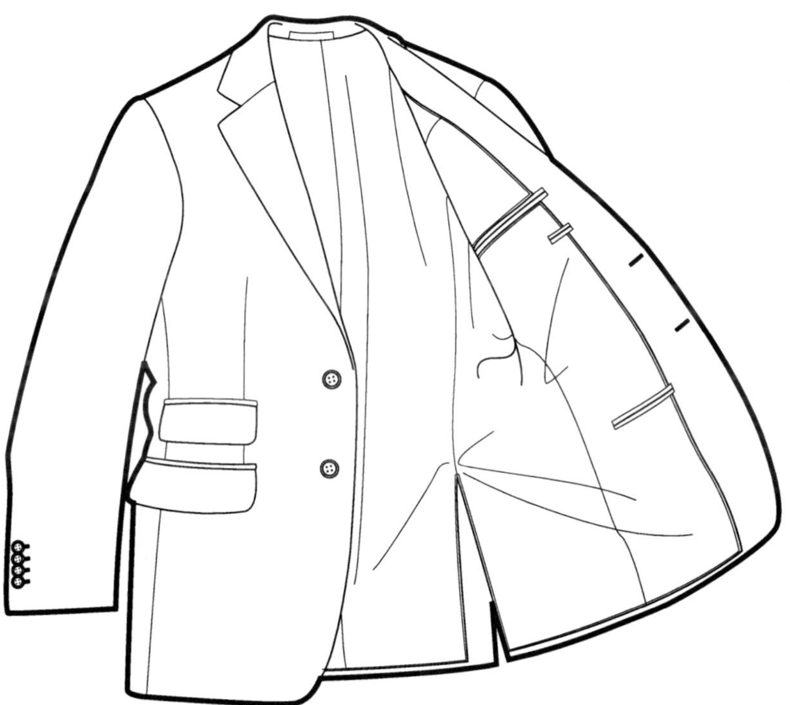

Men's Suit Jacket:

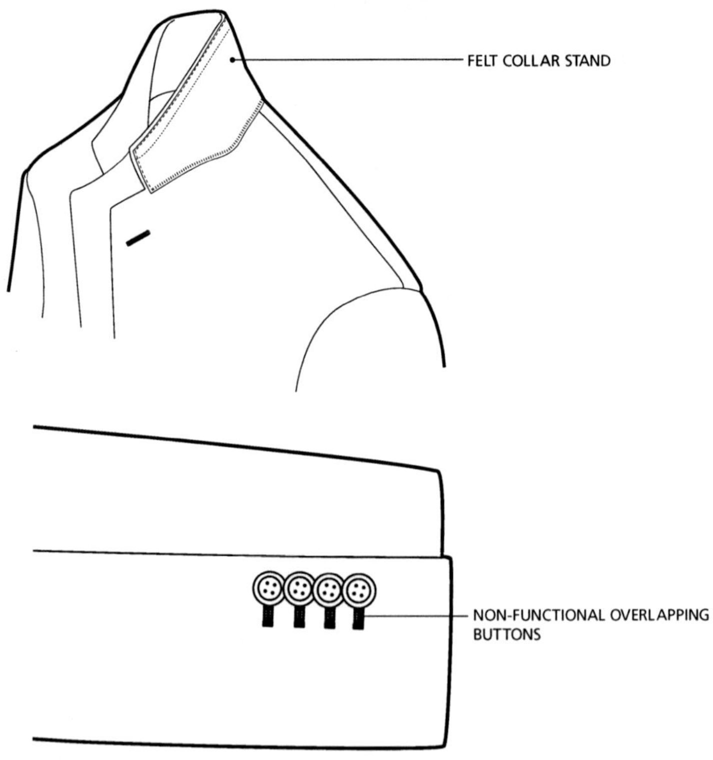

Jeans: Bartack and Rivet Placement

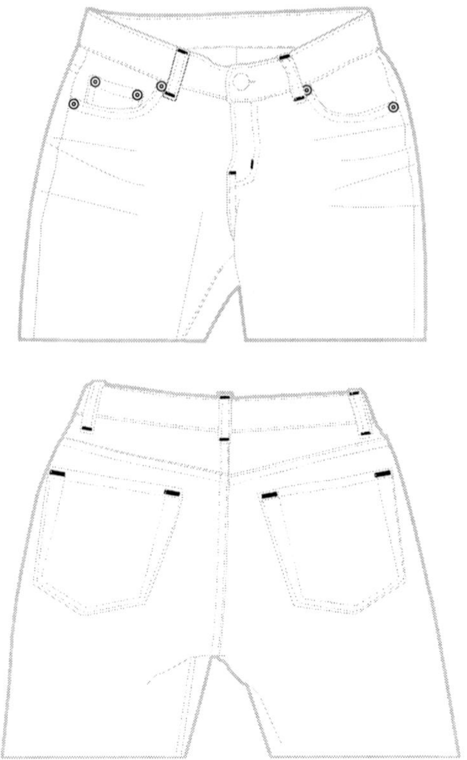

Men's or Boy's Swim Trunks:

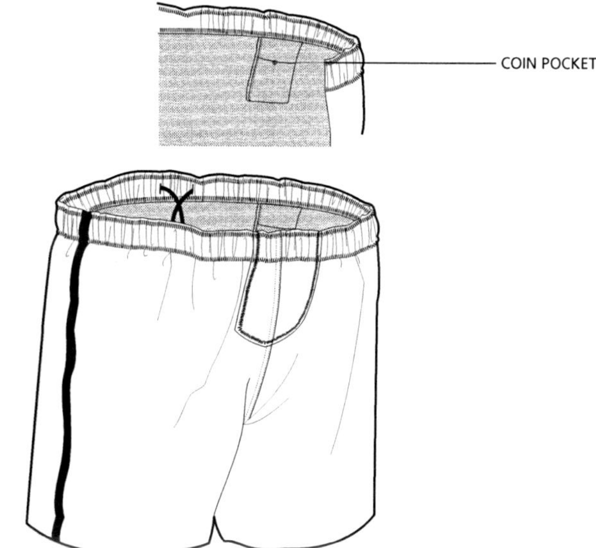

Showing Mesh Lining

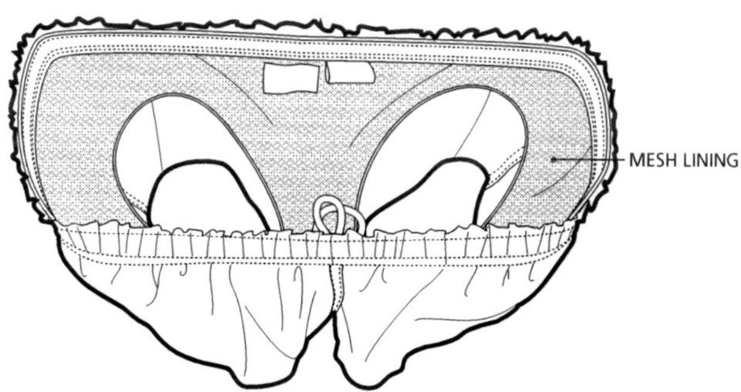

Toddler Bottom:

GRADING STANDARDS

Grade rules establish the proportional increase or decrease (grading) in measurements for various parts and elements of a garment. These grading standards will vary according to the category of merchandise, the sizes offered in a particular style and the company's overall standards for fit and styling.

To follow, are grading guidelines for two styles, to be used as examples of grading standards on completed Grade Rule Sheets. Specific grades will depend on overall grade rules for each style, and may vary per company. Grading also affects detail placement and other proportional issues. For a complete range of grade rules by market, consult The Apparel Production Handbook (A Technical Reference), published by Fashiondex.

GRADE RULES

The grade rules noted here are an example from men's outerwear, offered in XXS (extra/extra small) to XXL (extra/extra large) sizes. This is a zipper and pocket detail grade.

Zipper grade for pullovers with half-zip, center front placket, and yoke grade:

- Grading is a 1/4 inch for every 2 sizes.

  For example, if M = 10", then grade is as follows:

  (Men's) XS and S = 9 3/4" M and L = 10" XL and XXL = 10 1/4"

Zipper grade for full zipper:

- Grading is a 1/2 inch for each size.

  For example, if M = 26", then grade is as follows:

  (Men's) XXS=24 1/2", XS=25, S=25 1/2", M=26, LG=26 1/2", XL=27", XXL=27 1/2"

Pocket grade:

- Grading is 1/2 inch for every two sizes:

  For example, if M=7", then grade as follows:

  (Men's) XS and S = 6 1/2" M and L = 7" XL and XXL = 7 1/2"

Grade Rule Sheet (An example from Men's Wear)

GRADE RULES						PROTO NO.		
Garment Measurements in Inches						STYLE NO.		
MEASUREMENTS:				Sample Size		Description: Mens' Jacket		
SIZE:	XXS	XS	S	M	L	XL	XXL	TOL
1) Center Back Length	-1 1/2	-1	- 1/2	0	1/2	1	1 1/2	1/2
2) Chest/Bust	-6	-4	-2	0	3	6	9	3/4
3a) Bottom Opening - Relax	-6	-4	-2	0	3	6	9	3/4
3b) Bottom Opening - Extended	-6	-4	-2	0	3	6	9	3/4
4) Side Seam Length	0	0	0	0	0	0	0	1/4
5) Shoulder to Shoulder	-2 1/4	-1 ½	- 3/4	0	1	2	3	1/2
6) Shoulder Length	0	0	0	0	0	0	0	1/4
7) Yoke Depth at CB	0	0	0	0	0	0	0	1/8
8) Armhole	-3	-2	-1	0	1	2	3	1/2
9) Upper Arm	-3	-2	-1	0	1	2	3	1/2
10) Elbow	-1 1/2	-1	- 1/2	0	1/2	1	1 1/2	1/2
11) Sleeve Length CB	-3	-2	-1	0	1	2	3	1/2
12a) Sleeve Length Cap-Long	-1 7/8	-1 ¼	- 5/8	0	1	1	1 1/2	1/4
12b) Sleeve Length Cap-Short	- 3/4	- ½	- 1/4	0	1	1/4	3/8	1/4
13) Sleeve Placket Length	0	0	0	0	0	0	0	1/4
14a) Sleeve Cuff Opening-Relax	-1 1/2	-1	- 1/2	0	1/2	1	1 1/2	1/4
14b) Sleeve Cuff Opening-Extend	-1 1/2	-1	- 1/2	0	1/2	1	1 1/2	1/4
15) Cuff Width	0	0	0	0	0	0	0	1/8
16) Front Placket Width	0	0	0	0	0	0	0	1/8
17) Collar Width CB	0	0	0	0	0	0	0	1/8
18) Collar Length Top	-2 1/4	-1 ½	- 3/4	0	1	2	3	1/8
19) Collar Point	0	0	0	0	0	0	0	1/8
20) Collar Spread	0	0	0	0	0	0	0	1/4
21) Collar Stand/Band Width CB	0	0	0	0	0	0	0	1/8
22) Neck Circumference	-2 1/4	-1 ½	- 3/4	0	1	2	3	3/8
23) Front Neck Drop	- 3/8	- ¼	- 1/8	0	1/8	1/4	3/8	1/4
24) Neck Width CB	- 3/4	- ½	- 1/4	0	1/4	1/2	3/4	1/4
25) Zipper Length CF	0	0	0	0	0	0	0	1/2
26) Collar Stand Length	0	0	0	0	0	0	0	1/8
27) Hood Length CB	-1 1/2	-1	- 1/2	0	1/2	1	1 1/2	1/2
28) Hood Width Horizontal	-3	-2	-1	0	1	2	3	3/8
29) Hood Height CF	0	0	0	0	0	0	0	1/8
30) Difference Between CF and CB	0	0	0	0	0	0	0	1/8

Grade Rule Sheet (An example from Children's Wear)

GRADE RULES Garment Measurements in Inches						PROTO NO. STYLE NO.
MEASUREMENTS			SAMPLE SIZE			DESCRIPTION: Sleeper
SIZE		0/3 Months	3/6 Months	6/9 Months		TOLERANCE
Measurements taken on the flat.						
1)	Total Vertical Trunk - HPS to Crotch	-2	0	1		3/4
2)	Front Vertical Trunk - HPS to Center of Snap	-1	0	1/2		3/8
3)	Back Vertical Trunk – HPS to Center of Snap	-1	0	1/2		3/8
4)	Chest - at Armhole	-3/8	0	1/2		1/2
5)	Across Shoulder	-1	0	1/4		1/4
6)	Armhole Circumference	-1/2	0	1/4		1/4
7)	Sleeve Length – CB Neck to Hem	-1 5/8	0	3/4		1/2
8)	Sleeve Opening	-1/4	0	1/8		1/4
9)	Neck Width - Seam to Seam	0	0	0		1/8
10)	Front Neck Drop - HPS to Seam	0	0	0		1/8
11)	Back Neck Drop - HPS to Seam	0	0	0		1/8
12)	Roll Up Cuff Width	0	0	0		1/8
13)	Hip - at Leg Opening	-1	0	1/2		1/2
14)	Leg Opening Relaxed	-1/2	0	1/4		1/4
15)	Crotch Width	0	0	0		1/8
16)	Shoulder Slope	0	0	0		1/8
17)	Binding Width on Leg Opening	0	0	0		0
18)	Collar Width at CB	0	0	0		1/4
19)	Front Placket Overlap	0	0	0		1/8
20)	Tie LxW	0	0	0		1/8
21)	Tie Place from HPS	0	0	0		1/8
22)	Facing of Front Placket Width	0	0	0		1/8
23)	Number of Snaps at Crotch	0	0	0		0

NOTES:

1) Add Reinforcement Tape to Shoulder Seam

CHAPTER 10

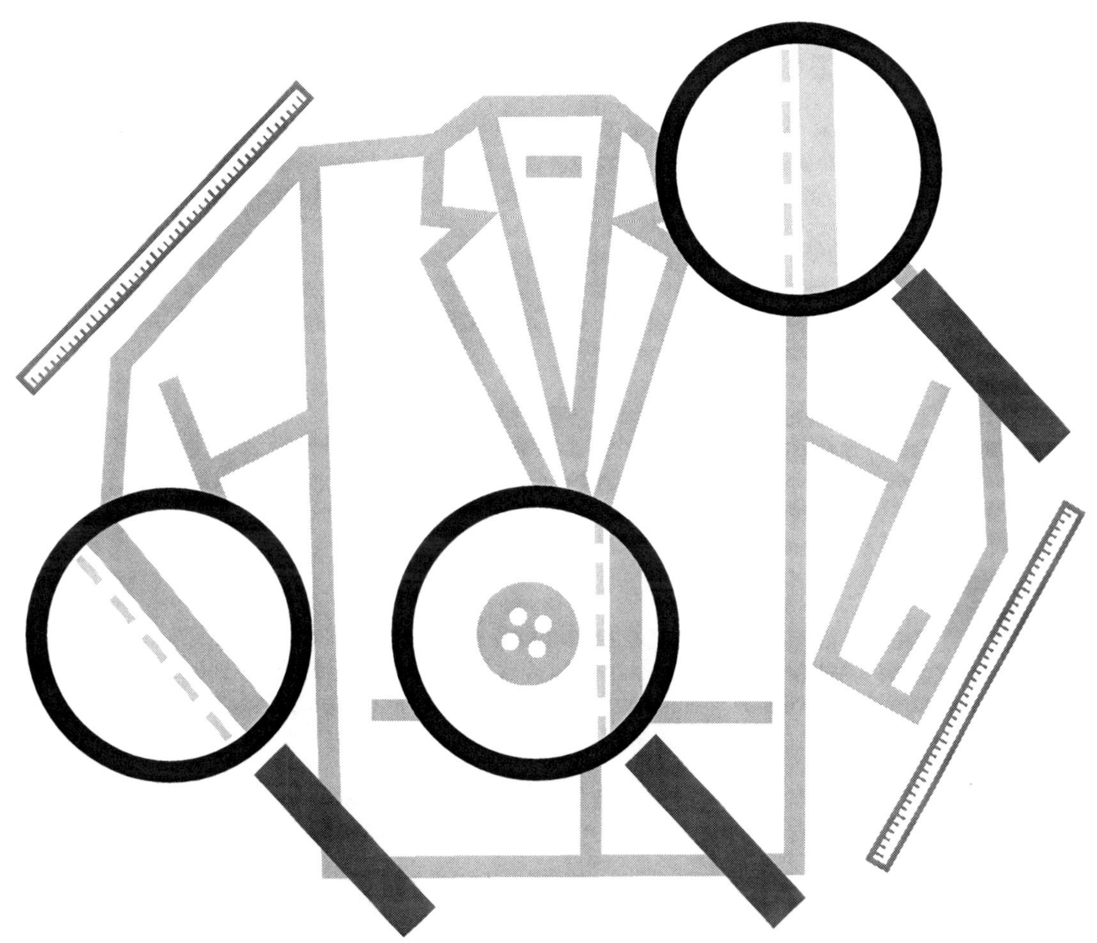

GARMENT INSPECTION STANDARDS

This chapter looks at the Garment Inspection/Audit Process that occurs once the production is completed. Sample lots from bulk production are pulled, and workmanship and quality standards are checked against Acceptable Quality Level Standards. Lots should be inspected and any defects corrected before shipping to the warehouse and again before shipping to the retailers.

GARMENT AUDIT INSPECTION PROCEDURE

PURPOSE

The purpose of the **Garment Audit** is to identify quality problems at the contractor and/or warehouse location before garments are shipped to distributors and final customers.

PROCEDURE

The customer's production or quality control staff or designated agent should conduct audits on all purchase orders (PO) when practical. A PO should not be released for shipment until a product passes audit. An additional audit should be performed upon receipt into warehouse.

The standardized MIL STD 105E "Sampling Procedures and Tables for Inspection by Attributes" (as taken from ANSI/ASQC Z1.4-1993), should be used as the method of auditing receipts. Attached are two tables to use as guidelines of this double sampling plan. The inspection/audit should use the AQL plan. **AQL** has two different definitions due to standard changes:

1. **Acceptable Quality Level (MIL-STD-105E, ISO 2859-1 (1999)**
   The acceptable quality level (AQL) is defined as the maximum percent defective (or the maximum number of defects per hundred units) that, for purpose of sampling inspection, can be considered satisfactory as a process average. The sampling plans most frequently used by the Department of Defense are based on the AQL.

2. **Acceptance Quality Limit (ANSI/ASQC Z1.4-2003)**
   The acceptance quality limit (AQL) is the quality level that is the worst tolerable process average when a continuing series of lots is submitted for acceptance sampling.

INSPECTIONS BASED ON ACCEPTABLE QUALITY LEVEL (AQL)

An AQL of 4% and AQL of 2.5% are the most commonly used standards.

NORMAL, TIGHTENED, REDUCED

Normal, Tightened or Reduced inspection levels are determined by Apparel Quality Control, Production and Inventory Management Departments according to the guidelines outlined below:

Normal:

- Normal inspection should be used as criteria for all first incoming shipments from each contractor.
- Normal inspection should be used when a lapse of 6 months or more occurs between shipments.
- Normal inspection should be used when a contractor changes manufacture location.
- Inspection should remain at the normal level until such time as tightened or reduced is deemed necessary.

Tightened:

- Tightened inspection should be implemented when 2 out of 5 consecutive shipments have failed audit.
- Normal inspection should be reinstituted once 5 consecutive shipments have been accepted.

Reduced:

- Reduced inspection should be implemented when either 5 consecutive shipments have been accepted or no more than 3 months has elapsed since last shipment.
- Normal inspection should be reinstituted if one shipment is rejected.
- Normal inspection should be reinstituted if more than 3 months have elapsed since last shipment.

SAMPLING PROCEDURES FOR AQL

Using the grid to follow, determine the sample lot size to be audited. Lot size is defined as the total number of units received in one shipment consisting of one style, but may include multiple sizes and colors.

The audit sample must include a representation of all sizes and colors received. The proportion of sizes and colors sampled should match proportion of size and color breakdown of shipment.

EXAMPLES

The following examples are based on 4% AQL Normal Inspection.

Example 1:

- Shipment is received containing 800 units, across 3 colors.
- Sample lot to audit is 50 units.

Color	Units	Sample	Reject
A	200	12	0
B	300	19	1
C	300	19	1
Total	800	50	2

Since acceptance rate for this lot size is 3 units or less, this shipment is accepted.

Example 2:

- Shipment is received containing 800 units, across 3 colors.
- Sample lot to audit is 50 units.

Color	Units	Sample	Reject
A	200	12	1
B	300	19	2
C	300	19	2
Total	800	50	5

Since number of rejects falls between the accept and reject criteria (3 and 7), an additional sample of 50 units must be audited. If cumulative number of rejects is 8 or less, lot is accepted.

DOUBLE SAMPLING PLAN

AQL 4%

	Lot Size	Sample Size		Normal		Tightened		Sample Size		Reduced	
		Initial	Cumulative	Accept	Reject	Accept	Reject	Initial	Cumulative	Accept	Reject
A	2-8	2	2	0	1	0	1	2	2	0	1
B	9-15	2	2	0	1	0	1	2	2	0	1
		2	4								
C	16-25	3	3	0	1	0	1	2	2	0	1
		3	6								
D	26-50	5	5	0	2	0	2	2	2	0	2
		5	10	1	2	1	2	2	4	0	2
E	51-90	8	8	0	2	0	2	3	3	0	2
		8	16	1	2	1	2	3	6	0	2
F	91-150	13	13	0	3	0	2	5	5	0	3
		13	26	3	4	1	2	5	10	0	4
G	151-280	20	20	1	4	0	3	8	8	0	4
		20	40	4	5	3	4	8	16	1	5
H	281-500	32	32	2	5	1	4	13	13	0	4
		32	64	6	7	4	5	13	26	3	6
I	501-1,200	50	50	3	7	2	5	20	20	1	5
		50	100	8	9	6	7	20	40	4	7
J	1,201-3,200	80	80	5	9	3	7	32	32	2	7
		80	160	12	13	11	12	32	64	6	9
K	3,201-10,000	125	125	7	11	6	10	50	50	3	8
		125	250	18	19	15	16	50	100	8	12
L	10,001-35,000	200	200	11	16	9	14	80	80	5	10
		200	400	26	27	23	24	80	160	12	16
M	35,001-50,000	500	500	11	16	9	14	125	125	5	10
		500	1,000	26	27	23	24	125	250	12	16

DOUBLE SAMPLING PLAN
AQL 2.5%

	Lot Size	Sample Size Initial	Sample Size Cumulative	Normal Accept	Normal Reject	Tightened Accept	Tightened Reject	Sample Size Initial	Sample Size Cumulative	Reduced Accept	Reduced Reject
A	2-8	2	2	0	1	0	1	2	2	0	1
B	9-15	2	2	0	1	0	1	2	2	0	1
		2	4								
C	16-25	3	3	0	1	0	1	2	2	0	1
		3	6								
D	26-50	5	5	0	1	0	1	2	2	0	1
		5	10					2	4		
E	51-90	8	8	0	2	0	2	3	3	0	2
		8	16	1	2	1	2	3	6	0	2
F	91-150	13	13	0	2	0	2	5	5	0	2
		13	26	1	2	1	2	5	10	0	2
G	151-280	20	20	0	3	0	2	8	8	0	3
		20	40	3	4	1	2	8	16	0	4
H	281-500	32	32	1	4	0	3	13	13	0	4
		32	64	4	5	3	4	13	26	1	5
I	501-1,200	50	50	2	5	1	4	20	20	0	4
		50	100	6	7	4	5	20	40	3	6
J	1,201-3,200	80	80	3	7	2	5	32	32	1	5
		80	160	8	9	6	7	32	64	4	7
K	3,201-10,000	125	125	5	9	3	7	50	50	2	7
		125	250	12	13	11	12	50	100	6	9
L	10,001-35,000	200	200	7	11	6	10	80	80	3	8
		200	400	18	19	15	16	80	160	8	12
M	35,001-50,000	500	500	11	16	9	14	125	125	5	10
		500	1,000	26	27	23	24	125	250	12	16

AREAS REVIEWED DURING AUDIT

PACKAGING AND SHIPPING COMPLIANCE

- Carton size
- Carton bar code
- Carton marking
- Carton count
- Mix
- Poly-bag sticker
- Fold
- Bar code ticket
- Hangtags
- Cardboard and packaging materials

GENERAL APPEARANCE

- Thread tails
- Soil
- Holes
- Skipped stitches
- Markings
- Fabric defects
- Repairs
- Embroidery/screen printing alignment and quality

GARMENT MEASUREMENT COMPLIANCE

TOPS:

- Chest
- CB or HPS length
- Sleeve length
- Neckline or neck circumference
- Shoulder

BOTTOMS:

- Waist
- Inseam
- Hip
- Front and back rise

Note: *Critical measurements are listed above. Measurements taken during audit include, but are not limited to, the above measurement points.*

FABRIC COMPLIANCE

- Shading
- Crocking
- Fabric hand
- Water repellency (when applicable)

SPECIFICATION COMPLIANCE

- Seams/Stitching
- Trims
- Construction
- Plaid/stripe match
- Labels
- Finishing

Written documentation should be provided to each vendor on a regular basis indicating compliance level for each area measured.

THE DEFINITION OF A DEFECT

MAJOR

A **major defect*** is any defect that in the customer's judgment:

- Renders a garment unacceptable due to its conspicuous nature.
- May affect the salability of the garment.
- Has a negative impact on the serviceability of the garment.
- Deviates significantly from the customer's established standards and specifications.
- Is a justifiable cause for a retail customer return.

*** If the defect is visible from a distance of 36 inches, the customer believes it is a major defect.**

MINOR

A **minor defect** is any defect that would not in the customer's judgment render a garment to be second quality, but when combined with other minor defects on the same garment may cause the garment to be rejected. Minor defects should be noted and used as a tool to eliminate the possibility of more significant defects in subsequent production.

Note: Regardless of the outcome of in-line audits and/or finished product audits at the factory, the final acceptance of any shipment lies with the customer, the customer's distributors, and/or the customer's customers.

ZONE DEFINITIONS

ZONES - TOPS

Zone 1: **Top front of the garment, neck/collar (inside and outside), top of shoulders, front sleeve, inclusive of visible packaged area.**

- No defects accepted in this critical area.

Zone 2: **Middle section of front in a conspicuous or visible area, and the top back area.**

- One very faint or small mark may be acceptable in this region. A contractor and/or agent supervisor should determine if any mark in this area is acceptable.

Zone 3: **Bottom front and back area.**

- Small, inconspicuous marks may be acceptable in this lower hem region if they are not clustered together.

Zone 4: **The area inside the garment that is not typically seen unless turned inside out. This does not include the inside neck area as seen when folded.**

- Seam repair work, small soil marks, or unclipped threads up to 1/4" in length may be considered acceptable.

Note: Under no circumstances are holes in the fabric or broken/open seams acceptable in any zone.

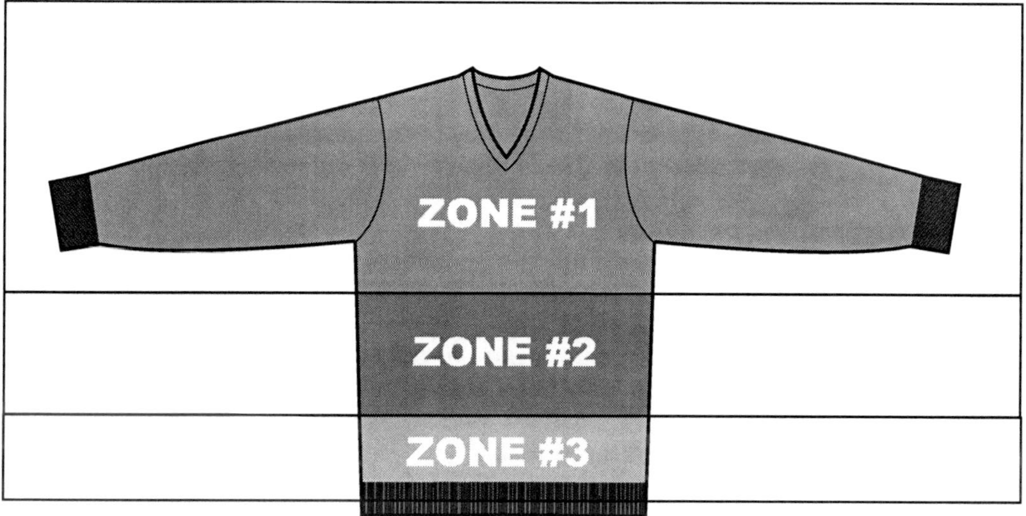

ZONES - BOTTOMS

Zone 1: **Top front half of the garment, waistband (inside and outside), inclusive of visible packaged area.**

- No defects accepted in this critical area.

Zone 2: **Top back half of the garment.**

- One very faint or small mark may be acceptable in this region. A contractor and/or agent supervisor should determine if any mark in this area is acceptable.

Zone 3: **Bottom front and back area.**

- Small inconspicuous marks may be acceptable in this lower hem region if they are not clustered together.

Zone 4: **The area inside the garment that is not typically seen unless turned inside out. This does not include the inside waistband area as seen when folded.**

- Seam repair work, small soil marks, or unclipped threads up to 1/4" in length may be considered acceptable.

Note: Under no circumstances are holes in the fabric or broken/open seams acceptable in any zone.

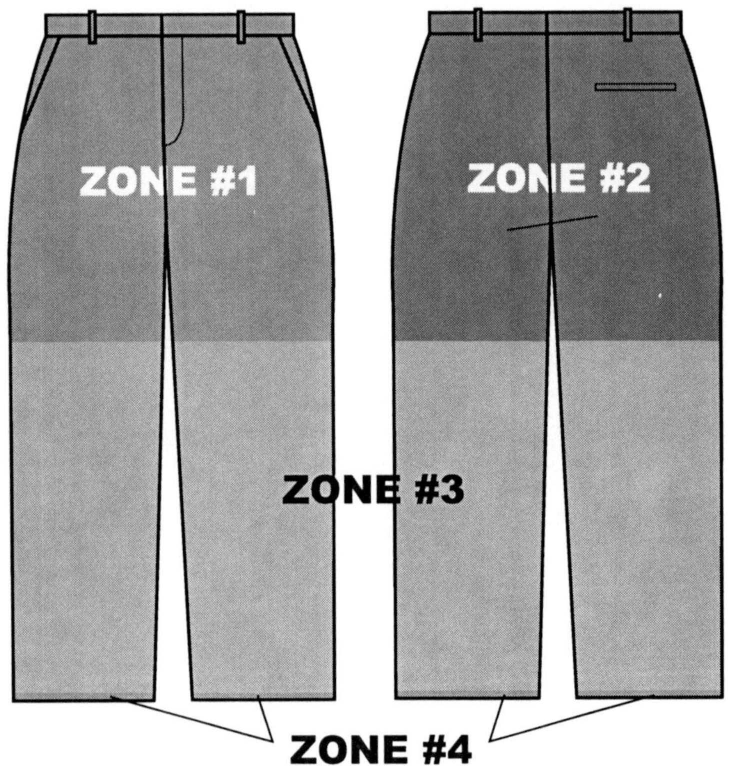

DEFECT CLASSIFICATION

The following is a list of defects for comparison when auditing the customer's apparel that is:

- In production (in-line inspection)
- Inspected before packing (trim/pressing/inspection)
- In-plant contractor and/or agent statistical inspection
  (AQL 4% or AQL 2.5%)
  or
- In the customer's warehouse inspection
  (AQL 4% or AQL 2.5%)

All defects should be repaired or cleaned when possible. The customer does not accept any second quality garments packed in first quality shipments. Only first quality garments should be packed in first quality cartons. Chargebacks should be processed for failure to comply with this standard. This is of great importance since the customer often is representing the retailer's Specifications and Compliance Standards and should be held liable by the retailer in the form of retail chargebacks.

PACKAGING AND SHIPPING NON-COMPLIANCE ISSUES

Carton size:

- Improper dimensions and/or weight of shipping carton.

Bar codes:

- Incorrect data printed on bar code or missing bar code sticker for hangtags, poly bags or outer-cartons.
- Un-scanable bar codes:
  - Poor print
  - Folded sticker
  - Bar code not face out in poly-bag.

Carton marking:

- Hand-written packing list.

Carton count:

- Discrepancy between packing list and contents of carton.

Mix:

- Mixed styles and/or sizes in same carton (see Chapter 10: Packaging and Shipping for mixed carton compliance).
- Second Quality goods shipped in same carton as First Quality.
- Improper direct shipment packaging.

Stickers / Tickets:

- Missing, incorrectly positioned, or incorrect hangtags, or tickets.

Cardboard and Packaging Materials:

- Missing or incorrect cardboard, pins, butterflies, buttons covers, or other packaging.

GENERAL APPEARANCE NON-COMPLIANCE

Threads:

- Loose threads and debris in packaging.
- Any threads not trimmed down to 1/4 inch (inside and outside of garment). **All threads MUST be trimmed in ZONE 1.**
- No threads hanging below hemline.

Soil:

- Any soiling / spots / stains on the garment affecting appearance
- Any cleaning stains
- Sewing machine oil.

Holes:

- Needle holes, needle cuts, machine-feed abrasion.

Skipped stitches:

- Skipped stitches (anywhere in or out of garment)
  - ⊡ One skipped stitch on a seam: **Minor** (lockstitch)**, Major** (chain stitch).
  - ⊡ Two skipped stitches together or on the same seam: **Major** in ZONES 1 and 2**.**
  - ⊡ Two single skipped stitches on one garment: M**inor.**

- One cut or broken stitch of any type.

Markings:

- Any chalk marks, pen marks, etc.
- Any staples, pins or swift tacks left in the garment not serving a useful purpose.
- Any tape or seconds stickers on a garment not serving a useful purpose.

Fabric Defects:

- Hole, runner, dropped stitch, or misweave
- Excessive scratch marks, tick bites, blemishes in leather skins
- Snagged or pulled yarns, or excessive pilling
- Nap, slub, mote or other surface blemish
- Torque
- Conspicuous horizontal barré
- Poor rib stretch and recovery.

Embroidery / Screen Printing Alignment and Quality:

- Skew or slant out of tolerance
- Incorrect placement
- Deviation of graphic from approved sample or strike-off
- Incorrect art or size
- Poor thread color / shade matching or wrong color used
- Skipped stitches
- Puckering / pulling of fabric
- Insufficient trimming of threads and backing
- Poor registration
- Heavy hand or poor coverage
- Poor ink color / shade matching or incorrect color
- Ink spots, flops, or smudges
- Stretched/deformed print
- Insufficiently cured
- Not following flashing instructions as specified on graphic design sheet.

Repairs:

- Any repair adversely affecting serviceability/appearance.
- Any broken stitch repair that is not sewn exactly stitch-on-stitch with an overlap of at least three stitches on each end.
- Any repair that is not complete, clean of threads, or resewn in a way that adversely affects appearance.

MEASUREMENT NON-COMPLIANCE

- Any measurements out of tolerance, per Specification Sheet.

FABRIC NON-COMPLIANCE

Shading:

- Shade variance within garment
- Shade variance between fabric and thread
- Dye spots, fading or streaks
- Use of AZO dyestuffs.

Crocking:

- Failure to meet wet or dry crocking requirements.
- Failure to meet colorfastness requirements as noted in "Physical Testing and Fabric Performance" section. (See Chapter 8)

Fabric Hand:

- Deviation from approved hand standard.

Water Repellency:

- Failure to meet water repellency requirements.

Note: Acceptable lot shading is a slight color variance from garment to garment. This is a minor defect and should be noted. Leather will have a range of color shades within each color. This is normal and acceptable within shade range established.

SPECIFICATION NON-COMPLIANCE

Seams/Stitching:

- Seam construction not as specified in the customer's specification package.
- Seams twisted, puckered, or pleated (1) affecting appearance.
- Ends of stitching not properly secured, tied in, or caught in other seams (back stitched).
- Raw fabric edge anywhere on outside of the garment unless part of the original design.
- Stitches per inch deviation of more than two-per-inch + / - as specified.
- Edge stitch margin irregularity / unevenness.
- Bar- and running tacks missing, or not placed as specified.
- Any seams with uneven allowance or margin.
- Loose stitching causing grinning seams.
- Any stitching run-off over one needle puncture.

Trims:

- Any defective component or part that affects the serviceability or appearance of the garment.
- Any specified component or part omitted from the garment.
- Any required operation omitted or improperly performed.

CONSTRUCTION NON-COMPLIANCE

Center Front or Fly Construction:

- Skipped, broken, cut or run-off stitches.
- Omitted, back tack or bartack.
- Exposed drill holes or chalk marks.
- Misaligned button and buttonhole or fastener.

Pockets/Flaps:

- One skipped, cut, broken, or run-off stitch.
- Horizontal or vertical placement of pocket off by more than a 1/4 inch.
- Side edge of pocket exposed from under side of flap.
- Under flap: Any amount of raw edge at flap turnover.
- Excessive puckering or pleating (one pleat).
- Omitted back tack or bartack.
- Exposed drill holes, chalk marks.
- Raw edge leather pen hole/buttonholes (unless otherwise specified).
- Misaligned buttonhole covering/cutting stitching.
- Misaligned buttonholes/snaps seriously affecting appearance + / - 1/8 inch: (Button/buttonholes see button/buttonhole construction).
- Poorly shaped pockets or flaps, not following pattern and / or adversely affecting appearance.
- Edge seam of pocket flap (underside) rolled forward (beading) 1/32 of an inch.
- Face or underply of flap tight or twisted causing tightness, twisting, fullness, or curling flap.
- Any raw edge on pocket or flap.
- Flap contours turned out (guttered), or top stitched down in a way that adversely affects appearance.
- A run off of no more than one stitch on the start and stop of the *flap only.*
- Hi / lo pockets or flaps more than 1/4 inch.
- Edge margin of topstitching not uniform or balanced between left and right pockets.
- Left and right pockets not the same size / shape.
- Tipped or slanted pocket or flaps.

Collar:

- Poorly shaped collar seriously affecting appearance.
- Collar points not fully turned out (guttered) and topstitched down in a way that adversely affects appearance or construction.
- Topstitch margin deviates more than 1/16 inch from spec.
- Raw edges, or punched out collar tips.
- Face or underply of collar tight or twisted causing fullness, twisting, or curling of the collar.
- Length of collar points uneven more than 1/8 inch.
- Interlining in collar or collar band or fusing tight, puckered, or full, causing unacceptable visual distortion.
- Any pleat, pucker, or crease causing unacceptable visual distortion.
- Underside of collar edge exposed (beaded, no tolerance).
- Collar stay(s) missing (when specified).
- Any foreign matter sewn into collar.
- Width of collar insufficient to cover collar band when folded down.
- Collar band ends short or long causing unbalanced or puckered appearance.

Placket/Vent/Sleeve Facing:

- Any raw edge in placket / vent construction.
- Excessive twisting or roping of placket / sleeve facing adversely affecting appearance.
- Excessive puckering or pleating of sleeve facing or sleeve placket.
- Vent tack causing pleating, puckering or excessive fullness in sleeve.
- Placket point rounded, not sewn to a point.

Hem:

- Roping hem that seriously affects visual appearance.
- Broken stitches on bottom hem.
- Pleats or puckering on the outside of hem affecting visual appearance or serviceability.
- Small pleats (half pleat), and puckers that do not affect visual appearance or serviceability.
- Incorrectly shaped bottom hem, does not follow pattern.
- Uneven front panels / placket at bottom hem, beyond tolerance.

Plaid/Stripe Match:

- Any deviation from plaid or stripe match.
  - Balance - mirrored image from left to right, side to side.
  - Match - something exactly corresponding to another, across a portion of a garment.

Labels:

- Sewn crooked.
- Off-center (at least 1/3 of the label must be in center of back neck).
- Poor quality of printed label.
- Improper fiber content.
- Uncut labels on irregulars.
- Improper size.
- Incorrect country of assembly or origin.
- Improper insertion of label in neck seam.
- Missing RN #.
- Missing care instructions.
- Incorrect / missing joker tag if required.

Finishing:

- Any burn or scorch marks.
- Fabric discoloration / color change due to pressing.
- Unpressed garments or sections of garments.
- Pressed in pleats.
- Improper pressing, adversely affecting garment appearance.
- Shine marks in fabric from pressing.

CHAPTER 11

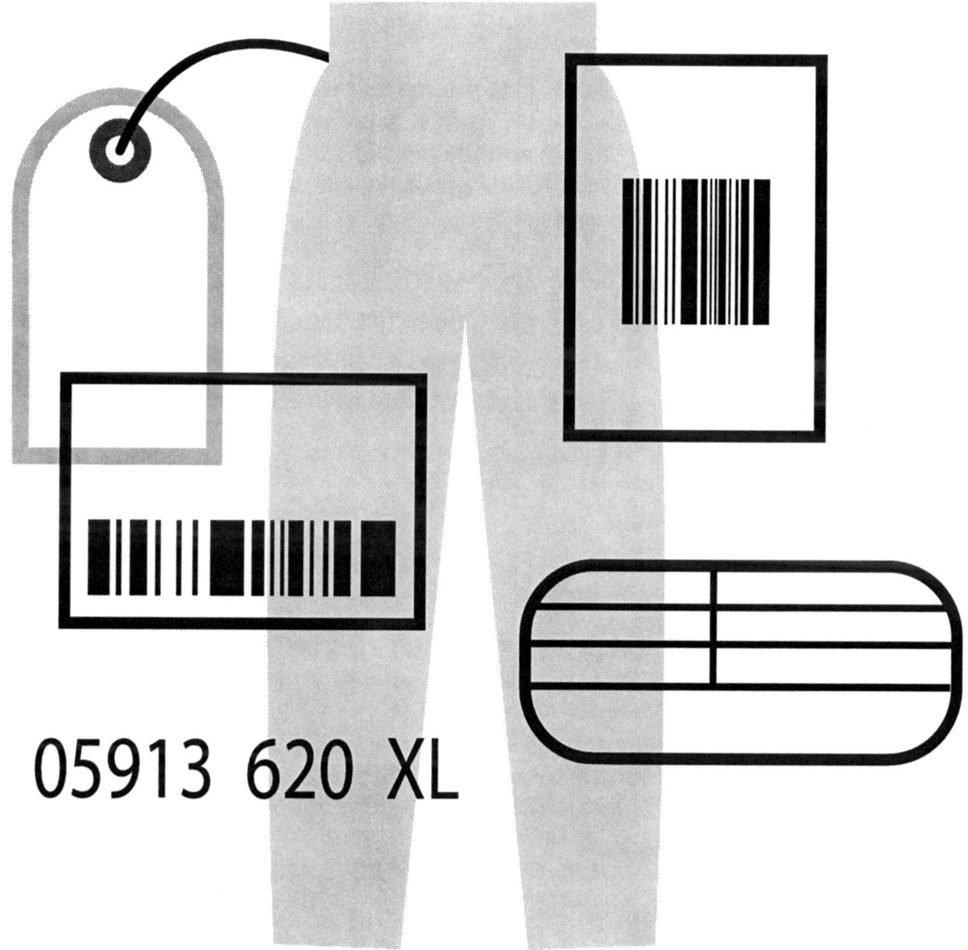

UPC LABELS

This chapter talks about Universal Product Codes (UPC Codes), and where they must be placed on garments and on garment packaging prior to shipping. The specifications and non-compliance rules of UPC codes are strict, from the quality of the printing to the height of the bars and the placement of the UPC tickets or stickers.

UPC LABELS

UPC labels are the easiest way to control what you have in stock; what you are shipping; the contents of the box you are shipping; what sizes are included; and, at the request of the customers, the suggested price your garments should be sold at.

This process is a must for large retailers. You will not be able to bypass this step no matter what your relationship is with the retailer.

Before shipping, make sure that each bar reads into the bar-tag reader. At times, the correct number will appear underneath the bar, but it may not be legible. To avoid this problem, before shipping to large retailers, have them provide you with the already printed tags from their own supplier or give you the supplier info. This will help you avoid future problems with them. For smaller stores, the above might not apply.

BAR CODE TICKETS, UPC POLY-BAG STICKERS, UPC CARTON LABELS

All the customer's products should have the following three UPC tags and/or labels affixed to the garments prior to shipment:

1) A UPC bar code ticket

2) UPC bar code poly-bag sticker

3) UPC carton label

ORDERING PROCEDURE

1. PURCHASE ORDER INFORMATION IS DOWNLOADED TO CONTRACTOR AND/OR AGENT

- The customer downloads production PO information (i.e., style, color, size, quantity) to our UPC ticket/UPC sticker/carton label contractor on a weekly basis.
- Hard copies of POs are also sent to the contractor and/or agent concurrent to the download.

2. CONTRACTOR and/or AGENT ORDERS TICKETS, STICKERS AND LABELS FROM LABEL MAKER

- Upon receipt of the PO, the contractor and/or agent must contact the customer's label maker to order the appropriate UPC ticket, UPC sticker, and carton labels.
- Lead times for paper trim production typically run from 10-14 business days.
- **Allow sufficient time for the order.**
- If the customer's production orders have been placed worldwide, it is highly recommended that the contractor and/or agent order the appropriate hangtags and bar codes 8 weeks prior to shipping, so that garment delivery is not impacted.
- The customer's label maker should fax an order form to the contractor and/or agent immediately to allow them to place the order with proper "bill to" and "ship to" information.
- The customer's PO # and style # is required on the order form (additional faxed copy of the PO is not required).
- The customer's label maker should ship to and bill each contractor and/or agent for the UPC ticket, UPC poly-bag sticker, and carton labels that are needed.

Note: Orders should not be called out earlier than 8 weeks prior to PO date. If contractor and/or agent requires tickets, stickers or labels earlier, customer's production department should be contacted.

It is critical that the above UPC bar code ticket, UPC bar code sticker, and UPC bar code carton label procedures are followed by each contractor and/or agent. **Bar codes are required on every garment shipped out of each contractor and/or agent**. The customer should not accept any substitute tickets, stickers, or labels. (Non-compliance should result in chargebacks - see Chapter on Chargeback, Irregular and Overrun Purchase Policy).

UPC BAR CODE TICKET

EXAMPLE

The UPC bar code tickets should look like the following:

Customer U.S. Destinations

Customer Non-U.S. Destinations

Please note that these are visual samples, not actual UPC bar code tickets.

SUGGESTED PLACEMENT

- All UPC tickets should be attached with a 3" plastic fastener (e.g. Swiftachment® plastic fastener) through the cutout on the tag and ticket.

- A 5"-loop plastic fastener (e.g. Secur-A-Tach® plastic fasteners) should be used when it is not possible to use a 3" plastic fastener (e.g. Swiftachments® plastic fasteners).

The UPC hangtag location is very important for industry standards and consistency. The following UPC symbol location guidelines published by the Uniform Code Council (UCC) should be used for apparel ticketing.

Women's/Girls' Apparel	Location of Tags
Coats/Outerwear *	At the bottom of the left sleeve at the seam
Hanging Tops/Shirts	At the bottom of the left sleeve at the seam
Packaged/Folded Tops	Through main label at neck
Bottoms *	On the waistband at the left seam
Sleepwear	At the bottom of the left sleeve at the seam
Vests (Fabric and Leather)	Through main label at neck

Men's/Boys' Apparel	Location of Tags
Leather Outerwear	Through main label at neck
Coats/Outerwear (non-leather) *	At the bottom of the left sleeve at the seam
Suits/Jackets	At the bottom of the left sleeve at the seam
Hanging Tops/Shirts	At the bottom of the left sleeve at the seam
Packaged/Folded Tops	Through main label at neck
Vests (Fabric and Leather)	Through main label at neck
Pants/Bottoms *	On the waistband at the left seam
Robes	At the bottom of the left sleeve at the seam
Ties	Through label on the back of the tie
Belts *	Secur-A-Tach® plastic fasteners through the first belt hole
Hats/Headwear *	Through the sweatband to right of back opening

* Ticketing of waterproof items should not interfere with the waterproofing ability of the material (e.g. waterproof storm pants must be Swiftached through the manufacturer's label on the inside waistband). Special consideration also applies to all leather outerwear. Ticketing should not adversely affect the appearance of the leather (i.e. permanent holes).

UPC POLY-BAG STICKER
EXAMPLE

The UPC poly-bag stickers should look like the following:

Please note that this is a visual sample, not an actual UPC poly-bag sticker.

PLACEMENT

FLAT-PACKED GARMENTS	
• Each individual garment must have a UPC poly-bag sticker affixed to the lower left corner of the poly-bag (garment's right-hand side).	

HANGING GARMENTS

- Each individual garment must have a UPC poly-bag sticker affixed to the upper right corner of the poly-bag (garment's left side).

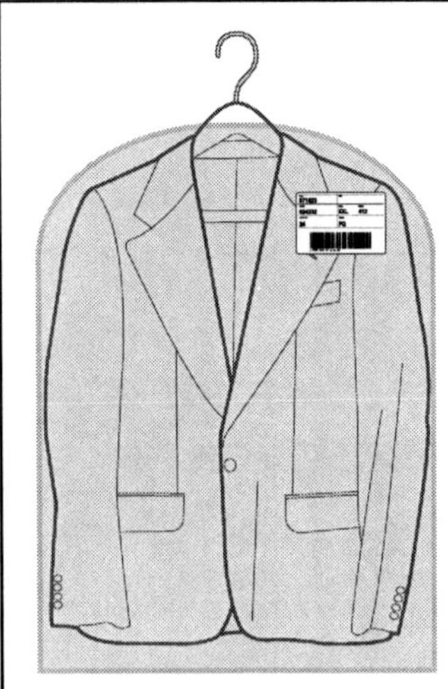

UPC CARTON LABEL EXAMPLE

The UPC label should be printed using Code 128 symbology and should use the following generation specifications:

Field Name	Bar Code: All Fields Concatenated	Human Readable: Spaces Between Fields
Data Identifier	Literal "A" one character	Literal "A" one character
PO Number	Six digits padded with leading zeros	Six digits padded with leading zeros
Style Number	Five digits padded with leading zeros	Five digits padded with leading zeros
Color Number	Three digits padded with leading zeros	Three digits padded with leading zeros
Quality	Two characters	Two characters
Size	Three characters padded with trailing spaces	Three characters padded with trailing spaces
Carton Quantity	Three digits padded with leading zeros	Three digits padded with leading zeros

Data	Position	Scan Sample
Data Identifier	(1)	A
PO Number	(2-7)	071623
Customer Style #	(8-12)	02432
Color	(13-15)	412

Quality	(16-17)	FQ
Size	(18-20)	XXL
Quantity	(21-23)	024

The bar coded carton label should use 9/16" lettering and overall label size should be at least 6" in length and 4" in height.

SPECIFICATIONS FOR LABEL

Examples of the fields used for various sizes are as follows where '_' denotes a trailing space.

34_	Size 34
8_ _	Size 8
XXL	Size XXL

A. Density

Narrow element dimension = 0.020 inches.

B. Bar Height

The recommended minimum bar height is 1.250 inches to accomplish line scanning operations.

C. Quiet Zone

The quiet zone or clear area preceding and following the bar code shall be 0.25 inches (6.35 mm). The height of the clear area shall equal the height of the bar code.

D. Human Readable Characters

The 23 data characters of the code 128 symbology should be printed in human readable form directly below the bar code. These human readable characters should be a minimum of 0.125 inches high, and not closer to the bar code than 0.04 inches. The spacing between data fields should look like the following example where a "_" denotes a blank space.

A_071623_02432_412_FQ_XXL_024

E. Substrates

The Code 128 Symbol is to be printed upon substrate that preserves the optical specifications as described in the *USS-128 Uniform Symbology Specification* and that meets ANSI grade A or B print quality. White label stock is to be used for label generation provided it is not glossy, prone to smearing, smudging, etc., and is not direct thermal.

F. Printing Process

A wide variety of printing processes are possible providing they meet or exceed the specification requirements and achieve the required degree of durability. The contractor and/or agent should consult with their equipment suppliers before purchase to ensure that Code 128 application compliance is achieved. The symbols must satisfy optical specifications for the spectral band centered at 633 nanometers (visible red).

For all printing processes (on or off-site), it is recommended that the symbols be tested to ensure that they meet specification requirements. This testing should initially cover 100% of test samples and then later the symbols should be intermittently tested to ensure compliance with specifications (i.e. 4% random testing of bulk production).

PLACEMENT

Label must be placed in the upper right hand corner on the end of the box.

CHAPTER 12

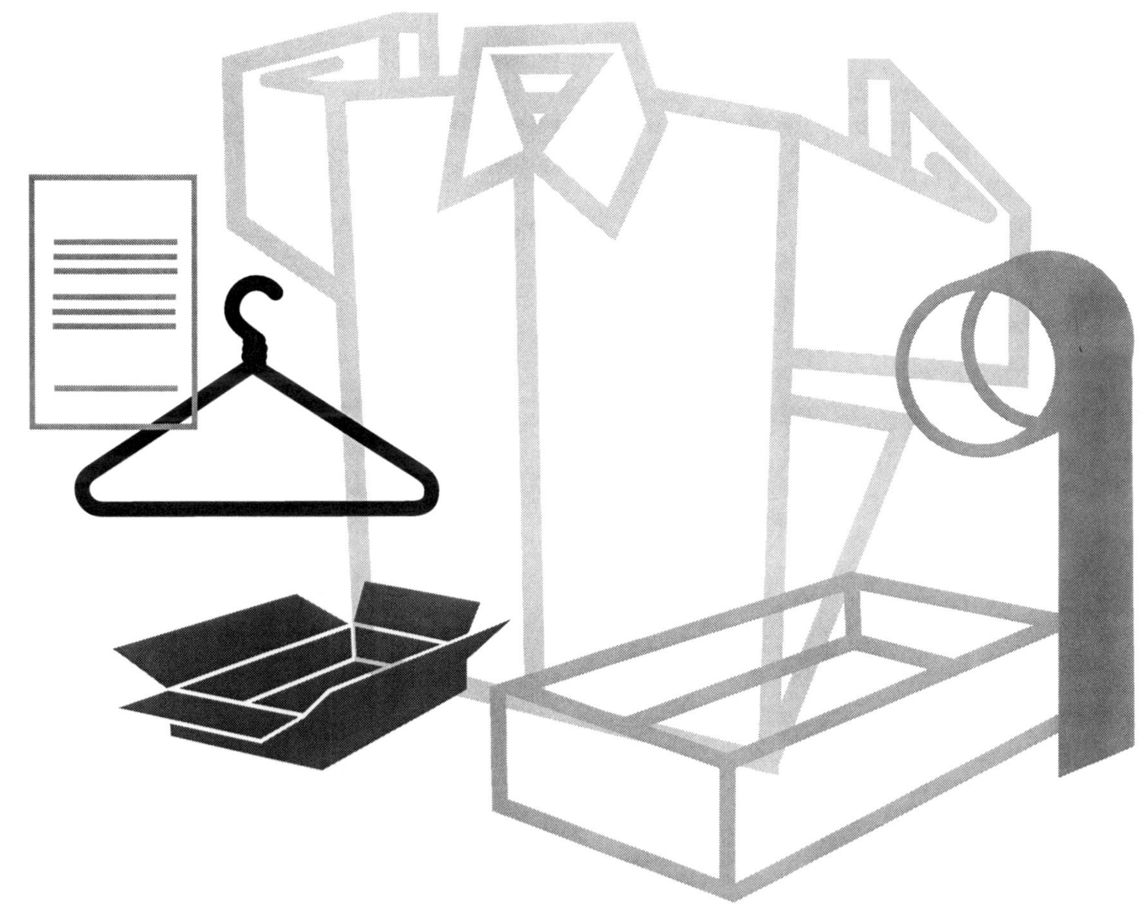

PACKAGING AND SHIPPING

This chapter outlines frequently encountered issues and standards for the packing and shipping of merchandise from a contractor or factory to you, the customer. These are accepted industry-wide practices, and can be adapted to a company's particular needs and type of business. All companies are entitled to expect compliance with these guidelines.

PACKAGING STANDARDS

PACKAGING AND SHIPPING

How many ways can you fold and ship a garment? The ones listed here are the most commonly used methods. Again, this will be determined by you and whomever is receiving the shipment. You should decide whether the garments will be folded and stacked or if they should be placed on hangers. You might come up with your own creative way of packaging. Please discuss this with your retailer to ensure that the shelf size or hanging size will work with their needs.

First, let's look at the standards for issues concerning folding methods and packaging of hanging and flat-packed garments. Second, we discuss the procedures and guidelines for cartons. Then last is the documentation and requirements for shipping the packed merchandise.

WOVEN PACKAGING

Below you will find an example of a woven shirt fold. This will vary depending on the style, shirt and category, i.e. women's, men's, children's, etc.

Tissue Paper Standards

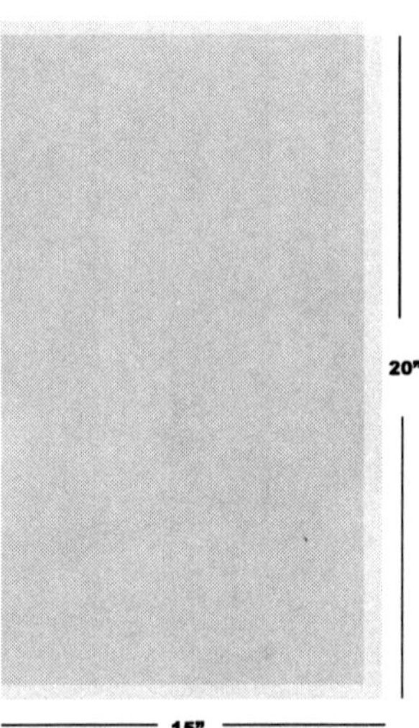

All woven fabric shirts must be folded utilizing the standard folding method to the specified finished dimension.

- ⇒ Men's X-Small and Small is 14 1/2" long (from top of collar) x 12 1/2" wide.
- ⇒ Men's Medium, Large and X-Large is 15 1/2" long (from top of collar) x 12 1/2" wide.
- ⇒ Women's, all sizes, is 12" long (from top of collar) x 11" wide.

Folding Methods

- Place the shirt face down.
- Place tissue at center back of shirt just beneath the collar. (Tissue should extend down approximately 3/4 of the length of the shirt.)
- Sleeves and shirt edges are then folded back across the tissue.
- **Each shirt must have two pins only**. One pin at each inner shoulder to secure shirttail to sleeve.

Poly-bag

- Poly-bags must be of a size that will easily accommodate the garment.
- The poly-bag should not compress the garment in any direction.
- All bags must be taped closed to help keep the garment clean, and to prevent the garment from sliding out of the bag during shipping and handling.
- The open end of the poly-bag must extend far enough beyond the length of the product to allow 2"-3" of plastic to be folded back and taped closed. Fold-lock bags can be used but opening should still be taped closed.

MEN'S SHIRT FOLD for sizes XXS, XS and S

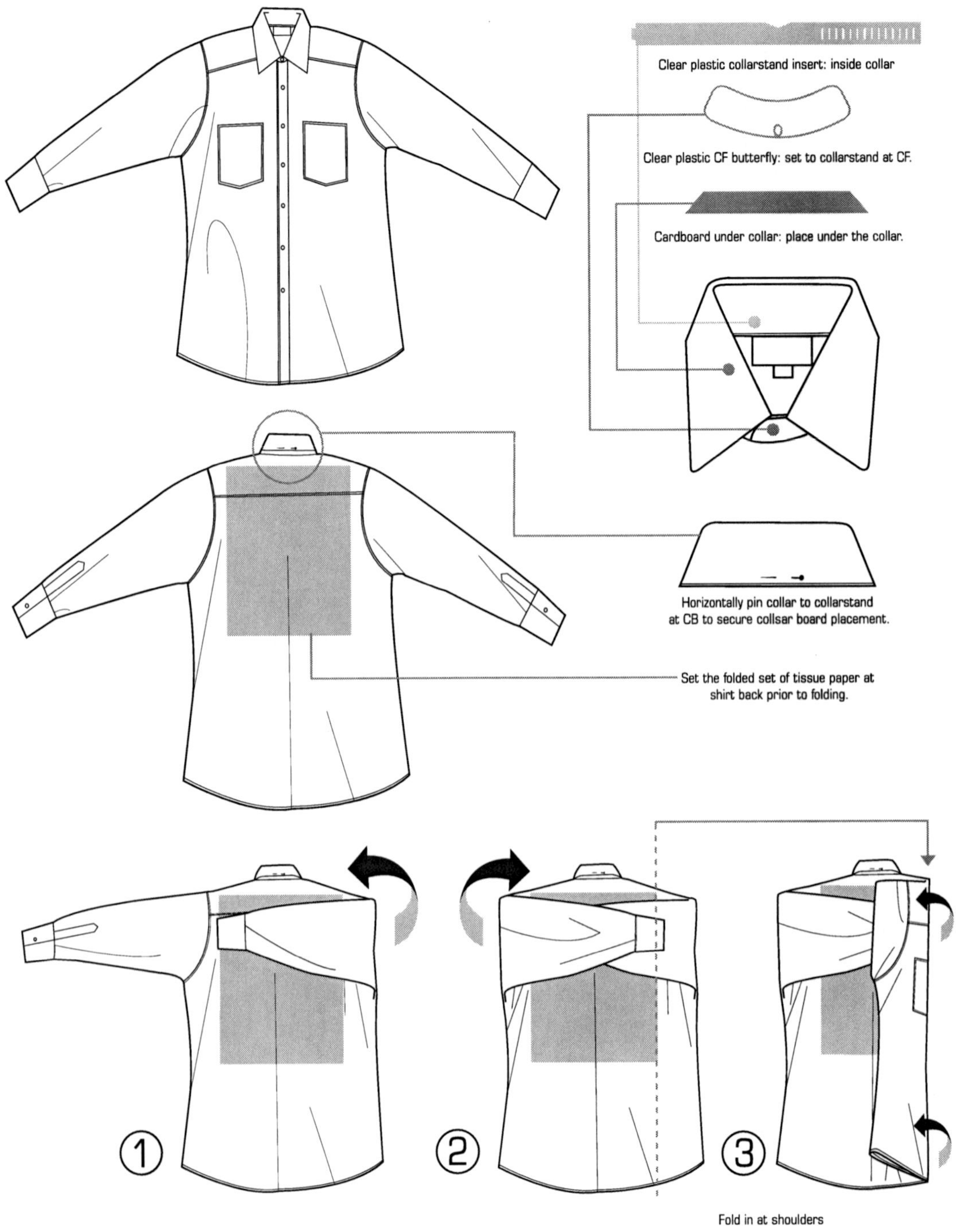

FOR MEN'S SIZES XXS, XS and S: Finished shirt measures 14 1/2" long x 12 1/2" wide.

MEN'S SHIRT FOLD for sizes M, L, XL and XXL

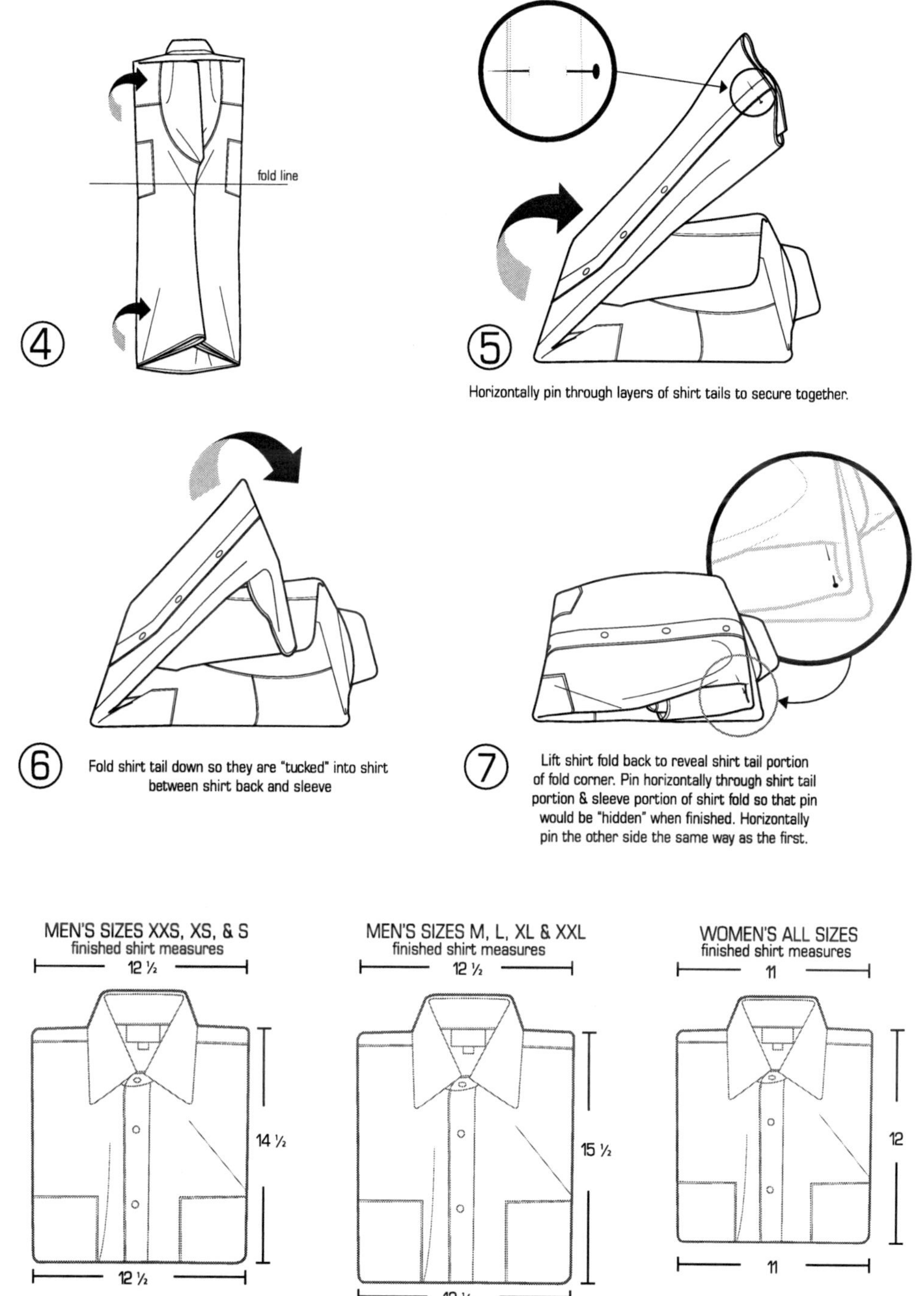

FOR MEN'S SIZES M, L, XL and XXL: Finished shirt measures 15 1/2" long x 12 1/2" wide.

WOMEN'S SHIRT FOLD for all sizes

FOR WOMEN'S ALL SIZES: Finished shirt measures 12″ long x 11″ wide.

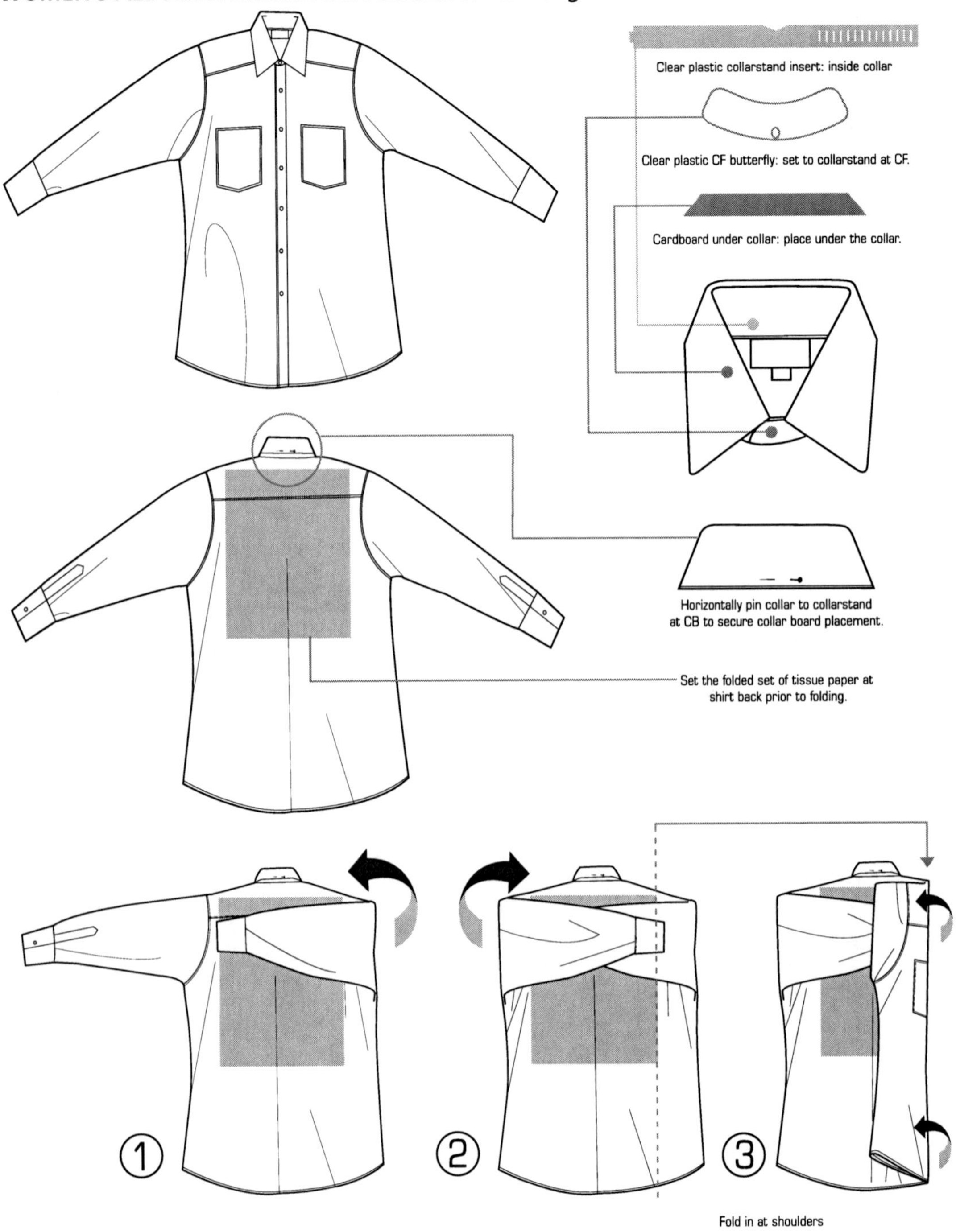

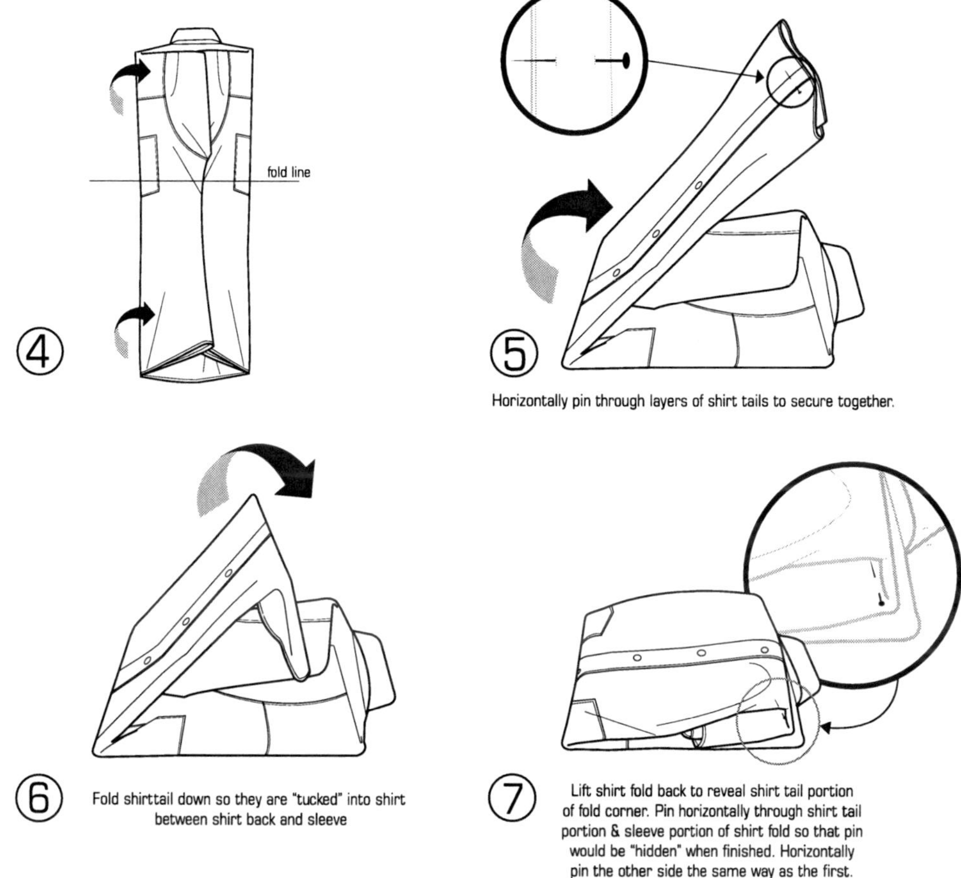

Size of folded shirt will depend upon style of garment.

SWEATER PACKAGING

Here is an example of a sweater fold. This will vary depending on the style and category, i.e. women's, men's, children's, etc.

Tissue Paper Standards

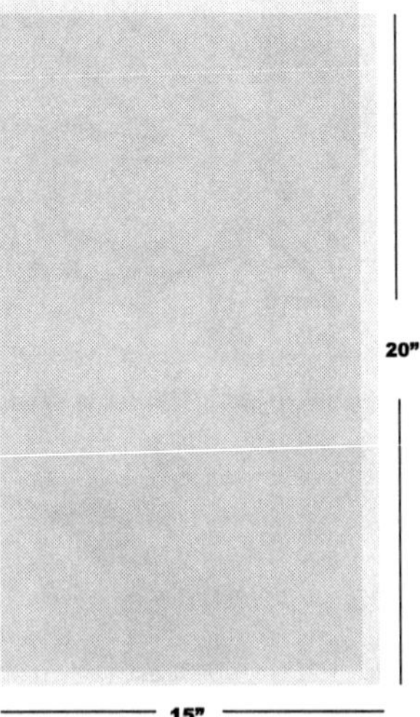

Folding Method

- Place the sweater face down.
- Place two pieces of tissue paper at back, and proceed with folding.
- Sleeves must be folded back across the body.
- If hooded, fold the hood back at neckline.
- Sweater is then folded back in half at the waist.

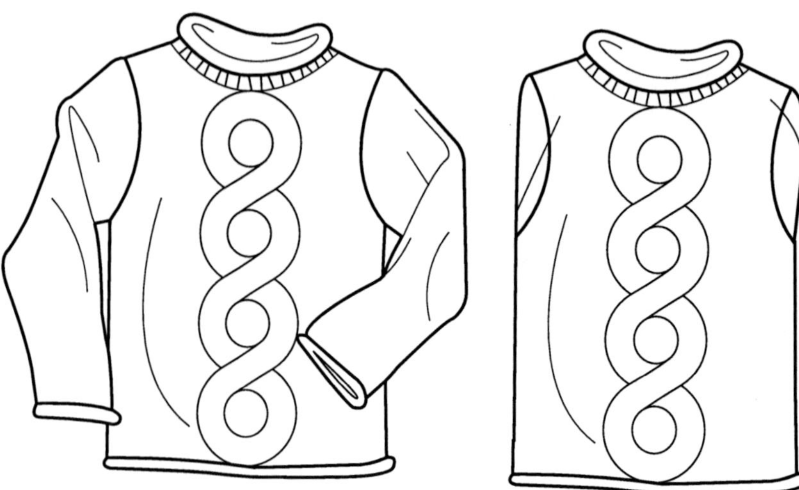

Poly-bag

- Place the sweater face down.
- Poly-bag must be of a size that will easily accommodate the garment.
- The poly-bag must not compress the garment in any direction.
- All bags should be taped closed to prevent the garment from sliding out of the bag during transit and handling.

KNIT SHIRT PACKAGING

Tissue Paper Standards

Below you will find an example of a knit shirt fold. This will vary depending on the style, shirt and category, i.e. women's, men's, children's, etc.

Folding Method

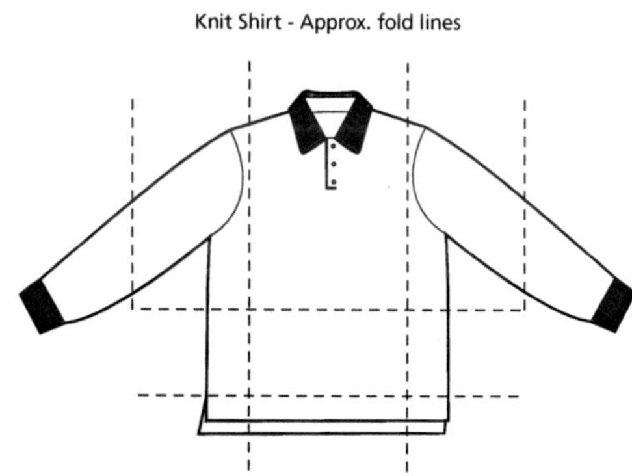

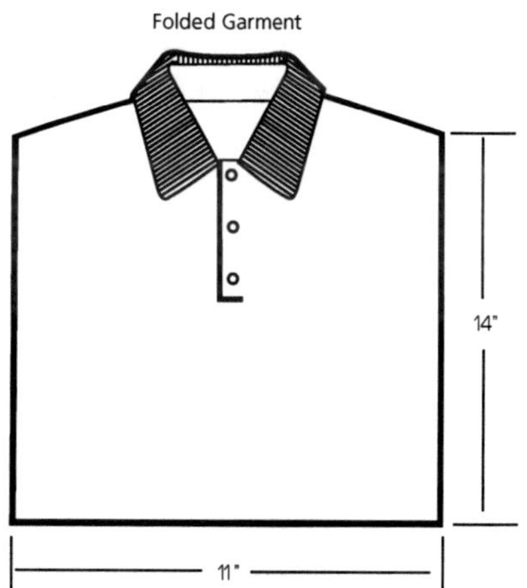

- Place the knit shirt/top face down.
- Place two pieces of tissue paper at shirt back, and proceed with folding.
- Place two plastic clips (of standard size) on either side of garment at shoulder as shown above.
- If hooded, fold hood to the back at the neck, then proceed with standard fold noted above.
- Knit shirts should be folded to standard shirt size approximately 14" tall by 11" wide.

SWEATSHIRTS
Folding Method

- Place the knit sweatshirt face down.
- Place two pieces of tissue paper at back, and proceed with folding.
- Sleeves must be folded back across the body.
- If hooded, fold hood back at neckline.
- Garment is then folded back in half at the waist.
- Sweatshirts should be folded to standard shirt size approximately 14" tall by 11" wide.

KNIT SHIRTS AND SWEATSHIRTS
Poly-bag

- Poly-bag must be of a size that will easily accommodate the garment.
- The poly-bag must not compress the garment in any direction.
- All bags should be taped closed to prevent the garment from sliding out of the bag during transit and handling.

OUTERWEAR AND DRESS PACKAGING

The following are the details of leather and non-leather outerwear (including: blazers, trench coats, jackets) and dresses. These standards will vary depending on the particular style and category, i.e. women's, men's, children's, etc.

LEATHER OUTERWEAR (Coats, jackets and trench coats)

- Leather outerwear must be packed on hangers.
- Hangers must be of a strength that will easily support the weight of the garment during shipping without breaking and without scratching or marking the garment.
- Hanger surfaces, edges and corners must be smooth. All hangers must be pre-approved by the customer.
- Individual buttons must be covered by cardboard to prevent them from marring the garment during shipping.

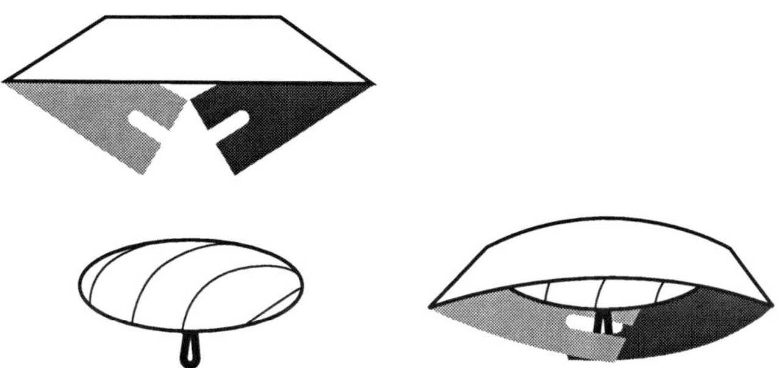

Poly-bag

- Poly-bag must be of a size that will easily accommodate the garment.
- The poly-bag must not compress the garment in any direction.
- All bags should be taped closed to prevent the garment from sliding out of the bag during transit and handling.
- The poly-bag for leather outerwear must extend beyond the length of the garment by no more than 4 inches.
- The bottom of the bag must be secured to protect the garment and allow ventilation.

NON-LEATHER OUTERWEAR (Rugged: jackets, coats and non-waterproof trench coats)

- Rugged non-leather outerwear must be flat-packed.
- All rugged outerwear must be flat-packed **without** hangers, including non-waterproof trench coats. The only exception may be wool outerwear. Please reference the product specification sheet for confirmation of need for hangers on specific wool styles.
- Fold sleeves at shoulder seam extending them across the back of the garment.
- Then fold jacket / coat in half at the waist.
- If garment folded in the manner described above does not fit into the carton dimensions required in the following section on packaging and shipping, contact Production Manager for review.

Poly-bag

- Poly-bag must be of a size that will easily accommodate the garment.
- The poly-bag must not compress the garment in any direction.
- All bags should be taped closed to prevent the garment from sliding out of the bag during transit and handling.
- The poly-bag for non-leather outerwear must extend beyond the length of the garment by no more than 4 inches.
- The bottom of the bag must be secured to protect the garment and allow ventilation.

NON-LEATHER OUTERWEAR (Hanging garments and flat-packed: waterproof trench coats, blazers, vests)

- Waterproof trenches must be flat-packed on hangers.
- All blazers and vests must be flat-packed on hangers.
- Vests must have no folds.
- Hangers must be of a strength that will easily support the weight of the garment during shipping without breaking and without scratching or marking the garment. Hanger surfaces, edges and corners must be smooth. All hangers must be pre-approved by the customer.

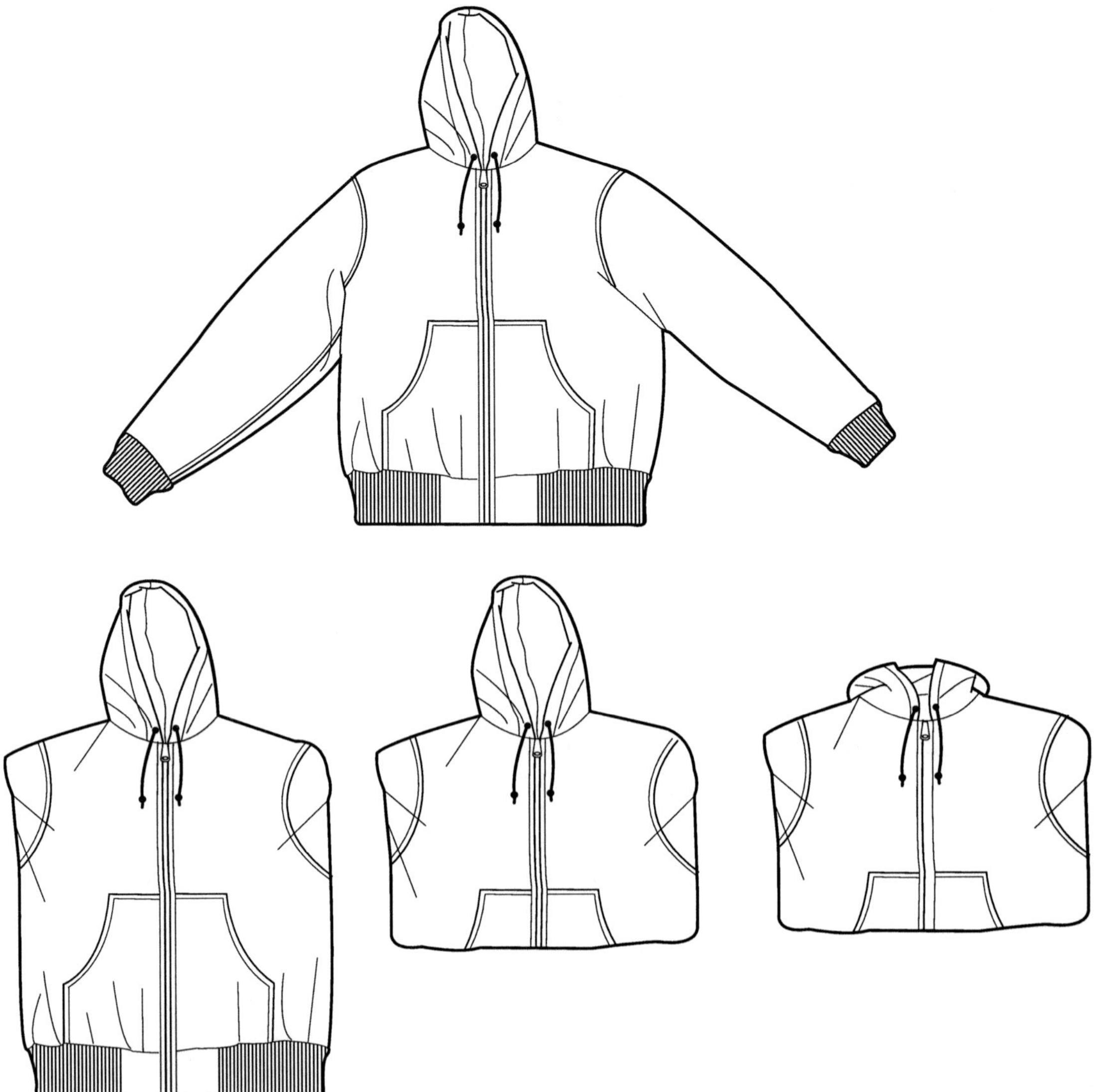

- Fold sleeves over the front of the cardboard separator and fold in half at waist.
- Care must be taken to avoid permanent creases in the sleeves and waist.
- When flat packing, the garments must be arranged in the carton with no folds or with as few folds as possible. Extreme care must be taken to avoid wrinkling or creasing in transit.
- When flat-packing coats longer than 41" (measuring from the top of the **hanger hook** to the bottom hem), each garment must be folded back in half at the waist. Cardboard inserts must still cover the entire front of the garment when folded.
- Garments must be packed with a protective cardboard layer covering the entire front body of the garment. Sleeves are to be folded across the protective cardboard layer as wrinkle-free as possible.

Cardboard Separators:

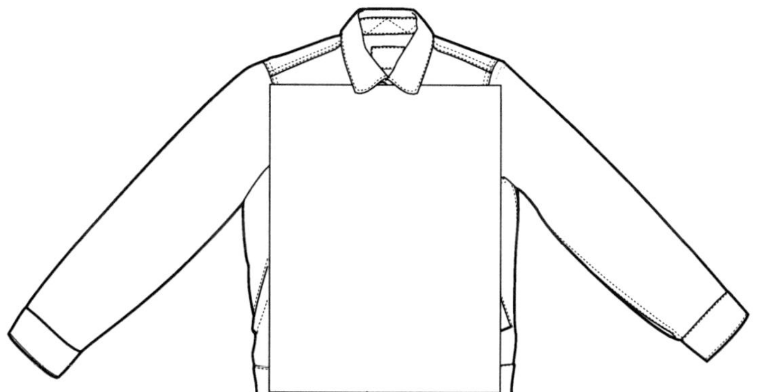

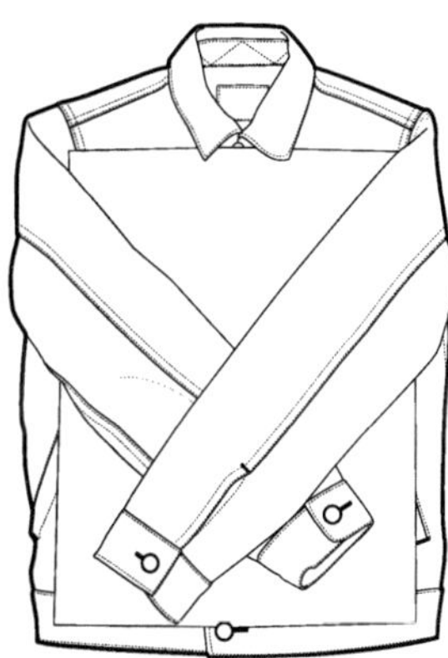

Poly-bag

- Poly-bag must be of a size that will easily accommodate the garment.
- The poly-bag must not compress the garment in any direction.
- All bags should be taped closed to prevent the garment from sliding out of the bag during transit and handling.
- The poly-bag for leather outerwear must extend beyond the length of the garment by no more than 2-3 inches.
- The bottom of the bag must be secured to protect the garment and allow ventilation.

CARTON CONSTRUCTION AND DIMENSIONS

For the cartons used in shipping finished garments, the specific packaging will vary, depending on your particular requirements for different styles or those required by your retail customer. The following examples are suggestions for various packaging* formats and measurements.

*** The customer should require all cartons and packaging to be recyclable.**

CARTONS FOR ALL APPAREL ITEMS, EXCLUDING OUTERWEAR

- The standard corrugated carton dimension (outside measurements) for all of the customer's apparel (excluding outerwear) should be **16"W x 24"L x 17"H** as illustrated below.

- Corrugated material used for all outer cartons should have a burst test rating of at least 275 lbs. per square inch with double-wall construction.

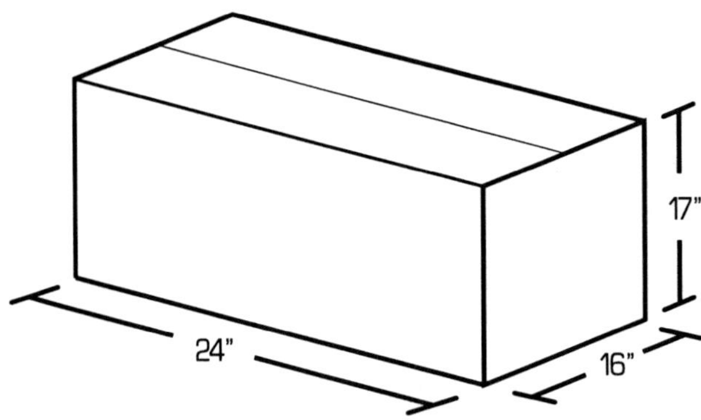

CARTONS FOR NON-LEATHER OUTERWEAR

- All non-leather outerwear should be flat-packed including those shipped on hangers.
- Corrugated material used for all outerwear cartons should have a burst test rating of at least 275 lbs. per square inch with double walled construction.
- Garments with hangers should be packed with few or no folds. Carton dimensions for these garments should not exceed 26"W x 42" L (and height not to exceed 10") determined by a weight restriction of 45 lbs. per carton.
- All other non-leather outerwear should be packed in cartons with a maximum dimension of 24" W x 24" L x 17" H. Maximum weight should not exceed 45 lbs.
- Flat-packed garments should be packed into the carton in an alternating "head-to-toe" manner. This will allow for packing that is even and balanced inside the carton as the tops of the garments (thickened by inserted hangers) will **not** all be at the same end of the carton. (See illustration below).

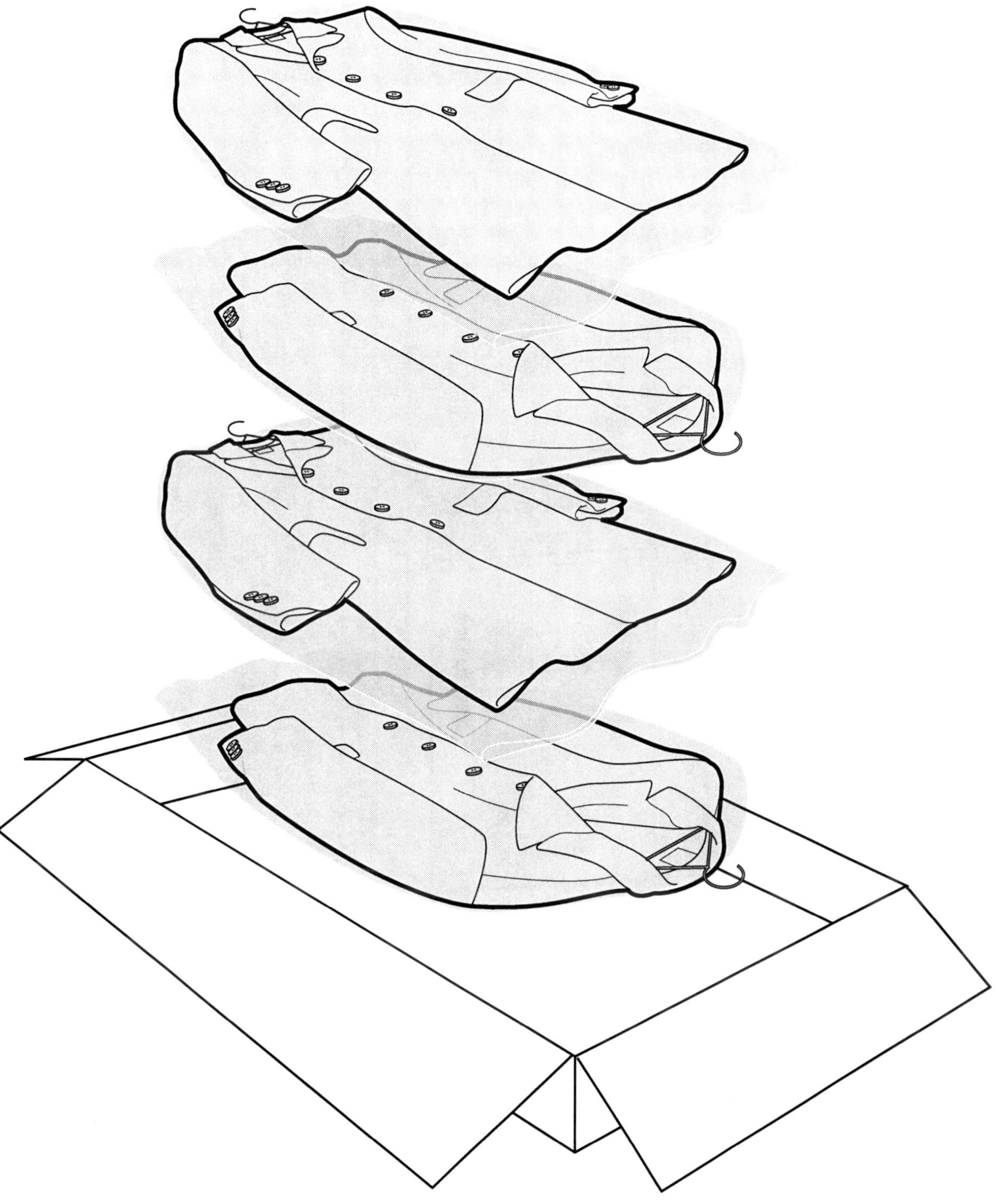

CARTONS FOR LEATHER OUTERWEAR

- Leather outerwear should be shipped in "hanging" cartons.

- The standard carton dimension (length and width) for leather garments is:
  24"L X 24"W X 50"H.

- The crossbar (see illustration) should be made of metal and able to support at least 150 lbs. in weight. The crossbar should be designed so that the hanger will be firmly attached to the bar and will not permit the hanger to slip or bounce off the crossbar during transit or handling.

- The carton should have side markings that indicate **"THIS END UP"** to help ensure that the carton stays vertical during transit.

- The corrugated material used for hanging cartons should have a burst test rating of at least 275 lbs. per square inch with double walled construction.

- Maximum weight per carton should not exceed 65 lbs.

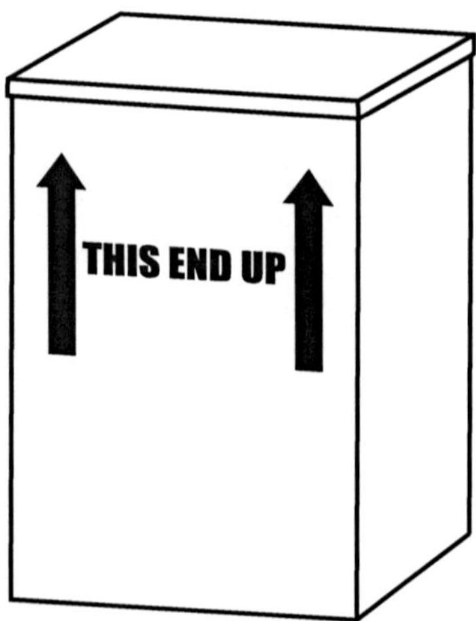

CARTON MARKINGS

In addition to the UPC carton label (see Chapter 11: UPC Labels), the customer's receiving procedures should require that additional information should have consistent placement, character size, and readability to facilitate the proper receipt of goods.

Customer approved methods for marking cartons should be:

1) Computer-generated label
   or
2) Stenciling

The computer-generated or stenciled carton-marking method should always identify:

- Destination
- Gross weight
- Dimensions
- Carton box number

Note: Handwritten carton markings should not be accepted. The customer may stipulate a penalty for such infractions. (This should be done in advance with the factory or contractor's understanding.)

END BOX MARKINGS

Each carton should clearly display the following information on one end (in addition to applying the UPC carton label):

- Destination: Final destination of shipment.
- Gross Weight: Gross weight of box.
- Dimensions: Metric measurements of outside box dimensions.

SIDE MARKINGS

Side markings are also necessary for all cartons.

- Each carton should clearly display a **"T"** symbol positioned in the quadrangle as shown to represent a customer shipment.
- Additional markings include:

  - Ship To Destination
  - Carton Number
  - Country of Origin

Note: the <u>Ship To Destination</u> and the <u>Final Destination</u> may not always be the same. Refer to the routing and consignee guide distributed by the customer for confirmation of proper address.

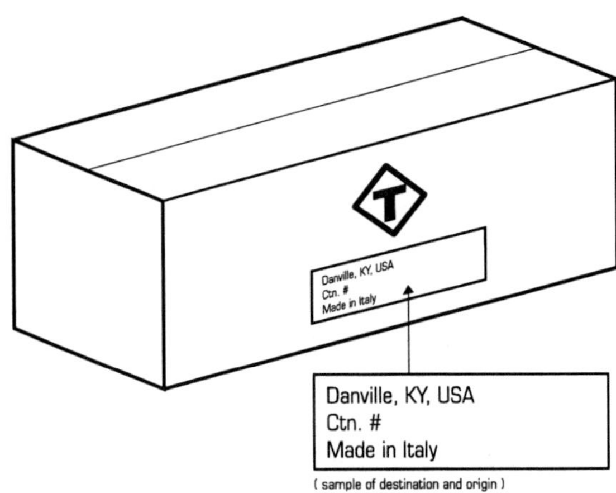

(sample of destination and origin)

CARTON BOX NUMBERING

The box number of the shipment should be printed, stenciled, or stamped in the designated area of the label (upper right-hand corner) by the factory.

- One acceptable method for applying the box number to each carton label is to preprint (via a computer) the box numbers on appropriately sized adhesive laser labels and placing them in the appropriate location on the UPC carton label.
- If this method is used, the laser label should easily fit in the designated area in the upper right-hand corner of the carton label and not cover any writing or bar code lines.

MIXED CARTON LABELING

In addition to the markings listed above, the following is required for marking **Mixed Cartons**:

END BOX MARKINGS

DEST.	Final Destination of shipment.
PO #	Purchase Order (PO) number.
STYLE #	Customer style/model number.
COLOR #	Color number of garment as indicated on customer PO.
SIZES/QUANTITY	Sizes and quantity of each size.
TOTAL QUANTITY	Total quantity in carton.
BOX #	Carton sequence number of the box in shipment.
GROSS WEIGHT	Gross weight of box.
DIMENSIONS	Metric measurements of outside box dimensions.

Note: Handwritten carton markings should not be accepted. The customer may stipulate (in advance) a penalty for such infractions.

SIDE MARKINGS

If the length of the carton is greater than 24," then one of the sides of the carton should restate the following:

- Style #
- Color #
- Size
- Quantity

GENERAL PACKING INSTRUCTIONS

COMPOSITION OF CARTON UNIFORMITY

- Cartons should be packed by all the same style, size, and color. Styles or colors should not be mixed in the same carton except at the end of a production run.

- The quantities packed per carton should be uniform throughout the style production (i.e., same quantities per carton).

- Cartons should not be overfilled so much that it makes them appear rounded or bulging. This condition encourages possible damage to the merchandise while in transit to the customer's offices, warehouse or distribution centers.

POLY-BAGS

- Every garment should be individually poly-bagged.

- Hanging apparel should be individually poly-bagged so that the poly-bag extends beyond the bottom of the garment by no more than 4 inches.

- The bottom of the poly-bag should be closed to protect the garment but should allow ventilation.

CARTON CLOSURES

- All cartons should have a piece of protective cardboard just inside the flaps to protect the contents from knife cuts when cartons are opened.

- Cartons should be sealed with a strong security tape*. The tape should have a logo **other** than the manufacturer's name to make it possible to detect pilferage. For security reasons, the logo should **not** identify the customer or the manufacturer in any way. An accepted logo may have the following printing on the tape:

Across width of tape, printing with the warning:

'IF THIS TAPE SHOWS SIGNS OF HAVING BEEN BROKEN AND RESEALED . . . DO NOT ACCEPT. ADVISE SHIPPER IMMEDIATELY.' Warning should be written in 1/4" lettering next to the logo. Logo and warning is to be repeated across the length of tape.

If manufacturer does not use security tape, the customer may charge back for any loss or damage in such carton(s).

- Lettering should be of a contrasting color from the background of the tape such as red lettering with a tan background. This tape should be used for sealing all carton seams along the top and bottom side as pictured below.

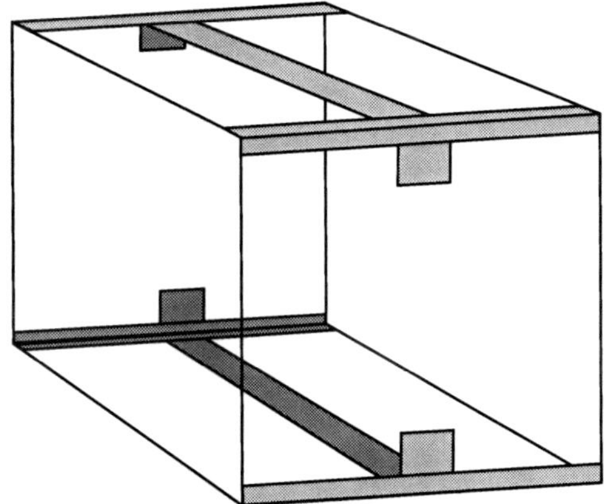

- Reflective tape should not be used.
- Staples or glue should not be used for top closure.
- LCL (Less-than-Container Load) shipments from the manufacturer are required to use nylon binding straps around the outer cartons for extra strength and security.

MIXED CARTONS

- End-of-production-run cartons should be mixed at the size level only. In such an instance, the word "MIXED" should be clearly marked on the outside of the carton in addition to all other required carton information (See "Chapter 7: Labeling" for mixed carton labeling specifications).
- The customer should not allow more than 3 mixed cartons for each color combination in a single shipment. The customer may stipulate (in advance) a penalty for such infractions.
- Furthermore, a chargeback may be issued against any shipment where the mixing of cartons is found to be unnecessary. A shipment is considered non-compliant if it is in the contractor and/or agent's power to avoid mixing cartons.

SHIPPING FACTORY SECONDS

Please refer to "Chapter 13: Chargeback, Irregular and Overrun Purchase Policies" for guidelines.

PACKING AND SHIPPING OF FACTORY SECONDS

These guidelines for packaging, invoicing and packing lists are the same for first and second quality goods. In addition, the following should also be noted:

- Factory seconds should not be shipped without prior approval and a PO from the customer.
- Factory seconds should be packed separately from first quality production.
- Factory seconds should be printed in bold on all cartons. The poly-bag bar code label, as well as the bar coded carton label, should have 'FACTORY SECOND' or 'FD' marked on it along with the proper UPC code.
- All packing lists and invoices should indicate "Factory Seconds" for U.S. Customs' purposes on imported goods.
- Cartons should be packed by all the same Style, Size and Color (SKU). The exception to this policy should be the use of mixed cartons with the same style and color (varying sizes) when there is not enough of one SKU to fill a carton.
- The word "IRREGULAR" should be stamped on or near the customer's main label per procedure in "Chapter 13: Chargeback, Irregular, and Overrun Purchase Policy."

COMMERCIAL INVOICE

A **Commercial Invoice** is normally required for every PO and destination. The following invoice illustrated may be used as a guideline for all invoices made out for the customer's shipments.

Invoices should be in English and be faxed or e-mailed along with packing lists at the time of shipment.

Every invoice should include the following information:

- Customer PO #.
- Breakdown by style # and color #.
- Garment description and composition.
- Harmonized code # per classification (if applicable).
- Unit price / total price in US dollars.
- Total number of pieces.
- Total number of cartons.
- Method of transport.
- Country of origin (for imported goods).
- FOB terms.

Please note that a **Raw Material Assist** should be included for all raw materials supplied by the customer as part of the total invoice value for U.S. Customs (for imported goods). See " Raw Material Assists" for additional information.

COMMERCIAL INVOICE EXAMPLE

MFG: ____________________
____
____

INVOICE DATE: __________

INVOICE # ________________

BILL TO: The Customer's Company
Some Street
Town, Some State 00000

DESTINATION/SHIP TO ADDRESS:
(Ship to Address)

FINAL DESTINATION:
(Country or Consignee/Customer)

SHIP VIA: (Air/Sea/Truck)

P.O. #: 12345

STYLE#	COLOR#	DESCRIPTION	QTY	UNIT PRICE	TOTAL PRICE
9999	10	Men's Woven Shirt 100% Cotton	70	$40.00	$2,800.00
9999	41	Men's woven Shirt 100% Cotton	42	$40.00	$1,600.00

					$4,400.00

Harmonized Code # ___________ (If applicable)

TOTAL CARTONS: ____________________
SHIPPER; ____________________
FOB TERMS: ____________________
COUNTRY OF ORIGIN: ____________________

RAW MATERIAL ASSISTS (Non-USA Manufacturers Only)
U.S. Customs requires that all material(s), provided free of charge or at a reduced cost to the foreign manufacturer and not included in the invoice price of the garment, should be declared, listed, and valued separately. These items can include, but are not limited to, fabrics, leathers, trims, packaging, tags, and bar code labels supplied to the factory, which are not reflected in the garment invoice price. Transportation costs for the raw material(s) to the factory should also be included in the assist value.

The Raw Material Assist Declaration shown below is an example of a 450-piece garment shipment. In this example, the leather trim, hang tags, and bar code labels were supplied by the customer to an offshore contractor free of charge and, therefore, were not included in the garment cost listed on the manufacturer's invoice. As stated above, the raw materials should be declared, listed, and valued separately. An acceptable format is as follows:

EXAMPLE:

RAW MATERIAL ASSIST STATEMENT

Raw Materials:

- Leather Trim:	450 pcs x 1.3mtrs / garment	=	585 mtrs x $2.92/mtr	=	$1,708.20
- Hang Tags:	450 pcs x 1 / garment	=	450 tags x .07 / tag	=	31.50
- Bar Code Labels:	450 pcs x 1 / garment	=	450 lbls x .04 / lbl	=	18.00
Total Value for U.S. Customs Purposes:		=			$ 1,757.70

PACKING LISTS

A copy of the **Packing List** should be required for each Purchase Order, destination and per container (for full container load shipments only). A copy of the packing list should accompany all shipments and be located in carton #1. The carton containing the Packing List should be marked: "PACKING LIST ENCLOSED."

A new packing list should be prepared whenever one of the following two data fields change: Invoice Number or Container Number. If any of these conditions change, a new Packing List is written.

All packing lists should be in English and clearly indicate the following information:

• Carton number	• Total pieces per Carton
• Customer PO #	• Carton measurement
• Style # (breakdown by color and size)	• Volume
• Color number	• Gross weight
• Size	• Net weight

IMPORTANT! All packing lists and invoices should be faxed or e-mailed to the customer at the time of shipment. This step is crucial to customer procedures and operations. Non-compliance may necessitate a charge back to the contractor and/or agent.

PREPARING THE PACKING LIST

1. Each contractor and/or agent should prepare a packing list with all the required information. An example is provided to show the format and data fields.

2. A packing list is required for every shipment leaving the factory. There should be one packing list for each container or less-than-container load (LCL). In the case of an LCL shipment, the contractor and/or agent should fill out the complete packing list except for the container number information.

3. A new packing list should be prepared whenever one of the following two data fields change: invoice number or container number. If any of these conditions change, a new packing list should be written.

4. The packing list number should be the same as the invoice number for a shipment on one container. If multiple containers are required to load a shipment on the same invoice, the packing list number should be designated by invoice number followed by a check digit (C1, C2, C3,...). An example for invoice number 12345 over three containers would look like the following: Packing List # 12345-C1, 12345-C2, and 12345-C3.

5. Packing list carton numbers should be arranged in ascending carton number (1,2,3,...etc.). POs should have only one carton #1 with labels printed consecutively for the entire PO.

FOR SHIPMENTS TO UNITED STATES

Contractor and/or agent's instructions for completing the packing list are as follows:

A. **Date** of the shipment leaving the contractor's factory in the format MM/DD/YY (i.e. 08/10/05).
B. **Sold To** - customer or client.
C. **Final Destination -** city and state.
D **Carrier Name** - name of trucking company.
E. **Page Number** for multiple page packing lists in the format showing page number sequence (example: 1 of 5, 2 of 5, ...etc.).
F. **Invoice Number** given by the contractor.
G. **Packing List Number** following the guidelines given above. It should be a unique number for all shipments down to the container level.
H. **Container Number** that the shipment is traveling aboard including the size of the container (example: 40', 20'). This should be left blank for less-than- container loads delivered to the freight consolidator.
I. **Trailer Number** that the shipment is traveling aboard, including the size of the trailer (ex. 53'). This should be left blank for less-than-trailer loads picked up by the customer's designated inland carrier.
J. **Carton Number Sequence** of the carton label ranges by size and in ascending order. The packing list contains examples of missing carton labels and how the numbers should be listed.
K. **Purchase Order Number** is the customer's PO number for this shipment.
L. **Style Number** of the apparel within the carton range.
M. **Color Number**.
N. **Size** of the style within the carton (indicating quantity per size).
O. **Total Number of Pieces** per carton.
P. **Carton Dimensions** of the factory-packed carton.
Q. **Volumetric Weight** in cubic meters (CBM's).
R. **Gross Weight** on a per-carton basis in kilograms (kgs).
S. **Net Weight** on per-item basis (kilo's or lbs.). If carton is mixed, individual items' net weight should be stated in ascending size order.
T. **Summary** of the total shipment by PO, style, color, size run and end destination. Units and cartons are totaled for each PO within the container.
U. **List Grand Totals:**

Total cartons in shipment.
Total pieces in shipment.
Total weight of shipment (in lbs. or kilo's).
Total cubic meters (CBM's) of the shipment.

PACKING LIST
EXAMPLE FOR SHIPMENTS TO UNITED STATES

Sold to: The Customer's Company
Some Street
P.O. Box ###
Town, Some State 00000 USA

Date: 08/24/95

Page No.: **1 of 1**

Invoice No.: 99999

End Destination: Somewhere, KY USA

Packing List: 99999-C1

Carrier: Name of Carrier

Trailer Number (Size): APLU450401 (53')

Carton #	PO #	Style #	Color #	XS	S	M	L	XL	Total Pieces	Ctn Meas	Vol	Gross Weight	Net Weight
#1	12345	9999	10	15					15	16x17x24	3.8'	42lbs	36.3
#2	"	"	10		15				15	"	"	"	"
#3	"	"	10			10			10	"	"	37 lbs	31.3
#4	"	"	10				10		10	"	"	"	"
#5	"	"	10					10	10	"	"	"	"
#6	12346	9991	41			10			10	"	"	"	"
#7	"	"	41				10		10	"	"	"	"
#8	"	"	41					12	12	"	"	40 lbs	34.3
#9	"	"	41		8				8	"	"	35 lbs	29.3
Carton #10 - Mixed Carton Example (FOR END OF SIZE RUN ONLY)													
#10	"	"	41	5					12	"	"	18 lbs	12.3
#10	"	"	41					7	12	"	"	22 lbs	16.3

SUMMARY:

PO#	Style #	Color #	XS	S	M	L	XL	Total
12345	**9999**	**#10**	**15**	**15**	**10**	**10**	**10**	**70**
12346	**9991**	**#41**	**5**	**8**	**10**	**10**	**19**	**42**
								112

TOTAL CARTONS: 10
TOTAL PIECES: 112
TOTAL WEIGHT: 384 lbs
TOTAL CBMS: 2.52m3

PRE-RECEIVING REQUIREMENTS / SHIPPING INSTRUCTIONS

DOMESTIC CONTRACTORS (within the USA)

In addition to a Commercial Invoice and Packing List, the following **additional documentation** should be required for each shipment:

A. **Certificate of origin**: For orders shipping internationally- outside of the US.
B. **Container manifest**: For vendor/contractor loaded, full ocean containers only, shipping internationally.
C. **Beneficiary's certificate(s)**: Per instructions under L/C.
D. **Inspection certificate**.
E. **Shippers letter of instruction**: International shipments only.
F. **Any other documents** specified under a customer Letter of Credit and/or instructions from the customer's transportation department.

FOREIGN CONTRACTORS

In addition to a Commercial Invoice and Packing List, the following **additional documentation** is required for each shipment:

A. **Certificate of origin**.
B. **Container manifest**: For contractor full-loaded ocean containers only.
C. **Forwarder's cargo receipt**: Issued by the customer's designated consolidator.
D. **Beneficiary's certificate(s)**: Per instructions under L/C.
E. **Export license-per shipment**: When required.
F. **Textile declaration**: For US destination shipments only.
G. **Inspection certificate**.
H. **Any other documents** specified under the Letter of Credit and/or instructions from the customer.

•For all Less-than-One-Container-Load Shipments

The contractor should deliver all cartons and documentation specified above for each shipment to the customer's consolidator who will coordinate the shipping to all retail customers. Upon receipt of the cartons and a complete set of original documents, the consolidator should issue cargo receipts to the contractor.

Original documents should be delivered to the consolidator and distributed to the appropriate parties per the customer's instructions.

•For all Full-Container-Load Shipments

The contractor should book all containers with the customer's designated consolidator.
The contractor should follow the customer's requirements for maximizing container loads as follows:

Container Utilization Factor	Standard Container Capacity
40' Container	35 - 55 CBM's
40' 9'6" (Hi Cube)	61 - 65 CBM's
45' Container	66 - 75 CBM's

If CBM's (cubic meters) per shipment do not meet the above capacity requirements, contractors should deliver all cartons as loose freight to the customer's designated consolidator, for consolidation.

The contractor should provide all original documentation specified above, for each shipment, to the customer's designated origin consolidator, who will coordinate the shipping to all countries. Upon receipt of a complete set of original documents, the consolidator should issue cargo receipt to vendor.

Original documents are to be delivered to the consolidator, who should distribute them to the appropriate parties per the customer's instructions.

•For Air Freight Shipments

The contractor should deliver all cartons and documentation as specified above for each shipment to the customer's designated airfreight forwarder, who should coordinate the shipping to the U.S. Upon receipt of the cartons and a complete set of original documents, the airfreight forwarder should issue a cargo receipt to the contractor.

Original documents should be delivered to the airfreight forwarder, who will distribute them to the appropriate parties per the customer's instructions.

Reminder! All packing lists and invoices must be faxed or emailed to the customer at the time of shipment. Non-compliance can result in a charge back to the contractor and/or agent.

AIR FREIGHT AUTHORIZATION

The customer should authorize all air freight shipments in writing. Unauthorized air freight shipments may be returned to the contractor (with no obligation to the customer) for its expense. If the customer decides to accept an unauthorized air freight shipment, a chargeback should be issued for the difference between air freight cost and surface freight cost. See "Chapter 13: Chargeback, Irregular and Overrun Purchase Policy."

Here is an example of the Air Freight Authorization Form.

CUSTOMER NAME

AIR FREIGHT AUTHORIZATION FORM

AIR FREIGHT REQUEST #

CONTRACTOR ACCT #:
SHIP FROM: ______ (Name) ______ (Address) ______ (City.State) (Country)

SHIP TO: ______ (Name) ______ (Address) ______ (City, State) (Country)

FOR RAW MATERIALS:

Dimensions:

Weight:

PARTY TO PAY DIFFERENCE BETWEEN SEA AND AIR:

BUDGET CODE (18 DIGIT):

REASON:

REQUESTOR: ______ Ext. ______
DATE: ______
X-FCTY DATE: ______
CARRIER: ______
AWB#: ______
ARIVAL DATE REQUIRED: ______

COLLECT: ______
PREPAID: ______
AIR RATE: ______
SEA RATE: ______

ORDER #	STOCK NUMBER	SQ FT OR UNITS	FINAL DEST. (U1,F1,G1,GC,etc)	ESTIMATED FREIGHT COST* OCEAN/TRUCK	AIR	DIFFERENCE
TOTAL						

SERVICE LEVEL REQUESTED **
Overnight AM: ______
Overnight PM: ______
2-Day: ______
Other: ______

______
TRAFFIC MANAGER

SHADED AREAS TO BE COMPLETED BY TRANSPORTATION DEPARTMENT.
* PORT TO PORT RATE ONLY, NO ACCESSORIAL CHARGES CONSIDERED
**DOMESTIC REQUESTS ONLY

______
CONTROLLER

CONTACT NAMES AND NUMBERS

ROUTING AND SHIPPING QUESTIONS

For any problems or questions concerning the routing of a shipment, carrier selection or consolidator, all domestic and foreign contractors and/or agents should contact the customer's distribution and/or warehouse at the address below:

Customer's Company
Attn.: Distribution (or) Warehouse
Contact: Name
Some Street
Some Town, Some State 00000
Tel: (000) 000-0000
Fax: (000) 000-0000

PACKAGING, HANDLING, MARKING, OR DOCUMENTATION QUESTIONS

For all contractor's and/or agent's problems or questions concerning the packaging, marking or handling specifications, or any problems or questions concerning the information required prior to shipment or other aspect of a shipment, domestic and foreign contractors and/or agents should contact:

The Customer's Company
Attn.: Production Department
Contact: Name
Some Street
Some Town, Some State 00000
Tel: (000) 000-0000
Fax: (000) 000-0000

CHAPTER 13

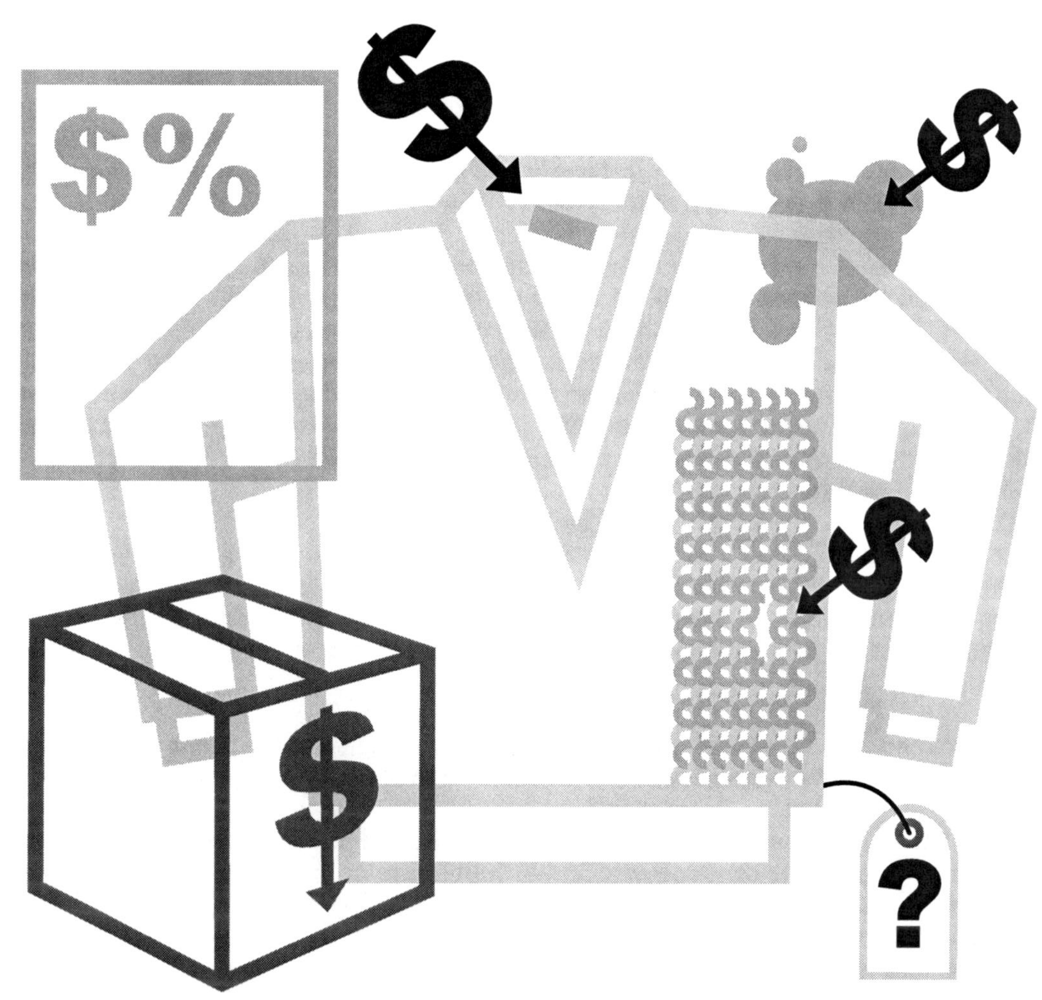

CHARGEBACKS, IRREGULAR AND OVERRUN PURCHASE POLICIES

This chapter serves as a format for an important part of the policy manual you should create for individual contractors and agents. Presented here are specific guidelines and circumstances where you are entitled to make chargebacks over issues of failure to follow specifications or directions, quality and delivery issues and other non-compliance issues, as well as proper disposal of second-quality merchandise and production overruns.

CHARGEBACK

This chapter will explain the things that can happen if you are not careful about understanding your retailer, and making sure your supplier understands the consequences. (You should try to make the factory or vendor responsible as well for this charge.)

In this chapter, you will see suggested dollar amounts and conditions where you might be forced to pay the retailer monies. Again, this is an example, and each retailer might have his or her own guidelines. If you decide to incorporate this as your working method, you should create a set of rules. This set of rules should be agreed upon with your factory stating that if not met, they will adhere to them. This will again help you ensure compliance for your factory and help you both minimize problems. This will make you both accountable in every step of the process.

Any merchandise that varies from the customer's specifications in any manner may, at the customer's discretion, be returned to the contractor and/or agent at their expense, with no further obligation on the customer's part. A chargeback to the contractor and/or agent should be made for the cost of any such return. These costs may include any direct or consequential damages suffered by the customer as a result of a contractor's and/or agent's failure to follow these guidelines and those on any Purchase Order or PO, including lost profits, damages resulting from delay to the customer's own customers, and any other damages suffered or incurred by the customer.

CHARGEBACK ASSESSMENTS

Generally a chargeback (suggested - $250.00) per Purchase Order should be assessed for the failure to comply with any requirement contained in this manual. Repeated violations may require additional charges. It should be noted that the imposition of a chargeback does not release any contractor and/or agent from future claims by the customer for damaged merchandise or other violations of the purchase contract.

In addition to any remedies the customer is entitled to by law or pursuant to the parties' Purchase Order(s), the customer should charge the contractor and/or agent who shall be liable, for the following:

- Merchandise that fails to meet the customer's quality control standards or product specifications.
- Merchandise that fails quality control inspection in warehouse or distribution centers, as well as the cost of auditing the full shipment (100% inspection).
- All handling and processing costs to repair manufacturing defects.
- Shipment quantities not following to Invoice Quantity or PO Quantity (beyond 3% of total PO).
- Defective merchandise discovered in the storage and freight costs to return the merchandise to the warehouse, distribution center or back to the contractor.
- Storage and handling costs incurred as a result of delays caused by contractor and/or agent not providing necessary documentation, information or other materials in a timely manner.
- All handling and processing costs associated with the contractor's and/or agent's failure to use and comply with carton standards specified in this manual.
- All handling and processing costs for failure to affix the proper price (UPC) ticket, hangtag or poly-bag sticker to the garment/item.
- All expenses related to any shipment refused, due to non-compliance, and all inbound collect freight chargebacks, should be the sole responsibility of the contractor and/or agent.
- Miscellaneous handling charges, not specified above, that are the result of administrative workload caused by the contractor and/or agent, when in advance of the initiation of the charge.

CONDITIONS THAT QUALIFY FOR A CHARGEBACK

The chargeback to a contractor and/or agent for a discrepant shipment (through debit note or invoice) should be calculated according to the following conditions:

1. **Quality Defects Exceeding Acceptable Rate**
   The customer should chargeback for defective products shipped as "first quality," which are later determined by quality control to be defective. The chargeback amount should be a negotiated discount, as listed in the Manufacturing Agreement between the customer and the contractor and/or agent, of the standard FOB cost (as listed on the customer's Purchase Order) and levied against **all** defective units. Negotiations should be between the customer's quality control and the contractor and/or agent.

   Case 1: Useable FD's should be paid at a rate by category or price of FOB.

   Case 2: Scrap or unusable should not be paid for by the customer.

2. **Labor for 100% Inspections**
   A 100% inspection should be performed by the customer's quality control when a product fails the standard audit (as defined in "Chapter 10: Garment Inspection Standards") used by the customer. There is no charge for this standard audit. If a product fails this audit and the supplier is unable to inspect the shipment, the customer should perform a 100% inspection to separate the factory defects from first quality product. The cost of this 100% inspection should be charged, in addition to the charges for any defective products. The chargeback for the inspection should be at a rate of $25.00 per inspection hour, per inspector, plus an administration cost of $100.00 per 100% inspection. (*See Quality Defects Exceeding Acceptable Rate above.*)

3. **Repairs to Correct Manufacturing Defects**
   Defective products may be repairable by the customer's staff or an outside contractor. The contractor and/or agent should be given the option to make the repairs when possible. The customer should discuss the course of action for a repair prior to implementation, but the customer should make the final decision on all repairs. The cost to repair defective products should be charged to the contractor and/or agent if they have caused the defect or have failed to match the approved specifications. The repair chargeback should include all raw materials used in the repair, washing, cleaning, refinishing costs, repackaging costs, transportation and labor costs associated with the repair.

4. **Shipments Without Approval**
   The customer should approve all shipments. Shipments made without the customer's authorization should result in a chargeback to the contractor and/or agent for all increased costs and lost revenues associated with the unauthorized shipment. Examples are (not all inclusive): increased transportation and storage fees. In addition, the customer should not pay for any units in excess of quantities indicated in the PO and shipped without permission from the customer. The contractor and/or agent should be responsible for all costs associated with returning these goods.

5. **Shipment Quantity Discrepant to Invoice Quantity or Purchase Order Quantity**
   A discrepant quantity is defined as being any quantity that is less than or more than the quantity indicated on the Supplier's Invoice or the customer's Purchase Order.

   -If a discrepant quantity exceeds 3%

   If a discrepant quantity exceeds 3% (shortage or excess) of the Purchase Order quantity, the customer should issue a chargeback. The chargeback rate for these discrepancies should be

negotiated based on quantities involved, by the customer's production department and the contractor and/or agent.

Discrepancies should be measured at the size and color level. For example, the total quantity on a Purchase Order may match the packing list/invoice but may be more than 3% discrepant due to shortages and excesses at the size and color level. If this discrepancy causes inventory or allocation problems, it is unacceptable.

-If a discrepant quantity is less than 3%

If a discrepant quantity is less than 3% (shortage or excess) of the Purchase Order quantity, the customer should accept all products and not issue a chargeback. The customer should not pay for products that have been invoiced but not shipped. Again the 3% excess or shortage is measured at the size and color level.

6. **Late Delivery**

A late delivery is defined as any shipment leaving the factory after the cancel date specified on the customer's Purchase Order. The customer should do everything possible to work with the contractor and/or agent to prevent late deliveries. Delivery beyond the Purchase Order cancel date should not accepted without specific written authorization by the appropriate customer's production manager. In addition, the customer reserves the right to negotiate a chargeback to offset any actual or estimated losses incurred by the customer due to:

- Extra freight costs to expedite delivery.
- Reduced gross margins.
- Lost revenue due to canceled orders.
- Any other losses or costs arising from the contractor's and/or agent's delay of shipment.

The formula for computing the chargeback for late delivery should be in accordance with the terms of the Manufacturing Agreement between the customer and the contractor and/or agent, not to exceed:

1% per day for all units that ex-factory after the Purchase Order cancel.

The customer reserves the right to refuse or cancel all or any portion of a Purchase Order that is shipped after the cancel date specified on the customer's Purchase Order.

7. **Pre-shipment**

A pre-shipment is defined as any shipment that leaves the factory or is delivered to a consolidator, port, airport or distribution center prior to the ex-factory date indicated on the customer's Purchase Order. Pre-shipments can only be made with the express written authorization of the appropriate customer's production manager. If a contractor and/or agent ships goods before the ex-factory date without such approval, the customer reserves the right to refuse or return these goods, and delay or withhold payment until such time as payment was due if the goods were shipped on time. The contractor and/or agent also may be held responsible for any additional handling and storage charges incurred as a result of pre-shipment.

8. **Failure to Follow Packaging, Labeling, Shipping, and Documentation Requirements**
   The contractor and/or agent should be charged for all merchandise improperly packaged, labeled, shipped or documented according to the customer's specifications and causing delays at the customer's warehouse or distribution centers or requiring additional labor to correct the non-compliance or extra expenses. The chargeback for the repackaging/labeling should be at a rate of $25.00 per inspection hour, per person, plus an administration cost of 100.00 per job. Any discrepancy to documentation requirements should result in a minimum $250.00 chargeback.

CHARGEBACK FORMAT AND PAYMENT

Details of the reason for a chargeback should be supplied by the customer's quality control to their accounts payable. A chargeback, with a brief summary of the reasons, should be issued by the customer's quality control in the form of a debit note. The debit note should be sent directly to the contractor and/or agent.

Chargebacks should be paid via check or wire transfer upon receipt.

The customer reserves the right to offset these charges against any amounts due to the contractor and/or agent, including amounts due under Purchase Orders covering first quality merchandise.

DEFECTIVE PRODUCTS POLICY

The customer should only accept first quality merchandise that is shipped against open, First Quality Purchase Orders. In the case of defective products, the customer's production department should be notified prior to shipment for approval and direction as to the disposition of the defective products. The customer reserves the "right of first refusal" to purchase some, or all, of the defective products.

If the customer chooses not to purchase the defective products, the contractor and/or agent should dispose of the products in accordance with the manufacturing agreement.

CUSTOMER SELL-OFF AND DISPOSAL PROCEDURES (Irregulars and Over-Runs)

The customer's suppliers should not produce excess product (first quality or irregular) with intent to sell outside of the customer's approved and authorized distribution channels. To do so would constitute a violation of the manufacturing agreement or the Purchase Order contract and would require the customer to pursue legal action.

The disposition of all products should be in accordance with the manufacturing agreement between the customer and the contractor and/or agent.

It is crucial that each contractor and/or agent identify all overruns (excess beyond ordered quantity) and irregulars (defective product) at the completion of each Purchase Order. Do not accumulate overruns or irregulars!

If a contractor and/or agent receives written authorization to utilize the customer sell-off and disposal procedures, the following steps should be followed:

REMOVAL OF CUSTOMER LOGO

The seller should remove the customer's main label from all their branded apparel items, according to the following guidelines:

A. Leather and leather-like labels sewn on apparel items should be completely removed, or, if sewn on four sides, cut from stitch to stitch or, if sewn on two sides, cut in half.

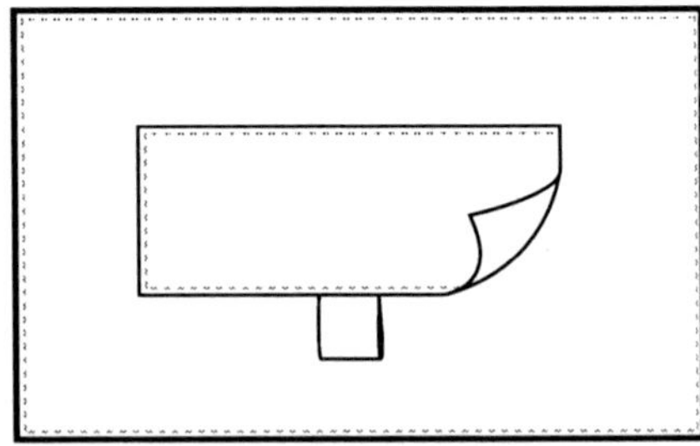

B. Woven labels sewn on only one side are to be completely removed.

C. Woven labels sewn only on two sides are to be cut out between the attaching stitches so that the customer's name or logo is no longer visible.

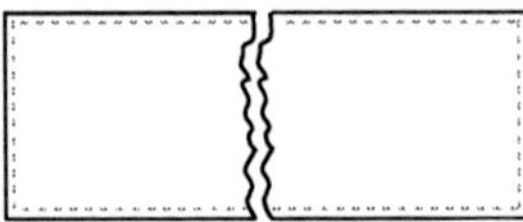

D. Woven labels sewn on all four sides should be cut lengthwise from stitch to stitch.

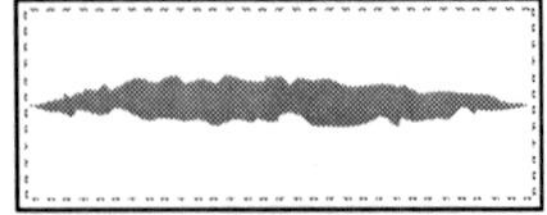

E. For loop labels including both the loop label used on jeans and all other loop type labels that contain the customer's logo plus the size, or care instructions, or fabric content, or the RN number, only the logo should be cut out with all other information left intact.

F. For all other apparel and apparel-related items with other types of labels, hardware, decorative logos, embroidery, screen print, etc., you should contact the customer's production managers or quality control for written instructions regarding removal.

IDENTIFICATION OF "IRREGULAR" GOODS

The word "IRREGULAR" should be stamped on each unit in the location specified below with an approved indelible ink. This guideline requirement applies to all seconds, rejected goods and overruns that should not go into normal first-quality distribution.

The entire word "IRREGULAR" is to be stamped on each apparel unit in a minimum size of 1 1/2" X 1/4". The indelible ink color should contrast with the color of the fabric to which it is applied. The location of the stamp should be as follows:

A. **Pants, Jeans, Shorts and Skirts**
- On the inside waistband on left front.
- If there is no waistband, 1" from top of inside left front.

B. **Outerwear, Knit and Woven Shirts**
- Inside the collar band 2" from center back.
- If there is no collar band, inside 1" below collar and 2" from center back, or if stamp should show through, inside button-stay 4" from top.

C. **Sweaters and Sweatshirts**
- On the inside 1" below collar and 2" from center back.
- If there is no collar, inside 2" below top of back and 2" from center back.

D. **All Other Apparel and Apparel-Related Items**
- Instructions for the specific location of the "IRREGULAR" stamp should be requested in writing from the customer's production or quality control department.

HANGTAGS AND LABEL REQUIREMENTS

The contractor and/or agent should remove and destroy all paper tickets and/or hangtags that identify the customer.

The label containing fabric content, fabric care instructions, and the RN number should remain on the apparel item (garment size should remain if possible).

NOTIFICATION OF DEFECTIVE PRODUCTS

The contractor and/or agent should notify the customer of the intended ship date of defective products at least 14 days prior to shipping. During this 14-day period, the customer reserves the right to inspect the goods at the contractor's and/or agent's facility, for compliance with these guidelines. Goods that do not comply should be rejected and should not be shipped until they comply with the procedures.

The contractor and/or agent should provide the customer's agent or production manager with the name and address of the purchaser as well as the selling price of the "irregular" products that are subject to the customer's approval. The customer should not allow off-price or off-quality apparel products to be sold through unacceptable channels of distribution.

> ***Note:*** There may be exceptions to these procedures for items that are purchased by the customer. The customer's production manager or quality control manager should advise and approve any exceptions in writing.

SHIPMENT OF DEFECTIVE PRODUCTS

There are two categories of defective products:

1. **Defective Products Identified Prior to Shipment:**
   Products that have been identified as defective by the contractor and/or agent or the customer prior to shipment should be reported to the customer's production department or to the customer's agent, with an exact size, color and quantity breakdown. If the customer elects to purchase the defective products, such sale should be in accordance with the Manufacturing Agreement between the customer and the contractor and/or agent.

   For packing, carton marking, packing list and invoice instructions for "seconds," please refer to: "Chapter 12: Packaging and Shipping."

2. **Defective Products Identified after Shipment:**
   For defective products that are shipped as first quality and are found to be defective by the customer's quality control or by the customer's customers, the customer should notify the contractor and/or agent of all seconds discovered during the quality control audit process. In addition to charging back the standard FOB cost (as listed on the customer Purchase Order) for all seconds, the customer should chargeback the costs of locating and sorting seconds (100% inspection) at the rate* of $25.00 per inspection hour per inspector, plus an administration cost of $100.00 per 100% inspection, as noted previously in this chapter.

*These are suggested dollar amounts for labor/nuisance costs and may be adjusted by the customer to suit specific circumstances.

PAYMENT FOR DEFECTIVE GOODS

The customer should negotiate a discounted price based on the standard FOB cost (as listed on the customer Purchase Order) for products that are identified by the contractor and/or agent as defective. Negotiations should be made on a case-by-case basis and should be directed by the customer's production department.

Refer to "Conditions that Qualify for a Chargeback, 1. Quality Defects Exceeding Acceptable Rate", earlier in this chapter, for guidelines.

CHAPTER 14

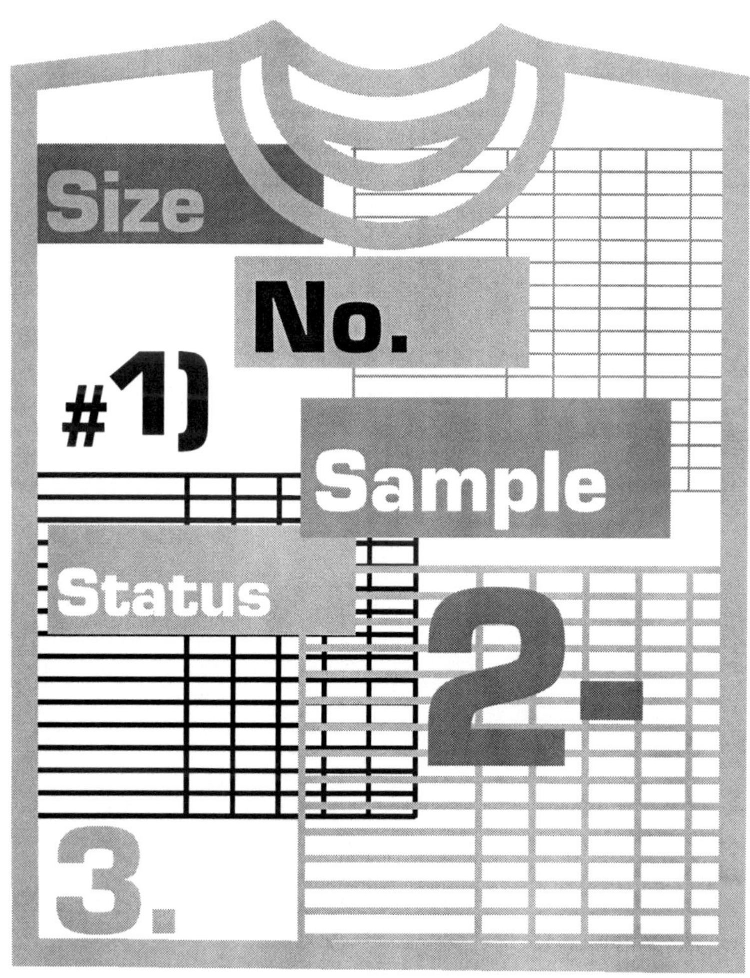

FORMS AND DATA TEMPLATES

This Chapter includes various Forms and Data Sheets that are frequently used in Product Development and may used as Templates in an Apparel Company.

SPECIFICATIONS LEAD SHEET					
COMPANY NAME:			COMPANY ADDRESS:		
DATE:					
PROTO NO.:		SEASON:		MAIN LABEL:	
STYLE NO.:		DELIVERY:		CONTENT:	
PATTERN NO.:		CATEGORY:		CARE:	
SIZE RANGE:		DESCRIPTION:			
SAMPLE SIZE:					
front view sketch			back view sketch		
FABRIC 1:		SUPPLIER:			
FABRIC 2:		SUPPLIER:			
FABRIC 3:		SUPPLIER:			
LINING 1:		SUPPLIER:			
LINING 2:		SUPPLIER:			
POCKETS:		SUPPLIER:			
WAISTBAND:		SUPPLIER:			
BUTTON:		SUPPLIER:			
TRIM 1:		SUPPLIER:			
TRIM 2:		SUPPLIER:			
TRIM 3:		SUPPLIER:			
DETAILS:					

SIZE SPECIFICATIONS - OUTERWEAR

SPECIFICATION MEASUREMENT SHEET (Garments Measured in Inches)									
Sample Size		Proto No.				Style No.			
SAMPLE STATUS		ORIGINAL SAMPLE		PROTO SAMPLE		SALES SAMPLE		PRE-PRODUCTION SAMPLE	
SAMPLE SIZE REQUEST									
MEASUREMENTS		Actual	Request	Actual	Request	Actual	Request	Actual	Request
1)	Center Back Length								
2)	Chest - 1" Below Armhole								
3a)	Bottom Opening - Relaxed								
3b)	Bottom Opening - Extended								
4)	Side Seam Length								
5)	Shoulder Point-to-Point								
6)	Shoulder Length - HSP to Armhole								
7)	Yoke Depth at CB								
8)	Armhole								
9)	Upper Arm - 1" Below Armhole								
10)	Elbow - 13" Down from Top of Arm								
11)	Sleeve Length from CB Neck								
12a)	Sleeve Length Long from Cap								
12b)	Sleeve Length Short from Cap								
12c)	Sleeve Cap Height								
13a)	Sleeve Placket Length								
13b)	Sleeve Placket Width								
14a)	Sleeve Cuff Opening - Relaxed								
14b)	Sleeve Cuff Opening - Extended								
15)	Cuff Width								
16)	Front Placket Width								
17)	Collar Height CB								
18)	Collar Length Top								
19)	Collar Point Front								
20)	Collar Spread								
21)	Collar Stand/Band Width CB								
22)	Neck Circumference								
23)	Front Neck Drop								
24)	Neck Width CB								
25)	Zipper Length CF								
26)	Collar Stand Length								
27)	Hood Length CB								
28)	Hood Width Horizontal								
29)	Hood Height CF								
30)	Difference Between CF and CB								

Bold writing = changed measurements

SIZE SPECIFICATIONS - DRESSES

SPECIFICATION MEASUREMENT SHEET (Garments Measured in Inches)									
Sample Size		Proto No.				Style No.			
SAMPLE STATUS		ORIGINAL SAMPLE		PROTO SAMPLE		SALES SAMPLE		PRE-PRODUCTION SAMPLE	
SAMPLE SIZE REQUEST									
MEASUREMENTS		Actual	Request	Actual	Request	Actual	Request	Actual	Request
1)	Center Back Length								
2)	Chest/Bust								
3a)	Bottom Opening/Sweep - Relaxed								
3b)	Bottom Opening - Extended								
4)	Shoulder - Point-to-Point								
5)	Across Back – 5" Down from CB Neck								
6)	Shoulder Length								
7)	Yoke Depth at CB								
8)	Armhole – Circumference								
9)	Upper Arm – 1" Below Armhole								
10)	Elbow								
11)	Cap Height								
12a)	Sleeve Length CB								
12b)	Sleeve Length from Cap-Long								
12c)	Sleeve Length from Cap-Short								
13	Sleeve Placket Length								
14a)	Sleeve (Cuff) Opening - Relaxed								
14b)	Sleeve (Cuff) Opening - Extended								
15)	Cuff Width								
16)	Front Placket Width								
17)	Collar Height CB								
18)	Collar Length Top								
19)	Collar Point Front								
20)	Collar Spread								
21)	Collar Stand/Band Width CB								
22)	Neck Circumference								
23)	Front Neck Drop								
24)	Neck Width CB								
25)	Collar Stand Lengt								
26)	Zipper Length								

Bold writing = changed measurements

SIZE SPECIFICATIONS - KNIT TOPS AND SWEATERS

SPECIFICATION MEASUREMENT SHEET (Garments Measured in Inches)									
Sample Size		**Proto No.**				**Style No.**			
SAMPLE STATUS		**ORIGINAL SAMPLE**		**PROTO SAMPLE**		**SALES SAMPLE**		**PRE-PRODUCTION SAMPLE**	
SAMPLE SIZE REQUEST MEASUREMENTS		**Actual**	**Request**	**Actual**	**Request**	**Actual**	**Request**	**Actual**	**Request**
1)	Shoulder - Point-to-Point								
2)	Chest/Bust - 1" Below Armhole								
3)	Shoulder - Point-to-Point								
4a)	Chest/Bust - 1" Below Armhole								
4b)	Across Chest - 5" Down from HPS								
5)	Bottom Opening								
6)	Sleeve Length								
8)	Armhole								
9)	Upper Arm - 1" Below Armhole								
10)	Cuff/Sleeve Opening								
11)	Cuff Height/Sleeve Hem Height								
12)	Neck Width – at Seam								
13)	Front Neck Drop - HPS to Seam								
14)	Back Neck Drop - HPS to Seam								
15)	Front Yoke Depth - HPS to Seam								
16)	Back Yoke Depth - CB Neck to Seam								
17)	Back Facing Depth at CB								
18)	CF Placket Width								
19)	CF Placket Length								
20)	Placket Box Height								
21)	Collar Height CF								
22)	Collar Height CB								
23)	Collar Stand Height CF								
24)	Collar Stand Height CB								
25)	Collar Spread								
26)	Pocket Width								
27)	Pocket Length								
28)	Pocket Placement- HPS to Top Edge								
29)	Pocket Placement from CF								
30)	Length of Side Vent								
31)	Bottom Hem Height								

Bold writing = changed measurements

SIZE SPECIFICATIONS - WOVEN TOPS AND BLOUSES

SPECIFICATION MEASUREMENT SHEET (Garments Measured in Inches)									
Sample Size		Proto No.				Style No.			
SAMPLE STATUS		ORIGINAL SAMPLE		PROTO SAMPLE		SALES SAMPLE		PRE-PRODUCTION SAMPLE	
SAMPLE SIZE REQUEST									
MEASUREMENTS		Actual	Request	Actual	Request	Actual	Request	Actual	Request
1)	Center Back Length								
2)	Center Front Length								
3a)	Chest - 1" Below Armhole								
3b)	Chest - 5" Down from HPS								
4)	Waist - 8" Below Armhole								
5)	Bottom Opening								
6)	Side Seam Length								
7)	Shoulder-to-Shoulder								
8)	Shoulder Seam								
9)	Yoke Depth at CB								
10)	Armhole								
11)	Biceps - 1" Below Armhole								
12)	Elbow - 9 " Above Cuff Seam								
13)	Sleeve Length CB								
14)	Sleeve Length Cap								
15)	Cuff/Sleeve Opening								
16)	Cuff/Topstitching Width								
17)	Front Placket Width								
18)	Collar Width CB								
19)	Collar Length								
20)	Collar Point								
21)	Collar Spread - Buttoned & Folded								
22)	Tie Space - Buttoned & Folded								
23)	Collar Stand Width CB								
24)	Collar Stand Length/Neck Circum.								
25)	Sleeve Placket Length								
26)	Sleeve Placket Width								
27)	Pocket Length								
28)	Pocket Width								
29)	Pocket Placement from CF								
30)	Pocket Placement from Shoulder Seam at Neck								
31)	Pocket Flap Length (Depth)								
32)	Pocket Flap Width								
33)	Neck Drop								

Bold writing = changed measurements

SIZE SPECIFICATIONS - BOTTOMS & TROUSERS

SPECIFICATION MEASUREMENT SHEET (Garments Measured in Inches)									
Sample Size		Proto No.				Style No.			
SAMPLE STATUS		ORIGINAL SAMPLE		PROTO SAMPLE		SALES SAMPLE		PRE-PRODUCTION SAMPLE	
SAMPLE SIZE REQUEST									
MEASUREMENTS		Actual	Request	Actual	Request	Actual	Request	Actual	Request
1)	Waist Relaxed								
2)	Waist Extended								
3)	Waistband Width								
4)	High Hip - 3" Down from Waist Seam								
5)	Hip - 7" Down from Waist Seam								
6)	Front Rise Not Including Waistband								
7)	Back Rise Not Including Waistband								
8)	Front Rise - From Top Edge of Waist								
9)	Back Rise - From Top Edge of Waist								
10)	Thigh - 1" Down from Crotch Seam								
11)	Knee - 13" Down from Crotch Seam								
12)	Leg Opening								
13)	Inseam								
14)	Hem Width								
15)	Cuff Width								
16)	Fly Length (To Outer Row of Topstitch)								
17)	Fly Width (To Outer Row of Topstitch)								
18)	Front Pocket Opening								
19)	Front Pocket Depth/Length								
20)	Coin Pocket from Side Seam								
21)	Coin Pocket from Waistband								
22)	Coin Pocket Opening								
23)	Back Pocket Opening								
24)	Back Pocket Depth/Length								
25)	Pocket Flap Depth/Length								
26)	Pocket Flap Width								
27)	Back Pocket from Side Seam								
28)	Back Pocket from Waistband								
29)	Belt Loop Length								
30)	Belt Loop Width								
SHORTS LINER:									
31)	Front Rise (Not Including Waistband)								
32)	Back Rise (Not Including Waistband)								
33)	Leg Opening Relaxed								
34)	Leg Opening Stretched								
35)	Outseam								
36)	Crotch Width								

Bold writing = changed measurements

COST CALCULATION SHEET		Date:		Style No.:	
		Label:		Size Range:	
		Season:		On Line: ______	Estimate: ____ ___
Category:	**Description:**	**Yield/Style:**	**Cost/Yard:**	**Cost/Garment:**	**Total/Garment:**
Fabric 1					
	Freight				
Fabric 2					
	Freight				
Fabric 3					
	Freight				
Trim 1					
	Freight				
Trim 2					
	Freight				
Notions 1					
Notions 2					
Notions 3					
Category:	**Direct Labor:**	**Mfg. Overhead:**	**Contract Wk.:**	**Excess:**	
Cutting					
Sewing					
Finishing					
Special Finish					
Special Finish					
Transportation					
Total Manufacturing Cost:					
Expense Category		**Total Manufacturing Cost x ____%**			
Administrative				10%	
Selling				4%	
Shipping				2%	
Insurance					
Close-Outs				1%	
Total Make and Sell Cost:					
Variable Marketing Expenses					
Total Make and Sell Cost:					
			A	B	C
Selling Price					
Net-Profit (Selling Price less Make and Sell):					
Net-Profit % (Net-Profit div. by Selling Price):					

SAMPLE PLAN AND ACTION CALENDAR FOR DESIGNERS				
Example: Fall I – In store and on the Floor 7/15 Future Seasonal Development Cycles will Overlap this Cycle				
DEADLINES	**Retailer's Calendar**	**Mills and Yarn Calendar**	**Manufacturing Calendar**	**Designer Calendar**
15 May				Review Color Services and Forecasts.
15 Jun				Establish Color Palettes and Themes.
15 Jul		Fall Preview for Yarn and Color Direction.		Begin Lab Dipping. Shop Print and Yarn-Dye Collections.
15 Aug		Fall Previews for Base Fabrics and Styling Direction.	Models.	Begin Proto and Model Development. Preview Collections.
15 Sep		Textile Shows. Take Sample Fabric Orders.	Develop Protos and Models.	Textile Shows. Sample Fabrics. Sample Yarns.
15 Oct		Ship Sample Fabrics-Wovens. Bulk Production Orders.	Develop Protos and Models. Begin Sales Samples	Review Protos and 1st Samples. Order Samples.
15 Nov	Preview Lines.	Ship Sample Fabrics-Knits.	Make Sales Samples.	Make Sample Corrections. Preview w/ Buyers.
15 Dec		Bulk Production Orders.	Complete and Ship Sales Samples.	Review Final Samples. Line Edit.
15 Jan	Review Lines and Collections.	Ship Production Fabrics.		Final Costing. Sales Meeting.
15 Feb	Finalize Orders.	Ship Production Fabrics.	Begin Bulk Production.	Finalize Production and Fit Details.
15 Mar				Check Pre-Production Samples.
15 Apr			Ship Fall I to Warehouse.	
15 Jun			Ship to Retailer.	
15 Jul	Fall I - In Store Merchandise on Selling Floor.			

SAMPLE APPROVAL TRACKING			
Season:		Proto No.	Style No.
SALES SAMPLES			
APPROVED FOR FIT	DATE:		
APPROVED FOR CONSTRUCTION	DATE:		
APPROVED FOR FABRIC	DATE:		
APPROVED FOR EMBROIDERY	DATE:		
APPROVED FOR TRIMS	DATE:		
BULK			
APPROVED FOR FIT	DATE:		
APPROVED FOR CONSTRUCTION	DATE:		
APPROVED FOR FABRIC	DATE:		
APPROVED FOR EMBROIDERY	DATE:		
APPROVED FOR TRIMS	DATE:		
TEST REPORT SUBMITTED	DATE:		
CARE LABEL SUBMITTED	DATE:		

DATE	BY	SUBJECT	CHANGES/COMMENTS

BILL OF MATERIALS				Style No. Proto No.
MATERIALS	DESCRIPTION	PLACEMENT	QUANTITY	SOURCE/ COUNTRY
BUTTONS				
SNAPS				
ZIPPERS				
MAIN LABEL				
SECONDARY LABEL				
UPC TICKET				
UPC STICKER				
POCKET FLASHER				
JOKER TICKET				
COUNTRY OF ORIGIN LABEL				
SIZE TAB				
CARE/CONTENT LABEL				
HANGTAG				
HANGER				
POLY BAG				
BOX				
TISSUE				

Attach following:
***Packaging instructions**
***Label placement codes**
***Instructions for care/content labels**
***French translation for country of origin label**

Note: The vendor is responsible for accurate country of origin and care/content labels.

COLORWAYS

STYLE NO:	DESIGNER:
PROTO NO:	TECH DESIGN.:
SEASON:	

PATTERN	DESCRIPTION	COLOR #	COLOR #	COLOR #	COLOR #
Shell					
Lining 1					
Lining 2					
Thread Color 1					
Thread Color 2					
Thread Color 3					
Embroidery 1					
Embroidery 2					
Embroidery 3					
Trim 1					
Trim 2					
Trim 3					
Trim 4					
Trim 5					
Pocketing 1					
Pocketing 2					
Waistband					
Button 1					
Button 2					
Button 3					
Artwork					
Front					
Back					
Notes:					

COUNTER SAMPLE SPECIFICATIONS (All Measurements in Inches)											
SAMPLE STATUS		ORIGINAL SAMPLE		FIRST SAMPLE		SECOND SAMPLE		THIRD SAMPLE		FINAL	
STYLE NO.	SIZE										
	DATE										
MEASUREMENTS		Actual	Request	Actual	Request	Actual	Request	Actual	Request	Actual	Request
1)	Center Back Length										
2)	Center Front Length										
3)	Chest - 1" Below Armhole										
4)	Waist - 8" Below Armhole										
5)	Bottom Opening										
6)	Side Seam Length										
7)	Shoulder - Point to Point										
8)	Shoulder Seam										
9)	Yoke Depth at CB										
10)	Armhole										
11)	Bicep - 1" Below Armhole										
12)	Elbow - 9 1/2" Above Cuff Seam										
13)	Sleeve Length CB										
14)	Sleeve Length from Shoulder Point										
15)	Cuff/Sleeve Opening										
16)	Cuff or Topstitching Width										
17)	Front Placket Width										
18)	Collar Width CB										
19)	Collar Length										
20)	Collar Point										
21)	Collar Spread - Buttoned and Folded										
22)	Tie Space - Buttoned and Folded										
23)	Collar Stand Width CB										
24)	Collar Stand Length/Neck Circumference										
25)	Sleeve Placket Length										
26)	Sleeve Placket Width										
27)	Pocket Length										
28)	Pocket Width										
29)	Pocket Placement from CF										
30)	Pocket Placement from Shoulder Seam at Neck										
31)	Pocket Flap Length/Depth										
32)	Pocket Flap Width										
33)	Front Neck Drop										
34)	Logo Placement - CF										

GRADE RULES (An Example From Men's Wear)								PROTO NO. STYLE NO.
Garment Measurements in Inches								
MEASUREMENTS				SAMPLE SIZE				
SIZE		XS	S	M	L	XL	XXL	TOLERANCE
Measurements taken on the flat.								
1)	Center Back Length	-1	-1/2	0	1/2	1	1 1/2	1/2
2)	Center Front Length	-1	-1/2	0	1/2	1	1 1/2	1/2
3)	Chest 1" Below Armhole	-3	-1 1/2	0	1 1/2	3	4 1/2	1/2
4)	Waist 8" Below Armhole - Open Pleat	-3	-1 1/2	0	1 1/2	3	4 1/2	1/2
5)	Bottom Opening	-3	-1 1/2	0	1 1/2	3	4 1/2	1/2
6)	Side Seam Length	-1/2	-1/4	0	1/4	1/2	3/4	1/4
7)	Shoulder Point to Point	-1 1/2	-3/4	0	1 1/4	2 1/2	3 3/4	1/2
8)	Shoulder Seam	-1/2	-1/8	0	1/8	1/2	3/4	1/2
9)	Yoke Depth at CB	-1/2	0	0	0	1/2	1	1/4
10)	Armhole - Measured Straight	-2	-1	0	1 1/4	2 1/2	3 3/4	1/2
11)	Biceps - 1" Below Armhole	-2	-1	0	1	2	3	1/2
12)	Elbow - 9 1/2" Above Cuff Seam	-1	-1/2	0	1/2	1	1 3/4	1/2
13)	Sleeve Length CB	-2	-1	0	1	2	3	1/2
14)	Sleeve Length from Shoulder Point	-1 1/4	-5/8	0	3/4	1 1/2	2 1/4	1/2
15)	Cuff/Sleeve Opening	-1	-1/2	0	1/2	1	1 1/2	1/2
16)	Cuff or Topstitching Width	0	0	0	0	0	0	1/8
17)	Front Placket Width	0	0	0	0	0	0	1/8
18)	Collar Width CB	0	0	0	0	0	0	1/8
19)	Collar Length	-2	-1	0	1	2	3	3/8
20)	Collar Point	0	0	0	0	0	0	1/8
21)	Collar Spread - Buttoned and Folded	0	0	0	0	0	0	1/4
22)	Tie Space - Buttoned and Folded	0	0	0	0	0	0	1/8
23)	Collar Stand Width CB	0	0	0	0	0	0	1/8
24)	Collar Stand Length/Neck Circumference	-2	-1	0	1	2	3	3/8
25)	Sleeve Placket Length	0	0	0	0	0	0	1/4
26)	Sleeve Placket Width	0	0	0	0	0	0	1/8
27)	Pocket Length	0	0	0	0	0	0	1/8
28)	Pocket Width	0	0	0	0	0	0	1/8
29)	Pocket Placement from CF	-1/2	-1/4	0	1/4	1/2	3/4	1/8
30)	Pocket Placement from Shoulder Seam at Neck	-3/8	-1/8	0	1/8	3/8	1/2	1/8
31)	Pocket Flap Length (Depth)	0	0	0	0	0	0	1/8
32)	Pocket Flap Width	0	0	0	0	0	0	1/8
33)	Front Neck Drop	0	0	0	0	0	0	1/8
34)	Logo Placement-CF	-1/2	-1/4	0	1/4	1/2	3/4	1/8

CUTTER'S MUST			
BODY #	DESCRIPTION:	PATTERNMAKER:	
SIZE:	FABRIC#	COMPANY:	

ITEM #	PATTERNS				# PCS to cut

DATE:	SEASON:

SKETCH

ITEM#	PATTERN MARKERS				

TRIMMINGS

CUTTER'S MUST - SEWING INSTRUCTIONS

SEAMS:

TOP STITCHING:

ITEM #	PATTERN SIZE			GARMENT SIZE		YIELDS component / yield		

FABRIC SWATCH

YOUR COMPANY LLC				
ADDRESS:				
CITY, STATE:				
TEL:	FAX:		EMAIL:	

SALES SAMPLE PURCHASE ORDER			
PO NUMBER:		DATE:	
TO:			
ATTN:		FAX:	
FROM:		TEL:	

We confirm having ordered from you the following:

ITEM CODE	ITEM / DESCRIPTION	QUANTITY (YDS)	UNIT PRICE (USD)	AMOUNT (USD)

INVOICE INSTRUCTIONS AND DOCUMENTATIONS:		ADDRESSED TO:
		YOUR COMPANY
TOTAL ORDER VALUE:		
DELIVERY:		
TERMS OF PAYMENT:		
OTHER TERMS:		
REMARKS:		
ACCEPTED BY:		

SELLER'S SIGNATURE:

NAME

YOUR COMPANY, LLC

YOUR COMPANY LLC		
ADDRESS:		
CITY, STATE :		
TEL:	FAX:	EMAIL:

PURCHASE ORDER

PO NUMBER:		DATE:	
TO:			
ATTN:		FAX:	
FROM:		TEL:	

We confirm having ordered from you the following:

ITEM CODE	ITEM / DESCRIPTION	QUANTITY (YDS)	UNIT PRICE (USD)	AMOUNT (USD)

INVOICE INSTRUCTIONS AND DOCUMENTATIONS:		ADDRESSED TO:
		YOUR COMPANY
TOTAL ORDER VALUE:		
DELIVERY:		
TERMS OF PAYMENT:		
OTHER TERMS:		
REMARKS:		
ACCEPTED BY:		

SELLER'S SIGNATURE:

NAME	YOUR COMPANY, LLC

PURCHASE ORDER CONFIRMATION
PURCHASE ORDER #:
STYLE:
QUANTITY:
EX-MAKER DATE:
CANCELLATION DATE:
PRICE:
VENDOR NAME:
Signature and return by fax from Contractor acknowledges: **Receipt, Review and Agreement to Price, Quantity** by **Style / Color / Size** and **Delivery Date**, and receipt and understanding of the Customer's Contractor Compliance Manual.
signed / date Response and confirmation is anticipated within 48 hours of receipt. Date sent by customer is:
Return To:

CONTRACTOR INFORMATION SHEET

Contractor Name: ______________________________
(as appears on Purchase Order)

____

Contractor Address: ______________________________
(as appears on Purchase Order)

____

____

Country ______________________________

Mailing Address:
(if different than PO address)

Name ______________________________

Address ______________________________

____

Country ______________________________

Contractor Point of Contact:

Name ______________________________

Telephone ______________________________

Fax ______________________________

Product Origin: ______________________________

Payment Terms (e.g. Net 30, L/C): ______________________________

FOB Terms (e.g. FOB HK): ______________________________

Buying Agent: ______________________________

COST CALCULATION SHEET		Date:		Style No.:	
		Label:		Size Range:	
		Season:		On Line: ______	Estimate: ____ ___
Category:	**Description:**	**Yield/Style:**	**Cost/Yard:**	**Cost/Garment:**	**Total/Garment:**
Fabric 1					
	Freight				
Fabric 2					
	Freight				
Fabric 3					
	Freight				
Trim 1					
	Freight				
Trim 2					
	Freight				
Notions 1					
Notions 2					
Notions 3					
Category:	**Direct Labor:**	**Mfg. Overhead:**	**Contract Wk.:**	**Excess:**	
Cutting					
Sewing					
Finishing					
Special Finish					
Special Finish					
Transportation					
Total Manufacturing Cost:					
Expense Category		**Total Manufacturing Cost x ____%**			
Administrative				10%	
Selling				4%	
Shipping				2%	
Insurance					
Close-Outs				1%	
Total Make and Sell Cost:					
Variable Marketing Expenses					
Total Make and Sell Cost:					
			A	**B**	**C**
Selling Price					
Net Profit (Selling Price less Make and Sell):					
Net Profit % (Net-Profit div. by Selling Price):					

CHAPTER 15

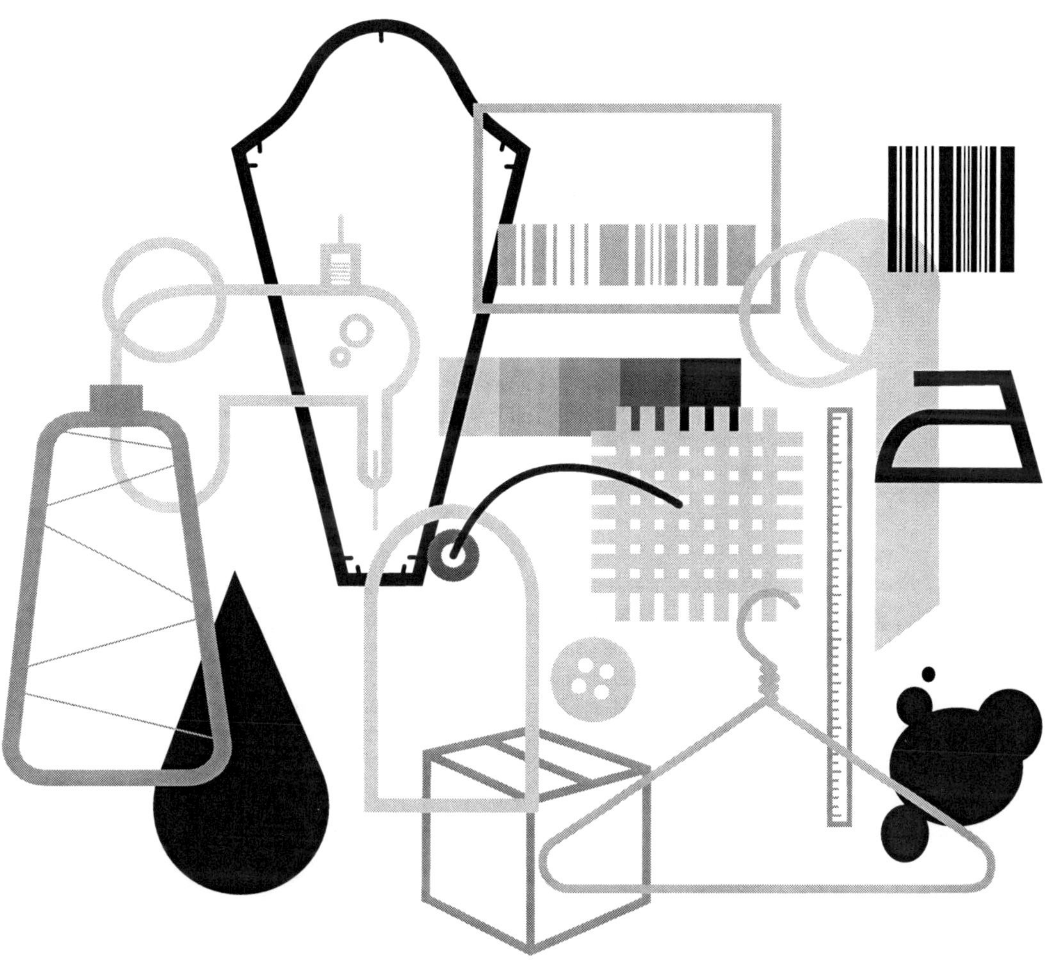

GLOSSARY

Glossary of frequently-used textile, manufacturing, development, production, and commercial shipping terms in the apparel industry.

AATCC	(**American Association of Textile Chemists and Colorists**) Worldwide association of professionals active in textile wet processing.
Abrasion Level	The level of (desired) fraying or worn areas on a garment caused by stones, abrading the garment during wash and usually heaviest at the thickest seams (pockets, hem, fly).
Abrasion Resistance	The degree to which a fabric can withstand surface rubbing, chafing and other forms of friction through normal wear and maintenance.
Acceptable Quality Level	(**AQL**) The maximum percent defective (or maximum number of defects per hundred units) that, for purpose of sampling inspection, can be considered satisfactory as a process average. MIL-STD-105E, ISO 2859-1 (1999).
Acceptance Quality Limit	(**AQL**) The quality level that is the worst tolerable process average when a continuing series of lots is submitted for acceptance sampling. ANSI/ASQC Z1.4-2003.
Advance Ship Notice	See: ASN
Airway Bill	(**AWB**) A non-negotiable contract covering domestic and international flights, used for the transportation of freight including shipping instructions, description of shipment and transportation charges. The air industry's equivalent to the motor carrier's (trucker's) Bill of Lading.
Approvals	Usually small hand woven, knitted or printed swatches or "strike-offs" sent to the customer for approval of weave, color, finish or print design, etc.
AQL	Has two different definitions due to standard changes, see: **Acceptable Quality Level**, see: **Acceptance Quality Limit**.
Art Work	Designs for textile printing, weaving or other forms of ornamentation, often purchased from outside artists or specialty studios that may be used for production purposes. Usually these designs are exclusive to the purchaser and are one of a kind. If a design is selected from a manufacturer's range and is made exclusive to a customer it is referred to as "confined."
ASN	(**Advance Ship Notice**) Electronic packing slip.
AWB	See: Airway Bill
AZO Dyestuffs	Dyestuffs that contain amino groups, which are known carcinogens or are likely carcinogens.
Bar Tack	A group of stitches used to reinforce specific areas on a garment, such as at the bottom of a fly opening or on either end of a pocket opening.
Bill of Lading	A contract of carriage between shipper and carrier. It serves three purposes: 1. To set the terms and conditions of the contract. 2. To serve as the receipt for the goods to be transported. 3. As documentary evidence of the party entitled to deliver.

Bill Receiver	Freight invoice payment term unique to Airborne Express; charges are billed to the recipients.
Blind Hem	A hand or machine operation where the hem is turned up and secured with stitches that are nearly invisible from the right side of the garment.
Bonded or Laminated	Textiles that have a secondary layer of material, often a non-woven structure applied or fused on the face or back to alter the hand and/or functionality of the primary fabric, such as: polyurethane (water resistance), foam (bulk and insulation), woven or knit fabrics (stabilizing), etc.
Bow	A fabric condition resulting when knitted courses are displaced from a line perpendicular to the selvages and form one or more arcs (waviness) across the width of the fabric. Similar conditions can occur in woven fabrics and are results of improper finishing.
Breaking Strength	The maximum force applied to a specimen in a tensile test carried to rupture.
Burn Out or Voided or Devore	Techniques that involve removing areas of fibers to create a design or pattern in a textile and still leave a fine supporting structure (weave or knit) so that some elements of the design appear opaque and some areas are translucent. This can be accomplished by using a secondary layer of fabric that is cut away and is the reverse of the design or by using special chemicals that dissolve only specific fibers in the design.
Burn Test	Burning a swatch, yarn or fibers taken from a textile in order to determine the fiber content. Flammability, smell and the quality of the residual ash or "bead" are reasonably accurate indicators of the fiber or blend.
Bursting Strength	The force or pressure required to rupture a textile by distending it with a force, applied at right angles to the plane of the fabric, under specified conditions.
C&F	(**Cost and Freight**... port of destination) The seller pays the costs and freight of the goods to the port of destination, with the risk of loss of or damage to the goods, as well as additional costs occurring after the time the goods are delivered on board the vessel. Responsibility is transferred from the seller to the buyer when the goods pass the ship's rail in the port of shipment. The seller usually chooses the forwarder.
C&I	(**Cost and Insurance**... port of destination) Shipping term included in a Contract of Sale where the seller agrees to arrange and pay for transportation and cargo insurance over the goods to the named destination. Such costs are included in the price of the goods. The buyer is responsible for the cost of the ocean freight and arranging the transportation from the port of discharge.
Cancel Date	The Cancel Date on the Purchase Order (PO). The last accepted day to ship. Commonly referred to as the Past Cancel Date.
Care Instructions	A series of directions describing which care practices should refurbish a product without adverse effects, and warning of those care practices expected to have a harmful effect. Covers washing, drying, pressing and dry-cleaning.
Cargo Claims	Claims written against a carrier for recoupment of merchandise cost and freight charges as a result of damage or shortage of goods delivered or non-delivery.
Carrier Liability	A contract carrier is liable for all loss, damage and delay with the exception of Act of God, Act of Public Enemy, Act of Public Authority, Act of the Shipper and the inherent nature of the goods.

Carton	A corrugated packaging type not usually to exceed 36" x 24" x 24" or 50 lbs.
CBM	(**Cubic Meter**) International measurement (metric) used in freight and warehousing.
Certificate of Origin	(**CO**) A document that certifies a specific country as the origin of specific goods. The U.S. and certain other countries require this certificate for tariff purposes.
CIF	(**Cost, Insurance and Freight**...port of destination) The seller has the same obligations as under C&F, but must also pay for marine insurance against loss or damage to the goods during transport. The seller pays for the insurance but only is required to obtain minimum coverage. Again, the seller usually chooses the freight forwarder. Delivery is made at the port of destination.
Circular Knitting	Machine knitting with a circular knitting bed. Each stitch is controlled by a separate knitting needle or sets of needles (called cylinders and dials). The knitted "fabric" comes out of the machine as a knitted tube that can be cut open and finished flat or left in tubular form. Circular knitting machines are very productive and can be set up fairly quickly. Many circular machines now interface with computers and can knit elaborate jacquard or fancy stitch patterns. Circular machines cannot fashion individual panels to size or shape or create true "cable" effects. Circular knits are usually cut-and-sewn.
Claim	A deduction processed against a vendor's account for merchandise returns, shortages, cost differences, markdowns, advertising co-op, rebates, etc.
CMT	(**Cut, Make and Trim**) A preliminary cost factor where a contractor provides services for cutting out the fabric and other components, assembling the parts and finishing the garment, including pressing, trimmings and labels.
CO	See: Certificate of Origin
Collect	Freight invoice payment terms; charges are billed to the recipient.
Color Approval	A customer's approval or rejection of lab dips or print strike-offs along with necessary comments for correction. These specific comments usually indicate errors in hue, value (lightness/darkness) and chroma (saturation/intensity).
Color Change	An undesirable change of color, whether in lightness, hue, or chroma, or any combination of these, and discernible by comparing the test specimen with a corresponding untested specimen.
Color Combo, Colorway, Color Pitch	All indicate distinct color combinations for a textile design or pattern, whether stripes, plaids, prints or multicolor jacquards. To "pitch colors" means to devise various new color combinations for a design based on the original color combination in the swatch or artwork.
Colorfastness	A material's resistance to change in any of its color characteristics, to transfer its colorant(s) to adjacent materials, or both, as a result of exposure to any environment that might be encountered during the processing, testing, storage, or use of the material.
Colorfastness to Light (Light Fastness)	The resistance of a material to a change in its color characteristics as a result of exposure to sunlight or an artificial light source.

Commercial Invoice	A document that generally contains the name and address of the seller and buyer, date of the sale, a description of the goods, quantity, unit price, terms of sale, amount due under the Letter of Credit and type of currency.
Commercial Laundering	A process by which textile products or specimens may be washed, rinsed, bleached, dried, and pressed in commercial laundering equipment, typically at higher temperatures, higher PHs and longer times than used for home laundering.
Consignee	The receiver of a freight shipment, usually the purchaser or buyer.
Consignor	The exporter that delivers the merchandise; also referred to as the shipper on a Bill of Lading.
Consolidation of Shipment	A requirement by the recipient that all purchase orders going to the same DC (Distribution Center) on the same day must be consolidated onto one Bill of Lading or sub-bill, depending on which carrier is being used.
Consolidator	Assembles the interliner or LTL (Less than Truckload) shipments, organizes the freight by DC and purchase order, manifests shipments by DC and transmits to each DC to pre-alert them of the merchandise and delivery date. Releases freight by assembly to the DC.
Construction (Fabric)	The specific base construction of a fabric: knit, woven, or non-woven. The type of structure within a category: Knits - Warp knit, weft knit, raschel; Wovens - Twill, poplin, satin, and jacquard. Also represented as a formula in wovens indicating the yarn sizes (yarn counts) in the warp and weft and the number of threads per inch in both.
Content	The percentage breakdown of the fiber contents in the primary fabric (e.g. 60% Cotton/40% Polyester). This will affect duty rates on imported fabrics or garments.
Contract Carrier	A for-hire carrier that does not serve the general public, but serves shippers or consignees with whom the carrier has a continuing contract.
Contractor	An individual or company that contracts to supply certain materials, work or a package of production for an agreed-upon sum and time frame.
Converter	A company that takes greige (grey) goods and uses one or more processes to finish the textile, such as: dyeing, printing, brushing, shrinking, bonding, etc.
Cost and Freight	See: C&F
Cost and Insurance	See: C&I
Cost, Insurance and Freight	See: CIF
Counter Sample	Pre-production samples sent from a vendor for purposes such as fitting, comments on execution or interpretation of a design or model. Samples sent for approval or confirmation.

Country of Origin	The country where garments or other items are manufactured or assembled. This must appear on the garment label.
Couture (Haute Couture)	The highest level of sewing and dressmaking techniques. Traditionally, custom-made clothing, largely made by hand. From the French.
Cover Stitch	A topstitched seam finish; raw edges are enclosed in covering threads on one or both surfaces. The appearance varies depending on the number of threads and type of stitch used.
Crocking	The transfer of colorant from the surface of a colored yarn or fabric to another surface or to an adjacent area of the same fabric principally by rubbing.
Cross Dye (Union Dye)	Dyeing a textile that is composed of 2 or more types of fiber with special dyestuffs that will be accepted by only one of the fibers respectively. This can be done to produce iridescent effects, heathers or the appearance of "yarn dye" looks, like gingham plaids and oxford weaves. Union dye uses the appropriate dye chemicals to dye all the different fibers within fabric the same color.
Cubic Feet	Length x width x height of the carton. Cubic measurement is required to provide for overshipments.
Customer's Owned Goods	Merchandise or material that has been sold to a customer. Customer's Owned Goods can also be a Repair Claim sent back to the contractor for repair.
Cuttable Width	The usable width of a fabric, excluding selvages or where textures and finishes do not cover the full width of the fabric. This is important in the figuration of the yield.
Cut-and-Sew	Usually refers to a factory or contractor that specializes in cutting and sewing knitted fabrics and knitted trims. These knit fabrics are in the form of yardage, rather than fully-fashioned panels. A cut-and-sew operation requires special attention in layout and cutting of the fabrics, as well as special sewing equipment for construction and finishing, owing to the fabric's stretch or elastic characteristics.
Cutter's Must	A production document that lists important information for laying out and cutting a garment. Listed items include: sewing and construction information; all pattern pieces for fabric, linings and components; key measurements; and yields for all fabrics and trims.
Cutting Ticket	A document like a Work Order used by a contractor or manufacturer to set up production details for a particular order, including customer, style number, fabric and trim information, quantities, etc.
Dart	A wedge or diamond shape removed from the body of a garment section by stitching or by cutting and stitching to aid in the shaping of the garment. A dart can be functional or used in various forms as a design element.
DC	A retailer's **Distribution Center** for its stores. The DC is usually the "Ship To" point on their Purchase Order.
Delivery (Dates)	Completion dates provided by the vendor or contractor for the latest date acceptable by the customer and indicated in the contract.

Department Number	The retailer's Department Number contains the type of merchandise belonging to a group of departments in their merchandise division.
Dimensional Change	A generic term for variation in length or width of a garment or fabric specimen subjected to specified conditions. The change is usually expressed as a percentage of the initial dimension of the specimen.
Discharge Printing	The process of pre-dyeing the background color in a printed textile to insure evenness and depth of color and then printing a chemical to "discharge" or bleach out the background. At the same time a new color is printed (dyestuff), in its place, all in one operation. This assures perfect registration of the print motifs on the ground color.
Distribution Center	See: DC
Dobby Weave	A fancy woven fabric with a small repeating pattern woven on a special dobby loom. The pattern and repeat are usually smaller than a jacquard pattern.
Dog Ears	The (undesirable) frayed seams present at the inside corners of the pockets caused when the pocket corners are turned back and stitched down improperly.
Double Knit	A group of knitted textiles that can be done on a variety of knitting equipment, but consists of two knitted structures knitting together simultaneously. Double knit fabrics can be plain like interlock and full Milano or multicolored and patterned as in double knit jacquards. Double knit fabrics are often more stable and less stretchy.
Double-Bed (Vee) Knitting	Knitting machines that have two opposing beds of knitting needles, each one controlling a stitch during the knitting process. Double bed machines make a higher quality rib construction and can often be used in full-fashioned knitting and elaborate stitch combinations. True "cable stitches" can only be done on double bed machinery.
Drape	The visual (perceived) structural or aesthetic effect a fabric has when made into a garment, such as: graceful, soft, fluid, stiff, crisp, heavy, bouffant, etc.
Dry-cleaning	The cleaning of fabrics with organic solvents such as petroleum solvents, perchloroethylene, or fluorocarbons. Note: The process also includes adding detergent and moisture to the solvent, up to 75% relative humidity, and hot tumble-drying to 71C (160F).
Duty	A government tax imposed on imported goods or manufacture, based on product categories, materials or fiber content and other consumer-based categories as outlined in the U.S. Harmonized Code. Originally applied to discourage outside or foreign competition.
Dyer / Dye House	A converter who specializes in preparing and dyeing a fabric to customer specifications. Dyes are chemical substances that produce a wide range of colors that penetrate and bond with the fibers of the cloth. The permanence of the dyeing process is dependent on the fibers, the dyestuffs, the "setting" process, environmental circumstances, etc. Dyes do not usually change the weight or hand of the fabric.

Ease	In fitting and styling - The amount of extra "room" included in the garment for purposes of comfort, movement or appearance. In sewing - Joining two pieces of fabric or trims of different lengths so that the longer length is "held in" against the shorter length without any obvious pleating or wrinkling along the seam. This form of Ease is used to mold the shape of the garment instead of extraneous seams or darts, as in tailoring.
Edge Stitch	A line of stitching through a folded edge, 1/32 of an inch away from, and parallel to, the edge.
Electronic Documents	Various documents processed electronically, such as: POs, Request Changes, UPC Catalogues, etc.
Electronic Jacquard	Circular or flat knitting machines that use a computer interface to create a variety of patterns and fancy stitches. The computer allows the designer to quickly draft and even plan the fashioning or shaping of the garment panels.
Ex-Works (Ex-factory)	A shipping arrangement that places a minimum responsibility on the seller. In an Ex-Works transaction, goods are made available for pickup at the beneficiary/seller's factory or warehouse and delivered to the buyer's freight forwarder. The buyer is responsible for making arrangements for insurance, export clearance and handling all other paperwork. Simply, the buyer takes possession (ownership) of goods as soon as it leaves the seller's facility. Port of loading.
Facings	A sewn-in panel or section of the exterior fabric that faces inward, toward the body, and provides a clean-finished edge, a finished opening or prevents seeing the interior construction of a garment.
FAS	(**Free Alongside Ship**...port of loading) The buyer bears all the transportation costs and the risk of loss of goods. Normally, buyers use their freight forwarder to clear the goods for export. Delivery is completed when the goods are turned over to the buyer's forwarder for insurance and transportation.
Fiber Content	The specific percentages, by fiber, used in constructing (weaving, knitting, etc.) the outer or "fashion fabric" of a garment. This is required by the U.S. government to appear on a label along with the Care and Country of Origin.
Filament Yarn	A relatively continuous length of fiber, usually manmade, created through an "extrusion process" where plastic materials are forced through small apertures (spinnerets) and then solidified into filaments. Silk is a natural form of a filament.
Finish (Fabric)	Refers to any special or customer-designated finishes or treatments.
Finisher	A converter who "finishes" a textile before use: brushing, glazing, napping, water-repellence, etc.
Fit Model	An individual whose general body measurements reflect the standard or sample size designated for development or production of a garment. Garments are tested on a Fit Model in order to check style, fit, movement and comfort issues, before continuing on to production.
Flammability	Those characteristics of a material that pertain to its ease of ignition and ability to sustain combustion. Flammability is of particular concern in children's and sleepwear or special uniforms.

Flat Knitting	Knitting on a single or double needle bed machine. A "carriage" carries the yarns back and forth across the knitting bed and forms the loop-like stitches needle-by-needle. Flat bed knitting can be more versatile and may have the ability to fully fashion a garment, but it is considerably slower than circular knitting.
Flats	Detailed design sketches used in product development that include front and back views as well as special details and treatments. Flats often include measurements indicating placement of details and exact proportions. Flats represent the garment as if laid flat on a table or hung on a wall to create a working diagram of the garment, without artistic expression or flourishes.
Fleece	A warp or weft knitted textile that has loops or floats on one or both surfaces that are bushed in the finishing for a plush effect. Fleece can be made from a variety of natural and manmade fibers. When unbrushed it is called french terry.
Float Jacquard	A fancy knit structure involving a multicolored pattern or design. The various yarn colors are carried on the back of the knit fabric (floats) until they are knitted into the design on the surface. Float jacquard is less bulky and firm as than double jacquard.
Floor Ready	Referring to merchandise that is received ready to be placed directly on the selling floor.
Fly closure	One-Piece Fly - The fly facing is an extension of the body, folded back to form a fly or lapped zipper application. The fly extension is single ply, usually over-edge finished. Two-Piece-Fly – A separate piece is used to form a fly or lapped zipper application. The fly extension is double ply with a fold at the outside edge. French Fly – An extension added to the right side fly stand to allow for an additional button and buttonhole on the inside waistband.
FOB	(**Free on Board**...port of loading) A term of sale that defines who is to incur transportation charges for the shipment; who is to control the movement of the shipment; or where the title to the goods passes to the buyer/purchaser.
Folder (Operation)	A labor saving attachment on a sewing machine that folds various layers of fabric and components together during the assembly process, eliminating the machine operator from manually producing the effect, such as: seam binding, placket attachment, flat-felling seams and hemming.
Free Alongside Ship	See: FAS
Free on Board	See: FOB
Freight Allowance	The amount (%) of freight the supplier or retailer pays per PO based on a Freight Partnership Contract.
Freight Chargeback	A supplier's freight deduction document; the two types of freight chargebacks are: Agreement – Supplier agrees to participate in sharing freight charges. Violation – Supplier is charged for full freight charges plus a handling fee. Violation is usually either of Purchase Order contract or the indicated carrier or routing selection.
Freight-Only Invoice	An invoice for prepaid freight charges sent to the DC.
Full Freight	The supplier/shipper agrees to pay 100% of the freight charges.

Fully Fashioned	A knitting term indicating that each section of the garment is "fashioned" or shaped to its finished dimensions for every size in the range. Usually the garment sections are then "linked" or "looped" together to finish. A Fully-Fashioned garment wastes very little yarn, often an important cost factor.
Fashioning Marks	A knitting term indicating the marks that fully-fashioned garments usually have near the seams, indicating where the individual panels were knitted to shape. See: Fully-Fashioned *above*.
Garment Dye	Greige fabric cut and sewn into garments, then dyed in the garment form.
Garment on Hanger	(**GOH**) A hanging packaging shipping type.
Garment Twist (Torquing)	A rotation, usually lateral, between panels of a garment resulting from the release of latent stresses during laundering of the woven or knitted fabric forming the garment. Twist may also be referred to as torque or spiraling.
Garment Wash	Dyed goods washed to tone down color, provide a distressed or weathered look, seam abrasion, or make fabric softer.
Gauge	In knitting, the number of needles (wales) per inch on the knitting machine (rather than the number of stitches per inch on the knitted textile). Some full fashioned knitting equipment still indicates the gauge as needles per 1-1/2". The more needles-per-inch indicates the fineness of the knitted fabric.
GOH	See: Garment on Hanger
Grade Rule	A standard set of increases or decreases for various body or garment measurements within a size range. This can be established or modified by the designer, the contractor or the retailer and usually reflects their standard "fit" for their customer.
Grading	Proportionately increasing or decreasing the dimensions of all the parts of a sample/proto/model garment according to the size ranges in a style intended for production. Grading is a significant step in garment production, in order to maintain proper fit in the full range of sizes, as well as determining the cutting layout (marker) for the fabric and trims.
Grain	As applies to woven fabrics: Straight Grain - Threads running down the length of the fabric and parallel to the selvage. Cross Grain - Across the width of the fabric. Bias - Diagonally across the fabric at a 45 degree angle. Off Grain - Not aligned with the Straight Grain or the grain indicated for the pattern piece.
Greige (Grey) Goods	Unfinished or "loom state" textiles, coming from a mill or knitter. Various "finishing" procedures follow like bleaching, dyeing, printing, brushing, etc.
Greige Goods	Knitted or woven cloth that has not received any dry or wet finishing such as bleaching, dyeing or printing.
Hand (Handfeel)	The way a fabric feels in the hands or to the touch: soft, harsh, stiff, silky, bouncy, dead, etc. This is an important aspect in the selection of fabric for both design and production. Fabric can be rejected for production if it is not to the standard of the original or specified "hand."

Hand Loom	A hand woven textile following a customer's design and used to approve colors and construction. Often used to "preview" a design with merchandisers and buyers. More and more replaced by computer-generated printed facsimiles.
Importer of Record	The company or individual who is listed as the importer with U.S. Customs at the time the goods are entered into the U.S. The Tax ID # or Social Security # of the "Importer of Record" must also be submitted to Customs.
Incoterms	See: International Commercial Terms
Inspection Certificate	A document that certifies that merchandise was in good condition and as specified in a contract prior to shipment. Often obtained from an independent testing organization.
Intarsia	A knitting process where different colors or yarns are inlaid within the body of the knitted panel so that they are contained in that specific design element or motif. The reverse side of an intarsia design will be single knitting throughout without floats or double knitting. Intarsias can be done by hand-frame knitting or on special intarsia machines.
Interfacing	A woven or non-woven material used between layers of fabric to change or improve the stylistic qualities of that section of the garment, or to improve durability and resistance to creasing, wrinkling or "drooping." Typical areas using interfacings are collars, cuffs, front openings, hems and lapels. Fusible Interfacings are attached to the garment sections or facings using high heat to temporarily melt a backing adhesive. The attachment to the garment is relatively permanent unless the garment is subjected to the same level of heat. Sew-in Interfacings are sandwiched between the layers of fabric during the construction process and "float." They do not change the hand or appearance of the fashion fabric, but add body or support.
Interlining	Provides additional weight and warmth in strategic areas of a garment.
Interlock	A specific double-knit circular knit fabric that can be piece-dyed or printed. The front and back of the fabric will appear the same (as plain jersey). It is versatile, tailors well and is more stable, though heavier, than plain jersey fabrics.
International Commercial Terms	(**Incoterms**) International terms of sale published by the International Chamber of Commerce that define the buyer's and seller's obligations in a transaction.
Jacquard	A mechanism used in knitting or weaving that allows the production of fancy stitches and weaves or elaborate patterning on the surface of the textile, similar to the mechanism in a music box or player piano. Modern electronic jacquards work in conjunction with a computer design system and allow quick pattern and structural changes.
Jersey	In machine knitting, plain knit fabric, formed on one set of needles. In hand knitting called "knit"; on the reverse side the stitch formation is called "purl".
Jobber	A person or company who buys textiles from manufacturers, mills, importers in quantity, as well as overruns and unused sample yardage and re-sells them to wholesalers, retailers and smaller garment manufacturers.
Knit-down	A knitted sample, used to demonstrate or present the specific color combos, yarns, stitches and/or pattern in a design. The knit-down is often used for approval purposes.

Knits	A family of textiles produced by a series of interlocking or interlacing loops. Knits are usually distinguishable from woven fabrics by greater stretch and recovery in the length and/or width of the fabric. Weft Knitting - Derived from hand-knitting and involves rows of interlocking loops formed across and back as the fabric is knitted. Machine weft knitting can be done on either flatbed machines that produce panels or on circular machines that produce lengths (large tubes) of knitted piece goods. Warp Knitting - Utilizes a "warp" of yarns but instead of interlacing these with weft yarns, the warp yarns make interlocking loops in a diagonal pattern back and forth across the fabric. Warp knits are usually employed for high volume knit textile production. Raschel and lace knitting are also warp knits.
L/C	See: Letter of Credit
Lab Dips	Color approvals sent to the customer by a dyer, spinner or printer on the appropriate fiber, yarn or fabric. The customer must approve, or reject the "dips" with appropriate comments for correction. Approved lab dips become color standards for production.
Landed Duty Paid	See: LDP
LDP	(**Landed Duty Paid**) The total cost of a product delivered to a given location; the cost of production plus the transportation, appropriate U.S. Customs duties and taxes to the customer/purchaser's location.
Lead Time	The time it takes to go from initial product development or design concept to completed item and can involve the time for prototyping, counter samples, approvals, weaving or knitting, etc.
Less than Truckload	See: LTL
Letter of Credit, Commercial	A bank-issued document (requested by the customer/applicant) to a specified beneficiary by which the bank substitutes its credit for that of the applicant. The bank makes payments to the beneficiary under conditions specified in the L/C.
Letter of Credit, Sight	A Letter of Credit, payable immediately upon shipment of the merchandise or on demand with accompanying documents of compliance (compare Letter of Credit, Usance).
Letter of Credit, Usance	A Letter of Credit payable at some future date, also called a Timed Letter of Credit because it allows the buyer a certain period of time to pay all drawings under the Letter of Credit (compare Letter of Credit, Sight). The bank accepts a draft and payment is made at a future point in time.
Ligne (Buttons)	The system of measuring the overall width (diameter) of a button. In the English Ligne System, there are 40 lignes to the inch. A 20-ligne button would be 1/2" in diameter.
Line (Merchandise) Plan	A plan developed by and for the design, and that merchandising staff outlining styles, by their categories, for a coming season and forms the basis of a seasonal collection. An outline or framework for product development. Line Plans are usually based on sales analysis of previous seasons. Also may involve an SKU count.
Lining	Fabrics used on the inside of a garment to hide seams or interior construction elements. Also to provide ease of removal, additional seam strength and/or warmth. A garment can be fully or partially lined.

Linking or Looping	An assembly technique most often used in fully-fashioned knits. The various sections and knit trims of the garment are joined together by a machine that produces a flexible, elastic chain-stitch seam. The machine operator matches each stitch along a seam to its counterpart on the other panel to be joined. It is a high quality, labor-intensive process.
Links-Links	Flat or circular knitting that forms a textile (yardage for cut-and-sew) that often has a horizontally ribbed surface of alternating courses of knit and purl stitches.
Loom	The mechanism for weaving a textile (woven fabric). A loom usually consists of a warp (a series of closely set threads running parallel to the selvage) and the weft or filling yarn that is woven from side to side creating the desired fabric. The warp (warp beam) on a modern power loom may hold thousands of yards of thread in preparation for weaving. Often used incorrectly for a knitting machine.
LTL	**(Less than Truckload)** A shipment weighing less than the minimum weight needed to use the lesser truckload rate.
Manufacturer ID	Numbers (digits) used to represent a vendor in the UPC (Universal Product Code) number.
Marker	A full-scale diagram, usually on paper, indicating the most economical placement for all the graded pattern pieces in a garment and used in cutting the fabric for production. A marker can be made manually or with the aid of a computer. The marker must take all variables in the garment and fabric into consideration: matching print or woven patterns, grain lines, directional cutting, etc.
Master Bill of Lading	A uniquely numbered Contract-of-Carriage document that summarizes more than one shipment or sub-bills of lading.
Matching (Match Points)	The choice to match various repeating elements in patterned fabric (prints, stripes, plaids or embellishments) across the garment in order to balance the visual "effect" of the pattern on the body. Match points can be at the front of the armhole, across the front opening, at various seams or applied details. Matching usually incurs additional cost and preparation time, but also indicates higher quality.
Mercerized	A process were cotton yarn or cloth is treated with a caustic soda solution which improves the strength of the goods, as well as improves dyeing and color intensity and usually imparts a permanent luster to the product.
Microfiber	Any manmade fiber where the diameter of each filament is less than 1 micron. Microfibers can remain in filament form or can be cut into staple lengths for spinning. Microfiber refers to the fineness of the fiber and not to a specific textile construction or weave.
Migration	The non-uniform movement and distribution of dyes, pigments, finishes, or other materials from one part to another - bleeding, crocking, etc.
Mill	A company that is responsible for the initial spinning of yarns or the knitting or weaving of textiles. A vertical mill refers to a company that can take the product from spinning to final finishing and then to the market.
Minimums	The minimum quantity that a vendor or mill requires of the customer in order to contract their goods as in: yardage, yarn poundage, finished piece goods, etc.
Mode	Method of transportation (type of service) used for shipments. Usually Surface or Air indicated on the PO.

Multimodal Transport	Transportation that includes at least two modes of transport, such as shipping by rail and by sea.
Muslin (Toile)	An inexpensive fabric (traditionally an un-bleached cotton sheeting) used to develop and test the prototype for design, fit and proportion. The muslin is often taken apart and used to make the first pattern for preliminary samples and patternmaking. Fabrics for the "muslin" are usually selected to approximate the final fabric choice in weight and drape. Construction notations are often written on the outside.
Natural Fibers	Any fiber that comes from a natural source and needs a minimum of processing to create yarns for textile production. The most common categories are: animal - silk, (wool, hair) and fur); vegetable - cotton, linen, ramie.
Notches	Cut-in markings on the pattern piece or "sloper" indicating matching points to facilitate sewing seams, seam allowances, easing or gathering and creating pattern/fabric (markers) layouts for cutting.
Package (Production)	An arrangement where a contractor agrees to purchase all piece goods and trims, etc., on behalf of the customer, in addition to providing the CMT (Cut, Make and Trim).
Packing List	A list prepared by the shipper that lists the quantity and kinds of items being shipped.
Piece (of Fabric)	A length of finished fabric in manageable pieces, usually determined by practical manufacturing or production considerations. A bolt or roll of cloth.
Piece Dye	Dyeing lengths of cloth for production, usually in solid colors.
Piece Goods	Textiles used in the apparel or accessories industry. Production fabric.
Pile Fabrics	A group of textiles composed of various fibers ranging from: terry towels, velvet, corduroy, and carpeting. Pile fabrics have a stable, supporting woven or knitted base fabric (ground) and loops formed on the surface that can be left uncut or cut and finished to create a smooth, plush surface. Pile fabrics can be plain, solid colors, fancy patterned or multicolored jacquards.
Pique	In knitting, a group of fabrics used in cut-and-sew that combines various simple patterns of "knit" and "tuck" stitches. A typical pique fabric has small bumps of tucked stitches on the face and is smooth on the back. Piques knit fabrics are popular in sports and active wear for their absorbency and wrinkle resistance.
Plain Weave	The simplest and most common woven construction (weave) produced on a loom, consisting of warp and weft (filling) threads interlacing in an alternating one-over and one-under arrangement throughout the fabric. Plain weaves can be composed of any fiber and range in weight from chiffon to canvas.
Plating	In knitting, the process of knitting two different yarns simultaneously so that one yarn is visible from the surface and the other yarn is carried underneath, directly behind it. This can be done to combine two colors for a mock "heather" effect, to hide a more functional yarn or fiber on the back of the textile (as in a stretch yarn) or to have a "performance" yarn next to the body (for absorbency, wicking, anti-rash, etc.).
Pleats	Folds of material included to allow expansion or provide styling features, such as: forward or reverse pleats, knife, box pleats, inverted box, accordion, crystal, Fortuny or sunburst pleats. Some fabrics can be permanently pleated.

PO	See: Purchase Order
Pocketing	Fabric used for the "bag" or pouch of the pocket. Usually a finer, lighter-weight, sturdy material, not the same as the fashion fabric or shell fabric.
POD	See: Proof of Delivery
Prepaid	Freight invoice payment term; charges are billed to the shipper or supplier.
Pre-Production	All parts of the process leading up to bulk production, includes garments made using the actual production patterns, sewing line and machinery. Pre-Production comes before Top-of-Production.
Pre-Production (P/P) Sample	Following the Sales Sample, submittals will be called Pre-Production (P/P) Samples until fit, construction, and all details are approved for bulk. Pre-Production samples should be made in actual fabric and trims, and must be made in the factory where bulk production is being placed. Factory may not proceed with bulk until this sample is approved.
Pre-Shipment	Any shipment that leaves the factory or is delivered to a consolidator, port, airport, or distribution center prior to the ex-factory date indicated on the customer's Purchase Order.
Pressing	The act of using heat and/or steam to smooth, shape or form a crease in the fabric or garment. There are a variety of specialized irons, pressing machines, etc., used in manufacturing. Hard Press - Heavy press, which forms a crisp crease line or durable shaping. Soft Press - Press to remove undesirable wrinkles, but not to form crisp crease line.
Printing (Textile)	The process of applying dyes or pigments to a textile in a pre-determined design or pattern. All commercially produced printed textiles involve a pattern repeated down the length of the fabric and often across the width, as well. The most common types of textile printing are: screen-printing, roller or rotary printing and heat transfer printing. Ink jet printing is also becoming more cost effective for small quantities, but remains very slow. Wet Printing uses chemical dye stuffs in a paste or ink form that is printed on the surface of the fabric and is then set with steam and/or heat to bond with the fibers. Wet printing does not usually change the hand or drape of the fabric. Pigment Printing uses colors mixed with a binder (as in paint) and is applied to the surface of the fabric. Without special treatments to the fabrics, pigment printing will affect the hand, weight and stiffness of the fabric.
Proof of Delivery	**(POD)** Proof that shipment was received with signature.
Prototype (Proto)	The initial sample produced for a given design. This can be made in muslin or an available fabric and trims for product development and assessment.
Punch (Mark)	A small hole in a pattern piece that will be transferred to the fabric indicating placement of a special sewing detail within the panel of fabric, such as: the apex of a dart, set-on or cut-in pocket placement, pleats, etc.
Purchase Order	**(PO)** A legal, binding contract between a buyer and a supplier.

Quick Response	The ability to replenish merchandise by sending sales information to a vendor and having the merchandise replenished immediately, using Electronic Data Interchange or a similar program.
QR	See: Quick Response
Racking	One of the basic functions of machine knitting where one or more stitches are transferred to another needle to the left or right of their current positions. This can produce a zigzag effect and is also one of the steps in making a cable stitch on a double bed machine.
Refusal	A Refusal may occur when a Purchase Order is delivered to a consolidator or buyer that does not comply with the terms of the Purchase Order contract. Refusals are put "on hand," and all expenses are borne by the seller. The seller usually has 30 days to give disposition to the party in possession of the shipment. After that, it is free to be salvaged in order to recover expenses.
Return Authorization	An authorization number that is obtained from the supplier prior to returning merchandise under a filed claim.
Rib Knit (Ribbing)	A group of stitches alternating jersey and reverse jersey (purl) to create a vertical ribbed effect and create a more elastic textile. Because of the additional elasticity, ribbed knits are often used at the openings or bottoms of a garment for a snug and comfortable fit.
Sales Sample	This sample should be an exact replica of what will be purchased and shipped to the retailer. This will be used by the salesperson for that purpose.
Sample Cuts (Yardage)	Fabric purchased to create sales or product development samples. Some mills will manufacture a number of fabrics from their range in limited colors or colorways. Otherwise, the customer must contract to make sample fabric or take a portion of fabric from their bulk production. There is usually a surcharge for sample fabrics.
Sample Loom	Looms in a mill given over to making a customer's sample yardage. A surcharge on the fabric is usually involved.
Sample Room	An area set aside in a design studio or at a contractor's facility for the purpose of making product development samples (protos) or counter samples and sales samples.
Samples	Merchandise not for resale but used as a selling tool (sales samples), a guide for development or manufacturing (first or counter sample), or as an example of production (top-of-production, etc.).
Sanding/Sand Wash	Intentional abrasion on a garment; originally achieved with a high-pressure sand blaster - now done with brushes or sand in the dry state or with chemicals and sand or grit in washing.
Satin/Sateen	One of the three basic woven constructions (weave). Satins have long "floating" yarns on the face (or both sides - "double faced") of the fabric and have a lustrous-to-shiny appearance. Satin is usually warp faced and sateen is usually weft faced. Satins can be made of any natural or manmade fiber.
Seam Allowance	The pre-determined amount of seam margin material between the edge of the component part of the garment and the seam line. Prevents seam slippage, seam bursting or fraying.

Seam Finishes	Bound Seam - where a narrow fold of bias fabric or a non-fraying material like a cloth tape covers the raw edges of the seam allowance. Enclosed Seam - where two or more layers are joined and then turned so that the seam allowances are hidden inside the garment section, such as a collar, cuff or facing. (Flat) Felled Seam - in which two panels are joined together by overlapping so both raw edges are folded under one another. Usually done with a folder and either a double or triple needle machine. Often used on men's shirts. French Seam - constructed so that a narrow seam is contained within a slightly larger one, producing a clean finish on the inside of the garment. (Pressed) Open Seam - a simple seam treatment where the seam allowances are pressed open and facing in opposite directions. Serged - where two or more layers of fabric or components are trimmed and joined using a type of serging machine. Also Overlock, Over-edging or Merrow. Welted Seam - when both seam allowances are pressed to one side and are held in position by topstitching.
Seam Slippage	In sewn fabrics, the displacement of the fabric yarn parallel and adjacent to the stitch line caused by stress or straining.
Seconds	Any textile that is not of first quality. Fabrics that have an excessive frequency of defects, damages or irregularities and cannot be marketed at full price.
Selvage	The woven or interlaced edge of a textile that runs parallel to the warp threads. The selvage maintains the fabric's correct width and prevents woven fabrics from unraveling. The selvage is also used to stabilize the fabric during further finishing processes.
Shading	Gradual changes in hue, chroma, and/or lightness lengthwise or widthwise. Note: When unintended, shading is considered a defect. It may be intentional for styling purposes (ombre or degrade).
Shipper	The sender of a freight shipment, usually the supplier, contractor, seller or seller's agent.
Short Shipments	Shipment contents that are less than the packing slip count, or a carrier's shipment, that has delivered less than the carton count on the Bill of Lading or freight delivery receipt.
Shrinkage	A dimensional change resulting in a decrease in the length or width of a textile or garment usually due to water, heat, steam, wet-cleaning or a combination of all.
Single Needle (Construction)	A term often used in men's wear for a high-quality construction technique that uses a lock-stitch to form a flat-felled seam at the side seams and the armhole of a shirt. Double Needle refers to a similar sewing technique that produces parallel lines of chain stitches in one operation and is less durable.
Size Run	Pre-production samples that are used to check the accuracy of all sizes to be produced in an order.

Skew	A fabric condition resulting when knitted courses are displaced angularly and from a line perpendicular to the edge or side of the fabric. A similar condition can occur in woven fabrics and is also a result of improper finishing.
SKU	**(Stock Keeping Unit)** Reference to a specific style, color, size by season or delivery. SKUs are used in planning, budgets, tracking, merchandising and retailing usually indicated by 5, 8 or 12 digit numbers and a bar code.
Sloper	Stiff paper or cardboard pattern pieces for a basic or "core" style that has been approved for fit and appearance, which may be used in the development of more complex styles and pattern pieces. Also called a Block Pattern.
Spec. Sheet (Specs)	A document indicating the complete specifications (specs) for a garment or accessory generated prior to production. The Spec Sheet or Spec Package may include: a general sketch or flats, fabric and construction details, measurement charts and other pertinent information for the manufacturer and QC.
Special Finishes	Any additional finishes that a customer contracts to be added to a textile, such as: water repellency, stain resistance, odor-blocking, UV protection, crease resistance, etc.
Stain	A localized deposit of soil or discoloration on a substrate that exhibits some degree of resistance to removal, as in laundering or dry-cleaning.
Standard (Color)	Colors that are submitted to a mill or converter that become the standard for future production. The mill or converter will in turn provide lab dips or strike-offs to the customer for approval or comments.
Stay	To limit stretch or distortion of a seam, shape or detail in a sewn garment.
Stitches (Sewing Operations)	<u>Chain Stitch</u> - A one or two thread structure that provides a row of stitches in the form of interlocking loops (similar to crochet). This stitch can be removed quickly by cutting and pulling from one end of the stitched seam. This seam is more elastic than a Lock Stitch seam and is used in seams requiring stretch. <u>Flatlock (Coverstitch)</u> - A seam that joins or finishes a lapped seam. The raw edges are covered on the upper and/or underside of the garment. Originally used in underwear and athletic wear. <u>Lock Stitch</u> - A two-thread operation combining a needle thread and a bobbin thread where the two threads are locked together between the plys of fabric. This seam is the least likely to open up along its length, but is the least elastic. <u>Serging</u> - A group of seam structures that involves a chain stitch seam combined with additional threads that over-edges (overcasts) seams at the same time. Usually a serger trims the edge of the seam as it sews. <u>Zigzag Stitch</u> - A variation of a Lock Stitch that produces a more elastic seam or topstitching resembling a stair step pattern.
Stitches per Inch	The recommended stitches per inch in constructing a garment; may vary according to specific parts of the garment (for durability), fabrics and components involved, or for appearance, as decorative in top-stitching.
Stock/Bulk	Fabric that is contracted and manufactured specifically for production purposes, as opposed to sample production.
Stock Keeping Unit	See: SKU

Store Pack	Packing a shipment to the retailer by style, color and size (SKU).
Sub-Bill	A Bill of Lading always used in conjunction with a Master Bill of Lading. It lists the detailed information for a DC shipment: POs, Dept. #, itemized by # of cartons and weight, etc.
Supplier Number	Identifying number for the individual supplier in the retailer's merchandising system or "vendor matrix."
Tearing Strength	The average force required to continue a tear previously started in a fabric.
Tech Package	A packet of technical specifications sent to a factory for each new style. Also called a spec package. A tech package includes the following forms and often more: Lead/Sketch Sheet, Specification Measurement Sheet and Fabric and Trim Sheet.
Time and Action Calendar	A seasonal calendar devised by the design team, merchandising, production and sales divisions of a company in order to keep each area in synch throughout the product development, sales and production cycles.
Top of Production (Top of Line)	The first units completed off the sewing/production line that are used for quality check. Bulk production follows Top of Production.
Topstitch Gauge	The measured distance between the rows of topstitching when two or more rows of parallel stitching are used; i.e., double-needle topstitch.
Topstitching	A wide variety of stitch effects that show on the surface of the garment for practical, structural or aesthetic reasons. Topstitching often occurs near the outer edge of a garment section, as on: pockets, collars, lapels, yokes, etc. Topstitching can attach one garment section (set-on) to another, keep seams flat and smooth or keep elements of the garment from shifting.
Top(s) Dyed	Dyeing the fibers before they are spun into yarn for weaving or knitting. This can be done to assure color consistency and depth or to achieve a "heathered " or "mélange"(mixy) effect in the textile. Often confused with over-dyeing.
Transfer	One of the basic functions of machine knitting where one or more stitches are transferred from the front or back bed of needles as the textile or panels are being knitted. This is done on double bed machines (front-to-back) or vise versa.
Transshipment	When products manufactured in one country, commercially enter another country, and are then exported for sale in a third country.
Trims (Trimmings)	A wide range of articles designed to add detail or to ornament a garment or accessory, usually made by a specialty manufacturer or supplier. Trims are usually applied to the item rather than form an integral part of the construction. Trims include: ribbons, braids, piping, bindings, appliqués, lace, decorative patches, logos, etc.
Tubular Knit - Tubular Start	A knitting technique where two separate layers or plys of fabric are created at the same time creating horizontal tubes or pockets between the layers. A tubular start is like a knitted-on hem at the beginning of knitting to stabilize a section of the garment, to prevent curling or over-stretching.
Tuck	A basic stitch formation that holds one or more stitches on an individual knitting needle through one or more courses (passes) in knitting. This causes the stitch to "pull up" the other stitches around it. It can be used for functional purposes or for design effects.

Twill	One of the three basic woven constructions (weaves). Twills have shorter floating threads on the surface of the fabric than satins and have a diagonal ribbed appearance even though the warp and weft (fill) yarns are weaving at a 90-degree angle. Twills often have a denser feel and softer drape than plain weave fabrics of the same type of yarn. A common example is jeans or denim.
Underlining	Used to back the fashion or shell fabric in order to modify the hand or visual effect of the garment; to add firmness, weight, opaqueness or stiffness. Usually sewn as one with the individual panels of the garment.
Under-stitching	A line of stitching that appears on the underside of a garment, usually around facings, flys, etc., that causes the top fabric to roll slightly over and hide the seam edge.
Universal Product Code	See: UPC
UPC	(**Universal Product Code**) A unique 12-digit vendor "SKU" number assigned by the retailer. Usually the first 6 digits represent the vendor's ID#, the next 5 digits are the specific product SKU and the last digit is the check digit.
VAN	(**Value Added Network**) A designated network used to transmit and receive EDI transactions.
Value Added Network	See: VAN
Vendor	An individual or company that sells finished goods, materials or components to another individual or company, contractors, intermediaries or retailer.
Vendor Number	The Vendor Number is found on the retailer's Purchase Order under "Pay to Vendor."
VICS	**Voluntary Inter-Industry Commerce Standards** for EDI transactions established by the UCC (Uniform Code Council).
VMR	(**Vendor Managed Replenishment**) Vendor "Basic Stock" system that automatically creates Purchase Orders and replenishes merchandise based on retail sales and SKU information.
Volume Shipments	A full load that exceeds the standard size/weight guidelines. Surface: 10,000 pounds or more, or over 1,200 cubic feet per consolidated shipment. Air: 1,000 pounds or over, per consolidated shipment. Volume Shipments are considered for possible Full Load shipment routing.
Waistband	Straight Waistband - The waistband pattern edges are parallel and cut on the straight grain. Contour Waistband - A band formed to fit the body's curve, accommodating differences in measurement between top edge of waistband and waistband seam. Curtain Waistband - A waistband with a self-fabric outer face supported by a bias strip designed to hang below the waistline seam. Used for tailored trousers and skirts.
Warp Knit	A wide range of machine-knitting techniques that involve a prepared "warp" of yarns, similar to weaving. This "warp" of parallel yarns is inter-looped in various diagonal, sideways and back and forth patterns to knit the fabric together. Warp knits include: tricots, raschel, power-nets, milanese, lace machines, etc. Warp knits can create both fashion and high performance fabrics and less expensive utilitarian fabrics depending on the equipment.

Washdown	A change in appearance to give a worn or laundered look resulting from washing, scouring, chemical, mechanical, or other treatments, or combination of treatments.
Water Repellency	The characteristic of a fiber, yarn, or fabric to resist wetting or saturation.
Water Resistance	The characteristic to resist wetting and or easy penetration by water. This treatment is often non-permanent.
Waterproofing	A garment made with water-resistant fabric with the addition of taping or flexible cement on all seams or stitching lines to prevent water penetration at those points.
Weaving	The process of interlacing yarns at a 90-degree angle. The mechanism for weaving textiles is a loom. Warp threads (yarn) run the length of the fabric and are usually prepared on a drum or "beam." The warp yarns can be thousands of yards in length (often determining the minimum customer order). The warp yarns can be dyed for creating fancy patterns or left undyed for piece dyeing or other treatments. Weft (fill) threads interlace or "weave" the warp threads together and run back and forth across the fabric from selvage to selvage.
Weight (Fabric)	Usually given in weight per sq. yard or sq. meter.
Welt Jacquard	A weft knitting technique that carries the various colors and yarns for a fancy textile on the reverse side until they are required in the surface design. The reverse side of the fabric looks like horizontal colored stripes. Birds-eye-back is a similar technique but the reverse side looks like multicolored dots.
Welt Pocket	A pocket that is set-in or cut-in and has one or two folds of fabric that bind or pipe the opening. It is also called a Besom or Reece Pocket.
Wicking	The ability for a fiber or fabric to draw moisture or perspiration away from the body in order to improve evaporation and comfort.
Width (Fabric)	The cuttable width of a given fabric. This will affect the "yield" in cutting out the garment pieces.
WIP	(**Work-in-Progress Report**) This shows an update of each step involved in a season's production.
Work in Progress	See: WIP
Worsted	Long staple woolen fibers that go through the additional process of combing prior to spinning and produce a smoother, more lustrous and harder finished fabric.
Yarn Count	The size of a given yarn and the number of "ends" (strands) plied together in spinning. This is usually given as a fraction such as 2/20. There are several "count systems" but NM (New Metric) is gaining favor as a universal system that deals in the diameter of yarn based on a set length.

Yarn Dyed	A knitted or woven textile that uses yarns dyed prior to construction. Usually this is done to create various patterns or designs during the actual knitting or weaving, as in: jacquards, stripes, plaids and dobbies.
Yield	Amount of fabric (yardage) used to cut one garment, or, when referring to knit fabric, yield = weight of fabric. The yield is used as a costing factor.
Zipper	A device for closing and opening, or attaching and removing a part of a garment and uses a pair of interlocking teeth and a "slider." The teeth of the zipper can be made of various kinds of metal or plastic and come in a wide range of colors, finishes and sizes. The "slider" and the "pull" can be functional or decorative. Zipper Teeth can be cast into shape, molded, or in coil form. Zippers can have a stop at one or both ends to prevent the slider from disengaging. Separating Zippers are used on jacket or coat fronts and on removable hoods and linings. 2-Way Zippers have two sliders that allow the zipper to be open fully or partially open from either end. Invisible Zippers are used in seams where the appearance of a zipper opening is unacceptable. The garment fabric creates a covering fold over the zipper teeth and there is no visible topstitching from the outside. They are less durable than regular zippers.

INDEX

ABOUT THE AUTHOR

David Secul was born in Caracas, Venezuela and grew up in Southern California. He has worked in the fashion industry for over twenty years.

David began his career working as a fashion designer in New York City. Working closely with some of the world's leading fashion designers such as Geoffrey Beene and Carolina Herrera, David's fascination for creating apparel continued to grow. After designing he moved into other areas of fashion including sourcing, production, and manufacturing. He is currently the president of Vicunha U.S.A., which is a subsidiary of Vicunha Brazil.

This is David's first book, but he hopes to continue writing and helping people in the industry find their way in what is, and continues to be, a very difficult and competitive industry.

FOOTNOTES

Gray Scale is a scale that measures colorfastness of textile dyes. Gray Scale shows the amount of staining of adjacent materials that happens with washing of a sample.

AATCC stands for the American Association of Textile Chemists and Colorists. The AATCC is the worldwide association of professionals active in textile wet processing. AATCC provides the textile wet processing industry with a communication center and a clearinghouse for new ideas and innovation in textile chemistry and color science. AATCC has published more than 175 test methods addressing such topics as colorfastness, staining, laundering, and electrostatics.

http://www.techstreet.com/contact.html

Email:
techstreet.service@thomson.com
Please allow one business day for a reply.
Phone:
(800) 699-9277 - Toll free in US & Canada
(734) 913-3930 - International
Fax:
(734) 913-3946

AQL
AQL has two different definitions due to standard changes.

MIL-STD-105E, ISO 2859-1 (1999)
Acceptable Quality Level. The acceptable level (AQL) is defined as the maximum percent defective (or the maximum number of defects per hundred units) that, for purpose of sampling inspection, can be considered satisfactory as a process average. The sampling plans most frequently used by the department of Defense are based on the AQL.

ANSI/ASQC Z1.4-2003
Acceptance Quality Limit. The AQL is the quality level that is the worst tolerable process average when a continuing series of lots is submitted for acceptance sampling.
The following note on the meaning of AQL was introduced with the ANSI/ASQ Z1.4-2003 revision.
The concept of AQL only applies when an acceptance-sampling scheme with rules for switching between normal, tightened and reduced inspection and discontinuance of sampling inspection is used. These rules are designed to encourage suppliers to have process averages consistently better than the AQL. If suppliers fail to do so, there is a high probability of being switched from normal inspection to tightened inspection where lot acceptance becomes more difficult. Once on tightened inspection, unless corrective action is taken to improve product quality, it is very likely that the rule requiring discontinuance of sampling inspection will be invoked.
Although individual lots with quality as bad as the AQL can be accepted with fairly high probability, the designation of an AQL does not suggest that this is necessarily a desirable quality level. The AQL is a parameter of the sampling scheme and should not be confused with a process average, which describes the operating level of a manufacturing process. It is expected that the product quality level will be less than the AQL to avoid excessive nonaccepted lots.

http://www.aqlinspectorsrule.com/manual/dictionary.htm
Copyright 2002 Coyote Technologies Inc

Breinigsville, PA USA
16 August 2010
243665BV00004B/3/P